Clashing Views
on Controversial
Moral Issues

3rd edition

Clashing Views
on Controversial
Moral Issues

3rd edition

Edited, Selected, and with Introductions by

Stephen Satris
Clemson University

The Dushkin Publishing Group, Inc.

To my mother and father

Taking Sides ® is a registered trademark of
The Dushkin Publishing Group, Inc.

Library of Congress Catalog Card Number:
91-72146
Manufactured in the United States of America
Third Edition, First Printing
ISBN: 1-56134-057-X

 Printed on Recycled Paper

The Dushkin Publishing Group, Inc.
Sluice Dock, Guilford, CT 06437

PREFACE

This text contains 40 essays, arranged in *pro* and *contra* pairs, that address 20 controversial issues in morality and moral philosophy. Each of the issues is expressed in terms of a single question in order to draw the lines of debate more clearly.

Some of the questions that are included here have been in the mainstream of moral philosophy for hundreds of years and are central to the discipline. I have not shied away from abstract questions about relativism, subjectivism, and the relationship between morality and religion. Other questions relate to specific topics of contemporary concern, such as euthanasia, abortion, affirmative action, and modern warfare.

The authors of the articles included here take a strong stand on a given issue and provide their own best defenses of a pro or contra position. The articles were selected for their usefulness in defending a position and for their accessibility to students. The authors are philosophers, scientists, lawyers, doctors, theologians, and social critics. Each successfully makes clear to us a determinant answer on an issue—even if we ultimately cannot accept the answer as our own.

Each issue is accompanied by an *introduction*, which sets the stage for debate, and each issue concludes with a *postscript* that summarizes the debate, considers other views on the issue, and suggests additional readings. The introductions and postscripts do not preempt what is the reader's own task: to achieve a critical and informed view of the issue at stake.

Taking Sides: Clashing Views on Controversial Moral Issues is a tool to encourage critical thought on important moral issues. Readers should not feel confined to the views expressed in the articles. Some readers may see important points on both sides of an issue and may construct for themselves a new and creative approach, which may incorporate the best of both sides or provide an entirely new vantage point for understanding.

Changes to this edition This new edition is significantly different from the second edition. Part 2, on the theme Morality and Contemporary Social Thought, is a new section. Part 5, on Morality and the International Scene, has been newly organized to incorporate two new issues on terrorism and modern war. Altogether there are five completely new issues: *Should Environmental Ethics Be Human Centered?* (Issue 6); *Is Feminism a Harmful Ideology?* (Issue 7); *Does Morality Require a Vegetarian Way of Life?* (Issue 8); *Is Terrorism Ever Justified?* (Issue 19); and *Can Modern War Be Just?* (Issue 20). For one issue, the issue question has been rephrased because the topic has been modified and one of the readings replaced: *Is Morality Relative to Culture?* (Issue 1). There are two issues that have remained the same, but in order to add clarity to the debate or to bring it up to date, I have changed one of each of their readings: *Is Abortion Immoral?* (Issue 12) and *Is Affirmative Action Morally Justifiable?* (Issue 17). In all, there are 13 new readings in this edition.

Supplements An *Instructor's Manual with Test Questions* (multiple-choice and essay) is available through the publisher for the instructor using *Taking Sides* in the classroom. A general guidebook, *Using Taking Sides in the Classroom*, which discusses methods and techniques for using the pro-contra approach in any classroom setting, is also available.

Acknowledgments I would like to thank Mimi Egan of the Dushkin Publishing Group for her valuable editorial assistance and sound advice. In working on this revision, I also received useful suggestions from many of the users of the second edition, and I was able to incorporate several of their recommendations in this edition. I particularly wish to thank the following:

Wayne G. Boulton
Hope College

Kenneth L. Brown
Manchester College

Don J. C. Carmichael
University of Alberta

David Carter
Pan American University

Dasiea Cavers-Huff
Riverside Community College

James E. Chesher
Santa Barbara City College

Donald F. Duclow
Gwynedd-Mercy College

Wesley L. Fisher
Gloucester County College

Samuel D. Fohr
University of Pittsburgh

Gary Fuller
Central Michigan University

Theodore Gracyk
Moorhead State University

Robert Hollinger
Iowa State University

C. Stephen Layman
Seattle Pacific University

Joseph Martos
Allentown College of St. Francis de Sales

Joseph M. McLachlan
Western Carolina University

Malcolm Munson
Greenville Technical College

Thomas Michael Norton-Smith
Kent State University

Leonard Olson
Modesto Junior College

Blaine Robinson
South Dakota School of Mines and Technology

Matthias Schulte
Montgomery College-Rockville

Mike Thomson
University of Texas at Austin

Finally, a special debt of thanks is owed to those who tolerated my strange hours and the time spent away from them as this book was being prepared and revised: Kim, Angela, and Michelle.

Stephen Satris
Clemson University

CONTENTS IN BRIEF

CONTENTS

American anthropologist Melville J. Herskovits (1895–1963) takes the position that morality has no absolute identity but is a social and cultural phenomenon that varies according to the customs and beliefs of different cultural groups. In his view, the great enemy of relativism is ethnocentrism, especially as expressed by European colonialism. Philosopher James Rachels claims that a general relativism about moral matters is false and that certain particular values must be maintained by *every* society.

British philosopher Renford Bambrough defends the view that some things are right and some things are wrong and contends that sometimes we have positive knowledge of which is which, no matter that other individuals or groups of people might think. Australian philosopher John L. Mackie (1917–1981) argues that people project their own moral values on the world and then delude themselves into thinking that morality is a matter of objective fact.

British philosopher Bertrand Russell (1872–1970) holds that morality is subjective, moral judgments express personal emotions, and differences in value judgments are due to differences in taste. American philosopher Brand Blanshard (1892–1987) rejects all of these views and maintains that subjectivism in ethics is untenable. He argues that when one makes a moral judgment about something, one is making a judgment about that object (an objective judgment), not simply expressing one's (subjective) feelings.

Professor of philosophy Jack Bemporad argues that only in religion is there a true foundation for ethics. He claims that if ethical questions are pushed far enough, they must eventually go beyond themselves into the religious realm; and here, the Judeo-Christian monotheistic tradition is particularly relevant. Philosopher John Arthur claims that morality is independent of religion. He does not claim that religious doctrines are false but, rather, that both the believer and the nonbeliever have to approach moral questions in the same way: by considering the merits of the case.

Professor of philosophy J. J. C. Smart defends the principle that one ought to act in such a way as to promote the greatest happiness for the greatest number. It is this end result that justifies doing even things that might seem wrong when judged by a traditional moral perspective. Professor of philosophy Paul W. Taylor objects to the utilitarianism of Smart and others on the ground that the theory does not take proper notice of the principles of justice. In particular, utilitarianism cannot rightfully support injustice even if an unfair act would supposedly lead to greater happiness in the end.

Professor of law William F. Baxter argues that environmental problems must be addressed and solved from a human point of view. He further claims that any resources, such as money, that are committed to environmental purposes will result in less available resources for other good purposes, such as education, health, and art. Philosopher Lawrence E. Johnson argues that wilderness areas, ecosystems, and even the entire biosphere are all self-maintaining systems that have interests. He warns that human beings, who have a tendency to exploit the environment, must be careful not to make such systems worse off.

Professor of philosophy Michael Levin argues that feminism ignores innate differences between men and women. Any attempt to enforce sexual equality would violate nature and would violate liberal values. Novelist and literary critic Marilyn French argues that feminism requires a thorough change in people's attitudes. Feminism is not the simple claim that women be allowed admittance to a previously male-only social world; it calls for that social world itself to be changed.

Professor of philosophy Tom Regan addresses the morality of raising animals for food. He considers the situation from three different points of view, which he calls the utilitarian, holist, and rights views, and concludes that all three points of view support the practice of vegetarianism. Professor of philosophy Philip E. Devine takes the view that the defenses of vegetarianism that have been offered by utilitarians and others fail to establish what they set out to prove. In light of this failure, eating meat remains a strong option for human beings.

Canadian philosopher Trudy Govier argues that society does have an obligation to care for the less well off, and welfare should be provided without being made contingent upon something (a willingness to work, for example). Author and social critic Irving Kristol argues that society should not redistribute wealth to the less well off but should promote economic growth in general.

PART 3 MORALITY, SEX, AND REPRODUCTION   167

Professor of philosophy Richard D. Mohr argues that homosexuals suffer from unjust discrimination and defends homosexuality against charges that it is immoral and unnatural. Psychologist Paul Cameron claims that homosexuality is associated with many negative personal traits. He argues that society would be making a mistake to allow homosexuality equal status with heterosexuality.

Professor of philosophy Ann Garry argues that pornography—as it exists today—degrades women and therefore is immoral. Pornographic materials violate principles of respect, and they send a message that calls for the violation of respect for women. G. L. Simons, a British writer on sex and social issues, claims that while it would be almost impossible to show that pornography (or anything else) is totally harm-free, some people enjoy pornography and some even learn from it. There is no evidence to show some great harm that would outweigh these acknowledged goods.

Professor of philosophy Don Marquis argues that abortion is generally wrong for the same reason that killing an innocent adult human being is generally wrong: we deprive the individual of a future that he or she would otherwise have. Philosopher Jane English (1947–1978) argues that there is no well-defined line dividing persons from nonpersons. She claims that both the conservative and the liberal positions are too extreme and that some abortions are morally justifiable and some are not.

Professor of law Herbert T. Krimmel argues that the fundamental wrong in surrogate motherhood lies in a woman's intention to have a baby not because she wants it but because she wants to give it away. In addition, numerous practical problems arise from surrogate arrangements. Philosopher Ruth Macklin argues that once we put purely emotional responses and "gut reactions" aside—and that is indeed necessary—the only thing wrong with the current practice of surrogate motherhood is the commercial aspect.

Psychiatrist Karl Menninger (1893–1990) argues that people have a double
attitude toward crime. We condemn crime, but we also seem to need to keep
it around. We hold criminals in prison, make little or no effort to rehabilitate
them, and then release them back into society. A therapeutic attitude should
replace this vindictiveness, and treatment of criminals should replace punishment. Religious writer C. S. Lewis (1898–1963) argues that this so-called
humanitarian approach is not really merciful and not really just. It does not
consider criminals to be human beings but "cases" to be "cured." Criminals
deserve, and should receive, punishment, not treatment.

Professor of philosophy Hugo Adam Bedau argues that the idea of "an eye
for an eye" (of retribution in kind) has not historically supported capital
punishment; in actuality, a wide variety of offenses have been punished by
death. The death penalty claims the lives of the least well defended (including some innocent people) rather than the most serious criminals. Ernest van
den Haag, legal professor and social critic, argues that capital punishment is
a fitting punishment for murder and that there are some crimes that are so
terrible that the most appropriate response is the death penalty.

J. Gay-Williams believes that euthanasia is immoral because it violates one's personal will to survive. In addition, he points out, a public policy that allows euthanasia would have severely negative practical effects. Moral philosopher Richard Brandt argues that killing human beings ordinarily injures them and violates their preferences. In cases of euthanasia, when both of these conditions are lacking, the killing could be allowable.

Professor of philosophy Richard Wasserstrom, in defense of affirmative action programs, refutes criticisms designed to persuade that, however well-intentioned affirmative action programs might be, they are fundamentally flawed. Philosopher Barry R. Gross argues that programs of affirmative action fail to fit any reasonable model of reparation or compensation, and they introduce undesirable consequences of their own. They are all cases of reverse discrimination and are all fundamentally unjust.

Professor of philosophy Peter Singer argues that citizens of rich nations can help those in poor nations without great harm to themselves and that, therefore, they *should* help. Biologist Garrett Hardin argues that since birthrates in poorer nations are high and the Earth can provide only finite resources, future generations of all nations will be hurt if wealthy nations help poor nations.

Professor of philosophy Virginia Held admits that a limited terrorism, directed to those in political power or their protectors, may be justifiable. She agrees that no violent, illegal acts *should* be morally justifiable, but if a terrorist act is the only way to counter state-inspired terrorism and if it is likely to succeed, then it may be justified. Professor of philosophy Alfred Louch argues that terrorism of any sort cannot be justified. He believes that terrorists' concerns, which seem only to extend to the destruction of present institutions and not to the possible good that may or may not result from their actions, are not sufficient motives to warrant the type of violence that they employ.

Professor of philosophy Robert L. Phillips argues that modern war, like any other war, can indeed be just if it is initiated and conducted within the requirements for a just war, which he specifies. Professor of philosophy Robert L. Holmes argues that war in the modern world is not justified. He dissociates himself from an absolute pacifism and argues that modern war involves means that always violate justice.

INTRODUCTION

Thinking About Moral Issues
Stephen Satris

GETTING STARTED

If you were asked in your biology class to give the exact number of bones in the average human foot, you could consult your textbook, or you could go to the library and have the librarian track down the answer, or you could ask your friend who always gets A's in biology. Most likely you haven't previously had any reason to consider this question, but you do know for certain that it has one right answer, which you will be expected to provide for the final exam.

What do you do, however, when faced with a moral question like one of the ones raised in this text? Where do you begin when asked, for example, does society have an obligation to care for the less well off? Maybe this is something you have already thought about, particularly if you have been stopped by a streetperson and asked for money. You may already have formed some opinions or made some assumptions—or maybe you even have conflicting opinions. Whereas it is a relatively straightforward matter to find out how many bones there are in the human foot, in addressing moral issues, understanding cannot be acquired as easily. Someone cannot report back to you on the right answer. You will have to discuss the ideas raised by these moral questions and determine the answers for yourself. And you will have to arrive at an answer through reason and careful thought; you cannot just rely on your *feelings* to answer these questions. Keep in mind, too, that these are questions you will be facing your entire life—understanding will not end with the final exam.

In approaching the issues in this book, one should maintain an open mind toward both sides of the question. Many readers will already have positions on many of the issues raised in this book. But if you are committed to one side of an issue, it will be more difficult for you to see, appreciate, and, most importantly, learn from the opposing position. Therefore, you first ought to ask yourself what are your own assumptions about an issue; become aware of any preconceived notions you may have. And then, after such reflection, you ought to assume the posture of an impartial judge. If you have a strong prior attachment to one side, that should not prevent you from giving a sympathetic ear to the opposing side.

Once the arguments have been laid out and you have given them careful consideration, you do not want to remain suspended in the middle. *Now* is the time for informed judgment.

A natural dramatic sequence is played out for each of the 20 issues discussed in *Taking Sides: Clashing Views on Controversial Moral Issues*. A question is posed, and you must open yourself to hear the arguments, reasons, and examples, which are meant to be persuasive. But then comes the second part of the drama. Having heard and considered both sides of an issue, what will *you* say? What understanding of the issue can *you* achieve?

You can choose aspects of the "yes" answer and aspects of the "no" answer and weave them together, if you can construct a coherent whole in such fashion. You can accept one answer and build some qualifications or limitations into it. Or you might be stimulated to think of a completely new angle on the issue.

Be aware of two dangers. The first is a premature judgment or fixed opinion that rules out a fair hearing of the other side. The second danger is to lack a judgment after having considered the issue. In this case, two contrary positions simply cannot both be right, and it is up to the reader to make an effort to distinguish what is acceptable from what is unacceptable in the arguments and positions that have been defended.

FUNDAMENTAL QUESTIONS

The 20 issues in this book are divided into four sections, or parts. The first section deals with fundamental questions about morality considered as a whole. It is in this context that one sometimes hears "it's all subjective" or "it's all relative." The issues in the first part do not directly confront specific moral problems; they question the nature of morality itself.

A few words of caution are in order about some of the issues in Part 1. The following three questions are interrelated: Is morality relative to culture? Is morality subjective? and Is morality grounded in religion? A positive answer to any one of them would establish society, the individual, or God, respectively, as the final court of appeal in morality. Since, in general, there cannot be more than one final court of appeal, a positive answer to one of these questions seems to require a negative answer to the other two.

A further point, and one that applies not only to these three issues but to controversial issues in general, is this: In evaluating any position, you should do so on the merits (or lack of merit) of the specific case that is made. Do not accept or reject a position on the basis of what the position (supposedly) tells you about the author, and do not criticize or defend a position by reducing it to simplistic slogans. The loss of articulation and sophistication that occurs when a complex position is boiled down to a simple slogan is significant and real. For example, a "no" answer to the question, Is morality grounded in religion? might be superficially labeled as "antireligion" and a "yes" answer as "proreligion." Yet, Saint Thomas Aquinas, who has always been regarded as the foremost theologian of the Christian tradition, would respond with a "no" to that question. Moral questions are complex, and the reduction of answers to superficial slogans will not be helpful. The questions and issues that are raised here require careful analysis, examination, and argumentation.

MORALITY AND CONTEMPORARY SOCIAL THOUGHT

Part 2 includes several questions that have to do with ways of looking at the world, including the biological world and the social world. In many respects, these issues are basic to an understanding of one's own place within the world and one's relationship to other people, animals, and things. Issues considered in Part 2 are: Should environmental ethics be human centered? Is feminism a harmful ideology? Does morality require a vegetarian way of life? and Does society have an obligation to care for the less well off?

When we turn our attention to the environment, there is general agreement that we should be aware of threats to the environment. For example, we *should* be concerned about various types of pollution. But why? Is it because (regardless of the pollution's effects on human beings) wildlife and natural habitats might be destroyed? Or is it because (regardless of the pollution's effects on wildlife and natural habitats) human life might be adversely affected? In many cases, of course, since we are ourselves part of the living environment, matters of ecological concern affect both wildlife and ourselves. But suppose there is a threat to a species that few people care about. Or suppose people clear land (and destroy animal habitats) in order to make homes for themselves. Here is where people become divided. Should we start paying more attention to the state of the environment because a lack of such concern will have a negative impact on people, or because a lack of such concern will have a negative impact on wildlife (or ecosystems)?

The question of whether feminism is a harmful ideology is different in that it deals with people and social life. This issue is not about the relationship of a particular person to another one of the opposite sex. It explores the social roles that are maintained by society and into which society demands that all males and females must fit. Feminism forces us to question what has often been taken for granted in our culture.

Does morality require a vegetarian way of life? is a question that challenges much that has been taken for granted in our culture and also challenges the way that animals are currently treated in our culture. Is there such a thing as cruelty to animals and mistreatment of animals? Can animals suffer wrongfully? Are animals that are raised for human consumption subjected to cruelty, mistreatment, and wrongful suffering? The new consciousness inspired by environmental awareness should inspire us to take a second look at meat-eating and vegetarianism.

We also ask: Does society have an obligation to care for the less well off? Those who support a "yes" answer to this question would have society, primarily through government agencies, care directly for the needs of the poor. If the poor need food, shelter, and medicine, then this is what would be supplied. Those who support the "no" position deny that these items should simply be supplied (given) to the needy. Our relation to the needy, they say, should not be one of caring directly for them; rather, we are to create a thriving economic system in which the poor and needy can find ways to take care of themselves.

MORALITY, SEX, AND REPRODUCTION

Part 3 introduces questions about particular moral issues that relate specifically to individuals as sexual and reproductive beings. The questions here are: Should homosexuality be accepted by society? Is pornography immoral? Is abortion immoral? and Is surrogate motherhood wrong?

Only in the last 20 years or so in the United States has a movement for "gay rights" and "gay liberation" even dared to be active and visible. Prior to that time, public pressure with regard to homosexuality had been consistently negative. It is still largely negative, but there is also a strong belief that what consenting adults do in private is their own business (and not society's business). Homosexuality does not just involve private acts, however. In order to see this, consider the fact that a person who is celibate (one who abstains from sexual intercourse) may be either a homosexual or a heterosexual (or a bisexual). Sexual orientation has at least as much to do with perceptions, with how one views one's own sexual identity and how one sees others, as it does with private *acts*. This issue is worth exploring not only for possible insights into homosexuality, but also for possible insights into wider social arrangements and institutions.

A similar recommendation can be made about the question: Is pornography immoral? An exploration of this question, and associated social observations, might lead not only to insight into pornography itself but also to insight into larger social phenomena. Recent feminist criticism of pornography, represented in Issue 11 by Ann Garry's article, must be recognized as quite different from more traditional complaints about such things as "dirty pictures." Garry and others invite us to consider the matter in a new light; and when we do, that light may be turned onto other social phenomena too.

The question: Is abortion immoral? is not at all a new one. It threatens to polarize people into "pro-life" and "pro-choice" camps, but it is best to leave such labels and superficial slogans behind. Whenever an issue seems to demand answers very quickly, as this one might, it is better to go slowly and to first consider the arguments, examples, and rationale of each position before making up your mind.

The last question in this section, which is about surrogate motherhood, is not as familiar as the previous question. One of the troubling aspects of surrogate motherhood has been the idea that women would bear babies for money. Our question asks whether surrogate motherhood itself is wrong, and it does not explore the commercial angle.

MORALITY, LAW, AND SOCIETY

The first two questions in Part 4 are: Do we have a moral responsibility to rehabilitate criminals? and Should capital punishment be abolished? These questions ask about our social response to criminal activity. One approach to criminal activity would be to provide treatment for criminals, in order that they might freely enter into society again. Another approach is to punish criminals, usually by imprisonment.

The second question addresses a more extreme aspect of criminal punishment: the death penalty. Many subsidiary questions enter into this issue. Does the death penalty deter crime? Is it the only way to give some criminals what they deserve? Is there a worldwide contemporary movement away from the death penalty? And, finally, even if we had the answers to all of these questions, is there a way of using those answers to answer the overarching question of whether capital punishment should be abolished?

Is euthanasia immoral? is another question of life and death. In addressing this question, it might be useful to keep in mind the distinction between voluntary euthanasia (where the person who is killed has specifically requested this) and involuntary euthanasia (where no such request has been made). An important factor is also the physical, mental, and emotional condition of the person who makes this request. We might want to make a distinction between a young, healthy person who is suffering from emotional pain and an older, dying person, whose suffering is physical. In the first case, *we* might see that there is indeed life beyond the emotional trauma or depression, although the person actually going through the experience might not be able to see this. But in the second case, the judgment of the dying person might be entirely reasonable and correct. Could it be that suicide prevention is called for in one case and euthanasia in the other? Or is euthanasia always wrong?

Another topic raised in this section is that of affirmative action, a policy that is intended to address problems due to the history and the legacy of race relations in this country. There are at least two general ways of regarding affirmative action: it can be seen as backward-looking or forward-looking. If it is a form of compensation or a response to previous injustice, then it is backward-looking. It aims to justify itself by looking at the past. If it is a method for promoting a more racially integrated and just society, then it is forward-looking. Programs of affirmative action have attracted opposition, however—not opposition to the charge that previous discrimination was unjust, nor to the ideal of a racially integrated and just society in the future, but opposition to affirmative action itself as reverse discrimination. Sometimes affirmative action is thought of as an unjust means to a just end—an unfair tilting of the playing field in order to help certain players.

MORALITY AND THE INTERNATIONAL SCENE

Since many legal matters only extend as far as a country's boundaries, and morality is often associated with legality, moral concerns might be thought to be confined within one country's boundaries. But this would be a mistaken view. In the absence of any special theory to the contrary, it seems that moral issues do not radically change—as the law might well change—when we cross international borders.

Opponents of abortion, for example, who work for the abolition of legal abortions in this country, do not generally believe that it is entirely all right if other countries continue to allow abortions. They think that it is wrong wherever it occurs—whether in the United States, England, Japan, or the Soviet Union. Likewise, those who support a woman's right to have an abortion do not consider themselves to be restricted by nationality.

The three issues considered in Part 5 are by no means the only issues that involve the world outside one's own country, but they do raise issues that *specifically* address the relationship between countries and between the people of different countries. The questions are: Do rich nations have an obligation to help poor nations? Is terrorism ever justified? and Can modern war be just?

Catastrophic natural disasters and political turmoil bring suffering and even starvation to the people of some nations. Is there an obligation on the part of more financially stable government to assist in such cases? Or is there a reason to control or resist sympathetic responses?

Asking whether terrorism is ever justified forces us to confront extremely difficult issues. On the one hand, we tend to feel that terrorists are unsavory characters who unjustly take the law into their own hands or violate the established law. On the other hand, it seems possible that a political system could be so corrupt or so noncognizant of people's rights that potential terrorists present themselves as the only solution. But are there some actions that would always be wrong? Must terrorism never be an option, or are there situations where resorting to terrorism is justified?

These lines of thought are also relevant to the final question: Can modern war be just? Terrorists can claim that they aim to achieve their political goals with far less bloodshed than would be caused by a modern war. Those who support the idea of war, but not terrorism, can point out that wars are declared by proper authorities while terrorists (like outlaws) act on their own. Christians who support the idea of war have a particular problem since they are committed to the Old Testament commandment "Thou shalt not kill." Over the centuries, partly in response to the difficulty of reconciling warfare with such teachings, there has developed a Christian theory of just war. Recently, this theory has been found to be useful by Christians and non-Christians alike. It does not make war necessarily acceptable, but it does describe what to look for if a war is to be morally permissible. Is the theory of just war applicable in the modern world?

LE PENSEVR
DE RODIN OFFERT
PAR SOVSCRIPTION
PVBLIQVE AV PEVPLE

PART 1

Fundamental Issues in Morality

Even before confronting particular moral issues, we find that there are several conflicting claims that have been made about morality considered as a whole. Relativists claim that morality is different for different cultural groups: one culture determines what is right or wrong for that culture, and another culture determines what is right or wrong for itself. The ideas of "moral fact" and "moral truth" have been radically questioned. One side affirms that there are indeed moral facts, the other side denies this. Subjectivists claim that all moral talk is simply the expression of subjective feelings, which vary from person to person. These and other points of view are discussed in this section.

Is Morality Relative to Culture?

Are There Moral Facts?

Is Morality Subjective?

Is Morality Grounded in Religion?

Do the Ends Justify the Means?

ISSUE 1

Is Morality Relative to Culture?

YES: Melville J. Herskovits, from "Cultural Relativism and Cultural Values," in Frances Herskovits, ed., *Cultural Relativism: Perspectives in Cultural Pluralism* (Random House, 1986)

NO: James Rachels, from *The Elements of Moral Philosophy* (Random House, 1986)

ISSUE SUMMARY

YES: American anthropologist Melville J. Herskovits (1895–1963) takes the position that morality has no absolute identity but is a social and cultural phenomenon that varies according to the customs and beliefs of different cultural groups. In his view, the great enemy of relativism is ethnocentrism, especially as expressed by European colonialism.
NO: Philosopher James Rachels claims that a general relativism about moral matters is false and that certain particular values must be maintained by every society.

As the social sciences began to be recognized during the last century, many thinkers developed a particular interest in the customs and morals of other groups of people. In 1865 (six years after Darwin's *Origin of Species* and six years before his *Descent of Man*), Sir Edward Tylor (1832–1917), one of the great leaders in the scientific study of humans, published his *Researches into the Early History of Mankind.* Tylor believed that the study of ancient pagans, and the study of uncivilized people and various heathen groups that lived outside the scope of civilized Victorian culture, would throw light on English culture itself. It was Tylor's view that all people shared the same human capacities and mental potentialities and that there had been a progression, or positive development, from ignorant savagery to civilized culture. This was a daring view at the time. Many people (especially defenders of religious orthodoxy) believed both that Darwin was seriously wrong to affirm a development or evolution of man from animals and that Tylor was seriously wrong to affirm a development or evolution of intelligent civilized Christians from ignorant uncivilized pagan savages. The conventional view held by many was that God had created man in his image as a rational and moral being; any savages who existed in the nineteenth century must have fallen into that state through a neglect of reason, a lack of morality, and an absence of faith. Surely, this view continued, God's initial creation of man was not the creation of an ignorant savage who wore beads (if anything at all) and followed a pagan life of promiscuity and superstition.

Sir James Frazer (1854–1941) was greatly stimulated by his reading of Tylor. He too wrote extensively about the customs of primitive people, and believed that such people exhibited "the rudimentary phases, the infancy and childhood, of human society." To the question whether he had actually seen any of the savages that he had written so much about, Frazer is said to have replied, "God forbid!" Frazer and most social scientists of the late nineteenth century studied books, read the diaries of travelers, and corresponded with those in distant lands. Field study had not yet established itself as a necessary social scientific technique. The armchair studies of Frazer are by no means manifestations of laziness or lack of commitment; Frazer devoted his life to the scientific study of humankind and is said to have spent 12 hours a day for over 50 years reading, taking notes, and writing.

During this century several well-known social scientists have endorsed a sophisticated type of cultural relativism. The armchair studies have been replaced by years of field studies that include a sympathetic involvement with the lives of the people one is studying. Gone is the view that so-called primitive people are standing on the lower rungs of the same ladder that leads to modern Western culture. There is no separation of the "civilized" and the "uncivilized." There are *various* civilizations and *various* cultures, and our own culture is only one of many.

Melville J. Herskovits was a champion of cultural relativism, which he saw as an antidote to European colonial attitudes and the ethnocentrism that they express. Herskovits was, in particular, a student of African societies and of the experience of blacks in the New World. He regarded it as a great mistake and a great tragedy that Europeans thought that they were the civilized ones and that the Africans were not. It was by force, not by civilization, that Europeans imposed themselves upon African culture. According to cultural relativism, it is false to think that in matters of morality our own Western culture is uniquely in a position to make absolute moral judgments. The fact is, different cultures simply have different moralities. The moral precepts of a given culture might appear as absolute to the individual who is enculturated in that culture, but this is a common error. Such is the view that Herskovits expresses in the following selection.

James Rachels responds critically to cultural relativism. He never challenges Herskovits on the question of colonialism, but argues that cultural relativism, at least with respect to morality, has several highly implausible consequences. And these consequences, when understood, should lead to the rejection of moral relativism. Moreover, he provides some reasons to think that certain particular practices must be supported by any society in any time and any place.

YES
Melville J. Herskovits

CULTURAL RELATIVISM AND CULTURAL VALUES

All peoples form judgments about ways of life different from their own. Where systematic study is undertaken, comparison gives rise to classification, and scholars have devised many schemes for classifying ways of life. Moral judgments have been drawn regarding the ethical principles that guide the behavior and mold the value systems of different peoples. Their economic and political structures and their religious beliefs have been ranked in order of complexity, efficiency, desirability. Their art, music, and literary forms have been weighed.

It has become increasingly evident, however, that evaluations of this kind stand or fall with the acceptance of the premises from which they derive. In addition, many of the criteria on which judgment is based are in conflict, so that conclusions drawn from one definition of what is desirable will not agree with those based on another formulation.

A simple example will illustrate this. There are not many ways in which the primary family can be constituted. One man may live with one woman, one woman may have a number of husbands, one man may have a number of wives. But if we evaluate these forms according to their function of perpetuating the group, it is clear that they perform their essential tasks. Otherwise, the societies wherein they exist would not survive.

Such an answer will, however, not satisfy all those who have undertaken to study cultural evaluation. What of the moral questions inherent in the practice of monogamy as against polygamy, the adjustment of children raised in households where, for example, the mothers must compete on behalf of their offspring for the favors of a common husband? If monogamy is held to be the desired form of marriage, the responses to these questions are predetermined. But when we consider these questions from the point of view of those who live in polygamous societies, alternative answers, based on different conceptions of what is desirable, may be given.

Let us consider, for example, the life of a plural family in the West African culture of Dahomey.[1] Here, within a compound, live a man and his wives.

From Melville J. Herskovits, "Cultural Relativism and Cultural Values," in Frances Herskovits, ed., *Cultural Relativism: Perspectives in Cultural Pluralism* (Random House, 1972). Copyright © 1972 by Frances Herskovits. Reprinted by permission.

The man has his own house, as has each of the women and her children, after the basic African principle that two wives cannot successfully inhabit the same quarters. Each wife in turn spends a native week of four days with the common husband, cooking his food, washing his clothes, sleeping in his house, and then making way for the next. Her children, however, remain in their mother's hut. With pregnancy, she drops out of this routine, and ideally, in the interest of her child's health and her own, does not again visit her husband until the child has been born and weaned. This means a period of from three to four years, since infants are nursed two years and longer.

The compound, made up of these households, is a cooperative unit. The women who sell goods in the market, or make pottery, or have their gardens, contribute to its support. This aspect, though of great economic importance, is secondary to the prestige that attaches to the larger unit. This is why one often finds a wife not only urging her husband to acquire a second spouse but even aiding him by loans or gifts to make this possible.

Tensions do arise between the women who inhabit a large compound. Thirteen different ways of getting married have been recorded in this society, and in a large household those wives who are married in the same category tend to unite against all others. Competition for the regard of the husband is also a factor, when several wives try to influence the choice of an heir in favor of their own sons. Yet all the children of the compound play together, and the strength of the emotional ties between the children of the same mother more than compensates for whatever stresses may arise between brothers and sisters who share the same father but are of different mothers. Cooperation, moreover, is by no means a mere formality among the wives. Many common tasks are performed in friendly unison, and there is solidarity in the interest of women's prerogatives, or where the status of the common husband is threatened.

We may now return to the criteria to be applied in drawing judgments concerning polygamous as against monogamous families. The family structure of Dahomey is obviously a complex institution. If we but consider the possible lines of personal relations among the many individuals concerned, we see clearly how numerous are the ramifications of reciprocal right and obligation of the Dahomean family. The effectiveness of the Dahomean family is, however, patent. It has, for untold generations, performed its function of rearing the young; more than this, the very size of the group gives it economic resources and a resulting stability that might well be envied by those who live under different systems of family organization. Moral values are always difficult to establish, but at least in this society marriage is clearly distinguished from casual sex relations and from prostitution, in its supernatural sanctions and in the prestige it confers, to say nothing of the economic obligations toward spouse and prospective offspring explicitly accepted by one who enters into a marriage.

Numerous problems of adjustment do present themselves in an aggregate of this sort. It does not call for much speculation to understand the plaint of the head of one large compound when he said: "One must be something of a diplomat if one has many wives." Yet the sly digs in proverb and song, and the open quarreling, involve no greater stress than is found in any small rural community where people are also thrown closely together for long periods of time. Quarrels between co-wives are not greatly different from disputes over the back fence between neighbors. And Dahomeans who know European culture, when they argue for their system, stress the fact that it permits the individual wife to space her children in a way that is in accord with the best precepts of modern gynecology.

Thus polygamy, when looked at from the point of view of those who practice it, is seen to hold values that are not apparent from the outside. A similar case can be made for monogamy, however, when it is attacked by those who are enculturated to a different kind of family structure. And what is true of a particular phase of culture such as this, is also true of others. Evaluations are *relative* to the cultural background out of which they arise.

2

Cultural relativism is in essence an approach to the question of the nature and role of values in culture. It represents a scientific, inductive attack on an age-old philosophical problem, using fresh, cross-cultural data, hitherto not available to scholars, gained from the study of the underlying value-systems of societies having the most diverse customs. The principle of cultural relativism, briefly stated, is as follows: *Judgments are based on experience, and experience is interpreted by each individual in terms of his own enculturation.* Those who hold for the existence of fixed values will find materials in other societies that necessitate a reinvestigation of their assumptions. Are there absolute moral standards, or are moral standards effective only as far as they agree with the orientations of a given people at a given period of their history? We even approach the problem of the ultimate nature of reality itself. Cassirer[2] holds that reality can only be experienced through the symbolism of language. Is reality, then, not defined and redefined by the ever-varied symbolisms of the innumerable languages of mankind?

Answers to questions such as these represent one of the most profound contributions of anthropology to the analysis of man's place in the world. When we reflect that such intangibles as right and wrong, normal and abnormal, beautiful and plain are absorbed as a person learns the ways of the group into which he is born, we see that we are dealing here with a process of first importance. Even the facts of the physical world are discerned through the enculturative screen, so that the perception of time, distance, weight, size, and other "realities" is mediated by the conventions of any given group.

No culture, however, is a closed system of rigid molds to which the behavior of all members of a society must conform. In stressing the psychological reality of culture, it was made plain that a culture, as such, can *do* nothing. It is but the summation of the behavior and habitual modes of thought of the persons who make up a particular society. Though by learning and habit these individuals conform to the ways of the group into which they have been born, they nonetheless vary in their reactions to the situations of living they commonly meet. They vary, too, in the degree to which they desire change, as whole cultures vary. This is but another way in which we see that culture is flexible and holds many possibilities of choice within its framework, and that to recognize the values held by a given people in no wise implies that these values are a constant factor in the lives of succeeding generations of the same group. . . .

[W]hile recognizing the role of both father and mother in procreation, many peoples have conventions of relationship that count descent on but one side of the family. In such societies, it is common for incest lines to be so arbitrarily defined that "first cousins," as we would say, on the mother's side call each other brother and sister and regard marriage with one another with horror. Yet marriage within the same degree of biological relationship on the father's side may be held not only desirable, but sometimes mandatory. This is because two persons related in this way are by definition not considered blood relatives.

The very definition of what is normal or abnormal is relative to the cultural frame of reference. As an example of this, we may take the phenomenon of possession as found among African and New World Negroes. The supreme expression of their religious experience, possession, is a psychological state wherein a displacement of personality occurs when the god "comes to the head" of the worshipper. The individual thereupon is held to be the deity himself. This phenomenon has been described in pathological terms by many students whose approach is nonanthropological, because of its surface resemblance to cases in the records of medical practitioners, psychological clinicians, psychiatrists, and others. The hysteria-like trances, where persons, their eyes tightly closed, move about excitedly and presumably without purpose or design, or roll on the ground, muttering meaningless syllables, or go into a state where their bodies achieve complete rigidity, are not difficult to equate with the neurotic and even psychotic manifestations of abnormality found in Euroamerican society.

Yet when we look beneath behavior to meaning, and place such apparently random acts in their cultural frame of reference, such conclusions become untenable. For *relative to the setting in which these possession experiences occur, they are not to be regarded as abnormal at all,* much less psychopathological. They are *culturally patterned,* and often induced by learning and discipline. The dancing or other acts of the possessed persons are so stylized that one who knows this religion can identify the god possessing a devotee by the behavior of the individual possessed. Furthermore, the possession experience does not seem to be confined to emotionally unstable persons. Those who "get the god" run the gamut of personality types found in the group. Observation of persons who frequent the cults, yet who, in the idiom of worship "have nothing in the head" and thus never experience possession, seems to show that they are far less adjusted than those who do get possessed. Finally, the nature of the possession experience in these cultures is so disciplined that it may only come to a given devotee under particular circumstances. In West Africa and Brazil the gods come only to those who have been designated in advance by the priest of their group, who lays his hands on their heads. In Haiti, for an initiate not a member of the family group giving a rite to become possessed at a ceremony is considered extremely "bad form" socially and a sign of spiritual weakness, evidence that the god is not under the control of his worshipper.

The terminology of psychopathology, employed solely for descriptive purposes, may be of some utility. But the connotation it carries of psychic instability, emotional imbalance, and departure from normality recommends the use of other words that do not invite such a distortion of cultural reality. For in these Negro societies, the meaning this experience holds for the people falls entirely in the realm of understandable, predictable, *normal* behavior. This behavior is known and recognized by all members as an experience that may come to any one of them, and is to be welcomed not only for the psychological security it affords, but also for the status, economic gain, aesthetic expression, and emotional release it vouchsafes the devotee.

3

The primary mechanism that directs the evaluation of culture is *ethnocentrism*. Ethnocentrism is the point of view that one's own way of life is to be preferred to all others. Flowing logically from the process of early enculturation, it characterizes the way most individuals feel about their own culture, whether or not they verbalize their feeling. Outside the stream of Euroamerican culture, particularly among nonliterate peoples, this is taken for granted and is to be viewed as a factor making for individual adjustment and social integration. For the strengthening of the ego, identification with one's own group, whose ways are implicitly accepted as best, is all-important. It is when, as in Euroamerican culture, ethnocentrism is rationalized and made the basis of programs of action detrimental to the well-being of other peoples that it gives rise to serious problems.

The ethnocentrism of nonliterate peoples is best illustrated in their myths, folk tales, proverbs, and linguistic habits. It is manifest in many tribal names whose meaning in their respective languages signifies "human beings." The inference that those to whom the name does not apply are outside this category is, however, rarely, if ever, explicitly made. When the Suriname Bush Negro, shown a flashlight, admires it and then quotes the proverb: "White man's magic isn't black man's magic," he is merely reaffirming his faith in his own culture. He is pointing out that the stranger, for all his mechanical devices, would be lost in the Guiana jungle without the aid of his Bush Negro friends.

A myth of the origin of human races, told by the Cherokee Indians of the Great Smoky Mountains, gives another instance of this kind of ethnocentrism. The Creator fashioned man by first making and firing an oven and then, from dough he had prepared, shaping three figures in human form. He placed the figures in the oven and waited for them to get done. But his impatience to see the result of this, his crowning experiment in the work of creation, was so great that he removed the first figure too soon. It was sadly underdone—pale, an unlovely color, and from it descended the white people. His second figure had fared well. The timing was accurate, the form, richly browned, that was to be the ancestor of the Indians, pleased him in every way. He so admired it, indeed, that he neglected to take out of the oven the third form, until he smelled it burning. He threw open the door, only to find this last one charred and black. It was regrettable, but there was nothing to be done; and this was the first Negro.[3]

This is the more usual form that ethnocentrism takes among many peoples—a gentle insistence on the good qualities of one's own group, without any drive to extend this attitude into the field of action. With such a point of view, the objectives, sanctioned modes of behavior, and value systems of peoples with whom one's own group comes into contact can be considered in terms of their desirability, then accepted or rejected without any reference to absolute standards. That differences in the manner of achieving commonly sought objectives may be permitted to exist without a judgment being entered on them involves a reorientation in thought for those in the Euroamerican tradition, because in this tradition, a difference in belief or behavior too often implies something is worse, or less desirable, and must be changed.

The assumption that the cultures of nonliterate peoples are of inferior quality is the end product of a long series of developments in our intellectual history. It is not often recalled that the concept of progress, that strikes so deep into our thinking, is relatively recent. It is, in fact, a unique product of our culture. It is a part of the same historic stream that developed the scientific tradition and that developed the machine, thus giving Europe and America the final word in debates about cultural superiority. "He who makes the gun-powder wields the power," runs a Dahomean proverb. There is no rebuttal to an argument, backed by cannon, advanced to a people who can defend their position with no more than spears, or bows and arrows, or at best a flint-lock gun.

With the possible exception of technological aspects of life, however, the proposition that one way of thought or action is better than another is exceedingly difficult to establish on the grounds of any universally acceptable criteria. Let us take food as an instance. Cultures are equipped differently for the production of food, so that some peoples eat more than others. However, even on the subsistence level, there is no people who do not hold certain potential foodstuffs to be unfit for human consumption. Milk, which figures importantly in our diet, is rejected as food by the peoples of southeastern Asia. Beef, a valued element of the Euroamerican cuisine, is regarded with disgust by Hindus. Nor need compulsions be this strong. The thousands of cattle that range the East African highlands are primarily wealth to be preserved, and not a source of food. Only the cow that dies is eaten—a practice that, though abhorrent to us, has apparently done no harm to those who have been following it for generations.

Totemic and religious taboos set up further restrictions on available foodstuffs, while the refusal to consume many other edible and nourishing substances is simply based on the enculturative conditioning. So strong is this conditioning that prohibited food consumed unwittingly may induce such a physiological reaction as vomiting. All young animals provide succulent meat, but the religious abhorrence of the young pig by the Mohammedan is no stronger than the secular rejection of puppy steaks or colt chops by ourselves. Ant larvae, insect grubs, locusts—all of which have caloric values and vitamin content—when roasted or otherwise cooked, or even when raw, are regarded by many peoples as delicacies. We never eat them, however, though they are equally available to us. On the other hand, some of the same peoples who feed on these with gusto regard substances that come out of tin cans as unfit for human consumption. . . .

4

Before we terminate our discussion of cultural relativism, it is important that we consider certain questions that are raised when the cultural-relativistic position is advanced. "It may be true," it is argued, "that human beings live in accordance with the ways they have learned. These ways may be regarded by them as best. A people may be so devoted to these ways that they are ready to fight and die for them. In terms of survival value, their effectiveness may be admitted, since the group that lives in accordance with them continues to exist. But does this mean that all systems of moral values, all concepts of right and wrong, are founded on such shifting sands that there is no need for morality, for proper behavior, for ethical codes? Does not a relativistic philosophy, indeed, imply a negation of these?"

To hold that values do not exist because they are relative to time and place is to fall prey to a fallacy that results from a failure to take into account the positive contribution of the relativistic position. For cultural relativism is a philosophy that recognizes the values set up by every society to guide its own life and that understands their worth to those who live by them, though they may differ from one's own. Instead of underscoring differences from absolute norms that, however objectively arrived at, are nonetheless the product of a given time or place, the relativistic point of view brings into relief the validity of every set of norms for the people who have them, and the values these represent.

It is essential, in considering cultural relativism, that we differentiate absolutes from universals. *Absolutes* are fixed, and, as far as convention is concerned, are not admitted to have variation, to differ from culture to culture, from epoch to epoch. *Universals*, on the other hand, are those least common denominators to be extracted from the range of variation that all phenomena of the natural or cultural world manifest. If we apply the distinction between these two concepts in drawing an answer to the points raised in our question, these criticisms are found to lose their force. To say that there is no absolute criterion of values or morals, or even, psychologically, of time or space, does not mean that such criteria, in differing *forms*, do not comprise universals in human culture. Morality is a universal, and so is enjoyment of beauty, and some standard for truth. The many forms these concepts take are but products of the particular historical experience of the societies that manifest them. In each, criteria are subject to continuous questioning, continuous change. But the basic conceptions remain, to channel thought and direct conduct, to give purpose to living.

In considering cultural relativism, also, we must recognize that it has three quite different aspects, which in most discussions of it tend to be disregarded. One of these is methodological, one philosophical, and one practical. As it has been put:

As method, relativism encompasses the principle of our science that, in studying a culture, one seeks to attain as great a degree of objectivity as possible; that one does not judge the modes of behavior one is describing, or seek to change them. Rather, one seeks to understand the sanctions of behavior in terms of the established relationships within the culture itself, and refrains from making interpretations that arise from a preconceived frame of reference. Relativism as philosophy concerns the nature of cultural values, and, beyond this, the implications of an epistemology that derives from a recognition of the force of enculturative conditioning in shaping thought and behavior. Its practical aspects involve the application—the practice—of the philosophical principles derived from this method, to the wider, cross-cultural scene.

We may follow this reasoning somewhat further.

In these terms, the three aspects of cultural relativism can be regarded as representing a logical sequence which, in a broad sense, the historical development of the idea has also followed. That is, the methodological aspect, whereby the data from which the epistemological propositions flow are gathered, ordered and assessed, came first. For it is difficult to conceive of a systematic theory of cultural relativism—as against a generalized idea of live-and-let-live—without the pre-existence of the massive ethnographic documentation gathered by anthropologists concerning the similarities and differences between cultures the world over. Out of these data came the philosophical position, and with the philosophical position came speculation as to its implications for conduct.[4]

Cultural relativism, in all cases, must be sharply distinguished from concepts of the relativity of individual behavior, which would negate all social controls over conduct. Conformity to the code of the group is a requirement for any regularity in life. Yet to say that we have a right to expect conformity to the code of our day for ourselves does not imply that we need expect, much less impose, conformity to our code on persons who live by other codes. The very core of cultural relativism is the social discipline that comes of respect for differences—of mutual respect. Emphasis on the worth of many ways of life, not one, is an affirmation of the values in each culture. Such emphasis seeks to understand and to harmonize goals, not to judge and de-

stroy those that do not dovetail with our own. Cultural history teaches that, important as it is to discern and study the parallelisms in human civilizations, it is no less important to discern and study the different ways man has devised to fulfill his needs.

That it has been necessary to consider questions such as have been raised reflects an enculturative experience wherein the prevalent system of morals is not only consciously inculcated, but its exclusive claim to excellence emphasized. There are not many cultures, for example, where a rigid dichotomy between good and evil, such as we have set up, is insisted upon. Rather it is recognized that good and evil are but the extremes of a continuously varied scale between these poles that produces only different degrees of greyness. We thus return to the principle enunciated earlier, that "judgments are based on experience, and experience is interpreted by each individual in terms of his enculturation." In a culture where absolute values are stressed, the relativism of a world that encompasses many ways of living will be difficult to comprehend. Rather, it will offer a field day for value judgments based on the degree to which a given body of customs resembles or differs from those of Euroamerican culture.[5]

Once comprehended, however, and employing the field methods of the scientific student of man, together with an awareness of the satisfactions the most varied bodies of custom yield, this position gives us a leverage to lift us out of the ethnocentric morass in which our thinking about ultimate values has for so long bogged down. With a means of probing deeply into all manner of differing cultural orientations, of reaching into the significance of the ways of living of different peoples, we can turn again to our own culture with fresh perspective, and an objectivity that can be achieved in no other manner.

NOTES

1. Cf. M. J. Herskovits, 1938b, Vol. I, pp. 137-55, 300-51.

2. E. Cassirer, 1944, p. 25.

3. This unpublished myth was told to F. M. Olbrechts of Brussels, Belgium, in the course of field work among the Cherokee. His having made it available is gratefully acknowledged. A similar tale has been recorded from the Albany Cree, at Moose Factory, according to information received from F. Voget.

4. M. J. Herskovits, 1951, p. 24.

5. Instances of the rejection of relativism on philosophical grounds, by writers who attempt to reconcile the principle of absolute values with the diversity of known systems, are to be found in E. Vivas, 1950, pp. 27-42, and D. Bidney, 1953a, pp. 689-95, 1953b, pp. 423-9. Both of these discussions, also, afford examples of the confusion that results when a distinction is not drawn between the methodological, philosophical, and practical aspects of relativism. For a critical consideration of relativism that, by implication, recognizes these differences, see R. Redfield, 1953, pp. 144 ff.

NO   James Rachels

THE CHALLENGE
OF CULTURAL RELATIVISM

> Morality differs in every society, and is a convenient term for socially approved habits.
>
> — Ruth Benedict, *Patterns of Culture* (1934)

HOW DIFFERENT CULTURES HAVE DIFFERENT MORAL CODES

Darius, a king of ancient Persia, was intrigued by the variety of cultures he encountered in his travels. He had found, for example, that the Callatians (a tribe of Indians) customarily ate the bodies of their dead fathers. The Greeks, of course, did not do that—the Greeks practiced cremation and regarded the funeral pyre as the natural and fitting way to dispose of the dead. Darius thought that a sophisticated understanding of the world must include an appreciation of such differences between cultures. One day, to teach this lesson, he summoned some Greeks who happened to be present at this court and asked them what they would take to eat the bodies of their dead fathers. They were shocked, as Darius knew they would be, and replied that no amount of money could persuade them to do such a thing. Then Darius called in some Callatians, and while the Greeks listened asked them what they would take to burn their dead fathers' bodies. The Callatians were horrified and told Darius not even to mention such a dreadful thing.

This story, recounted by Herodotus in his *History*, illustrates a recurring theme in the literature of social science: different cultures have different moral codes. What is thought right within one group may be utterly abhorrent to the members of another group, and vice versa. Should we eat the bodies of the dead or burn them? If you were a Greek, one answer would seem obviously correct; but if you were a Callatian, the opposite would seem equally certain.

It is easy to give additional examples of the same kind. Consider the Eskimos. They are a remote and inaccessible people. Numbering only about

From James Rachels, "The Challenge of Cultural Relativism," *The Elements of Moral Philosophy* (Random House, 1986) pp. 12–22. Copyright © 1986 by McGraw-Hill Publishing Company. Reprinted by permission.

25,000, they live in small, isolated settlements scattered mostly along the northern fringes of North America and Greenland. Until the beginning of this century, the outside world knew little about them. Then explorers began to bring back strange tales.

Eskimo customs turned out to be very different from our own. The men often had more than one wife, and they would share their wives with guests, lending them for the night as a sign of hospitality. Moreover, within a community, a dominant male might demand—and get—regular sexual access to other men's wives. The women, however, were free to break these arrangements simply by leaving their husbands and taking up with new partners—free, that is, so long as their former husbands chose not to make trouble. All in all, the Eskimo practice was a volatile scheme that bore little resemblance to what we call marriage.

But it was not only their marriage and sexual practices that were different. The Eskimos also seemed to have less regard for human life. Infanticide, for example, was common. Knud Rasmussen, one of the most famous early explorers, reported that he met one woman who had borne twenty children but had killed ten of them at birth. Female babies, he found, were especially liable to be destroyed, and this was permitted simply at the parents' discretion, with no social stigma attached to it. Old people also, when they became too feeble to contribute to the family, were left out in the snow to die. So there seemed to be, in this society, remarkably little respect for life.

To the general public, these were disturbing revelations. Our own way of living seems so natural and right that for many of us it is hard to conceive of others living so differently. And when we do hear of such things, we tend immediately to categorize those other peoples as "backward" or "primitive." But to anthropologists and sociologists, there was nothing particularly surprising about the Eskimos. Since the time of Herodotus, enlightened observers have been accustomed to the idea that conceptions of right and wrong differ from culture to culture. If we assume that *our* ideas of right and wrong will be shared by all peoples at all times, we are merely naive.

CULTURAL RELATIVISM

To many thinkers, this observation—"Different cultures have different moral codes"—has seemed to be the key to understanding morality. The idea of universal truth in ethics, they say, is a myth. The customs of different societies are all that exist. These customs cannot be said to be "correct" or "incorrect," for that implies we have an independent standard of right and wrong by which they may be judged. But there is no such independent standard; every standard is culture-bound. The great pioneering sociologist William Graham Sumner, writing in 1906, put the point like this:

> The "right" way is the way which the ancestors used and which has been handed down. The tradition is its own warrant. It is not held subject to verification by experience. The notion of right is in the folkways. It is not outside of them, of independent origins, and brought to test them. In the folkways, whatever is, is right. This is because they are traditional, and therefore contain in themselves the authority of the ancestral ghosts. When we come to the folkways we are at the end of our analysis.

This line of thought has probably persuaded more people to be skeptical about ethics than any other single thing. *Cultural Relativism*, as it has been called, challenges our ordinary belief in the objectivity and universality of moral truth. It says, in effect, that there is no such thing as universal truth in ethics; there are only the various cultural codes, and nothing more. Moreover, our own code has no special status; it is merely one among many. . . .

THE CULTURAL DIFFERENCES ARGUMENT

Cultural Relativism is a theory about the nature of morality. At first blush it seems quite plausible. However, like all such theories, it may be evaluated by subjecting it to rational analysis; and when we analyze Cultural Relativism we find that it is not so plausible as it first appears to be.

The first thing we need to notice is that at the heart of Cultural Relativism there is a certain *form of argument*. The strategy used by cultural relativists is to argue from facts about the differences between cultural outlooks and a conclusion about the status of morality. Thus we are invited to accept this reasoning:

1. The Greeks believed it was wrong to eat the dead, whereas the Callatians believed it was right to eat the dead.
2. Therefore, eating the dead is neither objectively right nor objectively wrong. It is merely a matter of opinion, which varies from culture to culture.

Or, alternatively:

1. The Eskimos see nothing wrong with infanticide, whereas Americans believe infanticide is immoral.
2. Therefore, infanticide is neither objectively right nor objectively wrong. It is merely a matter of opinion, which varies from culture to culture.

Clearly, these arguments are variations of one fundamental idea. They are both special cases of a more general argument, which says:

1. Different cultures have different moral codes.
2. Therefore, there is no objective "truth" in morality. Right and wrong are only matters of opinion, and opinions vary from culture to culture.

We may call this the *Cultural Differences Argument*. To many people, it is very persuasive. But from a logical point of view, is it a *sound* argument?

It is not sound. The trouble is that the conclusion does not really follow from the premise—that is, even if the premise is true, the conclusion still might be false. The premise concerns what people *believe*: in some societies, people believe one thing; in other societies, people believe differently. The conclusion, however, concerns *what really is the case*. The trouble is that this sort of conclusion does not follow logically from this sort of premise.

Consider again the example of the Greeks and Callatians. The Greeks believed it was wrong to eat the dead; the Callatians believed it was right. Does it follow, *from the mere fact that they disagreed*, that there is no objective truth in the matter? No, it does not follow; for it *could* be that the practice was objectively right (or wrong) and that one or the other of them was simply mistaken.

To make the point clearer, consider a very different matter. In some societies, people believe the earth is flat. In other societies, such as our own, people believe the earth is (roughly) spherical. Does it follow, *from the mere fact that they disagree,* that there is no "objective truth" in geography? Of course not; we would never draw such a conclusion because we realize that, in their beliefs about the world, the members of some societies might simply be wrong. There is no reason to think that if the world is round everyone must know it. Similarly, there is no reason to think that if there is moral truth everyone must know it. The fundamental mistake in the Cultural Differences Argument is that it attempts to derive a substantive conclusion about a subject (morality) from the mere fact people disagree about it. . . .

THE CONSEQUENCES OF TAKING CULTURAL RELATIVISM SERIOUSLY

Even if the Cultural Differences Argument is invalid, Cultural Relativism might still be true. What would it be like if it were true?

In the passage quoted above, William Graham Sumner summarizes the essence of Cultural Relativism. He says that there is no measure of right and wrong other than the standards of one's society: "The notion of right is in the folkways. It is not outside of them, of independent origin, and brought to test them. In the folkways, whatever is, is right."

Suppose we took this seriously. What would be some of the consequences?

1. *We could no longer say that the customs of other societies are morally inferior to our own.* This, of course, is one of the main points stressed by Cultural Relativism. We would have to stop condemning other societies merely because they are "different." So long as we concentrate on certain examples, such as the funerary practices of the Greeks and Callatians,

this may seem to be a sophisticated, enlightened attitude.

However, we would also be stopped from criticizing other, less benign practices. Suppose a society waged war on its neighbors for the purpose of taking slaves. Or suppose a society was violently anti-Semitic and its leaders set out to destroy the Jews. Cultural Relativism would preclude us from saying that either of these practices was wrong. We would not even be able to say that a society tolerant of Jews is *better* than the anti-Semitic society, for that would imply some sort of transcultural standard of comparison. The failure to condemn *these* practices does not seem "enlightened"; on the contrary, slavery and anti-Semitism seem wrong *wherever* they occur. Nevertheless, if we took Cultural Relativism seriously, we would have to admit that these social practices also are immune from criticism.

2. *We could decide whether actions are right or wrong just by consulting the standards of our society.* Cultural Relativism suggests a simple test for determining what is right and what is wrong: all one has to do is ask whether the action is in accordance with the code of one's society. Suppose a resident of South Africa is wondering whether his country's policy of *apartheid*—rigid racial segregation—is morally correct. All he has to do is ask whether this policy conforms to his society's moral code. If it does, there is nothing to worry about, at least from a moral point of view.

This implication of Cultural Relativism is disturbing because few of us think that our society's code is perfect—we can think of ways it might be improved. Yet Cultural Relativism would not only forbid us from criticizing the codes of *other* societies; it would stop us from criticizing our *own*. After all, if right and wrong are relative to culture, this must be true for our own culture just as much as for others.

3. *The idea of moral progress is called into doubt.* Usually, we think that at least some changes in our society have been for the better. (Some, of course, may have been changed for the worse.) Consider this example: Throughout most of Western history the place of women in society was very narrowly circumscribed. They could not own property; they could not vote or hold political office; with a few exceptions, they were not permitted to have paying jobs; and generally they were under the almost absolute control of their husbands. Recently much of this has changed, and most people think of it as progress.

If Cultural Relativism is correct, can we legitimately think of this as progress? Progress means replacing a way of doing things with a *better* way. But by what standard do we judge the new ways as better? If the old ways were in accordance with the social standards of their time, then Cultural Relativism would say it is a mistake to judge them by the standards of a different time. Eighteenth-century society was, in effect, a different society from the one we have now. To say that we have made progress implies a judgment that present-day society is better, and that is just the sort of transcultural judgment that, according to Cultural Relativism, is impermissible.

Our idea of social *reform* will also have to be reconsidered. A reformer such as Martin Luther King, Jr., seeks to change his society for the better. Within the constraints imposed by Cultural Relativism, there is one way this might be done. If a society is not living up to its own ideals, the reformer may be regarded as acting for the best: the ideals of the society are the standard by which we judge his or her proposals as worthwhile. But the "reformer" may not challenge the ideals themselves, for those ideals are by definition correct. According to Cultural Relativism, then, the idea of social reform makes sense only in this very limited way.

These three consequences of Cultural Relativism have led many thinkers to reject it as implausible on its face. It does make sense, they say, to condemn some practices, such as slavery and anti-Semitism, wherever they occur. It makes sense to think that our own society has made some moral progress, while admitting that it is still imperfect and in need of reform. Because Cultural Relativism says that these judgments make no sense, the argument goes, it cannot be right.

WHY THERE IS LESS DISAGREEMENT THAN IT SEEMS

The original impetus for Cultural Relativism comes from the observation that cultures differ dramatically in their views of right and wrong. But just how much do they differ? . . .

Consider a culture in which people believe it is wrong to eat cows. This may even be a poor culture, in which there is not enough food; still, the cows are not to be touched. Such a society would *appear* to have values very different from our own. But does it? We have not yet asked why these people will not eat cows. Suppose it is because they believe that after death the souls of humans inhabit the bodies of animals, especially cows, so that a cow may be someone's grandmother. Now do we want to say that their values are different from ours?

No; the difference lies elsewhere. The difference is in our belief systems, not in our values. We agree that we shouldn't eat Grandma; we simply disagree about whether the cow *is* (or could be) Grandma.

The general point is this. Many factors work together to produce the customs of a society. The society's values are only one of them. Other matters, such as the religious and factual beliefs held by its members and the physical circumstances in which they must live, are also important. We cannot conclude, then, merely because customs differ, that there is a disagreement about values. The difference in customs may be attributable to some other aspect of social life. Thus there may be less disagreement about values than there appears to be.

Consider the Eskimos again. They often kill perfectly normal infants, especially girls. We do not approve of this at all; a parent who did this in our society would be locked up. Thus there appears to be a great difference in the values of our two cultures. But suppose we ask *why* the Eskimos do this. The explanation is not that they have less affection for their children or less respect for human life. An Eskimo family will always protect its babies if conditions permit. But they live in a harsh environment, where food is often in short supply. A fundamental postulate of Eskimo thought is: "Life is hard, and the margin of safety small." A family may want to nourish its babies but be unable to do so.

As in many "primitive" societies, Eskimo mothers will nurse their infants over a much longer period of time than mothers in our culture. The child will take nourishment from its mother's breast for four years, perhaps even longer. So even in the best of times there are limits to the number of infants that one mother can sustain. Moreover, the Eskimos are a nomadic people—unable to farm, they must move about in search of food. Infants must be carried, and a mother can carry only one baby in her parka as she travels and goes about her outdoor work. Other family members can help, but this is not always possible.

Infant girls are more readily disposed of because, first, in this society the males are the primary food providers—they are the hunters, according to the traditional division of labor—and it is obviously important to maintain a sufficient number of food gatherers. But there is an important second reason as well. Because the hunters suffer a high casualty rate, the adult men who die prematurely far outnumber the women who die early. Thus if male and female infants survived in equal numbers, the female adult population would greatly outnumber the male adult population. Examining the available statistics, one writer concluded that "were it not for female infanticide . . . there would be approximately one-and-a-half times as many females in the average Eskimo local group as there are food-producing males."

So among the Eskimos, infanticide does not signal a fundamentally different attitude toward children. Instead, it is a recognition that drastic measures are sometimes needed to ensure the family's survival. Even then, however, killing the baby is not the first option considered. Adoption is common; childless couples are especially happy to take a more fertile couple's "surplus." Killing is only the last resort. I emphasize this in order to show that the raw data of the anthropologists can be misleading; it can make the differences in values between cultures appear greater than they are. The Eskimos' values are not all that different from our values. It is only that life forces upon them choices that we do not have to make.

HOW ALL CULTURES HAVE SOME VALUES IN COMMON

It should not be surprising that, despite appearances, the Eskimos are protective of their children. How could it be otherwise? How could a group survive that did *not* value its young? This suggests a certain argument, one which shows that all cultural groups must be protective of their infants:

1. Human infants are helpless and cannot survive if they are not given extensive care for a period of years.

2. Therefore, if a group did not care for its young, the young would not survive, and the older members of the group would not be replaced. After a while the group would die out.

3. Therefore, any cultural group that continues to exist must care for its young. Infants that are *not* cared for must be the exception rather than the rule.

Similar reasoning shows that other values must be more or less universal. Imagine what it would be like for a society to place no value at all on truth telling. When one person spoke to another, there would be no presumption at all that he was telling the truth—for he could just as easily be speaking falsely. Within that society, there would be no reason to pay attention to what anyone says. . . . Communication would then be extremely difficult, if not impossible. And because complex societies cannot exist without regular communication among their members, society would become impossible. It follows that in any complex society there *must* be a presumption in favor of truthfulness. . . .

Could a society exist in which there was no prohibition on murder? What would this be like? Suppose people were free to kill other people at will, and no one thought there was anything wrong with it. In such a "society," no one could feel secure. Everyone would have to be constantly on guard. . . . Of course, people might band together in smaller groups with others that they *could* trust not to harm them. But notice what this means: they would be forming smaller societies that *did* acknowledge a rule against murder. The prohibition of murder, then, is a necessary feature of all societies.

There is a general theoretical point here, namely, that *there are some moral rules that all societies will have in common, because those rules are necessary for society to exist.* The rules against lying and murder are two examples. And in fact, we do find these rules in force in all viable cultures. Cultures may differ in what they regard as legitimate exceptions to the rules, but this disagreement exists against a background of agreement on the larger issues. Therefore, it is a mistake to overestimate the amount of difference between cultures. Not *every* moral rule can vary from society to society.

POSTSCRIPT

Is Morality Relative to Culture?

Rachels argues that the thesis of cultural relativism is false; nevertheless he claims that there are positive lessons to be learned from the view. In fact, he says, the view is based on an *insight*. The insight is that much of what we think of as the only way (or the only natural way, or the only correct way) to arrange social matters is really arbitrary or the result of historical forces that could just as well have been otherwise. Sumner would probably agree with that observation, although he and other relativists might want to change the word *much* to *all*.

Rachels endeavors to show that certain particular values must be held by any group if the group is to survive and reproduce both physically and culturally. One might wonder, however, whether Rachels has demonstrated the point that every society must maintain these values as moral values. Even if we prove that care of the young is of value for the survival of any given society, why would this be considered a *moral* value? Why couldn't this be compared to the value that attaches to the care of one's body for one's own continued personal existence? Do we think for example, that someone who eats healthy foods and exercises regularly is thereby *morally* better than someone who does not?

Antirelativists might argue that these considerations are really beside the point. Even if the relativists are correct in their view that moral disagreement *is* widespread, this does not *prove* that no one knows any truths in morality, or that there is no truth in morality. The fundamental point to which anti-relativists return is this: the thesis that "there is no truth about matters of X" simply does not follow from the premise that "there is widespread disagreement about X." All that follows from the premise about disagreement is that there is no consensus.

Classic social scientific views in the relativistic tradition are Ruth Benedict, *Patterns of Culture* (Pelican, 1946), and M. Herskovits, *Man and His Works* (Knopf, 1948). Ruth Benedict has also published a relevant article, "Anthropology and the Abnormal," *Journal of General Psychology* (1934).

The relevance of the anthropological data to philosophical issues is discussed by Kai Nielsen in his article "Ethical Relativism and the Facts of Cultural Relativity," *Social Research* (1966).

At least one scientist, Irenäus Eibl-Eibesfeldt, argues that ethical norms are biologically innate and not culturally varying. His views are found in his book *Love and Hate* (Methuen, 1971).

Gilbert Harman, a philosopher, has provided a sophisticated defense of moral relativism in his "Moral Relativism Defended," *Philosophical Review* (1975).

Further sources are Robert Arrington, *Rationalism, Realism, and Relativism: Perspectives in Contemporary Moral Epistemology* (Cornell University Press, 1989), David Wong, *Ethical Relativity* (University of California Press, 1984), and Michael Krausz and Jack W. Meiland, eds., *Relativism: Cognitive and Moral* (University of Notre Dame Press, 1982).

ISSUE 2

Are There Moral Facts?

YES: Renford Bambrough, from *Moral Scepticism and Moral Knowledge* (Humanities Press, 1979)

NO: John L. Mackie, from "A Refutation of Morals," *Australasian Journal of Philosophy* (1946)

ISSUE SUMMARY

YES: British philosopher Renford Bambrough defends the view that some things are right and some things are wrong and contends that sometimes we have positive knowledge of which is which, no matter what other individuals or groups of people might think.
NO: Australian philosopher John L. Mackie (1917–1981) argues that people project their own moral values on the world and then delude themselves into thinking that morality is a matter of objective fact.

One of the central questions of our age is whether there are such things as moral facts. If so, is it possible to learn what these facts are? The skepticism of modern times is great. We question everything; neither science nor religion nor morality is immune from this questioning.

We have been brought up with various beliefs and ideas that probably seem to us to be just common sense. As Renford Bambrough relates in the following selection, it was G. E. Moore (1873–1958), a leading British philosopher, who earlier in this century defended common sense against what he regarded as strange philosophical claims. When a philosopher declared that time was unreal, G. E. Moore made this reply: He had eaten his breakfast just that morning; since it was now later in the day, it was a mistake to say that time is unreal. Common sense told him that time marches on, and a philosopher who claimed that time didn't even exist was strange indeed. Moore applied his famous defense of common sense against those philosophers who expressed doubts about the existence of the external world. Moore offered proof that the external world does exist: he held up his hands and said, "Here is one hand, and here is another." Since hands are clearly part of the external world, Moore's case was made.

Does such an approach work when what is doubted is not the existence of a physical world and physical facts, but, rather, the existence of a moral reality and moral facts? In the case of right and wrong, is there such a thing as knowledge?

Suppose it is physically true that an oven is hot. It is possible to tell children about this; it is also possible to let them touch the oven and find out for themselves that it is hot. In either case, evidence and proof are certainly available for the claim that the oven is hot.

What about the moral claim that parents with more than one child in their family make to their children when they say, "You should not hit the baby"? Siblings can be told this, and they can be punished if they fail to obey. But is there such a thing as proof or evidence for young brothers or sisters that hitting the baby is wrong? It is not enough to note the coercion factor—to say that the children will be punished if they persist in behavior that the parents have ruled out. The point to consider is whether "You should not hit the baby" is a fact, just as "The oven is hot" is a fact.

In ancient times the Romans threw Christians to the lions on account of the Christians' faith. Does getting into trouble with authorities prove that one has done something morally wrong?

In such cases as those postulated above, one tends to be drawn to these conclusions: hitting the baby is just wrong, and throwing Christians to the lions is just wrong. According to this view, these are not optional behaviors; as a matter of "fact," these things are wrong. This allows us to deduce that indeed there are moral facts and there is moral knowledge, as Bambrough asserts.

According to Moore, it is obviously false to say that time is not real or that the external world does not exist. We do not need a sophisticated theory to show that time exists (the existence of morning and afternoon is enough here), and we do not need a sophisticated theory to show that the external world is real (look at your hands). Similarly, one may conclude that no sophisticated theories are necessary to show that moral facts exist (all we need is a simple example—like the "fact" that one should not hit a baby).

Strictly speaking, this sort of commonsense argument actually provides too much information. In order to support the claim that there *are* moral facts, it is not even necessary to claim that people know them or will recognize them once they are explained. But two points remain. First, just because people do not recognize facts does not mean that these facts do not exist. Second, it has always been thought that parents should teach their children the difference between right and wrong. If there is nothing to learn here—if there are no moral facts anyway—then what are parents really doing when they are apparently giving their children a moral education?

John L. Mackie, in the second of the following selections, sees himself as a moral skeptic. He suggests that although many people—in fact, most people—believe in morals (they believe that morality is objective and that some moral judgments are true and some are false), there are only personal feelings involved, and no moral facts. People objectify their feelings and then *say* that morality is objective and that moral facts exist. Mackie argues that such people are under a misapprehension and that this error is widespread.

23

YES

Renford Bambrough

MORAL SCEPTICISM AND MORAL KNOWLEDGE

PROOF

It is well known that recent British philosophy, under the leadership of Moore and Wittgenstein, has defended common sense and common language against what seem to many contemporary philosophers to be the paradoxes, the obscurities and the mystifications of earlier metaphysical philosophers. The spirit of this work is shown by the titles of two of the most famous of Moore's papers: 'A Defence of Common Sense' and 'Proof of an External World'. It can be more fully but still briefly described by saying something about Moore's defence of the commonsense belief that there are external material objects. His proof of an external world consists essentially in holding up his hands and saying, 'Here are two hands; therefore there are at least two material objects'. He argues that no proposition that could plausibly be alleged as a reason in favour of doubting the truth of the proposition that I have two hands can possibly be more certainly true than that proposition itself. If a philosopher produces an argument against my claim to *know* that I have two hands, I can therefore be sure in advance that *either* at least one of the premises of argument is false, *or* there is a mistake in the reasoning. . . .

It is also well known that many recent British philosophers have rejected objectivist accounts of the nature of moral reasoning. The most famous and fashionable of recent British moral philosophers . . . agree in drawing a sharp contrast between moral reasoning on the one hand, and mathematical, logical, factual and scientific reasoning on the other hand. They sharply contrast *fact* with *value*. They attach great importance to Hume's doctrine, or what they believe to have been Hume's doctrine, that *is* never entails *ought*, that from no amount of factual evidence does any evaluative proposition logically follow; that no set of premises about what is the case, unless they are combined with at least one premise about what is good or what ought to be the case, can yield any conclusion about what is good or what ought to be the case. . . . We are repeatedly told that there are no moral *truths*, that there is no moral *knowledge*, that in morals and politics all that we can ultimately do is to *commit* ourselves, to declare where we stand, to try by persuasion and rhetoric to bring others to share our point of view. . . .

What is apparently not very well known is that there is a conflict between the fashionable allegiance to common sense and common language and the fashionable rejection of objectivism in moral philosophy. . . .

If we can show by Moore's argument that there is an external world, then we can show *by parity of reasoning*, by an exactly analogous argument, that we have moral knowledge, that there are some propositions of morals which are *certainly* true, and which we *know* to be true.

My proof that we have moral knowledge consists essentially in saying, 'We know that this child, who is about to undergo what would otherwise be painful surgery, should be given an anaesthetic before the operation. Therefore we know at least one moral proposition to be true'. I argue that no proposition that could plausibly be alleged as a reason in favour of doubting the truth of the proposition that the child should be given an anaesthetic can possibly be more certainly true than that proposition itself. If a philosopher produces an argument against my claim to *know* that the child should be given an anaesthetic, I can therefore be sure in advance that *either* at least one of the premises of his argument is false, *or* there is a mistake in the reasoning by which he purports to derive from his premises the conclusion that I

do not know that the child should be given an anaesthetic.

When Moore proves that there is an external world he is defending a commonsense belief. When I prove that we have moral knowledge I am defending a commonsense belief. . . .

The commonsense view is that we *know* that stealing is wrong, that promise-keeping is right, that unselfishness is good, that cruelty is bad. Common language uses in moral contexts the whole range of expressions that it also uses in non-moral contexts when it is concerned with knowledge and ignorance, truth and falsehood, reason and unreason, questions and answers. We speak as naturally of a child's not knowing the difference between right and wrong as we do of his not knowing the difference between right and left. We say that we do not know what to do as naturally as we say that we do not know what is the case. We say that a man's moral views are unreasonable as naturally as we say that his views on a matter of fact are unreasonable. In moral contexts, just as naturally as in non-moral contexts, we speak of thinking, wondering, asking; of beliefs, opinions, convictions, arguments, conclusions; of dilemmas, problems, solutions; of perplexity, confusion, consistency and inconsistency, of errors and mistakes, of teaching, learning, training, showing, proving, finding out, understanding, realising, recognising and coming to see. . . .

Those who reject the commonsense account of moral knowledge, like those who reject the commonsense account of our knowledge of the external world, do of course offer arguments in favour of their rejection. In both cases those who reject the commonsense account offer very much the same arguments whether or not they recognise that the account they are rejecting is in fact the commonsense account. If we now look at the arguments that can be offered against the commonsense account of moral knowledge we shall be able to see whether they are sufficiently similar to the arguments that can be offered against the commonsense account of our knowledge of the external world to enable us to sustain our charge of inconsistency against a philosopher who attacks common sense in one field and defends it in the other. . . .

'Moral disagreement is more widespread, more radical and more persistent than disagreement about matters of fact'.

I have two main comments to make on this suggestion: the first is that it is almost certainly untrue, and the second is that it is quite certainly irrelevant.

The objection loses much of its plausibility as soon as we insist on comparing the comparable. We are usually invited to contrast our admirably close agreement that there is a glass of water on the table with the depth, vigour and tenacity of our disagreements about capital punishment, abortion, birth control and nuclear disarmament. But this game may be played by two or more players. A sufficient reply in kind is to contrast our general agreement that this child should have an anaesthetic with the strength and warmth of the disagreements between cosmologists and radio astronomers about the interpretation of certain radio-astronomical observations. If the moral sceptic then reminds us of Christian Science we can offer him in exchange the Flat Earth Society.

But this is a side issue. Even if it is true that moral disagreement is more acute and more persistent than other forms of disagreement, it does not follow that moral knowledge is impossible. However long and violent a dispute may be, and however few or many heads may be counted on this side or on that, it remains possible that one party to the dispute is right and the others wrong. Galileo was right when he contradicted the cardinals; and so was Wilberforce when he rebuked the slave-owners. . . .

[A] question about the actual extent of agreement or disagreement has no bearing on the question of the objectivity of the enquiry. If this were not so, the objectivity of every enquiry might wax and wane through the centuries as men become more or less disputatious or more or less proficient in the arts of persuasion.

'Our moral opinions are conditioned by our environment and upbringing'.

It is under this heading that we are reminded of the variegated customs and beliefs of Hottentots, Eskimos, Polynesians and American Indians, which do indeed differ widely from each other and from our own. But this objection is really a special case of the general argument from disagreement, and it can be answered on the same lines. The beliefs of the Hottentots and the Polynesians about straightforwardly factual matters differ widely from our own, but that does not tempt us to say that science is subjective. . . .

'After every circumstance, every relation is known, the understanding has no further room to operate, nor any object on which it could employ itself'.

This sentence from the first Appendix to Hume's *Enquiry Concerning the Principles of Morals* is the moral sceptic's favourite quotation, . . . [But if] it is true that there may or must come a point in moral enquiry beyond which no further reasoning is possible, it is in that same sense equally true that there may or must be a point in *any* enquiry at which the reasoning has to stop. Nothing can be proved to a man who will accept nothing that has not been proved. . . . Not even in pure mathematics, that paradigm of strict security of reasoning, can we *force* a man to accept our premises or our modes of inference; and therefore we cannot force him to accept our conclusions. Once again the moral sceptic counts as a reason for doubting the objectivity of morals a feature of moral enquiry which is exactly paralleled in other departments of enquiry where he does not count it as a reason for scepticism. If he is to be consistent, he must either withdraw his argument against the objectivity of morals or subscribe also to an analogous argument against the objectivity of mathematics, physics, history, and every other branch of enquiry.

But of course such an argument gives no support to a sceptical conclusion about any of these enquiries. However conclusive a mode of reasoning may be, and however accurately we may use it, it always remains possible that we shall fail to convince a man who disagrees with us. . . . It is notorious that even an expert physicist may fail to convince a member of the Flat Earth Society that the earth is not flat, but we nevertheless *know* that the earth is not flat. . . .

'A dispute which is purely moral is inconclusive in principle. The specifically moral element in moral disputes is one which cannot be resolved by investigation and reflection'.

This objection brings into the open . . . the assumption that whatever is a logical or factual dispute, or a mixture of logical

and factual disputes, is necessarily *not* a moral dispute; that nothing is a moral dispute unless it is *purely* moral in the sense that it is a dispute between parties who agree on *all* the relevant factual and logical questions. But the *purely moral* dispute envisaged by this assumption is a pure fiction. The search for the 'specifically moral element' in moral disputes is a wild-goose chase, and is the result of the initial confusion of supposing that no feature of moral reasoning is *really* a feature of moral reasoning, or is *characteristic* of moral reasoning, unless it is peculiar to moral reasoning. It is as if one insisted that a ginger cake could be fully characterised, and could only be characterised, by saying that there is ginger in it. It is true that ginger is the peculiar ingredient of a ginger cake as contrasted with other cakes, but no cake can be made entirely of ginger, and the ingredients that are combined with ginger to make ginger cakes are the same as those that are combined with chocolate, lemon, orange or vanilla to make other kinds of cakes; and ginger itself, when combined with other ingredients and treated in other ways, goes into the making of ginger puddings, ginger biscuits and ginger beer.

To the question 'What is the place of reason in ethics?' why should we not answer: 'The place of reason in ethics is exactly what it is in other enquiries, to enable us to find out the relevant facts and to make our judgements mutually consistent, to expose factual errors and detect logical inconsistencies'? . . .

Here again the moral sceptic is partial and selective in his use of an argument of indefinitely wide scope: if it were true that a man must accept unprovable moral premises before I could prove to him that there is such a thing as moral knowledge it would equally be true that a man must accept an unprovable material object proposition before Moore could prove to him that there is an external world. Similarly, if a moral conclusion can be proved only to a man who accepts unprovable moral premises then a physical conclusion can be proved only to a man who accepts unprovable physical premises.

'There are recognised methods for settling factual and logical disputes, but there are no recognised methods for settling moral disputes'.

This is either false, or true but irrelevant, according to how it is understood. Too often those who make this complaint are arguing in a circle, since they will count nothing as a recognised method of argument unless it is a recognised method of logical or scientific argument. If we adopt this interpretation, then it is true that there are no recognised methods of moral argument, but the lack of such methods does not affect the claim that morality is objective. One department of enquiry has not been shown to be no true department of enquiry when all that has been shown is that it cannot be carried on by exactly the methods that are appropriate to some other department of enquiry. We know without the help of the sceptic that morality is not identical with logic or science.

But in its most straightforward sense the claim is simply false. There *are* recognised methods of moral argument. Whenever we say 'How would you like it if somebody did this to you?' or 'How would it be if we all acted like this?' we are arguing according to recognised and established methods, and are in fact appealing to the consistency requirement to which I have already referred. It is true

that such appeals are often ineffective, but it is also true that well-founded logical or scientific arguments often fail to convince those to whom they are addressed. If the present objection is pursued beyond this point it turns into the argument from radical disagreement.

The moral sceptic is even more inclined to exaggerate the amount of disagreement that there is about methods of moral argument than he is inclined to exaggerate the amount of disagreement in moral belief as such. One reason for this is that he concentrates his attention on the admittedly striking and important fact that there is an enormous amount of immoral *conduct*. But most of those who *behave* immorally appeal to the very same methods of moral argument as those who condemn their immoral conduct. Hitler broke many promises, but he did not explicitly hold that promise-breaking as such and in general was permissible. When others broke their promises to him he complained with the same force and in the same terms as those with whom he himself had failed to keep faith. And whenever he broke a promise he tried to *justify* his breach by claiming that other obligations overrode the duty to keep the promise. He did not simply deny that it was his duty to keep promises. He thus entered into the very process of argument by which it is possible to condemn so many of his own actions. He was *inconsistent* in requiring of other nations and their leaders standards of conduct to which he himself did not conform, and in failing to produce *convincing reasons* for his own departures from the agreed standards. . . .

Many of the forms of moral scepticism that are special cases of sceptical theories of potentially wider scope are based on confusions between the concepts of relativity and subjectivity and those of absoluteness and objectivity. To suggest that there is a *right* answer to a moral problem is at once to be accused of or credited with a belief in moral absolutes. But it is no more necessary to believe in moral absolutes in order to believe in moral objectivity than it is to believe in the existence of absolute space or absolute time in order to believe in the objectivity of temporal and spatial relations and of judgements about them.

The trouble here is partly due to a recurrence of the difficulty about criteria or standards which, as we have seen, has as much or as little force as a sceptical argument in moral as in non-moral contexts. If we think of the objectivity of ethics as being bound up with the possibility of stating unexceptionably correct rules or moral principles, we shall be liable to regard the evident fact that circumstances alter cases as a refutation of objective theories. The confusion may be dispelled by looking at some closely comparable cases which nevertheless offer no temptation to any analogous confusion. The fact that a tailor needs to make a different suit for each of us, and that no non-trivial specification of what a suit has to be like in order to fit its wearer will be without exceptions, does not mean that there are no rights and wrongs about the question whether your suit or mine is a good fit. On the contrary: it is precisely because he seeks to provide for each of us a suit that will have the *right* fit that the tailor must take account of our individualities of build. In pursuit of the objectively correct solution of his practical problem he must be decisively influenced by the relativity of the fit of clothes to wearer.

Similar examples may be indefinitely multiplied. Children of different ages require different amounts and kinds of food; different patients in different conditions need different drugs and operations; the farmer does not treat all his cows or all his fields alike. Circumstances objectively alter cases.

Some of the cases that are objectively altered by circumstances are cases calling for moral choice or judgement. If we need examples we can find them in the sceptic's own armoury of differences of moral practice and belief between one time or place and another. In collecting them he makes one of his many indirect and inadvertent contributions to the objective description of the objectivity of moral thought. When he reminds us that the ancient Greeks exposed unwanted children and left them to die, whereas we place them in orphanages or have them adopted, he does not, as he thinks, point to a clear case of conflict of moral belief. The effect of his citing such an instance is to open an investigation into the facts and circumstances of ancient Greek life, and how they compare and contrast with those of modern life, and a debate about whether the differences are such as to justify a difference of practice. If they are, then it will have turned out that in spite of superficial appearances there is no moral conflict between the ancients and ourselves. If there turns out to be a residual conflict, large or small, it may be that part of the difference is accounted for by differences in non-moral belief. If a man believes that a finite and temporal torment is the only way of saving a heretic from infinite and eternal torment, he may be prompted by motives of charity to reinforce his reasoning with the rack. And we may believe that charity would require the use of the rack in such circumstances without believing that such circumstances have ever arisen or could ever arise. Our disagreement with the Inquisitor, which is represented by the moral sceptic as an irresoluble dispute about moral principles, is then seen to be a dispute which, whether resoluble or not, is not about fundamental moral principles, but about the truth or falsehood of some non-moral propositions—historical, psychological and theological. . . .

INTEGRITY

I have reserved for separate treatment an objection which is usually felt to have special if not conclusive force against objectivism. . . .

This . . . objection is expressed by P. H. Nowell-Smith when he remarks that 'It is no accident that religious persecutions are the monopoly of objective theorists' (*Ethics*, p. 47). William James makes the same objection to 'the doctrine of certitude' (i.e. to the idea that knowledge is obtainable in moral and religious contexts) when he alleges that one of its clearest consequences has been 'the conscientious labors of the Holy Office of the Inquisition' (*The Will to Believe and Other Essays*, p. 17). . . .

The suggestion is that if we believe . . . that there *are* moral distinctions (Right and Wrong, Good and Evil) we shall become dogmatic and authoritarian. . . .

Once again the point can be put most economically by making the necessary comparison between ethics and science.

John Stuart Mill's resounding statement of the principle of free and open enquiry makes no distinction between opinions on one kind of question and opinions on another: 'If all mankind minus one were of one opinion, and only one person were of the contrary opinion,

mankind would be no more justified in silencing that one person than he, if he had the power, would be justified in silencing mankind'. (Mill, *On Liberty*, chapter II). . . .

[Mill] believed in freedom of scientific enquiry because he believed that the establishment and dissemination of scientific truth would be hampered by any form of censorship, repression, or inquisition, and by the imposition of any orthodoxy, however certainly true the content of its creed might be. The same reason has the same force and points to the same conclusion when we apply it to freedom of expression about questions of morals, politics, philosophy and religion. The man who is in a minority of one may be right, and that is why, or is at least one of the main reasons why, it is important not to suppress his opinion.

Mill was himself an objectivist in moral philosophy, and he rightly saw no conflict between his objectivism and his liberalism. On the contrary, his belief that knowledge was obtainable was here again one of the grounds of his adherence to the principle of free enquiry. Suppression of opinion and enquiry and criticism is objectionable because it leads to the maintenance of illusion and the propagation of errors. . . .

It is the objective theorist of morals who has the strongest reason to favour freedom of moral enquiry, just as it is the physicist or astronomer, who believes that answers to questions of physics and astronomy are in principle obtainable and establishable, who sees the greatest merit in freedom of scientific enquiry. To claim that there is such a thing as knowledge, or knowledge of such and such a kind, is not to claim to possess such knowledge, or to claim the right to impose one's opinion on others or to suppose that the possession of knowledge would confer such a right. If any theory in the epistemology of morals does give colour to dogmatism and the exercise of tyrannical authority it is a subjective theory, according to which nothing is objectively wrong, and hence the exercise of tyranny is not objectively wrong.

NO

John L. Mackie

A REFUTATION OF MORALS

[In this paper I do not pretend to be advancing any particularly new ideas: hardly any of the arguments are original, and indeed most are the stock instruments of all modern discussions of morals. But I think I am justified in offering this re-statement of them, because it is seldom realised how they may be brought together and interrelated, or how radically destructive they are of all common views of morality, when this is done.]

We all have moral feelings: all of us find that there are human actions and states of affairs of which we approve and disapprove, and which we therefore try to encourage and develop or to oppose. (This emotion of approval is different from liking, one difference being that its object is more general. If someone stands me a pint, I like it: if someone stands an enemy of mine a pint, I dislike it: but I should approve of a state of society which provided free beer all round. So if I hear of someone whom I have never met and to whom I am personally indifferent being stood a pint, I should not say that I like it, for I am not directly affected, but I may well approve of it, because it is an instance of the sort of thing I want to see everywhere. A thorough distinction of approval from liking and other relations would require further discussion, but perhaps this will serve to indicate a contrast between classes with which we are all in fact acquainted. I shall suggest later a possible source of these generalised emotions.) But most of us do not merely admit that we have such *feelings*, we think we can also *judge* that actions and states are right and good, just as we judge about other matters of fact, that these judgments are either true or false, and that the qualities with which they deal exist objectively. This view, which almost everyone holds, may be crudely called "believing in morals". A few sceptics, however, think that there are only feelings of approval, no objective moral facts. (Of course the existence of a feeling is an objective fact, but not what is commonly called a moral fact.) One of their main arguments is that moral facts would be "queer", in that unlike other facts they cannot be explained in terms of arrangements of matter, or logical constructions out of sense-data, or whatever the particular theorist takes to be the general form of real things.

From John L. Mackie, "A Refutation of Morals," *Australasian Journal of Philosophy*, vol. 24 (1946). Copyright © 1946 by the *Australasian Journal of Philosophy*. Reprinted by permission.

This argument is not in itself very strong, or even very plausible, for unless we have good *a priori* grounds for whatever is taken as the basic principle of criticism, the criterion of reality, the mere fact that we seem to observe moral qualities and facts would be a reason for modifying that principle. Their other main argument, which is both older and more convincing, though not logically conclusive, is that although at any one time, in a particular social group, there is fairly complete agreement about what is right, in other classes, other countries, and above all in other periods of history and other cultures, the actual moral judgments or feelings are almost completely different, though perhaps there are a few feelings so natural to man that they are found everywhere. Now feelings may well change with changing conditions, but a judgment about objective fact should be everywhere the same: if we have a faculty of moral perception, it must be an extremely faulty one, liable not only to temporary illusions, as sight is, but to great and lasting error. Of course it may be that every society except our own is mistaken, that savages are morally backward because they lack our illuminating experience of the long-term effects of various kinds of action, and so on. But this complacent view (not indeed very popular now) is shaken by the observation that the variations in moral feelings can be explained much more plausibly not as being due to mistakes, but as reflections of social habits. This moral relativity would be less alarming if we could say that the varying judgments were not ultimate, but were applications to different circumstances of a single principle or a small number of principles, which were everywhere recognised—for example, that whatever

produces pleasure is good, that whatever society commands is right, or, at the very least, that we should always do what we believe to be right. But these principles are not commonly laid down first, and the particular judgments deduced from them: rather the particular judgments are made by ordinary people, whereas the principles are later invented by philosophers and manipulated in order to explain them. In any case there is just as little agreement about principles as about particular judgments.

We find on further enquiry that most, perhaps all, actual moral judgments are fairly closely correlated with what we may call social demands: any society or social group has regular ways of working, and, in order to maintain these, requires that its members should act in certain ways: the members—from whatever motive, perhaps mainly habit, which has compelled them to adapt their desires to the established customs—obey these requirements themselves and force their fellows to do so, or at least feel obliged to obey and approve of others obeying. They call "right" and "good" whatever accords with these ways of working. Moreover as the science of social history develops, it is more and more strongly suggested that ways of working and institutions have their own laws of growth, and that the desires or moral views of individuals do not so much control the history of society as arise out of it.

Belief in the objectivity of moral qualities is further undermined when we remark that whenever anyone calls an action or activity or state of affairs right or good (unless he is speaking in an ironical tone or puts these words in inverted commas) he himself either has a feeling of approval, or desires that the action should be done or the activity pursued or the state of affairs come into existence. (Only one of these alternatives is necessary, but they are often found together.)

None of these considerations is conclusive, but each has a certain weight: together they move the moral sceptic (who is often of a scientific and inductive turn of mind, and less devoted than some others to the clear light of intuition or the authority of reason) to conclude that in all probability we do not recognise moral facts, but merely have feelings of approval and disapproval, which arise in general from social demands and therefore vary from one society to another. This view I intend to examine and re-state, and to advance what I regard as decisive arguments for one of its more important aspects.

The simplest formulation of this view is that when someone says "this act is right" he means merely "I approve of this act". The well-known reply simply leaps into the reader's mind: when one person says that an act is right, another that the same act is wrong, they would not on this theory be disagreeing, whereas in fact they think they are. It will not do to say, with Stevenson,[1] that there is a disagreement in attitude, but not in belief: they think, at any rate, that they disagree in belief. Nor does one mean that "society approves of this act", since we frequently meet people who say "I know society approves of this, but it is wrong all the same". But there is no need for argument: direct introspection shows that when we use the terms "right", "good", and the rest, we never intend merely to state that there are feelings of approval. An improved formulation of the sceptical view is that in saying "this is right", and so on, we are not *stating*

any approval, but only *expressing* one, that words like "right" and "wrong", "good" and "bad" are to be compared not with "red" and "square" but with exclamations or ejaculations like "ow!", "boo!", and "hurray!" This is certainly nearer the truth, and avoids the previous difficulties, but is, in another way, just as unplausible. For we do not think that we are merely ejaculating when we talk in moral terms. If we did, and if someone disagreed with us, we should merely disapprove of his approvals, and either try to coax him into a different emotional attitude, or if he proved obstinate, knock him down. In fact we reason with him. These facts, and the logical tangles that we get into when we try to re-state fairly complex moral situations in the "boo-hurray" language, prove that we think, at least, that we are not merely expressing our emotions but are describing objective facts, and therefore that the meaning of moral terms is not parallel with that of ejaculations. Many refutations of the "boo-hurray" theory have been worked out, but they all depend upon and illustrate the fact that we *think* that we are doing things of quite different sorts when we say "right" and when we say "ow!" Now if philosophy could do no more than elucidate the meaning of the terms of common speech, remove confusions and rationalise the thought of ordinary men, there would be nothing more to be said. Moral terms do mean objective qualities, and everyone who uses them does so because he believes in objective moral facts. But if the very terms of common speech may include errors and confusions within themselves, so that they cannot be used at all without falsity, if, we may add, philosophy may be permitted to enquire into these errors by observing a few facts for itself and founding inductive conclusions on them, the moral sceptic need not be so soon disheartened.

But he must modify his view again, and say that in using moral terms we are as it were objectifying our own feelings, thinking them into qualities existing independently of us. For example, we may see a plant, say a fungus, that fills us with disgust, but instead of stating that we have this feeling, or merely expressing and relieving it by an exclamation, we may ascribe to the fungus a semimoral quality of foulness, over and above all the qualities that a physical scientist could find in it. Of course, in objectifying our feelings we are also turning them inside out: our feeling about the fungus is one of being disgusted, while the foulness we ascribe to the fungus means that it is disgusting. The supposed objective quality is not simply the feeling itself transferred to an external object, but is something that would inevitably arouse that feeling. (No one would say, "That fungus is foul, but I feel no disgust at it".) The feeling and the supposed quality are related as a seal or stamp and its impression.

This process of objectification is, I think, well known to psychologists and is not new in philosophy. . . .

There are strong influences which might lead us thus to objectify moral feelings. As I have mentioned, our moral judgments seem to arise from approvals borrowed from society, or from some social group, and these are felt by the individual as external to himself. It is for this reason that they are universal in form, applying equally to himself and to others. They are thus formally capable of being objective laws, in contrast to the "selfish" desires of the individual. This generality or universality, which I men-tioned as characteristic of the emotion of approval, is reflected in Rousseau's doctrine that the general will and therefore law must be general in their object, and in Kant's criterion of the possibility of universalisation of a moral law. Since we inevitably tend to encourage what we approve of, and to impose it upon others, we want everyone to adopt our approvals, and this will most surely come about if they have only to perceive a genuinely existing objective fact, for what we feel is in general private, what we perceive may be common to all. Suppose that we approve of hard work: then if as well as a feeling of approval in our own minds there were an objective fact like "hard work is good", such that everyone could observe the fact and such that the mere observation would arouse in him a like feeling of approval, and even perhaps stimulate him to work, we should eventually get what we want done: people would work hard. And since what we want does not exist in fact, we naturally construct it in imagination: we objectify our feelings so thoroughly that we completely deceive ourselves. I imagine that this is the reason why our belief in moral objectivity is so firm: we much more readily admit that the foulness of a fungus is an objectification than the depravity of people who break our windows is. If moral predicates were admitted to be what the moral sceptic says they are, we should never be able to extol a state of affairs as good in any sense which would induce people to bring it about, unless they already wanted it, though we might point out that this state had features which in fact they did desire, though they had not realised this: we should never be able to recommend any course of action, except in such terms as "if you want to be rich, be economical"; nor could we give commands by any moral authority, though we might again advise "if you don't want a bullet through your brains, come quietly"; and we should never be able to lecture anyone on his wickedness—an alarming prospect. The temptations to objectify feelings of approval, and to retain our belief in morals, are clearly strong ones.

This process of objectifying our feelings, is, then, neither impossible nor improbable: there is also abundant evidence that it is just what has occurred. . . .

In attempting to give an account of the origin of moral terms in this process of objectification, I do not, of course, claim that it is complete or precise in all respects. It is still open to discussion and correction on empirical grounds. We might go on to consider this process as a psychological process, investigating its causes, its similarities and contrasts with other mental processes, and the steps of which it is made up. We might ask whether "objectification" or some other name is really the most suitable, and also what are the precise motives objectified: we might consider, for example, Westermarck's argument[2] that "ought" normally expresses a conation, is sometimes but not necessarily or essentially imperative, and has its origin in disapproval rather than approval.

My discussion in this paper is intended to open the way for such discussions, not to settle them once and for all. What I am concerned to establish is simply the logical status of moral terms, not the psychological details of their origin; in effect I am asserting only that there are no facts of the form "this is right", that when we use such words the only fact is the existence of some feelings in ourselves or in others or in both, but that in using these terms we are falsely postulating or asserting something of the simple, objective form "this is right". . . .

This re-statement does away with the logical difficulties previously encountered by moral scepticism. Nor are there, I think, any non-logical difficulties in the way of our accepting this view, except the persistence of the belief that moral facts are objective. It might be claimed that this firm belief is based on an intuition, but it has no further arguments to support it, and we have indicated social and psychological causes which would produce such a belief even if it had no foundation. However firm the belief may be, therefore, it is not valid evidence for the existence of moral facts. But the true moralist will not be deterred by lack of evidence: he will perhaps be compelled to admit that moral judgments are evolved, historically, by objectification of feelings. But none the less, he will maintain, when evolved they *are* valid. But now we remind him of their variability, their correlation with social demands. Actual moral judgments, en masse, cannot be valid, since they are mutually contradictory: in fact all the evidence suggests that not only are moral judgments derived from feelings, but there are no objective moral facts: the feelings are *all* that exists. We may now legitimately be influenced by the "queerness" of the alleged moral facts, their striking differences from most of the other objects of knowledge and belief. . . .

We may now sum up the progress that we have made. We have discovered how we can state the traditional view of moral sceptics without logical contradiction or denial of the observable facts of moral thinking, by saying that we have only moral feelings, but objectify these and think we are recognising objective facts and qualities. But we were not sure how much of our moral thought was made up of these objectifications, whether there might not be, say, an objective quality of goodness, with which these objectifications have been confused. . . . obligation, as we commonly use the term, cannot be an objective fact, but our notion of it must be derived from objectification. The same is true of everything necessarily connected with it, the te; is "should", "duty", and "right". Exhortation and recommendation can have no absolute validity when obligation is removed: we can only advise people how to attain what they already desire. With these we place those notions that bear plainly the marks of the process of objectification or of their emotional origin: the notion of value, the notion that goodness, if there is such an objective quality, has any necessary relation to desire, or to happiness and pleasure, since it is through desire that it is connected with these. Also, if there is such a quality, it will be such that we can recognise it without feeling impelled to approve of it or to pursue it. In fact, without going into further detail we may say that there may be an objective quality which we have confused with our objectifications of moral feelings, but if so it has few of the relations and other features that we have been in the habit of associating with goodness. But in any case we have shown that the great mass of what is called moral thought is, not nonsense, but error, the imagining of objective facts and qualities of external things where there exists nothing but our feelings of desire and approval.

NOTES

1. *Ethics and Language,* Chapter I.
2. *The Origin and Development of the Moral Ideas,* Chapter VI.

POSTSCRIPT

Are There Moral Facts?

Bambrough argues that the same commonsense support for believing in physical knowledge can also be brought to bear in support of the belief that there is moral knowledge. The very strength of Bambrough's commonsense approach can also be considered its weakness. Clearly, even if Bambrough is right, there is ample evidence that common sense has been wrong in the past. Is his argument another case in which common sense is wrong?

Mackie suggests that this is indeed the case and contends that although common sense accepts the *existence* of moral facts, there are not really any moral facts at all. He says that certain psychological and social phenomena operate so as to make us *think*, mistakenly, that moral facts exist; we tend to objectify our subjective feelings. Mackie concludes that most of what we regard as moral thought is not nonsense, but error. He seems to mean by this that most of our moral talk ("This is good," "This is bad") is not crazy or irrational, but is based on a mistake.

If Mackie is correct, what follows? If moral language is largely based on error, should we stop committing this error and stop using moral language? Should we stop sayings things like "This is good" or "This is bad"? And what about raising children? Should we teach them about right and wrong or good and evil? Bambrough expresses the idea that children should be brought up in such a way that they come to know the difference between right and wrong. Does a view like Mackie's regard all of this as a big mistake?

Further discussions of these and related ideas can be found in the following books: John L. Mackie, *Ethics: Inventing Right and Wrong* (Penguin, 1977); Ted Honderich, ed., *Morality and Objectivity: A Tribute to J. L. Mackie* (Routledge & Kegan Paul, 1985); David Copp and David Zimmerman, eds., *Morality, Reason and Truth* (Rowman & Allanheld, 1985); Geoffrey Sayre-McCord, ed., *Essays on Moral Realism* (Cornell University Press, 1988); and David O. Brink, *Moral Realism and the Foundations of Ethics* (Cambridge University Press, 1989). In some of this literature the claim that moral facts exist is called *moral realism*.

ISSUE 3

Is Morality Subjective?

YES: Bertrand Russell, from *Religion and Science* (Oxford University Press, 1935)

NO: Brand Blanshard, from "The New Subjectivism in Ethics," *Philosophy and Phenomenological Research* (March 1949)

ISSUE SUMMARY

YES: British philosopher Bertrand Russell (1872–1970) holds that morality is subjective; moral judgments express personal emotions; and differences in value judgments are due to differences in taste.

NO: American philosopher Brand Blanshard (1892–1987) rejects all of these views and maintains that subjectivism in ethics is untenable. He argues that when one makes a moral judgment about something, one is making a judgment about that object (an objective judgment), not simply expressing one's (subjective) feelings.

Subjectively, you may like strawberry ice cream but not oysters; and you may agree with the ideology of feminism but not vegetarianism. You realize that not everyone will share these tastes and values, and there is a tendency to treat values as a kind of taste. Many lines of thought seem to converge on the idea that morality, too, is a matter of taste and is therefore subjective. But let us further explore subjectivity by introducing a distinction between subjectivity and objectivity: subjectivity applies in matters of taste, objectivity applies in scientific matters.

The thought here is that anything objective (the boiling point of water or the presence of black swans in Australia, for example) can be determined by scientific means, such as ordinary sense perception or experimental inquiry. Where we have such objective means of answering questions, we say that the questions and the answers are themselves objective. In these cases, unlike the question of whether oysters are good to the taste, or the question of whether vegetarianism is (morally) good, there is no room for subjectivity. Anyone who follows scientific procedures correctly, without making any mistakes, will arrive at the objectively right results.

If, for example, the question is how close the sun is to the earth, and the answer is scientifically determined to be approximately 93,000,000 miles, it would be unreasonable to protest that you nevertheless feel that the answer is actually around 1,000,000 miles, or that you do not approve of the scientific answer, or that you simply do not like the idea of the sun being so far away! *Feeling* that the sun must be 1,000,000 miles away clearly does not *put* the sun 1,000,000 miles away. Feelings about these matters are not so much wrong as they are irrelevant. One's subjective feelings and responses simply do not enter into objective matters at all.

Sometimes a subjectivist says that in the case of moral issues and value issues, "It's all a matter of feelings." But an opponent of subjectivism would not agree. Why not? Although an objectivist (antisubjectivist) would admit that feelings and personal responses might often accompany the expression of strong moral views, he or she would insist that it is not *all* a matter of feelings, for the following reasons. First, these feelings are not even necessary to the expression of moral judgments, since such judgments can also be made in a very rational and unemotional way. Second, and more importantly, an objectivist would say that even in cases in which there is both a moral judgment and the presence of feelings, it is the judgment that leads to the feelings (not the feelings that lead to the judgment).

Consider, for example, some serious moral violations, like murder or rape. The objectivist would argue that we are not morally against these acts on account of the feelings that they cause in us when we contemplate them or find out that they have actually occurred. Rather, it is on account of our judgment that these are morally bad things that we have negative personal reactions to them. If the negative reactions were at the root of the moral judgment, then we would take care that we never experienced the negative reactions; we would not read the newspaper, for example. Instead, says the objectivist, realizing that these are bad things, we take measures against their occurrence.

In the following selections, Bertrand Russell denies objectivism and supports subjectivism. Brand Blanshard, arguing against subjectivism, suggests that if the world is morally neutral, and things are good or bad only by virtue of people's attitudes, then the solution to moral problems would never lie in changing the world (which is neutral) but in changing our attitudes. He maintains that moral judgments are not simply reflections of an individual's feelings.

YES   Bertrand Russell

SCIENCE AND ETHICS

Those who maintain the insufficiency of science . . . appeal to the fact that science has nothing to say about "values." This I admit; but when it is inferred that ethics contains truths which cannot be proved or disproved by science, I disagree. The matter is one on which it is not altogether easy to think clearly, and my own views on it are quite different from what they were thirty years ago. But it is necessary to be clear about it if we are to appraise such arguments as those in support of Cosmic Purpose. As there is no consensus of opinion about ethics, it must be understood that what follows is my personal belief, not the dictum of science. . . .

Different philosophers have formed different conceptions of the Good. Some hold that it consists in the knowledge and love of God; others in universal love; others in the enjoyment of beauty; and yet others in pleasure. The Good once defined, the rest of ethics follows: we ought to act in the way we believe most likely to create as much good as possible, and as little as possible of its correlative evil. The framing of moral rules, so long as the ultimate Good is supposed known, is matter for science. For example: should capital punishment be inflicted for theft, or only for murder, or not at all? Jeremy Bentham, who considered pleasure to be the Good, devoted himself to working out what criminal code would most promote pleasure, and concluded that it ought to be much less severe than that prevailing in his day. All this, except the proposition that pleasure is the Good, comes within the sphere of science.

But when we try to be definite as to what we mean when we say that this or that is "the Good," we find ourselves involved in very great difficulties. Bentham's creed that pleasure is the Good roused furious opposition, and was said to be a pig's philosophy. Neither he nor his opponents could advance any argument. In a scientific question, evidence can be adduced on both sides, and in the end one side is seen to have the better case—or, if this does not happen, the question is left undecided. But in a question as to whether this or that is the ultimate Good, there is no evidence either way; each disputant can only appeal to his own emotions, and employ such rhetorical devices as shall rouse similar emotions in others.

Take, for example, a question which has come to be important in practical politics. Bentham held that one man's pleasure has the same ethical importance as another man's, provided the quantities are equal; and on this ground he was led to advocate democracy. Nietzsche, on the contrary, held that only the great man can be regarded as important on his own account, and that the bulk of mankind are only means to his well-being. He viewed ordinary men as many people view animals: he thought it justifiable to make use of them, not for their own good, but for that of the superman, and this view has since been adopted to justify the abandonment of democracy. We have here a sharp disagreement of great practical importance, but we have absolutely no means, of a scientific or intellectual kind, by which to persuade either party that the other is in the right. There are, it is true, ways of altering men's opinions on such subjects, but they are all emotional, not intellectual.

Questions as to "values"—that is to say, as to what is good or bad on its own account, independently of its effects—lie outside the domain of science, as the defenders of religion emphatically assert. I think that in this they are right, but I draw the further conclusion, which they do not draw, that questions as to "values" lie wholly outside the domain of knowledge. That is to say, when we assert that this or that has "value," we are giving expression to our own emotions, not to a fact which would still be true if our personal feelings were different. To make this clear, we must try to analyse the conception of the Good.

It is obvious, to begin with, that the whole idea of good and bad has some connection with *desire*. *Prima facie*, anything that we all desire is "good," and anything that we all dread is "bad." If we all agreed in our desires, the matter could be left there, but unfortunately our desires conflict. If I say "what I want is good," my neighbour will say "No, what *I* want." Ethics is an attempt—though not, I think, a successful one—to escape from this subjectivity. I shall naturally try to show, in my dispute with my neighbour, that my desires have some quality which makes them more worthy of respect than his. If I want to preserve a right of way, I shall appeal to the landless inhabitants of the district; but he, on his side, will appeal to the landowners. I shall say: "What use is the beauty of the countryside if no one sees it?" He will retort: "What beauty will be left if trippers are allowed to spread devastation?" Each tries to enlist allies by showing that his own desires harmonize with those of other people. When this is obviously impossible, as in the case of a burglar, the man is condemned by public opinion, and his ethical status is that of a sinner.

Ethics is thus closely related to politics: it is an attempt to bring the collective desires of a group to bear upon individuals; or, conversely, it is an attempt by an individual to cause his desires to become those of his group. This latter is, of course, only possible if his desires are not too obviously opposed to the general interest: the burglar will hardly attempt to persuade people that he is doing them good, though plutocrats make similar attempts, and often succeed. When our desires are for things which all can enjoy in common, it seems not unreasonable to hope that others may concur; thus the philosopher who values Truth, Goodness and Beauty seems, to himself, to be not merely expressing his own desires, but pointing the way to the welfare of all mankind. Unlike the burglar, he is able to believe that his desires are for something that has value in an impersonal sense.

Ethics is an attempt to give universal, and not merely personal, importance to certain of our desires. I say "certain" of our desires, because in regard to some of them this is obviously impossible, as we saw in the case of the burglar. The man who makes money on the Stock Exchange by means of some secret knowledge does not wish others to be equally well informed: Truth (in so far as he values it) is for him a private possession, not the general human good that it is for the philosopher. The philosopher may, it is true, sink to the level of the stockjobber, as when he claims priority for a discovery. But this is a lapse: in his purely philosophic capacity, he wants only to enjoy the contemplation of Truth, in doing which he in no way interferes with others who wish to do likewise.

To seem to give universal importance to our desires—which is the business of ethics—may be attempted from two points of view, that of the legislator, and that of the preacher. Let us take the legislator first.

I will assume, for the sake of argument, that the legislator is personally disinterested. That is to say, when he recognizes one of his desires as being concerned only with his own welfare, he does not let it influence him in framing the laws; for example, his code is not designed to increase his personal fortune. But he has other desires which seem to him impersonal. He may believe in an ordered hierarchy from king to peasant, or from mine-owner to black indentured labourer. He may believe that women should be submissive to men. He may hold that the spread of knowledge in the lower classes is dangerous. And so on and so on. He will then, if he can, so

construct his code that conduct promoting the ends which he values shall, as far as possible, be in accordance with individual self-interest; and he will establish a system of moral instruction which will, where it succeeds, make men feel wicked if they pursue other purposes than his.* Thus "virtue" will come to be in fact, though not in subjective estimation, subservience to the desires of the legislator, in so far as he himself considers these desires worthy to be universalized.

The standpoint and method of the preacher are necessarily somewhat different, because he does not control the machinery of the State, and therefore cannot produce an artificial harmony between his desires and those of others. His only method is to try to rouse in others the same desires that he feels himself, and for this purpose his appeal must be to the emotions. Thus Ruskin caused people to like Gothic architecture, not by argument, but by the moving effect of rhythmical prose. *Uncle Tom's Cabin* helped to make people think slavery an evil by causing them to imagine themselves as slaves. Every attempt to persuade people that something is good (or bad) in itself, and not merely in its effects, depends upon the art of rousing feelings, not upon an appeal to evidence. In every case the preacher's skill consists in creating in others emotions similar to his own—or dissimilar, if he is a hypo-

* Compare the following advice by a contemporary of Aristotle (Chinese, not Greek): "A ruler should not listen to those who believe in people having opinions of their own and in the importance of the individual. Such teachings cause men to withdraw to quiet places and hide away in caves or on mountains, there to rail at the prevailing government, sneer at those in authority, belittle the importance of rank and emoluments, and despise all who hold official posts." Waley, *The Way and its Power,* p. 37.

crite. I am not saying this as a criticism of the preacher, but as an analysis of the essential character of his activity.

When a man says "this is good in itself," he *seems* to be making a statement, just as much as if he said "this is square" or "this is sweet." I believe this to be a mistake. I think that what the man really means is: "I wish everybody to desire this," or rather "Would that everybody desired this." If what he says is interpreted as a statement, it is merely an affirmation of his own personal wish; if, on the other hand, it is interpreted in a general way, it states nothing, but merely desires something. The wish, as an occurrence, is personal, but what it desires is universal. It is, I think, this curious interlocking of the particular and the universal which has caused so much confusion in ethics.

The matter may perhaps become clearer by contrasting an ethical sentence with one which makes a statement. If I say "all Chinese are Buddhists," I can be refuted by the production of a Chinese Christian or Mohammedan. If I say "I believe that all Chinese are Buddhists," I cannot be refuted by any evidence from China, but only by evidence that I do not believe what I say; for what I am asserting is only something about my own state of mind. If, now, a philosopher says "Beauty is good," I may interpret him as meaning either "Would that everybody loved the beautiful" (which corresponds to "all Chinese are Buddhists") or "I wish that everybody loved the beautiful" (which corresponds to "I believe that all Chinese are Buddhists"). The first of these makes no assertion, but expresses a wish; since it affirms nothing, it is logically impossible that there should be evidence for or against it, or for it to possess either truth or falsehood. The second sentence, instead of being merely optative, does make a statement, but it is one about the philosopher's state of mind, and it could only be refuted by evidence that he does not have the wish that he says he has. This second sentence does not belong to ethics, but to psychology or biography. The first sentence, which does belong to ethics, expresses a desire for something, but asserts nothing.

Ethics, if the above analysis is correct, contains no statements, whether true or false, but consists of desires of a certain general kind, namely such as are concerned with the desires of mankind in general—and of gods, angels, and devils, if they exist. Science can discuss the causes of desires, and the means for realizing them, but it cannot contain any genuinely ethical sentences, because it is concerned with what is true or false.

The theory which I have been advocating is a form of the doctrine which is called the "subjectivity" of values. This doctrine consists in maintaining that, if two men differ about values, there is not a disagreement as to any kind of truth, but a difference of taste. If one man says "oysters are good" and another says "*I* think they are bad," we recognize that there is nothing to argue about. The theory in question holds that all differences as to values are of this sort, although we do not naturally think them so when we are dealing with matters that seem to us more exalted than oysters. The chief ground for adopting this view is the complete impossibility of finding any arguments to prove that this or that has intrinsic value. If we all agreed, we might hold that we know values by intuition. We cannot *prove*, to a colour-blind man, that grass is green and not red. But there are various ways of proving to him that he lacks a power of discrimination which most men possess, whereas in the case of values there are no such ways, and disagreements are much more frequent than in the case of colours. Since no way can be even imagined for deciding a difference as to values, the conclusion is forced upon us that the difference is one of tastes, not one as to any objective truth.

The consequences of this doctrine are considerable. In the first place, there can be no such thing as "sin" in any absolute sense; what one man calls "sin" another may call "virtue," and though they may dislike each other on account of this difference, neither can convict the other of intellectual error. Punishment cannot be justified on the ground that the criminal is "wicked," but only on the ground that he has behaved in a way which others wish to discourage. Hell, as a place of punishment for sinners, becomes quite irrational.

In the second place, it is impossible to uphold the way of speaking about values which is common among those who believe in Cosmic Purpose. Their argument is that certain things which have been evolved are "good," and therefore the world must have had a purpose which was ethically admirable. In the language of subjective values, this argument becomes: "Some things in the world are to our liking, and therefore they must have been created by a Being with our tastes, Whom, therefore, we also like, and Who, consequently, is good." Now it seems fairly evident that, if creatures having likes and dislikes were to exist at all, they were pretty sure to like *some* things in their environment, since otherwise they would find life intolerable. Our values have been evolved along with the rest of our constitution, and nothing as to any

original purpose can be inferred from the fact that they are what they are.

Those who believe in "objective" values often contend that the view which I have been advocating has immoral consequences. This seems to me to be due to faulty reasoning. There are, as has already been said, certain ethical consequences of the doctrine of subjective values, of which the most important is the rejection of vindictive punishment and the notion of "sin." But the more general consequences which are feared, such as the decay of all sense of moral obligation, are not to be logically deduced. Moral obligation, if it is to influence conduct, must consist not merely of a belief, but of a desire. The desire, I may be told, is the desire to be "good" in a sense which I no longer allow. But when we analyse the desire to be "good" it generally resolves itself into a desire to be approved, or, alternatively, to act so as to bring about certain general consequences which we desire. We have wishes which are not purely personal, and, if we had not, no amount of ethical teaching would influence our conduct except through fear of disapproval. The sort of life that most of us admire is one which is guided by large impersonal desires; now such desires can, no doubt, be encouraged by example, education, and knowledge, but they can hardly be created by the mere abstract belief that they are good, nor discouraged by an analysis of what is meant by the word "good."

When we contemplate the human race, we may desire that it should be happy, or healthy, or intelligent, or warlike, and so on. Any one of these desires, if it is strong, will produce its own morality; but if we have no such general desires, our conduct, whatever our ethic may be, will only serve social purposes in so far as self-interest and the interests of society are in harmony. It is the business of wise institutions to create such harmony as far as possible, and for the rest, whatever may be our theoretical definition of value, we must depend upon the existence of impersonal desires. When you meet a man with whom you have a fundamental ethical disagreement—for example, if you think that all men count equally, while he selects a class as alone important—you will find yourself no better able to cope with him if you believe in objective values than if you do not. In either case, you can only influence his conduct through influencing his desires: if you succeed in that, his ethic will change, and if not, not.

Some people feel that if a general desire, say for the happiness of mankind, has not the sanction of absolute good, it is in some way irrational. This is due to a lingering belief in objective values. A desire cannot, in itself, be either rational or irrational. It may conflict with other desires, and therefore lead to unhappiness; it may rouse opposition in others, and therefore be incapable of gratification. But it cannot be considered "irrational" merely because no reason can be given for feeling it. We may desire A because it is a means to B, but in the end, when we have done with mere means, we must come to something which we desire for no reason, but not on that account "irrationally." All systems of ethics embody the desires of those who advocate them, but this fact is concealed in a mist of words. Our desires are, in fact, more general and less purely selfish than many moralists imagine; if it were not so, no theory of ethics would make moral improvement possible. It is, in fact, not by ethical theory, but by the cultivation of large and generous desires through intelligence, happiness, and freedom from fear, that men can be brought to act more than they do at present in a manner that is consistent with the general happiness of mankind. Whatever our definition of the "Good," and whether we believe it to be subjective or objective, those who do not desire the happiness of mankind will not endeavour to further it, while those who do desire it will do what they can to bring it about.

I conclude that, while it is true that science cannot decide questions of value, that is because they cannot be intellectually decided at all, and lie outside the realm of truth and falsehood. Whatever knowledge is attainable, must be attained by scientific methods; and what science cannot discover, mankind cannot know.

NO   Brand Blanshard

THE NEW SUBJECTIVISM IN ETHICS

By the new subjectivism in ethics I mean the view that when anyone says "this is right" or "this is good," he is only expressing his own feeling; he is not asserting anything true or false, because he is not asserting or judging at all; he is really making an exclamation that expresses a favorable feeling.

This view has recently come into much favor. With variations of detail, it in England, and by Carnap, Stevenson, Feigl, and others, in this country. Why is it that the theory has come into so rapid a popularity? Is it because moralists of insight have been making a fresh and searching examination of moral experience and its expression? No, I think not. A consideration of the names just mentioned suggests a truer reason. All these names belong, roughly speaking, to a single school of thought in the theory of knowledge. If the new view has become popular in ethics, it is because certain persons who were at work in the theory of knowledge arrived at a new view *there*, and found, on thinking it out, that it required the new view in ethics; the view comes less from ethical analysis than from logical positivism. . . .

Now I do not think their view will do. But before discussing it, I should like to record one vote of thanks to them for the clarity with which they have stated their case. It has been said of John Stuart Mill that he wrote so clearly that he could be found out. This theory has been put so clearly and precisely that it deserves criticism of the same kind, and this I will do my best to supply. The theory claims to show by analysis that when we say, "That is good," we do not mean to assert a character of the subject of which we are thinking. I shall argue that we do mean to do just that.

Let us work through an example, and the simpler and commoner the better. There is perhaps no value statement on which people would more universally agree than the statement that intense pain is bad. Let us take a set of circumstances in which I happen to be interested on the legislative side and in which I think every one of us might naturally make such a statement. We come upon a rabbit that has been caught in one of the brutal traps in common use. There are signs that it has struggled for days to escape and that in a frenzy of hunger, pain, and fear, it has all but eaten off its own leg. The

From Brand Blanshard, "The New Subjectivism in Ethics," *Philosophy and Phenomenological Research*, vol. 9 (1949), pp. 504–511. Copyright © 1949 by *Philosophy and Phenomenological Research*. Reprinted by permission.

attempt failed: the animal is now dead. As we think of the long and excruciating pain it must have suffered, we are very likely to say: "It was a bad thing that the little animal should suffer so." The positivist tells us that when we say this we are only expressing our present emotion. I hold, on the contrary, that we mean to assert something of the animal's experience itself, namely, that it was bad—bad when and as it occurred.

Consider what follows from the positivist view. On that view, nothing good or bad happened in the case until I came on the scene and made my remark. For what I express in my remark is something going on in me at the time, and that of course did not exist until I did come on the scene. The pain of the rabbit was not itself bad; nothing evil was happening when that pain was being endured; badness, in the only sense in which it is involved at all, waited for its appearance till I came and looked and felt. Now that this is at odds with our meaning may be shown as follows. Let us put to ourselves the hypothesis that we had not come on the scene and that the rabbit never was discovered. Are we prepared to say that in that case nothing bad occurred in the sense in which we said it did? Clearly not. Indeed we should say, on the contrary, that the accident of our later discovery made no difference whatever to the badness of the animal's pain, that it would have been every whit as bad whether a chance passer-by happened later to discover the body and feel repugnance or not. If so, then it is clear that in saying the suffering was bad we are not expressing our feelings only. We are saying that the pain was bad when and as it occurred and before anyone took an attitude toward it.

The first argument is thus an ideal experiment in which we use the method of difference. It removes our present expression and shows that the badness we meant would not be affected by this, whereas on positivist grounds it should be. The second argument applies the method in the reverse way. It ideally removes the past event, and shows that this would render false what we mean to say, whereas on positivist grounds it should not. Let us suppose that the animal did not in fact fall into the trap and did not suffer at all, but that we mistakenly believe it did, and say as before that its suffering was an evil thing. On the positivist theory, everything I sought to express by calling it evil in the first case is still present in the second. In the only sense in which badness is involved at all, whatever was bad in the first case is still present in its entirety, since all that is expressed in either case is a state of feeling, and that feeling is still there. And our question is, is such an implication consistent with what we meant? Clearly it is not. If anyone asked us, after we made the remark that the suffering was a bad thing, whether we should think it relevant to what we said to learn that the incident had never occurred and no pain had been suffered at all, we should say that it made all the difference in the world, that what we were asserting to be bad was precisely the suffering we thought had occurred back there, that if this had not occurred, there was nothing left to be bad, and that our assertion was in that case mistaken. The suggestion that in saying something evil had occurred we were after all making no mistake, because we had never meant anyhow to say anything about the past suffering, seems to me merely frivolous. If we did not mean to say this, why should we be so relieved on finding that the suffering had not occurred? On the theory before us, such relief would be groundless, for in that suffering itself there was nothing bad at all, and hence in its nonoccurrence there would be nothing to be relieved about. The positivist theory would here distort our meaning beyond recognition.

So far as I can see, there is only one way out for the positivist. He holds that goodness and badness lie in feelings of approval or disapproval. And there is a way in which he might hold that badness did in this case precede our own feeling of disapproval without belonging to the pain itself. The pain in itself was neutral; but unfortunately the rabbit, on no grounds at all, took up toward this neutral object an attitude of disapproval, and that made it for the first time, and in the only intelligible sense, bad. This way of escape is theoretically possible, but since it has grave difficulties of its own and has not, so far as I know, been urged by positivists, it is perhaps best not to spend time over it.

I come now to a third argument, which again is very simple. When we come upon the rabbit and make our remark about its suffering being a bad thing, we presumably make it with some feeling; the positivists are plainly right in saying that such remarks do usually express feeling. But suppose that a week later we revert to the incident in thought and make our statement again. And suppose that the circumstances have now so changed that the feeling with which we made the remark in the first place has faded. The pathetic evidence is no longer before us; and we are now so fatigued in body and mind that feeling is, as we say, quite dead. In these circumstances, since what was expressed by the remark when first made is, on the theory before us, simply absent, the remark now expresses nothing. It is as empty as the word "Hurrah" would be when there was no enthusiasm behind it. And this seems to me untrue. When we repeat the remark that such suffering was a bad thing, the feeling with which we made it last week may be at or near the vanishing point, but if we were asked whether we meant to say what we did before, we should certainly answer Yes. We should say that we made our point with feeling the first time and little or no feeling the second time, but that it was the same point we were making. And if we can see that what we meant to say remains the same, while the feeling varies from intensity to near zero, it is not the feeling that we primarily meant to express.

I come now to a fourth consideration. We all believe that toward acts or effects of a certain kind one attitude is fitting and another not; but on the theory before us such a belief would not make sense. Broad and Ross have lately contended that this fitness is one of the main facts of ethics, and I suspect they are right. But that is not exactly my point. My point is this: whether there is such fitness or not, we all assume that there is, and if we do, we express in moral judgments more than the subjectivists say we do. Let me illustrate.

In the novel *The House of the Dead*, Dostoyevsky tells of his experiences in a Siberian prison camp. Whatever the unhappy inmates of such camps are like today, Dostoyevsky's companions were about as grim a lot as can be imagined. "I have heard stories," he writes, "of the most terrible, the most unnatural actions, of the most monstrous murders, told with the most spontaneous, childishly merry laughter." Most of us would say that in this delight at the killing of others or the causing of suffering there is something very unfitting. If we were asked why we thought so, we should say that these things involve great evil and are wrong, and that to take delight in what is evil or wrong is plainly unfitting. Now on the subjectivist view, this answer is ruled out. For before someone takes up an attitude toward death, suffering, or their infliction, they have no moral quality at all. There is therefore nothing about them to which an attitude of approval or condemnation could be fitting. They are in themselves neutral, and, so far as they get a moral quality, they get it only through being invested with it by the attitude of the onlooker. But if that is true, why is any attitude more fitting than any other? Would applause, for example, be fitting if, apart from the applause, there were nothing good to applaud? Would condemnation be fitting if, independently of the condemnation, there were nothing bad to condemn? In such a case, any attitude would be as fitting or unfitting as any other, which means that the notion of fitness has lost all point.

Indeed we are forced to go much farther. If goodness and badness lie in attitudes only and hence are brought into being by them, those men who greeted death and misery with childishly merry laughter are taking the only sensible line. If there is nothing evil in these things, if they get their moral complexion only from our feeling about them, why shouldn't they be greeted with a cheer? To greet them with repulsion would turn what before was neutral into something bad; it would needlessly bring badness into the world; and even on subjectivist assumptions that does not seem very bright. On the other hand, to greet them with delight would convert what before was neutral into something good; it would bring goodness into the world. If I have murdered a man and wish to remove the stain, the way is clear. It is to cry, "Hurrah for murder." . . .

I come now to a fifth and final difficulty with the theory. It makes mistakes about values impossible. There is a whole nest of inter-connected criticisms here, some of which have been made so often that I shall not develop them again, such as that I can never agree or disagree in opinion with anyone else about an ethical matter, and that in these matters I can never be inconsistent with others or with myself. I am not at all content with the sort of analysis which says that the only contradictions in such cases have regard to facts and that contradictions about value are only differences of feeling. I think that if anyone tells me that having a bicuspid out without an anaesthetic is not a bad experience and I say it is a very nasty experience indeed, I am differing with him in opinion, and differing about the degree of badness of the experience. But without pressing this further, let me apply the argument in what is perhaps a fresh direction.

There is an old and merciful distinction that moralists have made for many centuries about conduct—the distinction between what is subjectively and what is objectively right. They have said that in any given situation there is some act which, in view of all the circumstances, would be the best act to do; and this is what would be objectively right. The notion of an objectively right act is the ground of our notion of duty: our duty is always to find and do this act if we can. But of course we often don't find it. We often hit upon and do acts that we think are the right ones, but we are mistaken;

and then our act is only subjectively right. Between these two acts the disparity may be continual; Professor Prichard suggested that probably few of us in the course of our lives ever succeed in doing *the* right act.

Now so far as I can see, the subjectivism would abolish this difference at a stroke. Let us take a case. A boy abuses his small brother. We should commonly say, "That is wrong, but perhaps he doesn't know any better. By reason of bad teaching and a feeble imagination, he may see nothing wrong in what he is doing, and may even be proud of it. If so, his act may be subjectively right, though it is miles away from what is objectively right." What concerns me about the new subjectivism is that it prohibits this distinction. If the boy feels this way about his act, then it is right in the only sense in which anything is right. The notion of an objective right lying beyond what he has discovered, and which he ought to seek and do is meaningless. There might, to be sure, be an act that would more generally arouse favorable feelings in others, but that would not make it right for him unless he thought of it and approved it, which he doesn't. Even if he did think of it, it would not be obligatory for him to feel about it in any particular way, since there is nothing in any act, as we have seen, which would make any feeling more suitable than any other.

Now if there is no such thing as an objectively right act, what becomes of the idea of duty? I have suggested that the idea of duty rests on the idea of such an act, since it is always our duty to find that act and do it if we can. But if whatever we feel approval for at the time is right, what is the point of doubting and searching further? Like the little girl in Boston who was asked if she would like to travel, we can answer, "Why should I travel when I'm already there?" If I am reconciled in feeling to my present act, no act I could discover by reflection could be better, and therefore why reflect or seek at all? Such a view seems to me to break the mainspring of duty, to destroy the motive for self-improvement, and to remove the ground for self-criticism. It may be replied that by further reflection I can find an act that would satisfy my feelings more widely than the present one, and that this is the act I should seek. But this reply means either that such general satisfaction is objectively better, which would contradict the theory, or else that, if at the time I don't feel it better, it isn't better, in which case I have no motive for seeking it. When certain self-righteous persons took an inflexible line with Oliver Cromwell, his very Cromwellian reply was, "Bethink ye, gentlemen, by the bowels of Christ, that ye may be mistaken." It was good advice. I hope nobody will take from me the privilege of finding myself mistaken. I should be sorry to think that the self of thirty years ago was as far along the path as the self of today, merely because he was a smug young jackanapes, or even that the paragon of today has as little room for improvement as would be allowed by his myopic complacency.

One final remark. The great problems of the day are international problems. Has the new subjectivism any bearing upon these problems? I think it has, and a somewhat sinister bearing. I would not suggest, of course, that those who hold the theory are one whit less public-spirited than others; surely there are few who could call themselves citizens of the world with more right (if "rights" have meaning any longer) than Mr. Russell. But Mr. Russell has confessed himself discontented with his ethical theory, and in view of his breadth of concern, one cannot wonder. For its general acceptance would, so far as one can see, be an international disaster. The assumption behind the old League and the new United Nations was that there is such a thing as right and wrong in the conduct of a nation, a right and wrong that do not depend on how it happens to feel at the time. It is implied, for example, that when Japan invaded Manchuria in 1931 she might be wrong, and that by discussion and argument she might be shown to be wrong. It was implied that when the Nazis invaded Poland they might be wrong, even though German public sentiment overwhelmingly approved it. On the theory before us, it would be meaningless to call these nations mistaken; if they felt approval for what they did, then it was right with as complete a justification as could be supplied for the disapproval felt by the rest of the world. In the present dispute between Russia and our own country over southeast Europe, it is nonsense to speak of the right or rational course for either of us to take; if with all the facts before the two parties, each feels approval for its own course, both attitudes are equally justified or unjustified; neither is mistaken; there is no common reason to which they can take an appeal; there are no principles by which an international court could pronounce on the matter; nor would there be any obligation to obey the pronouncement if it were made. This cuts the ground from under any attempt to establish one's case as right or anyone else's case as wrong. So if our friends the subjectivists still hold their theory after I have applied my little ruler to their knuckles, which of course they will, I have but one request to make of them: Don't make a present of it to Mr. Gromyko.

POSTSCRIPT

Is Morality Subjective?

Although the terms *relative* and *subjective* are sometimes used interchangeably, the issues placed at stake by these terms are significantly different. Relativism implies a standard *relative to which* judgments are to be measured. Thus, for example, head-hunting is considered wrong in America (whose standards it violates) but right for members of certain tribes in New Guinea (to whose standards it conforms). But what are we to say of a given tribesman who comes out against head-hunting, or of an American who comes out in favor of it? According to relativism, these individuals must be wrong since their views conflict with local standards, relative to which views must be measured.

It is this line of thinking that has generally caused serious objections to relativism. Relativism is supposed to be tolerant, but it is not. It tolerates *societies* to no limit, but not individuals, because the individual always has to be judged by the standards that society has laid down. Because it sets no limit on what societies may rightfully demand of individuals, relativism is authoritarian.

Subjectivism addresses this difficulty. According to the tenets of subjectivism, society has no special right to lay down standards relative to which individuals must be judged. Individuals are held accountable to nothing and to no one beyond themselves. Since moral response is personal or subjective, subjectivism allows such responses to vary from person to person.

Since subjectivism does not require conformity to standards (except perhaps to a person's own standards), it is thought that there is a connection between subjectivism and tolerance. We are supposed to be tolerant of each other's views, responses, and standards (if any) because morality is subjective and personal; it is based on individual feelings and responses.

But the relationship between subjectivism and tolerance is problematic. Suppose my own personal subjective view is highly intolerant of various people, their views, their races, and their religions. Do I then have the support of subjectivism when I persecute these people? If I do, the connection with tolerance is destroyed. If I don't, because I am supposed to tolerate others, then tolerance itself seems to emerge as an objective (not subjective) value.

A classic statement of the subjectivist view occurs in Alfred Jules Ayer, *Language, Truth, and Logic* (Gollancz, 1936; reprint by Peter Smith). A more recent critical discussion is in Bernard Williams, *Morality: An Introduction to Ethics* (Harper & Row, 1972).

ISSUE 4

Is Morality Grounded in Religion?

YES: Jack Bemporad, from "Morality and Religion," in H. Tristram Engelhardt, Jr., and Daniel Callahan, eds., *Knowledge, Value, and Belief* (Institute of Society, Ethics and the Life Sciences, 1977)

NO: John Arthur, from "Morality Without God," in Garry Brodsky et al., eds., *Contemporary Readings in Social and Political Ethics* (Prometheus Books, 1984)

ISSUE SUMMARY

YES: Professor of philosophy Jack Bemporad argues that only in religion is there a true foundation for ethics. He claims that if ethical questions are pushed far enough, they must eventually go beyond themselves into the religious realm; and here, the Judeo-Christian monotheistic tradition is particularly relevant.
NO: Philosopher John Arthur claims that morality is independent of religion. He does not claim that religious doctrines are false, but rather that both the believer and the nonbeliever have to approach moral questions in the same way: by considering the merits of the case.

There is a widespread feeling that morality and religion are connected. One view is that morality derives from religion. Religion provides a ground for morality, it is said, so that without religion there is no morality. A falling away from religion thus implies a falling away from morality.

Such thoughts have troubled many people in both the nineteenth and the twentieth centuries. The Russian novelist Dostoyevsky (1821–1881) wrote, "If there is no God, then everything is permitted." Many Americans today also believe that religious faith is important. They often believe that even if the doctrines and dogmas cannot after all be known for certain, religion nevertheless leads to morality and good behavior. President Dwight D. Eisenhower is reputed to have said that everyone should have a religious faith, but that it didn't matter what that faith was. And many daily newspapers throughout the country advise their readers to attend the church or synagogue of their choice. The implication is not that certain definite religious teachings or dogmas are being recommended, since any religion or faith will do. Apparently, the main reason why it is thought important to subscribe to a religion is that only in this way will one be able to attain morality. If there is no God, then everything is permitted and there is moral chaos. Moral chaos can be played out in societies and, on a smaller scale, within the mind of each individual. Thus, if there is no God for you, if you do not believe, then you will confront moral chaos; you will be liable to permit (and permit yourself to do) anything, and you will have no moral bearings at all.

Such a view seems to face several problems, however. For example, what are we to say of the morally good atheist, or of the morally good but completely nonreligious person? A true follower of the view that morality derives from religion might reply that we are simply begging the question if we believe that such people *could* be morally good. Such people might do things that are morally right and thus might *seem* good, the reply would go, but they would not be acting for the right reason (obedience to God). Such people would not have the same anchor or root for their seemingly moral attitudes that religious persons would have.

Another problem for the view that links morality with religion comes from the following considerations. If you hold this view, what do you say of devoutly religious people who belong to religious traditions and support moralities that are different from your own? If morality is indeed derived from religion, and if different people are thus led to follow different moralities, and if the original religions are not themselves subject to judgment, then it is understandable how different people arrive at different moral views. But the views will still be different and perhaps even incompatible. If so, the claim that morality derives from religion must mean that one can derive *a* morality from *a* religion (and not that one derives morality itself from religion). The problem is that by allowing this variation among religions and moralities back into the picture, we seem also to allow moral chaos back in too.

The view that holds that what God commands is good, what God prohibits is evil, and that without divine commands and prohibitions nothing is either good or bad in itself is called the divine command theory, or the divine imperative view. This view resists the recognition of any source of good or evil that is not tied to criteria or standards of God's own creation. Such a recognition is thought to go against the idea of God's omnipotence. A moral law that applied to God but was not of God's own creation would seem to limit God in a way in which he cannot be limited. But, on the other hand, this line of thought (that no moral law outside of God's own making should apply to him) seems contrary to the orthodox Christian view that God is good. For if good means something like in accordance with God's will, then when we say that God is good, we are only saying that he acts in accordance with his own will—and this just does not seem enough.

In the following selections, Jack Bemporad argues that ethical questions ultimately require a religious foundation, while John Arthur argues that such questions have an independent status, separate from all matters of religious belief.

YES

Jack Bemporad

MORALITY AND RELIGION

In this essay, I am concerned with delineating the interrelationship between ethics, science, and theology. This is an old and well-worn topic. However, what I shall endeavor to do here is to indicate where moral issues transcend those of ethics proper and constrain us to introduce religious questions. In particular I will be concerned with four issues.

I. The relationship of ethical questions to the development of a concept of an ideal self.

II. The significance of repentance.

III. The relationship between the good and the holy.

IV. The sense in which ethics and science demand a backdrop that more properly can be delineated as religious or theological.

I. ETHICS AND THE SELF

When we consider action, we cannot avoid questions of motives, goals, and results. We are immediately aware that reality is not homogeneous in all respects, or one-dimensional. We recognize that some actions or goals are better than others, we distinguish what is from what ought to be, and we recognize that our moral values are conceived independently of their actual concrete instances. They even seem to claim a certain preeminence over what actually is.

We continuously decide what is good or bad, right or wrong. This process is reflexive, for it affects not merely how we influence others (and we can never avoid influencing others by who we are and by what we do) but makes a difference to ourselves. Our acts contribute to our future selves. We, as it were, make ourselves in the sense that what we do will help to determine the self that will be, whether we want to be that self or not.

Every moral act not merely has its own intrinsic value but also directs us beyond the present act toward the horizon of something else, something larger and not fully exhausted in the particular act. This is true even in any

From Jack Bemporad, "Morality and Religion," in H. Tristram Engelhardt, Jr., and Daniel Callahan, eds., *Knowledge, Value, and Belief* (The Hastings Center, 1977). Copyright © 1977 by the Hastings Center. Reprinted by permission.

plausible hedonistic ethic which must take account of at least short-term consequences of actions. It is not enough just to seek pleasure since the particular experience of pleasure has to be seen in the context of a total life. We are forced to ask how any particular experience fits into the context or nexus of experiences which will determine the kind of self we want to be. There is a context to any act that forms a backdrop to it. Thus one can always ask: With respect to what total or whole self does this act or series of acts contribute?

Social mores and the teachings of our traditions offer guidelines for judging our particular acts through portrayals of what the whole self should be like. Such are the functions of taboos, rules, regulations, and moral codes. Yet there is always sufficient ambiguity in these that the individual must decide for himself what his overall unified self is, and how each act and experience applies to this unity. The less traditions constrain a society, the greater will be the ambiguity and the role of individual responsibility.

Now, for two reasons, I submit that what kind of self I want to be or produce through my actions is not simply a moral or ethical question. First, the search for the whole of the self requires categories that are not reducible to purely moral notions. They involve questions of hope and despair, of the purpose and significance of one's life, of self-realization and self-sacrifice. Second, when these issues are introduced, the ideal around which the self organizes itself becomes universal and all-encompassing. My point is that ethics may claim certain actions to be right or wrong. It may evaluate or order a hierarchy of values or goods. Yet when one asks the more radical questions of hope and faith, of the meaning of

it all and the meaning of one's life, then one transcends the strictly ethical and scientific pursuits. That is, one moves to a concept of an ideal in terms of which one judges particular actions.

The more one attempts to take familial and social considerations into account in one's actions, the more one is brought to judge one's actions in terms of an ideal self, and thus in terms of more than immediate satisfactions insofar as one judges in terms of overarching considerations. This ideal self gives a consistency to one's life and one's actions. Which is to say, one internalizes the surrounding mores.

But beyond that, one creates a portrait of oneself as a moral agent that can come into conflict with the moral ambience that inspired it, insofar as the mores one draws upon are not fully self-consistent. Such incompatibilities can culminate or display themselves as conflicts between one's view of oneself as a moral agent and one's generally accepted mores. This engenders what some have seen as the core of the genuine ethical dilemma, in distinction from a moral dilemma. Vivas, for example, claims that a genuine ethical dilemma does not consist of knowing what is right and wrong, but in lacking courage and willpower to choose the right.[1] In a genuine ethical dilemma a person does not know the right thing to do. For if he knew the right thing to do, but did not have the courage to do it, it is not a genuine ethical perplexity; it is rather a matter of failure of courage or will. A genuine ethical perplexity lies in a situation where an individual is undergoing stresses and strains in the organization of his inner values. It is one in which he must reconstitute those values through a radical decision involving a choice favorable not to our idea of our actual moral personality, but to our *ideal* moral personality. My contention is that there are situations in which he does not know what the right choice is, and where he has to refashion his moral decisions through a struggle and a creative act. Through an inward search for our essential moral personality we create an ideal person. We may act toward this ideal person as though he were real. A genuine moral perplexity invites a descent into the depths of our very being, a painful inquiry into our actual, rather than our ostensible, motivations and values. And since the formulation is constitutive of an ideal not yet fully formed, this is an act of self-creation.

The monotheistic vision of one God, one mankind, and one universal history, with a concomitant belief in the intrinsic dignity of every person as made in God's image, is an ideal which has furnished the means of judging and changing more parochial and limited ideals. It has been the corrective to various idolatries, chief among which are nationalism and the excessive use of power.

This insight should be seen in the context of the broadest and most universal ideals, and historically has led us to various religious visions. Isaiah was the first to give us a vision of international morality. It is not enough for Isaiah, for example, to have the sword forbidden to individuals. Isaiah claims it is incredible that murder is a crime but war is not. "Nation shall not lift up sword against nation neither shall they learn war anymore."[2] Isaiah's view of morality transcends nationalism—our class, our clan, our tribe—and is seen to be universal and applicable to all. In this fashion, monotheism provides grounds for universal values and functions as a corrective to narrower visions.

II. THE SIGNIFICANCE OF REPENTANCE

The attempt to fulfill ethical demands inevitably fails. And man's failure, his feelings of guilt and remorse at not having fulfilled his ethical goals, leads to contrition, repentance, and endeavors at self-transcendence and self-transformation. It often leads as well to a search for spiritual cleansing, purification, and forgiveness for one's sins.

This search for forgiveness and spiritual cleansing is not simply an ethical need but has numerous religious overtones. This is clear in the context of the self's awareness that ethically he has done wrong, and that yet there must be room for a new beginning, another chance, and not simply condemnation. Still, the more moral faults involve injury to persons generally, the more it becomes impossible to set aside moral debts within the ethical order. Especially as one comes to judge one's moral actions in terms of an ideal self, and the more that ideal self reflects a commitment to general goals of moral conduct, guilt for moral failure requires repentance and forgiveness in terms of that ideal self.

What comes to the fore is the consciousness of the connection of ethics with the self-transcendent aspect of man, his spiritual generation. It is here, as Hermann Cohen points out, that the correlation with God emerges.[3] The Psalmist phrases, "He restoreth my soul," or "Create in me a clean heart and *restore* a steadfast spirit within me," testify to man's need for spiritual healing and regeneration. One cannot refer to this need simply in ethical terms in the sense that ethics seeks general rules of correct behavior and does not give grounds for the very singular act of forgiveness—

especially when the offences involve justice generally, not simply particular individuals who could forgive the offence to them. What ethics does not fully confront, and here the religious element comes to the fore, is, as Hermann Cohen has indicated, the self-recognition of sin and failure and the need for repentance and self-transcendence. Repentance makes it possible to redeem the past. As Max Scheler states, " . . . there is no part of our past life which—while its component natural reality is of course less freely alterable than the future—might not still be genuinely altered in its *meaning* and *worth*, through entering our life's total significance as a constituent of the self-revision which is always possible."[4] Scheler continues,

> Repenting is equivalent to re-appraising part of one's past life and shaping for it a mint-new worth and significance. People tell us that Repentance is a senseless attempt to drive out something 'unalterable'. But nothing in this life is 'unalterable' in the sense of this argument. Even this 'senseless' attempt alters the 'unalterable' and places the regretted conduct or attitude in a new relation within the totality of one's life, setting it to work in a new direction.[5]

Thus Max Scheler sees repentance as the way in which one can "totally kill and extinguish the *reactive* effect of the deed within the human soul, and with it the root of an eternity of renewed guilt and evil." Repentance seeks "forgiveness of sin" and "an infusion of new strength from the center of things."[6]

The need for forgiveness and the recognition that we can be regenerated, start anew as it were, is the heart of repentance. It is an appeal to a transcendent source of power to give us strength, hope, and faith to continue. That is, it is an appeal beyond the ethical order for reinstatement within that order. The possibility for ethical failure, the reality of guilt, the lack of a ground for forgiveness for general moral failures signal beyond the ethical order. Forgiveness, as a general moral category, transcends the ethical in requiring a locus for the giving of forgiveness. One is returned thus to the concept of an ideal self, but now in correlation to the source of forgiveness—God.

III. THE RELATIONSHIP BETWEEN THE GOOD AND THE HOLY

There is another aspect of the ethical which, when fully amplified, transcends ethics and makes it enter the domain of the religious: the feeling of reverence and awe that is related to certain ethical acts, such as self-sacrifice. In such acts the individual often feels that his whole life and the meaning of his life are at stake. Here one has intimations of the holy and the sacred. . . . Even if one recognizes that one can only act coherently if one obeys the categorical imperative, still one may choose to act incoherently—especially if one's own life is at stake. How can the ethical order give adequate motivations for ethical action, especially when these are at the cost of self-sacrifice? Self-sacrifice requires an appeal to something of absolute value.

John Oman has argued that we cannot by building up natural, mundane values arrive at anything of absolute worth.[7] He claims that only in the experience of the holy does one stand in the presence of a reality before which one cannot simply seek one's own pleasure. What Oman distinguishes is the natural and supernatural; he indicates that it is in the recognition of absolute worth or of the holy that an intuition of the supernatural appears.

Hans Jonas also reinforces this concept when he states:

> We must, in other words, distinguish between moral obligation and the much larger sphere of moral value. (This, incidentally, shows up the error in the widely-held view of value theory that the higher a value the stronger its claim and the greater the duty to realize it. The highest are in a region beyond duty and claim.) The ethical dimension far exceeds that of the moral law and reaches into the sublime solitude of dedication and ultimate commitment, away from all reckoning and rule—in short, into the sphere of the holy. From there alone can the offer of self-sacrifice genuinely spring, and this—its source—must be honored religiously.[8]

In short, the search for an ideal focus in terms of which one's particular acts can be judged and given coherence, and the need for a source of forgiveness, coincide with the holy—the adequate ground for ultimate dedication and self-sacrifice. Reflection upon the ethical leads one beyond the ethical in order that coherence in the ethical life, repentance and forgiveness, and ultimate dedication and self-sacrifice can make sense. The argument is clearly not a strict one. It is rather an ascent from lesser to greater coherence of moral vision. The argument turns on an appeal to an interest in a moral life of greater compass and intensity. Thus, as Henry Slonimsky puts it, the religious man is:

> . . . one who is willing to bear the burdens—and on a higher and more difficult plane, the sorrows—and on the highest and most difficult and almost superhuman plane, the sins of the world. A religious person is one who feels responsible for every one else.[9]

This feeling of general responsibility and moral interest is one to which monotheism gives purpose and coherence. If God is one, then there is one moral history—grounded in that God. Moreover, this one God, as the God of all creation, suggests that there is one account or story of the world which is, in principle, a general story. Cosmology and moral history come to coincide in an appeal to universality and generality.

IV. ETHICS, SCIENCE AND THEOLOGY

Ethics makes a demand that the universe be such as to enable ethics to succeed. This is similar to the Kantian postulates in the *Critique of Practical Reason*. It is the task of theology to seek to determine the kind of universe wherein the presuppositions and demands of both science and ethics can be realized and fulfilled. That is, religion gives a view in terms of which the kingdom of nature and the kingdom of grace can be reconciled—in terms of which the otherwise senseless suffering of the innocent can have enduring meaning. Which is to say, religion makes a claim that morality at best can only leave as a postulate—that reality is, in fact, susceptible to morality—that being and goodness are not irreconcilable or opposed, but rather that at least in the Divine Being they are united in a supreme form.

Religion thus forwards an ideal of coherence that extends beyond that of giving unity to particular moral actions. It comes to include giving unity to both our descriptive and normative interests, both our interests in science and ethics. While science is primarily concerned with what is (i.e., with an accurate or true description of the state of things as they are), science as such is not concerned with that aspect of reality that needs changing and transformation. In this respect, science is concerned with what is, morality with what ought to be, and theology is concerned with the interrelationship of these two through an attempt to understand the structure of things as making possible both science and morality. As Montague has argued:

> Religion as we shall conceive it is the acceptance neither of a primitive absurdity nor of a sophisticated truism, but of a momentous possibility—the possibility namely that what is highest in spirit is also deepest in nature, that the ideal and the real are at least to some extent identified, not merely evanescently in our own lives but enduringly in the universe itself. If this possibility were an actuality, if there truly were at the heart of nature something akin to us, a conserver and increaser of values, and if we could not only know this and act upon it, but really feel it, life would suddenly become radiant. For no longer should we be alien accidents in an indifferent world, uncharacterized by-products of the blindly whirling atoms; and no longer would the things that matter most be at the mercy of the things that matter least.[10]

Implicit in Montague's characterization of religion are three concepts: meaning, order, and value. Religion is the assurance or reassurance that life and the universe have meaning and that meaning is impossible without order attuned to values.

Religion as the quest for meaning is not an abstract or intellectual pursuit but lies at the very depths of the human self. The quest for religion begins when man searches for the meaning of his existence, when he seeks the purpose and significance of his life, and when he judges himself by terms that transcend his finite self. This religious quest does not begin in wonder or amazement or in the ineffable, but in the self-questioning of the meaning and purpose of one's existence, and from questioning one's own existence to the existence of all that is. The question man ultimately asks himself is: Why is there something rather than nothing? What is the reason and meaning of the being that is? This question of meaning is never a question of fact. It is not raised by asking what is, but rather by asking the why for, the why.

It is necessary to point out that science makes certain presuppositions which are neither intelligible in themselves nor self-contained, but which require a metaphysical and theological context for their intelligibility. All science presupposes being and order. It takes them for granted and does not discuss the more radical question of the ground for the being and order of what is. But we are still inescapably aware of our contingency and of the contingency of all that is. We are still struck with the question: What is the ground of the being that is? Why is there order and not chaos? What is the ground of the order that is? No attempt at juggling theories of chance and randomness can successfully address itself to these questions. Being cannot come from nonbeing by chance. The laws of chance could intelligibly answer the question as to the probability of coming to be of a certain pattern with respect to a range of actualities. But they could never ask or answer the question about the universe, its coming into being. This question transcends the range and scope of science.

This religious quest for meaning, though, does not contradict science or ethics. After all, it stems from a concern to put science and ethics into a more encompassing framework. Religion in this sense affords a truly interdisciplinary, in fact, transdisciplinary perspective within which ultimate justifications are sought for both ethics and science, for both honoring obligations and having confidence in predictions. Religion offers a coincidence of the *termini ad quos* of our interests in an ideal vantage point for judging our particular moral actions, in a source of forgiveness, in a justification for moral self-sacrifice, and in grounds for confidence regarding our place as moral agents and knowers. A final authentication of ourselves as doers and knowers is to be found, if anywhere, only in religion. To quote Schubert Ogden:

Religious questions do not ask either about particular phenomena as do scientific questions, or about particular courses of action as do moral questions; they ask, rather, about the fundamental conditions that everything particular presupposes. Thus what gives rise to religious questions is the common experience of the apparent unreality and final meaninglessness of all that is and is done. . . . religion is a matter of enabling us so to understand our inalienable confidence in the worth of life that it may be reasonably affirmed.[11]

When one looks for foundations of ethics that also underlie science, I believe one finds them in religion. It is only in terms of a transcendent ground, a universal rationale underlying both the world of experience and the world of moral action, that the domains of ethics and science are assured of integration. Again, this is similar to Kant's suggestion—that only by presuming the existence of God does it become possible to be assured that the kingdoms of Grace and of Na-

ture, of autonomous action and scientific investigation, can be reconciled. The religious viewpoint looks beyond particular vantage points, which give fragmentary portrayals of the human condition, to affirm in one God a unity to being, and a unification to the diverse elements of human existence.

NOTES

1. Eliseo Vivas, *The Moral and the Ethical Life* (Chicago: Henry Regnery Co., 1963).
2. *Isaiah* 2:4b.
3. Hermann Cohen, *Religion of Reason* (New York: Unger Pub. Co., 1972), p. 168.
4. Max Sheler, *On the Eternal in Man* (London: SCM Press Ltd., 1960), p. 40.
5. Ibid., p. 41.
6. Ibid., p. 55.
7. John Oman, *The Natural and the Supernatural* (Cambridge: Cambridge University Press, 1931), p. 310.
8. Hans Jonas, *Philosophical Essays* (Englewood Cliffs, New Jersey: Prentice Hall, 1974).
9. Henry Slonimsky, *Essays* (Chicago: Quadrangle Press, 1967), p. 115.
10. W. P. Montague, *Belief Unbound* (New Haven: Yale University Press, 1930), pp. 6-7.
11. Schubert Ogden, personal communication.

NO
John Arthur

MORALITY WITHOUT GOD

The issue which I address in this paper is the nature of the connection, if any, between morality and religion. I will argue that although there are a variety of ways the two could be connected, in fact morality is independent of religion, both logically and psychologically. First, however, it will be necessary to say something about the subjects: just what are we referring to when we speak of morality and of religion? . . .

To have a moral code . . . is to tend to evaluate (perhaps without even expressing it) the behavior of others and to feel guilt at certain actions when we perform them. Religion, on the other hand, involves beliefs in supernatural power(s) that created and perhaps also control nature, along with the tendency to worship and pray to those supernatural forces or beings. The two—religion and morality—are thus very different. One involves our attitudes toward various forms of behavior (lying and killing, for example), typically expressed using the notions of rules, rights, and obligations. The other, religion, typically involves a different set of activities (prayer, worship) together with beliefs about the supernatural.

We come, then, to the central question: What is the connection, if any, between a society's moral code and its religious beliefs? Many people have felt that there must be a link of some sort between religious beliefs and morality. But is that so? What sort of connection might there be? In what follows I distinguish various ways in which one might claim that religion is necessary for a moral code to function in society. I argue, however, that such connections are not necessary, and indeed that often religion is detrimental to society's attempt to encourage moral conduct among its members.

One possible role which religion might play in morality relates to motives people have. Can people be expected to behave in any sort of decent way towards one another without religious faith? Religion, it is often said, is necessary so that people will DO right. Why might somebody think that? Often, we know, doing what is right has costs: you don't cheat on the test, so you flunk the course; you return the lost billfold, so you don't get the contents. Religion can provide motivation to do the right thing. God rewards those who follow His commands by providing for them a place in heaven

From John Arthur, "Morality Without God," in Garry Brodsky et al., eds., *Contemporary Readings in Social and Political Ethics* (Prometheus Books, 1984). Copyright © 1984 by John Arthur. Reprinted by permission of the author.

and by insuring that they prosper and are happy on earth. He also punishes with damnation those who disobey. Other people emphasize less selfish ways in which religious motives may encourage people to act rightly. God is the creator of the universe and has ordained that His plan should be followed. How better to live one's life than to participate in this divinely ordained plan? Only by living a moral life, it is said, can people live in harmony with the larger, divinely created order.

But how are we to assess the relative strength of these various motives for acting morally, some of which are religious, others not? How important is the fear of hell or the desire to live as God wishes in motivating people? Think about the last time you were tempted to do something you knew to be wrong. Surely your decision not to do so (if that was your decision) was made for a variety of reasons: "What if I get caught? What if somebody sees me—what will he or she think? How will I feel afterwards? Will I regret it?" Or maybe the thought of cheating just doesn't occur to you. You were raised to be an honest person, and that's what you want to be—period. There are thus many motives for doing the right thing which have nothing whatsoever to do with religion. Most of us in fact do worry about getting caught, about being blamed and looked down on by others. We also may do what is right just for that reason, because it's our duty, or because we don't want to hurt others. So to say that we need religion to act morally is mistaken; indeed it seems to me that most of us, when it really gets down to it, don't give much of a thought to religion when making moral decisions. All those other reasons are the ones which we tend to consider, or else we just don't consider

cheating and stealing at all. So far, then, there seems to be no reason to suppose that people can't be moral yet irreligious at the same time.

Another oft-heard argument that religion is necessary for people to do the right thing questions whether people would know how to do the right thing without the guidance of religion. In other words, however much people may want to do the right thing, it is only with the help of God that true moral understanding can be achieved. People's own intellect is simply inadequate to this task; we must consult revelation for help.

Again, however, this argument fails. Just consider what we would need to know in order for religion to provide moral guidance. First we must be sure that there is a God. And then there's the question of which of the many religions is true. How can anybody be sure his or her religion is the right one? After all, if you have been born in China or India or Iran your religious views would almost certainly not have been the ones you now hold. And even if we can somehow convince ourselves that the Judeo-Christian God is the real one, we still need to find out just what it is He wants us to do. Revelation comes in at least two forms, according to theists, and not even Christians agree which form is real. Some hold that God tells us what he wants by providing us with His words: the Ten Commandments are an example. Many even believe, as Billy Graham once said, that the entire *Bible* was written by God using 39 secretaries. Others doubt that every word of the *Bible* is literally true, believing instead that it is merely an historical account of the *events* in history whereby God revealed Himself. So on this view revelation is not understood as statements made by God but, instead, as

His intervening into historical events, such as leading His people from Egypt, testing Job, and sending His son as an example of the ideal life. But if we are to use revelation as a guide we must know what is to count as revelation—words given us by God, events, or both? Supposing that we could somehow solve all those puzzles, the problems of relying on revelation are still not over. Even if we can agree on who God is and on how and when He reveals Himself, we still must interpret that revelation. Some feel that the *Bible* justifies various forms of killing, including war and capital punishment, on the basis of such statements as "An eye for an eye." Others, emphasizing such sayings as "Judge not lest ye be judged" and "Thou shalt not kill," believe the *Bible* demands absolute pacifism. How are we to know which interpretation is correct?

Far from providing a short-cut to moral understanding, looking to revelation for guidance just creates more questions and problems. It is much simpler to address problems such as abortion, capital punishment, and war directly than to seek answers in revelation. In fact, not only is religion unnecessary to provide moral understanding, it can sometimes be a hindrance, leading people to look for answers where none are available. (My own hunch is that often those who are most likely to appeal to Scripture as justification for their moral beliefs are really just rationalizing positions they already believe.)

Far from religion being necessary for people to do the right thing, it often gets in the way. People do not need the motivation of religion; they for the most part are not motivated by religion as much as by other factors; and religion is of no help in discovering what our moral obli-

gations are. But others give a different reason for claiming morality depends on religion. They think religion, and especially God, is necessary for morality because without God there could BE no right or wrong. The idea was expressed by Bishop R. C. Mortimer: "God made us and all the world. Because of that He has an absolute claim on our obedience. . . . From [this] it follows that a thing is not right simply because we think it is. . . . It is right because God commands it."[1]

What Mortimer has in mind can best be seen by comparing moral rules with legal ones. Legal statutes, we know, are created by legislatures and judges. So if there had been no law passed requiring that people limit the speed they travel then there would be no such legal obligation. Without the commands of the legislature statutes simply would not exist. The view defended by Mortimer, often called the divine command theory, is that God has the same relation to moral law as the legislature does to statutes. Without God's commands there would be no moral rules.

Another tenet of the divine command theory, besides the belief that God is the author of morality, is that only the divine command theory is able to explain the objective difference between right and wrong. This point was forcefully argued by F. C. Copleston in a 1948 British Broadcasting Corporation radio debate with Bertrand Russell.

RUSSELL: But aren't you now saying in effect "I mean by God whatever is good or the sum total of what is good—the system of what is good, and, therefore, when a young man loves anything that is good he is loving God." Is that what you're saying, because if so, it wants a bit of arguing.

COPLESTON: I don't say, of course, that God is the sum total or system of what is good . . . but I do think that all goodness reflects God in some way and proceeds from Him, so that in a sense the man who loves what is truly good, loves God even if he doesn't avert to God. But still I agree that the validity of such an interpretation of man's conduct depends on the recognition of God's existence, obviously. . . . Let's take a look at the Commandant of the [Nazi] concentration camp at Belsen. That appears to you as undesirable and evil and to me too. To Adolph Hitler we suppose it appeared as something good and desirable. I suppose you'd have to admit that for Hitler it was good and for you it is evil.

RUSSELL: No, I shouldn't go so far as that. I mean, I think people can make mistakes in that as they can in other things. If you have jaundice you see things yellow that are not yellow. You're making a mistake.

COPLESTON: Yes, one can make mistakes, but can you make a mistake if it's simply a question of reference to a feeling or emotion? Surely Hitler would be the only possible judge of what appealed to his emotions.

RUSSELL: . . . you can say various things about that; among others, that if that sort of thing makes that sort of appeal to Hitler's emotions, then Hitler makes quite a different appeal to my emotions.

COPLESTON: Granted. But there's no objective criterion outside feeling then for condemning the conduct of the Commandant of Belsen, in your view. . . . The human being's idea of the content of the moral law depends certainly to a large extent on education and environment, and a man had to use his reason in assessing the validity of the actual moral ideas of his social group. But the possibility of criticizing the accepted moral code presupposes that there is an objective standard, that there is an ideal moral order, which imposes itself. . . . It implies the existence of a real foundation of God.[2]

God, according to Copleston, is able to provide the basis for the distinction, which we all know to exist, between right and wrong. Without that objective basis for defining human obligation we would have no real reason for condemning the behavior of anybody, even Nazis. Morality would be little more than an expression of personal feeling.

Before assessing the divine command theory, let's first consider this last point. Is it really true that only the commands of God can provide an objective basis for moral judgments? Certainly many philosophers . . . have felt that morality rests on its own, perfectly sound footing; to prejudge those efforts or others which may be made in the future as unsuccessful seems mistaken. And, second, if it were true that there is no nonreligious basis for claiming moral objectivity, then perhaps that means there simply is no such basis. Why suppose that there must be such a foundation?

What of the divine command theory itself? Is it reasonable, even though we need not do so, to equate something's being right with its being commanded by God? Certainly the expressions "is commanded by God" and "is morally required" do not mean the same thing; atheists and agnostics use moral words without understanding them to make any reference to God. And while it is of course true that God (or any other moral being for that matter) would tend to want others to do the right thing, this hardly shows that being right and being commanded by God are the same thing. Parents want their children to do the right thing, too, but that doesn't mean they, or anybody else, can make a thing right just by commanding it!

I think that, in fact, theists themselves if they thought about it would reject the divine command theory. One reason is because of what it implies. Suppose we grant (just for the sake of argument) that the divine command theory is correct. Notice what we have now said: Actions are right just because they are commanded by God. And the same, of course, can be said about those deeds which we believe are wrong. If God hadn't commanded us not to do them, they would not be wrong. (Recall the comparison made with the commands of the legislature, which would not be law except for the legislature having passed a statute.)

But now notice this. Since God is all-powerful, and since right is determined solely by His commands, is it not possible that He might change the rules and make what we now think of as wrong into right? It would seem that according to the divine command theory it is possible that tomorrow God will decree that virtues such as kindness and courage have become vices while actions which show cruelty and cowardice are the right actions. Rather than it being right for people to help each other out and prevent innocent people from suffering unnecessarily, it would be right to create as much pain among innocent children as we possibly can! To adopt the divine command theory commits its advocate to the seemingly absurd position that even the greatest atrocities might be not only acceptable but morally required if God were to command them.

Plato made a similar point in the dialogue *Euthyphro*. Socrates is asking Euthyphro what it is that makes the virtue of holiness a virtue, just as we have been asking what makes kindness and cour-

age virtues. Euthyphro has suggested that holiness is just whatever all the gods love.

SOCRATES: Well, then, Euthyphro, what do we say about holiness? Is it not loved by all the gods, according to your definition?
EUTHYPHRO: Yes.
SOCRATES: Because it is holy, or for some other reason?
EUTHYPHRO: No, because it is holy.
SOCRATES: Then it is loved by the gods because it is holy: it is not holy because it is loved by them?
EUTHYPHRO: It seems so.
SOCRATES: . . . Then holiness is not what is pleasing to the gods, and what is pleasing to the gods is not holy as you say, Euthyphro. They are different things.
EUTHYPHRO: And why, Socrates?
SOCRATES: Because we are agreed that the gods love holiness because it is holy: and that it is not holy because they love it.[3]

Having claimed that virtues are what is loved by the gods why does Euthyphro so readily agree that the gods love holiness *because* it's holy? One possibility is that he is assuming whenever the gods love something they do so with good reason, not just arbitrarily. If something is pleasing to gods, there must be a reason. To deny this and say that it is simply the gods' love which makes holiness a virtue would mean that the gods have no basis for their opinions, that they are arbitrary. Or to put it another way, if we say that it is simply God's loving something that makes it right, then what sense does it make to say God wants us to do right? All that could mean is that God wants us to do what He wants us to do. He would have no reason for wanting it. Similarly "God is good" would mean little more than "God does what He pleases." Religious people who find this an unacceptable consequence will reject the divine command theory.

But doesn't this now raise another problem? If God approves kindness because it is a virtue, then it seems that God discovers morality rather than inventing it. And haven't we then suggested a limitation on God's power, since He now, being a good God, must love kindness and command us not to be cruel? What is left of God's omnipotence?

But why should such a limitation on God be unacceptable for a theist? Because there is nothing God cannot do? But is it true to say that God can do absolutely anything? Can He, for example, destroy Himself? Can God make a rock so heavy that He cannot lift it? Or create a universe which was never created by Him? Many have thought that God's inability to do these sorts of things does not constitute a genuine limitation on His power because these are things which cannot logically be done. Thomas Aquinas, for example, wrote that, "whatever implies contradiction does not come within the scope of divine omnipotence, because it cannot have the aspect of possibility. Hence it is more appropriate to say that such things cannot be done than that God cannot do them."[4] Many theists reject the view that there is nothing which God cannot do.

But how, then, ought we to understand God's relationship to morality if we reject the divine command theory? Can religious people consistently maintain their faith in God the Creator and yet deny that what is right is right because He commands it? I think the answer to this is "yes." First, note that there is still a sense in which God could change morality (assuming, of course,

there is a God). Whatever moral code we decide is best (most justified), that choice will in part depend on such factors as how we reason, what we desire and need, and the circumstances in which we find ourselves. Presumably, however, God could have constructed us or our environment very differently, so that we didn't care about freedom, weren't curious about nature, and weren't influenced by others' suffering. Or perhaps our natural environment could be altered so that it is less hostile to our needs and desires. If He had created either nature or us that way, then it seems likely that the most justified moral code might be different in important ways from the one it is now rational for us to support. In that sense, then, morality depends on God whether or not one supports the divine command theory.

In fact, it seems to me that it makes little difference for ethical questions whether a person is religious. The atheist will treat human nature simply as a given, a fact of nature, while the theist may regard it as the product of divine intention. But in any case the right thing to do is to follow the best moral code, the one that is most justified. Instead of relying on revelation to discover morality, religious and nonreligious people alike can inquire into which system is best.

In sum, I have argued first that religion is neither necessary nor useful in providing moral motivation or guidance. My objections to the claim that without God there would be no morality are somewhat more complex. First, it is wrong to say that only if God's will is at its base can morality be objective. The idea of the best justified moral code—the one fully rational persons would support—may prove to provide sound means to evaluate one's own code as well as those of other societies. Furthermore, the divine command theory should not be accepted . . . by those who are religious. This is because it implies what clearly seems absurd, namely that God might tomorrow change the moral rules and make performing the most extreme acts of cruelty an obligation we all should meet. . . . Far from helping resolve moral disputes, religion does little more than sow confusion. Morality does not need religion and religion does not need morality.

NOTES

1. R. C. Mortimer, *Christian Ethics* (London: Hutchinson's University Library, 1950) pp. 7–8.

2. This debate was broadcast on the Third Program of the British Broadcasting Corporation in 1948.

3. Plato, *Euthyphro* tr. H. N. Fowler (Cambridge, Mass.: Harvard University Press, 1947).

4. Thomas Aquinas, *Summa Theologica*, Part I, Q. 25, Art. 3.

POSTSCRIPT

Is Morality Grounded in Religion?

As Arthur reminds us in his article, some of the earliest—and indeed some of the best—arguments on this issue can be found in Plato's dialogue called the *Euthyphro,* which was written in the fourth century B.C. His arguments were in terms of Greek religious practices and Greek gods, but we can reformulate the points and elaborate the arguments in Christian terms.

One key dilemma, in the original Greek version, asks us to consider whether holy things are: (i) holy because they please the gods, or (ii) please the gods because they are holy. In monotheistic terms, the dilemma would be whether holy things are: (i) holy because they please God, or (ii) please God because they are holy. The question can then be broadened and the dilemma posed in terms of goods things in general. We then ask whether good things are: (i) good because God wills them, or (ii) willed by God because they are good.

Plato believed that the gods love what is holy because it is holy (ii), just as Christians have traditionally believed that God wills good things because they are good (ii). Traditionally, a contrast is drawn between God, an infinite and all-good being who always wills the good, and humans, finite beings who are not all-good and do not always will the good.

We might also consider a parallel dilemma. Concerning truths, are these things true because God knows them, or does God know them because they are true? The traditional view is that God is all-knowing. God knows all truths because they are truths (and no truths lie outside divine knowledge), whereas people do not know all truths (and many truths lie outside human knowledge).

Nevertheless, there has also been in Christianity a tradition that the almighty power of God is not such as to be constrained by anything—even if we imagine that what constrains God are good things. This view holds that it is God who creates not only good things but the very fact that a good thing (such as honesty) is good while another thing (such as false witness against your neighbor) is not. Thus, in this view, God in his power determines what is good and what is bad.

An atheist who believes that only divine will could make something good or bad would conclude that nothing really is good or bad. But an atheist who believes that a divine will would always will the good could continue to believe both that there is no God and also that some things are good and some things are bad.

These issues are further discussed in Paul Helm, ed., *Divine Commands and Morality* (Oxford University Press, 1981) and Kai Nielsen, *Morality Without God* (Prometheus Books, 1973).

ISSUE 5

Do the Ends Justify the Means?

YES: J. J. C. Smart, from "An Outline of a System of Utilitarian Ethics," in J. J. C. Smart and Bernard Williams, *Utilitarianism: For and Against* (Cambridge University Press, 1973)

NO: Paul W. Taylor, from *Principles of Ethics: An Introduction* (Dickinson Publishing Co., 1975)

ISSUE SUMMARY

YES: Professor of philosophy J. J. C. Smart defends the principle that one ought to act in such a way as to promote, as a result, the greatest happiness for the greatest number. It is this end result that justifies doing even things that might seem wrong when judged by a traditional moral perspective.
NO: Professor of philosophy Paul W. Taylor objects to the utilitarianism of Smart and others on the ground that the theory does not take proper notice of the principles of justice. In particular, utilitarianism cannot rightfully support injustice even if an unfair act would supposedly lead to greater happiness in the end.

According to utilitarianism, the goodness or badness of an action is to be determined by its consequences. Actions that are good are those that promote the greatest happiness for the greatest number affected by the action. Utilitarianism gets its name from the fact that it often uses the term *utility* to mean happiness.

Utilitarianism first rose to prominence in the nineteenth century in the hands of a group known as the Philosophical Radicals. Their approach was to question all moral, social, and political practices. They asked, for example, why hang pickpockets? It didn't stop pickpocketing. In fact, as crowds gathered to watch the public hanging of a convicted pickpocket, many in the crowd had their pockets picked by clever pickpockets who had waited for just this opportunity.

John Stuart Mill (1806–1873), one of the most famous of the original utilitarian radicals, questioned the practice of requiring witnesses at a legal trial to swear belief in certain Christian doctrines before they were allowed to testify. Individuals who did not profess the approved beliefs were unable to give testimony and thus were dismissed. A believing Christian could of course profess the right beliefs and gain access to the witness stand. But, Mill asked, is there any greater guarantee that what was said was true than if the witness did not have those beliefs? Ignoring the possibility that a Christian could lie, Mill said let us place every trust in the testimony of the Christian anyway but let us then proceed to ask about the person who cannot swear that he holds certain religious beliefs. Mill pointed out that this individual, under strong social pressure, tells what he really thinks, and the law dismisses him. Finally, said Mill, consider the unbeliever who lies and *says* that he believes; this liar is then asked to stay to give legal testimony!

It *seemed* to many nineteenth-century English men and women that pickpockets should be hanged and that witnesses in legal cases should first qualify as trustworthy by virtue of having proper Christian beliefs. But utilitarians wanted to look at the *results* of acting on such suppositions. The results did not seem favorable, and utilitarians thought a better way (in each case) should be found. Mill complained that people's prejudices, feelings, and biases had been allowed to determine right and wrong. What was needed, however, was an impartial and scientifically informed assessment of the results of actions and policies. *Do* particular actions and policies actually lead to the greatest happiness for the greatest number, or are a great number of people's desires frustrated or denied? This line of questioning requires investigation and argument. Mill and other utilitarians did not advocate proceeding on traditional lines, doing the same things over and over because "this is the way we've always done it." Utilitarianism holds that traditional moralities are not reliable; they are merely cultural hand-me-downs.

Mill always thought that the traditional cultural role for women in Victorian times was outrageously limited and confining, and he produced a famous essay "On the Subjection of Women." Today, too, utilitarians argue for the elimination of all traces of sexism from society. The rationale, however, is not that women have certain rights, but that only by leaving sexism behind can we hope to progress to the greatest happiness for the greatest number. Jeremy Bentham, an early utilitarian and a teacher of Mill, said that rights were simply nonsense and the idea of natural human rights inherent in all people was "nonsense on stilts."

Utilitarians today generally defend measures that they believe will result in increased happiness, even though actions may be required that violate certain social rules. For example, we have in our society unwritten rules against killing, and written laws as well, but in the case of a dying patient who is in great pain and who begs to be killed, utilitarians tend to say that the best thing for all concerned is to kill the patient. To refrain from doing so, on the ground of the rule against killing, would appear to a utilitarian as a form of "rule worship," which simply does not promote utility. Utilitarians would argue that the laws and people's attitudes need to be changed.

A standard stumbling block for utilitarians, however, derives from the principles of justice. It seems that in concentrating on the desired *end* (happiness), utilitarians are too willing to violate principles of justice as a means to that end. In the following selections, J. J. C. Smart makes the case for utilitarianism, and Paul W. Taylor raises the objections from justice.

YES

J. J. C. Smart

AN OUTLINE OF
A SYSTEM OF UTILITARIAN ETHICS

The system of normative ethics which I am here concerned to defend is . . .
act-utilitarianism. Act-utilitarianism is to be contrasted with rule-utilitarianism. Act-utilitarianism is the view that the rightness or wrongness of an
action is to be judged by the consequences, good or bad, of the action itself.
Rule-utilitarianism is the view that the rightness or wrongness of an action is
to be judged by the goodness and badness of the consequences of a rule that
everyone should perform the action in like circumstances. . . .

An act-utilitarian judges the rightness or wrongness of actions by the
goodness and badness of their consequences. But is he to judge the goodness
and badness of the consequences of an action solely by their pleasantness
and unpleasantness? Bentham,[1] who thought that quantity of pleasure being
equal, the experience of playing pushpin was as good as that of reading
poetry, could be classified as a hedonistic act-utilitarian. Moore,[2] who
believed that some states of mind, such as those of acquiring knowledge, had
intrinsic value quite independent of their pleasantness, can be called an ideal
utilitarian. Mill seemed to occupy an intermediate position.[3] He held that
there are higher and lower pleasures. This seems to imply that pleasure is a
necessary condition for goodness but that goodness depends on other
qualities of experience than pleasantness and unpleasantness. I propose to
call Mill a quasi-ideal utilitarian. For Mill, pleasantness functions like x in the
algebraic product, $x \times y \times z$. If $x = o$ the product is zero. For Moore
pleasantness functions more like x in $(x + 1) \times y \times z$. If $x = o$ the product
need not be zero. Of course this is only a very rough analogy.

What Bentham, Mill and Moore are all agreed on is that the rightness of an
action is to be judged solely by consequences, states of affairs brought about
by the action. Of course we shall have to be careful here not to construe 'state
of affairs' so widely that any ethical doctrine becomes utilitarian. For if we
did so we would not be saying anything at all in advocating utilitarianism. If,
for example, we allowed 'the state of having just kept a promise', then a
deontologist who said we should keep promises simply because they are
promises would be utilitarian. And we do not wish to allow this. . . .

It is . . . necessary to remember that we are here considering utilitarianism as a *normative* system. The fact that it has consequences which conflict with some of our particular moral judgements need not be decisive against it. In science general principles must be tested by reference to particular facts of observation. In ethics we may well take the opposite attitude, and test our particular moral attitudes by reference to more general ones. The utilitarian can contend that since his principle rests on something so simple and natural as generalized benevolence it is more securely founded than our particular feelings, which may be subtly distorted by analogies with similar looking (but in reality totally different) types of case, and by all sorts of hangovers from traditional and uncritical ethical thinking.

If, of course, act-utilitarianism were put forward as a descriptive systematization of how ordinary men, or even we ourselves in our unreflective and uncritical moments, actually think about ethics, then of course it is easy to refute and I have no wish to defend it. Similarly again if it is put forward not as a *descriptive* theory but as an *explanatory* one. John Plamenatz, in his *English Utilitarians*, seems to hold that utilitarianism "is destroyed and no part of it left standing".[4] This is apparently on the ground that the utilitarian *explanation* of social institutions will not work: that we cannot *explain* various institutions as having come about because they lead to the maximum happiness. In this monograph I am not concerned with what our moral customs and institutions in fact are, and still less am I concerned with the question of *why* they are as they in fact are. I am concerned with a certain view about what they *ought* to be. The correctness of

an ethical doctrine, when it is interpreted as recommendatory, is quite independent of its truth when it is interpreted as descriptive and of its truth when it is interpreted as explanatory. In fact it is precisely because a doctrine is false as description and as explanation that it becomes important as a possible recommendation. . . .

UTILITARIANISM AND THE FUTURE

The chief persuasive argument in favour of utilitarianism has been that the dictates of any deontological ethics will always, on some occasions, lead to the existence of misery that could, on utilitarian principles, have been prevented. Thus if the deontologist says that promises always should be kept (or even if, like Ross, he says that there is a *prima facie* duty to keep them) we may confront him with a situation like the following, the well-known 'desert island promise': I have promised a dying man on a desert island, from which subsequently I alone am rescued, to give his hoard of gold to the South Australian Jockey Club. On my return I give it to the Royal Adelaide Hospital, which, we may suppose, badly needs it for a new X-ray machine. Could anybody deny that I had done rightly without being open to the charge of heartlessness? (Remember that the promise was known only to me, and so my action will not in this case weaken the general confidence in the social institution of promising.) Think of the persons dying of painful tumours who could have been saved by the desert island gold!

"But," the deontologist may still object, "it is my doctrine which is the humane one. You have accused me of inhumanity because I sometimes cause avoidable misery for the sake of keeping a rule. But it is these very rules, which you regard as so cold and inhuman, which safeguard mankind from the most awful atrocities. In the interests of future generations are we to allow millions to die of starvation, or still more millions to be sent to forced labour? Is it not this very consequentialist mentality which is at the root of the vast injustices which we see in the world today?" Two replies are relevant. In the first place the man who says this sort of thing may or may not be interested in the welfare of future generations. It is perfectly possible not to have the sentiment of generalized benevolence but to be moved by a localized benevolence. When this is localized in space we get the ethics of the tribe or the race: when it is localized in time we get an ethics of the present day and generation. It may well be that atrocities carried out for the sake of a Utopian future repel some people *simply* because they mortgage the present for the sake of the future. Here we have a difference about ultimate ends, and in this case I cannot accuse my opponent of being either confused or superstitious, though I may accuse him of being limited in his vision. Why should not future generations matter as much as present ones? To deny it is to be temporally parochial. If it is objected that future generations will only *probably* exist, I reply: would not the objector take into account a probably existing *present* population on a strange island before using it for bomb tests?

In the second place, however, the opponent of utilitarianism may have a perfectly disinterested benevolence, save for his regard for the observance of rules as such. Future generations may in fact mean as much to him as present ones. To

him the utilitarian may reply as follows. If it were known to be true, as a question of fact, that measures which caused misery and death to tens of millions today *would* result in saving from greater misery and from death hundreds of millions in the future, and if this were the only way in which it could be done, then it *would* be right to cause these necessary atrocities. The case is surely no different in principle from that of the battalion commander who sacrifices a patrol to save a company. Where the tyrants who cause atrocities for the sake of Utopia are wrong is, surely, on the plain question of fact, and on confusing probabilities with certainties. After all, one would have to be *very sure* that future generations would be saved still greater misery before one embarked on such a tyrannical programme. One thing we should now know about the future is that large-scale predictions are impossible. Could Jeremy Bentham or Karl Marx (to take two very different political theorists) have foreseen the atom bomb? Could they have foreseen automation? Can we foresee the technology of the next century? Where the future is so dim a man must be mad who would sacrifice the present in a big way for the sake of it. Moreover even if the future were clear to us, it is very improbable that large scale atrocities could be beneficial. We must not forget the immense side effects: the brutalization of the people who ordered the atrocities and carried them out. We can, in fact, agree with the most violent denouncer of atrocities carried out in the name of Utopia without sacrificing our act-utilitarian principles. Indeed there are the best of act-utilitarian reasons for denouncing atrocities. But it is empirical facts, and empirical facts only, which will lead the utilitarian to say this. . . .

UTILITARIANISM AND JUSTICE

So far, I have done my best to state utilitarianism in a way which is conceptually clear and to rebut many common objections to it. At the time I wrote the earlier edition of this monograph I did so as a pretty single-minded utilitarian myself. It seemed to me then that since the utilitarian principle expressed the attitude of generalized benevolence, anyone who rejected utilitarianism would have to be hard hearted, i.e. to some extent non-benevolent, or else would have to be the prey of conceptual confusion or an unthinking adherent of traditional ways of thought, or perhaps be an adherent of some religious system of ethics, which could be undermined by metaphysical criticism. Admittedly utilitarianism does have consequences which are incompatible with the common moral consciousness, but I tended to take the view "so much the worse for the common moral consciousness". That is, I was inclined to reject the common methodology of testing general ethical principles by seeing how they square with our feelings in particular instances.

After all, one may feel somewhat as follows. What is the purpose of morality? (Answering this question is to make a moral judgement. To think that one could answer the question "What is the purpose of morality?" without making a moral judgement would be to condone the naturalistic fallacy, the fallacy of deducing an 'ought' from an 'is'.) Suppose that we say, as it is surely at least tempting to do, that the purpose of morality is to subserve the general happiness. Then it immediately seems to follow that we ought to reject any putative moral rule, or any particular moral feeling, which conflicts with the utilitarian principle. It

is undeniable that we do have anti-utilitarian moral feelings in particular cases, but perhaps they should be discounted as far as possible, as due to our moral conditioning in childhood. (The weakness of this line of thought is that approval of the general principle of utilitarianism may be due to moral conditioning too. And even if benevolence were in some way a 'natural', not an 'artificial', attitude, this consideration could at best have persuasive force, without any clear rationale. To argue from the naturalness to the correctness of a moral attitude would be to commit the naturalistic fallacy.) Nevertheless in some moods the general principle of utilitarianism may recommend itself to us so much the more than do particular moral precepts, precisely because it *is* so general. We may therefore feel inclined to reject an ethical methodology which implies that we should test our general principles by our reactions in particular cases. Rather, we may come to feel, we should test our reactions in particular cases by reference to the most general principles. The analogy with science is not a good one, since it is not far off the truth to say that observation statements are more firmly based than the theories they test.[5] But why should our more particular moral feelings be more worthy of notice than our more generalized ones? . . .

The utilitarian, then, will test his particular feelings by reference to his general principle, and not the general principle by reference to his particular feelings. . . .

It is not difficult to show that utilitarianism could, in certain exceptional circumstances, have some very horrible consequences. In a very lucid and concise discussion note,[6] H. J. McCloskey has considered such a case. Suppose that the sheriff of a small town can prevent serious riots (in which hundreds of people will be killed) only by 'framing' and executing (as a scapegoat) an innocent man. In actual cases of this sort the utilitarian will usually be able to agree with our normal moral feelings about such matters. He will be able to point out that there would be some possibility of the sheriff's dishonesty being found out, with consequent weakening of confidence and respect for law and order in the community, the consequences of which would be far worse even than the painful deaths of hundreds of citizens. But as McCloskey is ready to point out, the case can be presented in such a way that these objections do not apply. For example, it can be imagined that the sheriff could have first-rate empirical evidence that he will not be found out. So the objection that the sheriff *knows* that the man he 'frames' will be killed, whereas he has only probable belief that the riot will occur unless he frames the man, is not a sound one. Someone like McCloskey can always strengthen his story to the point that we would just have to admit that if utilitarianism is correct, then the sheriff must frame the innocent man. (McCloskey also has cogently argued that similar objectionable consequences are also implied by rule-utilitarianism. That is, an unjust *system* of punishment might be more *useful* than a just one. Hence even if rule-utilitarianism can clearly be distinguished from act-utilitarianism, a utilitarian will not be able to avoid offensive consequences of his theory by retreating from the 'act' form to the 'rule' form.) Now though a utilitarian might argue that it is empirically unlikely that some such situation as McCloskey envisages would ever occur, McCloskey will point out that it is *log-ically* possible that such a situation will arise. If the utilitarian rejects the unjust act (or system) he is clearly giving up his utilitarianism. McCloskey then remarks: "But as far as I know, only J. J. C. Smart among the contemporary utilitarians, is happy to adopt this 'solution'." Here I must lodge a mild protest. McCloskey's use of the word 'happy' surely makes me look a most reprehensible person. Even in my most utilitarian moods I am not *happy* about this consequence of utilitarianism. Nevertheless, however unhappy about it he may be, the utilitarian must admit that he draws the consequence that he might find himself in circumstances where he ought to be unjust. Let us hope that this is a logical possibility and not a factual one. In hoping thus I am not being inconsistent with utilitarianism, since any injustice causes misery and so can be justified only as the lesser of two evils. The fewer the situations in which the utilitarian is forced to choose the lesser of two evils, the better he will be pleased. One must not think of the utilitarian as the sort of person who you would not trust further than you could kick him. As a matter of untutored sociological observation, I should say that in general utilitarians are more than usually trustworthy people, and that the sort of people who might do you down are rarely utilitarians.

It is also true that we should probably dislike and fear a man who could bring himself to do the right utilitarian act in a case of the sort envisaged by McCloskey. Though the man in this case might have done the right utilitarian act, his act would betoken a toughness and lack of squeamishness which would make him a dangerous person. We must remember that people have egoistic tendencies as well as beneficent ones, and should such a person be tempted to act wrongly he could act very wrongly indeed. A utilitarian who remembers the possible moral weakness of men might quite consistently prefer to be the sort of person who would not always be able to bring himself to do the right utilitarian act and to surround himself by people who would be too squeamish to act in a utilitarian manner in such extreme cases.

No, I am not happy to draw the conclusion that McCloskey quite rightly says that the utilitarian must draw. But neither am I happy with the anti-utilitarian conclusion. For if a case really *did* arise in which injustice was the lesser of two evils (in terms of human happiness and misery), then the anti-utilitarian conclusion is a very unpalatable one too, namely that in some circumstances one must choose the greater misery, perhaps the *very much* greater misery, such as that of hundreds of people suffering painful deaths.

Still, to be consistent, the utilitarian must accept McCloskey's challenge. Let us hope that the sort of possibility which he envisages will always be no more than a logical possibility and will never become an actuality. At any rate, even though I have suggested that in ethics we should test particular feelings by general attitudes, McCloskey's example makes me somewhat sympathetic to the opposite point of view. . . . It is perfectly possible to have conflicting attitudes within oneself. It is quite conceivable that there is *no* possible ethical theory which will be conformable with all our attitudes. If the theory is utilitarian, then the possibility that sometimes it would be right to commit injustice will be felt to be acutely unsatisfactory by someone with a normal civilized upbringing. If on the other hand it is not utilitarian but has deontological elements, then it will have the unsatisfactory implication that sometimes avoidable misery (perhaps very great avoidable misery) ought not to be avoided. It might be thought that some compromise theory, on the lines of Sir David Ross's, in which there is some 'balancing up' between considerations of utility and those of deontology, might provide an acceptable compromise. The trouble with this, however, is that such a 'balancing' may not be possible: one can easily feel pulled sometimes one way and sometimes the other. How can one 'balance' a serious injustice, on the one hand, and hundreds of painful deaths, on the other hand? Even if we disregard our purely self-interested attitudes, for the sake of interpersonal discussions, so as to treat ourselves neither more nor less favourably than other people, it is still possible that there is no ethical system which would be satisfactory to all men, or even to one man at different times. It is possible that something similar is the case with science, that no scientific theory (known or unknown) is correct. If so, the world is more chaotic than we believe and hope that it is. But even though the world is not chaotic, men's moral feelings may be. On anthropological grounds it is only too likely that these feelings are to some extent chaotic. Both as children and as adults, we have probably had many different moral conditionings, which can easily be incompatible with one another.

Meanwhile, among possible options, utilitarianism does have its appeal. With its empirical attitude to questions of means and ends it is congenial to the scientific temper and it has flexibility to deal with a changing world. This last consideration is, however, more self-recommendation than justification. For if flexibility is a recommendation, this is because of the utility of flexibility.

NOTES

1. Jeremy Bentham's most important ethical work is 'An Introduction to the Principles of Morals and Legislation,' in *A Fragment on Government and an Introduction to the Principles of Morals and Legislation*, ed. Wilfrid Harrison (Blackwell, Oxford, 1948). For the remark on poetry and pushpin see Bentham's *Works* (Tait, Edinburgh, 1843), vol. 2, pp. 253–4.

2. G. E. Moore, *Principia Ethica* (Cambridge University Press, London, 1962).

3. J. S. Mill, *Utilitarianism*, ed. Mary Warnock (Collins, London, 1962).

4. *The English Utilitarians*, 2nd ed. (Blackwell, Oxford, 1966), p. 145.

5. I say, 'not far off the truth' because observation statements are to some extent theory laden, and if they are laden with a bad theory we may have to reject them.

6. H. J. McCloskey, 'A note on utilitarian punishment,' *Mind* 72 (1963) 599.

NO   Paul W. Taylor

A PROBLEM FOR UTILITARIANISM

The objection raised against . . . utilitarian ethics is that *the principle of utility does not provide a sufficient ground for the obligations of justice*. Since the idea of justice is a fundamental moral concept, no normative ethical system can be considered adequate that does not show the basis for our duty to be just. The argument starts with a careful examination of the ultimate norm of utilitarian ethics, the principle of utility itself. Exactly what is utility? It has been described in the words, "the maximizing of intrinsic value and the minimizing of intrinsic disvalue." What, precisely, does this mean?

It will be helpful in answering this question to think of measurable units of intrinsic value and disvalue. We shall accordingly speak of units of happiness and unhappiness, respectively. This will enable us to see the difficulty more clearly, although no particular view of what is to be taken as the measurement of a unit of happiness or unhappiness will be presupposed. We all know in general what it means to be very happy, quite happy, not especially happy, rather unhappy, and extremely unhappy. Thus, the idea of degrees of happiness corresponds to something in our experience. We also know what it means to be happy for a brief moment, or for a day, and we use such phrases as "It was a happy two-week vacation," "I was not very happy during my early teens," and "He has led an unhappy life." There is some basis, therefore, in our everyday concept of happiness (and also of pleasure) for giving meaning to the idea of quantities or amounts of happiness, even though we do not ordinarily measure these quantities in arithmetical terms.

What, then, does the utilitarian mean by maximizing intrinsic value and minimizing intrinsic disvalue? There are three variables or factors that must be introduced in order to make this idea clear. First, it means to bring about, in the case of *one* person, the greatest balance of value over disvalue. Thus, if one act or rule yields +1000 of happiness and −500 units of unhappiness for a given person, while another act or rule yields +700 units and −100 units for that person, then all other factors being equal, the second alternative is better than the first, since the balance of the second (+600) is greater than the balance of the first (+500). Similarly, to "minimize disvalue" would mean that an act or rule which yielded +100 and −300 for a given person would be better than one that yielded +500 and −1000 for the same person, other things being equal (even though more happiness is produced by the second than by the first).

The second factor is that the happiness and unhappiness of *all persons* affected must be considered. Thus, if four persons, A, B, C, and D, each experience some difference of happiness or unhappiness in life as a consequence of the act or rule but no difference occurs in the lives of anyone else, then the calculation of maximum value and minimum disvalue must include the balance of pluses and minuses occurring in the experience of every one of the four persons. Suppose in one case the balance is +300 for A, +200 for B, −300 for C, and −400 for D. And suppose the alternative yields +200 for A, +100 for B, −400 for C, and +500 for D. Then if someone were to claim that the first is better than the second because D's happiness or unhappiness does not count (D, for example, might be a slave while A, B, and C are free men), this conclusion would not be acceptable to utilitarians. For them, the second alternative is better than the first because the second yields a higher total balance than the first when *all* persons are considered.

The third factor in the utilitarian calculus has been tacitly assumed in the foregoing discussion of the second factor. This is the principle that, in calculating the units of happiness or unhappiness for different persons, the same criteria for measuring quantity are used. If totals of +500 and −200 represent sums of happiness and unhappiness in the experience of A and +300 and −400 represent sums of happiness and unhappiness in the experience of B, then one unit of plus (or minus) for A must be equal to one unit of plus (or minus) for B. No differences between A and B are to be considered as grounds for assigning a different weight to one or the other's happiness or unhappiness. When utilitarians assert that everyone's happiness is to count *equally*, they mean that, in calculating consequences, it is irrelevant *whose* happiness or unhappiness is affected by the act or rule. This may be called the principle of the equality of worth of every person as a person. (It does not mean, of course, that everyone is just as morally good or bad as everyone else!)

Now when these three factors are used in calculating utility, it is still possible for some persons to be unfairly or unjustly treated. For the greatest total balance of pluses over minuses may be brought about in a given society by actions or rules which discriminate against certain persons on irrelevant grounds. Although a greater quantity of happiness and a lesser amount of unhappiness are produced, they are distributed unjustly among the persons affected. To illustrate this possibility, consider two societies, one of which distributes different amounts of happiness to people on the basis of their race or religion, the other dispensing them on the basis of people's different needs, abilities, and merits, where "merits" are determined by contributions to the common good or general happiness. In the first society, people belonging to one race or religion are favored in educational opportunities, comfortable housing, and high-paying jobs, while people of another race or religion are disfavored. Race and religion function in that society as grounds for discrimination. In the second society, on the other hand, race or religion do not matter as far as education, housing, and jobs are concerned. All that counts are such things as, Does the individual have a need for special treatment, a need which, if overlooked, would unfairly handicap him in matters of education, housing, or jobs? (For example, a blind person might be given special schooling and a special job, so that his blindness will not mean that he has less of a chance for happiness in life than others.) Or, has the individual, through fair and open competition, proven himself qualified for a high-paying job? Or, does he have exceptional abilities—such as musical genius or mathematical brilliance—which deserve the society's recognition, so that advanced education and scholarships are made available to him? Here race and religion do not function as grounds for discrimination, since they are not considered in determining the proper distribution of happiness and unhappiness throughout the population.

The problem of utility and justice arises when it is seen that, in the two societies described above, it is possible for the first to produce a greater total net balance of happiness over unhappiness than the second. Thus, suppose the first society can force the members of the disfavored race or religion to work long hours for little or no pay, so that they produce much more and use up much less of what is produced than they would without such coercion. Then, even if the calculation of utility includes the unhappiness of the disadvantaged, the total balance of happiness over unhappiness could be greater than that resulting from the second society's system of production and consumption. A utilitarian, it seems, would have to say in that case that the first society was morally better than the second, since its policies and rules yielded a higher net utility. Yet the first society, if not simply and self-evidently unjust, would at least be considered (even by utilitarians) to be less just than the second. Hence, utility and justice are incompatible when applied to certain types of societies under certain conditions.

Such conflicts between utility and justice can occur because, as far as utility alone is concerned, it is always morally right to increase one person's happiness at the expense of another's, if the total net balance of pluses over minuses is greater than would be the case were the two persons treated equally. It would seem, in contrast to this, that justice requires that no individual serve as a mere instrument or means to someone else's happiness. (If a person freely consents to sacrifice his happiness for the sake of another, he is not, of course, being used merely as a means to someone else's ends.) On this point the opposition between justice and utility appears to be fundamental.

It should be noted in this connection that utility not only permits but actually requires one individual's being made unhappy if doing so adds to a group's happiness *however small an increase in happiness might be experienced by each of its members*, as long as the total amount of happiness to the group outweighs the unhappiness of the individual in question. Thus, suppose an innocent man is made a scapegoat for the guilt of others and accordingly suffers punishment. If he experiences, say, −100 units of unhappiness and if there are 101 persons who, in victimizing him, gain +1 unit of happiness each (perhaps in relief at seeing another blamed for their own wrongdoing), then the principle of utility *requires* that the scapegoat be punished. This is not because the scapegoat's unhappiness is being ignored or is being assigned less intrinsic worth than the happiness of others. Each unit of unhappiness (-1) experienced by the scapegoat is equal in "weight" to a unit of happiness ($+1$) of someone in the group. It just happens that in the given situation the total quantity of the group's happiness is greater than that of the scapegoat's unhappiness. Consequently the principle of utility, when applied to this situation, entails that the scapegoat be made to suffer.

It is in this way that the idea of justice seems to present a major philosophical difficulty for all forms of utilitarianism. How might utilitarians reply to this criticism? They would begin by pointing out that, when we leave abstract speculations about theoretical possibilities behind and face the actual world around us, we find that any conflict between justice and utility is highly unlikely. The apparent plausibility of the cases given above, they would say, depends on their being abstracted from the real processes of historical and social development. They hold that when these processes are fully taken into account, it becomes clear that injustice inevitably yields great disutility.

In support of this claim, utilitarians ask us to consider how the principle of utility would apply to situations of social conflict, where one person's (or group's) interests can be furthered only if another person's (or group's) interests are frustrated. For this is where the concepts of justice and injustice are applicable. Now with regard to such situations, the principle of utility requires social rules which enable people to resolve their disagreements and live in harmony with one another. To live in harmony means, not that no social conflicts occur, but that whenever they do occur, there is a set of rules everyone can appeal to as a fair way to resolve them. Such rules will (a) take everyone's interests into account, (b) give equal consideration to the interests of each person, and (c) enable all parties to a dispute to decide issues on grounds freely acceptable by all. For it is only when everyone can appeal to such a system of conflict-resolving rules that the society as a whole can achieve its maximum happiness and minimum unhappiness.

This can be seen by referring to the condition of anyone who does *not* accept a set of conflict-resolving rules as fair. Such a person will simply consider himself to be under social coercion with respect to those rules. That is, he will conform to the rules only because he is forced to by society. If his interests are frustrated by their operation, he will believe he has legitimate moral complaints against the rest of society, and will then think any action necessary to right the wrongs carried out in the name of the rules to be justified. The greater the number of such disaffected persons, the deeper will be the state of social disharmony. It is obvious that very little happiness can be realized in such a society.

At this point the following might be raised. To make sure that social conflict will not get out of hand, let those who accept the rules establish a power structure which will ensure their domination over those who reject them. In this way, although some (the powerless) may suffer, those in power can maximize their happiness. To this the utilitarian replies, "History has shown us that no such power structure can last for long; even while it does last, the effort spent by the 'ins' on maintaining domination over the 'outs' makes it impossible for the 'ins' to obtain much happiness in life. A social system of this kind is constantly liable to break down. The need to preserve their position of power drives the 'ins' to ever greater measures of surveillance and repression. The society as a whole becomes a closed system in which the freedom of all individuals is diminished. Accompanying this curtailment of human freedom is a dwindling in the very conception of man and his creative powers. Inevitably, there develops an intolerance of diversity in thought, in speech, in styles of life. A narrow conformity of taste, ideas, and outward behavior becomes the main concern of everyone. What kind of 'happiness' is this? What amount of intrinsic value does such a narrow way of life really make possible for people, even people who have the power to advance their interests at the expense of others?"

The upshot of the argument is now apparent: Given a clearheaded view of the world as it is and a realistic understanding of man's nature, it becomes more and more evident that injustice will never have, in the long run, greater utility than justice. Even if the two principles of justice and utility can logically be separated in the abstract and even if they can be shown to yield contradictory results in hypothetical cases, it does not follow that the fundamental idea of utilitarianism must be given up. For it remains the case that, when we are dealing with the actual practice of people in their social and historical settings, to maximize happiness and minimize unhappiness requires an open, freely given commitment on the part of *everyone* to comply with the rules for settling conflicts among them. Anyone who is coerced into following the rules when he, in good conscience, cannot accept them as being fair to everyone (and consequently to himself) will not consider himself morally obligated to abide by

them. Since he will either feel unjustly treated himself or see himself as a participant in the unfair treatment of others, society stands condemned in his judgment. From his point of view he will have good reason to do what he can to change or abolish the rules. He will join with anyone else who rejects them as unfair, in an effort to overcome his powerlessness. Thus, injustice becomes, in actual practice, a source of great social disutility. If society's reaction to the challenge of its dissidents is only a stronger attempt to impose its rules by force, this response will, sooner or later, bring about a situation in which no one really benefits. Not only is it profoundly true that "might does not make right," it is equally true that might cannot create the maximum balance of human happiness over human misery, when the lives of everyone are taken into account.

Whether this argument provides a successful rebuttal to the criticism of utilitarianism when viewed in the light of justice is a matter for the reader's own reflection.

POSTSCRIPT

Do the Ends Justify the Means?

Utilitarianism's basic goal is to promote the greatest happiness for the greatest number of individuals. At first glance, this seems like a goal with which few could argue.

In taking the happiness of all as an end, however, utilitarianism allows this end to justify any means that it might take to bring about that end. Some of these means we might experience as liberating. For example, utilitarianism believes that systems of social caste, racial or sexual discrimination, and social persecution must be eradicated. If people were free to determine their own lives, it is anticipated that the increase in utility (happiness) would be great. More controversial is the utilitarian approach to "victimless crimes" (such as drug use, sexual acts between consenting adults, and so on). If there is no victim, it is said, then no one's happiness is sacrificed. Thus, people should be allowed to find their own happiness in these ways, and there should be no rules against drug use, homosexuality, or prostitution, for example.

One problem is that utilitarianism seems to go too far in its abandonment of rules. We can agree to the abandonment of such rules as "blacks sit in the back" and "women stay at home." These racist and sexist rules are easy to judge since they consistently deprive individuals of happiness. But what about abandoning a rule such as "an innocent person should *not* be condemned to die"? The question for utilitarians, as always, is whether observance of the rule would promote happiness or not. The rule about not condemning an innocent person to death probably promotes utility, at least for the most part. But is Smart correct in that there could be cases in which utility *could* be promoted by the judicial execution of an innocent person? Or is it possible to rule out such cases from the very beginning?

Opponents of utilitarianism say that even benevolent ends (such as the promotion of happiness) do not justify the means if the means are contrary to rules of justice. Utilitarians, however, still want to know why we have to observe rules if the observance of those rules does not promote happiness.

The classical statement of utilitarianism is in the essay *Utilitarianism* published by John Stuart Mill (1806–1873) in 1863. J. J. C. Smart and Bernard Williams have published *Utilitarianism: For and Against* (Cambridge University Press, 1973), in which Smart defends this point of view and Williams attacks it. Peter Singer, a contemporary utilitarian, has applied the theory of utilitarianism to a wide-ranging system of ethics in his book *Practical Ethics* (Cambridge University Press, 1979).

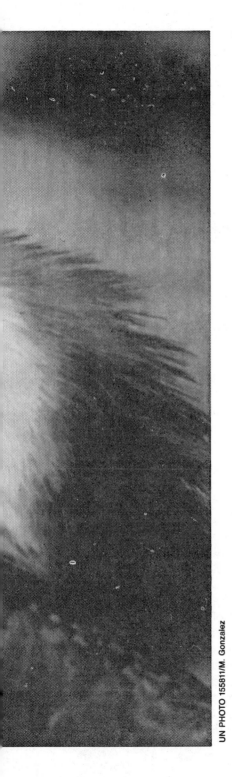

PART 2

Morality and Contemporary Social Thought

Although it is possible to find individual supporters of seemingly modern views in the ancient world, such views are exceptional. It is safe to say that the issues considered in this section are particular to modern society. Most people in early Western civilization did not question that men should rule over women, that the environment exists to serve human beings, and that people are morally permitted to eat animals. All of these assumptions are now being examined from modern perspectives. In addition, a special problem for us in the vast and impersonal world of modern society concerns our obligation to the poor. The issues considered in this section are not just limited or isolated issues; they affect one's whole way of looking at the world and of being part of society.

Should Environmental Ethics Be
　　Human Centered?
　　　　———————

Is Feminism a Harmful Ideology?
　　　　———————

Does Morality Require a Vegetarian
　　Way of Life?
　　　　———————

Does Society Have an Obligation to
　　Care for the Less Well Off?

ISSUE 6

Should Environmental Ethics Be Human Centered?

YES: William F. Baxter, from *People or Penguins: The Case for Optimal Pollution* (Columbia University Press, 1974)

NO: Lawrence E. Johnson, from *A Morally Deep World: An Essay on Moral Significance and Environmental Ethics* (Cambridge University Press, 1991)

ISSUE SUMMARY

YES: Professor of law William F. Baxter argues that environmental problems must be addressed and solved from a human point of view. He further claims that any resources, such as money, that are committed to environmental purposes will result in less available resources for other good purposes, such as education, health, and art.

NO: Philosopher Lawrence E. Johnson argues that wilderness areas, ecosystems, and even the entire biosphere are all self-maintaining systems that have interests. He warns that human beings, who have a tendency to exploit the environment, must be careful not to make such systems worse off.

Some of the claims that have been made about the state of the environment are: that the ozone layer over the Earth is deteriorating so that all life forms will suffer from the direct rays of the sun; that the quality of the air and water in many places is deteriorating; that acid rain is killing whole forests and making some lakes incapable of supporting any life at all; that there is a "global warming" phenomenon that is causing the Earth's temperature to rise (so that eventually the ice caps will melt and port cities like New York and San Francisco will be submerged); that certain species are endangered or becoming extinct; that plant and animal habitats are being eliminated with the draining of wetlands, the destruction of rain forests, and the development of formerly undeveloped areas; that human population growth threatens almost everything in the environment; that commercial farming relies far too much on the use of pesticides and also causes soil erosion. The list could go on. Even if only some of these claims turned out to be true, the situation would be serious, but many (if not all) of the claims are true. It may be that there are some things that are beyond human control, but human beings do have a large impact on most of the items on the list. In fact, it is becoming clear that everything that people do has some impact on the environment, and everything in the environment seems to be connected to other things in the environment. So the full extent of human impact on the environment is impossible to calculate.

In previous times it was easy to think that smoke would just blow away or that trash would just wash away in rivers or streams. Now it is known that resources like clean air and clean water are finite. There is only so much of each, and they are not capable of taking in all of the refuse that the human population can send their way.

Western civilization has generally proceeded from a faith that held the greatest values to be spiritual and eternal. It was far more important to an ordinary person to have his or her soul in a good relationship with God than to think about the welfare of animals or even, in many cases, of the condition of one's own body. The main strand of the Judeo-Christian tradition holds that physical and material things are not supposed to be worth worrying about. Generally, the biblical idea that human beings have "dominion" over all (other) animals of the Earth, and that human beings should "subdue" the Earth, was regarded as straightforward divine authorizations to use the Earth and all the living things on the Earth as resources for human beings.

Other religious traditions (such as those of Native Americans and some Eastern cultures) emphasize the interrelationship of all living things and the idea that human beings must find a place within nature, not subdue it.

In any case, even if it was true that in earlier times the land, the water, and the air were not affected much by what people did (for one thing, there were far fewer people and technologies were far less developed), today the situation is quite different. But what should be done?

Suppose acid rain or industrial pollution *is* killing the fish in a river. Suppose further that commercial fishermen downstream are unable to maintain their livelihood because the fish they would otherwise catch cannot survive in the polluted water. An anthropocentric (or human-centered) view would regard this as a catastrophe for the fishermen, especially if they were unable to secure employment or income in any other way. But is it also a catastrophe for the fish? Or for the ecology of the river?

In the following selections, William F. Baxter supports a human-centered point of view. For example, *if* those fish are important to us (we very much enjoy eating them), or *if* the river is important to us (we very much enjoy boating on the clear water), or *if* the employment of the fishermen is important to our economy, then we should work to maintain the cleanliness of the river so that the fish live, the water is clear, and the fishermen can fish. Lawrence E. Johnson argues that humans have to acknowledge that the ecology of the river itself has value and that the environment should be protected for the environment's sake.

YES
William F. Baxter

A "GOOD" ENVIRONMENT: JUST ONE OF THE SET OF HUMAN OBJECTIVES

I start with the modest proposition that, in dealing with pollution, or indeed with any problem, it is helpful to know what one is attempting to accomplish. Agreement on how and whether to pursue a particular objective, such as pollution control, is not possible unless some more general objective has been identified and stated with reasonable precision. We talk loosely of having clean air and clean water, of preserving our wilderness areas, and so forth. But none of these is a sufficiently general objective: each is more accurately viewed as a means rather than as an end.

With regard to clean air, for example, one may ask, "how clean?" and "what does clean mean?" It is even reasonable to ask, "why have clean air?" Each of these questions is an implicit demand that a more general community goal be stated—a goal sufficiently general in its scope and enjoying sufficiently general assent among the community of actors that such "why" questions no longer seem admissible with respect to that goal.

If, for example, one states as a goal the proposition that "every person should be free to do whatever he wishes in contexts where his actions do not interfere with the interests of other human beings," the speaker is unlikely to be met with a response of "why." The goal may be criticized as uncertain in its implications or difficult to implement, but it is so basic a tenet of our civilization—it reflects a cultural value so broadly shared, at least in the abstract—that the question "why" is seen as impertinent or imponderable or both.

I do not mean to suggest that everyone would agree with the "spheres of freedom" objective just stated. Still less do I mean to suggest that a society could subscribe to four or five such general objectives that would be adequate in their coverage to serve as testing criteria by which all other disagreements might be measured. One difficulty in the attempt to construct such a list is that each new goal added will conflict, in certain applications, with each prior goal listed; and thus each goal serves as a limited qualification on prior goals.

Without any expectation of obtaining unanimous consent to them, let me set forth four goals that I generally use as ultimate testing criteria in attempting to frame solutions to problems of human organization. My position regarding pollution stems from these four criteria. If the criteria appeal to you and any part of what appears hereafter does not, our disagreement will have a helpful focus: which of us is correct, analytically, in supposing that his position on pollution would better serve these general goals. If the criteria do not seem acceptable to you, then it is to be expected that our more particular judgments will differ, and the tasks will then be yours to identify the basic set of criteria upon which your particular judgments rest.

My criteria are as follows:

1. The spheres of freedom criterion stated above.

2. Waste is a bad thing. The dominant feature of human existence is scarcity—our available resources, our aggregate labors, and our skill in employing both have always been, and will continue for some time to be, inadequate to yield to every man all the tangible and intangible satisfactions he would like to have. Hence, none of those resources, or labors, or skills, should be wasted—that is, employed so as to yield less than they might yield in human satisfactions.

3. Every human being should be regarded as an end rather than as a means to be used for the betterment of another. Each should be afforded dignity and regarded as having an absolute claim to an evenhanded application of such rules as the community may adopt for its governance.

4. Both the incentive and the opportunity to improve his share of satisfactions should be preserved to every individual. Preservation of incentive is dictated by the "no-waste" criterion and enjoins against the continuous, totally egalitarian redistribution of satisfactions, or wealth; but subject to that constraint, everyone should receive, by continuous redistribution if necessary, some minimal share of aggregate wealth so as to avoid a level of privation from which the opportunity to improve his situation becomes illusory.

The relationship of these highly general goals to the more specific environmental issues at hand may not be readily apparent, and I am not yet ready to demonstrate their pervasive implications. But let me give one indication of their implications. Recently scientists have informed us that use of DDT in food production is causing damage to the penguin population. For the present purposes let us accept that assertion as an indisputable scientific fact. The scientific fact is often asserted as if the correct implication—that we must stop agricultural use of DDT—followed from the mere statement of the fact of penguin damage. But plainly it does not follow if my criteria are employed.

My criteria are oriented to people, not penguins. Damage to penguins, or sugar pines, or geological marvels is, without more, simply irrelevant. One must go further, by my criteria, and say: Penguins are important because people enjoy seeing them walk about rocks; and furthermore, the well-being of people would be less impaired by halting use of DDT than by giving up penguins. In short, my observations about environmental problems will be people-oriented, as are my criteria. I have no interest in preserving penguins for their own sake.

It may be said by way of objection to this position, that it is very selfish of people to act as if each person represented one unit of importance and nothing else was of any importance. It is undeniably selfish. Nevertheless I think it is the only tenable starting place for analysis for several reasons. First, no other position corresponds to the way most people really think and act—i.e., corresponds to reality.

Second, this attitude does not portend any massive destruction of nonhuman flora and fauna, for people depend on them in many obvious ways, and they will be preserved because and to the degree that humans do depend on them.

Third, what is good for humans is, in many respects, good for penguins and pine trees—clean air for example. So that humans are, in these respects, surrogates for plant and animal life.

Fourth, I do not know how we could administer any other system. Our decisions are either private or collective. Insofar as Mr. Jones is free to act privately, he may give such preferences as he wishes to other forms of life: he may feed birds in winter and do with less himself, and he may even decline to resist an advancing polar bear on the ground that the bear's appetite is more important than those portions of himself that the bear may choose to eat. In short my basic premise does not rule out private altruism to competing life-forms. It does rule out, however, Mr. Jones' inclination to feed Mr. Smith to the bear, however hungry the bear, however despicable Mr. Smith.

Insofar as we act collectively on the other hand, only humans can be afforded an opportunity to participate in the collective decisions. Penguins cannot vote now and are unlikely subjects for the franchise—pine trees more unlikely still. Again each individual is free to cast his vote so as to benefit sugar pines if that is his inclination. But many of the more extreme assertions that one hears from some conservationists amount to tacit assertions that they are specially appointed representatives of sugar pines, and hence that their preferences should be weighted more heavily than the preferences of other humans who do not enjoy equal rapport with "nature." The simplistic assertion that agricultural use of DDT must stop at once because it is harmful to penguins is of that type.

Fifth, if polar bears or pine trees or penguins, like men, are to be regarded as ends rather than means, if they are to count in our calculus of social organization, someone must tell me how much each one counts, and someone must tell me how these life-forms are to be permitted to express their preferences, for I do not know either answer. If the answer is that certain people are to hold their proxies, then I want to know how those proxy-holders are to be selected: self-appointment does not seem workable to me.

Sixth, and by way of summary of all the foregoing, let me point out that the set of environmental issues under discussion—although they raise very complex technical questions of how to achieve any objective—ultimately raise a normative question: what *ought* we to do. Questions of *ought* are unique to the human mind and world—they are meaningless as applied to a nonhuman situation.

I reject the proposition that we *ought* to respect the "balance of nature" or to "preserve the environment" unless the reason for doing so, express or implied, is the benefit of man.

I reject the idea that there is a "right" or "morally correct" state of nature to which we should return. The word "nature" has no normative connotation. Was it "right" or "wrong" for the earth's crust to heave in contortion and create mountains and seas? Was it "right" for the first amphibian to crawl up out of the primordial ooze? Was it "wrong" for plants to reproduce themselves and alter the atmospheric composition in favor of oxygen? For animals to alter the atmosphere in favor of carbon dioxide both by breathing oxygen and eating plants? No answers can be given to these questions because they are meaningless questions.

All this may seem obvious to the point of being tedious, but much of the present controversy over environment and pollution rests on tacit normative assumptions about just such nonnormative phenomena: that it is "wrong" to impair penguins with DDT, but not to slaughter cattle for prime rib roasts. That it is wrong to kill stands of sugar pines with industrial fumes, but not to cut sugar pines and build housing for the poor. Every man is entitled to his own preferred definition of Walden Pond, but there is no definition that has any moral superiority over another, except by reference to the selfish needs of the human race.

From the fact that there is no normative definition of the natural state, it follows that there is no normative definition of clean air or pure water—hence no definition of polluted air—or of pollution—except by reference to the needs of man. The "right" composition of the atmosphere is one which has some dust in it and some lead in it and some hydrogen sulfide in it—just those amounts that attend a sensibly organized society thoughtfully and knowledgeably pursuing the greatest possible satisfaction for its human members.

The first and most fundamental step toward solution of our environmental problems is a clear recognition that our objective is not pure air or water but rather some optimal state of pollution. That step immediately suggests the question: How do we define and attain the level of pollution that will yield the maximum possible amount of human satisfaction?

Low levels of pollution contribute to human satisfaction but so do food and shelter and education and music. To attain ever lower levels of pollution, we must pay the cost of having less of these other things. I contrast that view of the cost of pollution control with the more popular statement that pollution control will "cost" very large numbers of dollars. The popular statement is true in some sense, false in others; sorting out the true and false senses is of some importance. The first step in that sorting process is to achieve a clear understanding of the difference between dollars and resources. Resources are the wealth of our nation; dollars are merely claim checks upon those resources. Resources are of vital importance; dollars are comparatively trivial.

Four categories of resources are sufficient for our purposes: At any given time a nation, or a planet if you prefer, has a stock of labor, of technological skill, of capital goods, and of natural resources (such as mineral deposits, timber, water, land, etc.). These resources can be used in various combinations to yield goods and services of all kinds—in some limited quantity. The quantity will be larger if they are combined efficiently, smaller if combined inefficiently. But in either event the resource stock is limited, the goods and services that they can be made to yield are limited; even the most efficient use of them will yield less than our population, in the aggregate, would like to have.

If one considers building a new dam, it is appropriate to say that it will be costly in the sense that it will require x hours of labor, y tons of steel and concrete, and z amount of capital goods. If these resources are devoted to the dam, then they cannot be used to build hospitals, fishing rods, schools, or electric can openers. That is the meaningful sense in which the dam is costly.

Quite apart from the very important question of how wisely we can combine our resources to produce goods and services, is the very different question of how they get distributed—who gets how many goods? Dollars constitute the claim checks which are distributed among people and which control their share of national output. Dollars are nearly valueless pieces of paper except to the extent that they do represent claim checks to some fraction of the output of goods and services. Viewed as claim checks, all the dollars outstanding during any period of time are worth, in the aggregate, the goods and services that are available to be claimed with them during that period—neither more nor less.

It is far easier to increase the supply of dollars than to increase the production of goods and services—printing dollars is easy. But printing more dollars doesn't help because each dollar then simply becomes a claim to fewer goods, i.e., becomes worth less.

The point is this: many people fall into error upon hearing the statement that the decision to build a dam, or to clean up a river, will cost $X million. It is regrettably easy to say: "It's only money. This is a wealthy country, and we have lots of money." But you cannot build a dam or clean a river with $X million—unless you also have a match, you can't even make a fire. One builds a dam or cleans a river by diverting labor and steel and trucks and factories from making one kind of goods to making another. The cost in dollars is merely a shorthand way of describing the extent of the diversion necessary. If we build a dam for $X million, then we must recognize that we will have $X million less housing and food and medical care and electric can openers as a result.

Similarly, the costs of controlling pollution are best expressed in terms of the other goods we will have to give up to do the job. This is not to say the job should not be done. Badly as we need more housing, more medical care, and more can openers, and more symphony orchestras, we could do with somewhat less of them, in my judgment at least, in exchange for somewhat cleaner air and rivers. But that is the nature of the trade-off, and analysis of the problem is advanced if that unpleasant reality is kept in mind. Once the trade-off relationship is clearly perceived, it is possible to state in a very general way what the optimal level of pollution is. I would state it as follows:

People enjoy watching penguins. They enjoy relatively clean air and smog-free vistas. Their health is improved by relatively clean water and air. Each of these benefits is a type of good or service. As a society we would be well advised to give up one washing machine if the resources that would have gone into that washing machine can yield greater human satisfaction when diverted into pollution control. We should give up one hospital if the resources thereby freed would yield more human satisfaction when devoted to elimination of noise in our cities. And so on, trade-off by trade-off, we should divert our productive capacities from the production of existing goods and services to the production of a cleaner, quieter, more pastoral nation up to—and no further than—the point at which we value more highly the next washing machine or hospital that we would have to do without than we value the next unit of environmental improvement that the diverted resources would create.

Now this proposition seems to me unassailable but so general and abstract as to be unhelpful—at least unadministerable in the form stated. It assumes we can measure in some way the incremental units of human satisfaction yielded by very different types of goods. The proposition must remain a pious abstraction until I can explain how this measurement process can occur. . . . I insist that the proposition stated describes the result for which we should be striving—and again, that it is always useful to know what your target is even if your weapons are too crude to score a bull's eye.

ALL OF OUR ENVIRONMENTAL PROBLEMS are, in essence, specific instances of a problem of great familiarity: How can we arrange our society so as to make most effective use of our resources? I use the term "resources" broadly and mean to include within it not only all the physical components of our planet earth—its waters, its air envelope, its minerals, and its tillable soils—but also human energies, acquired human skills, which is to say technology, and finally our existing stock of tools—manufacturing plants and other forms of capital investment. There is some particular deployment of those resources which, at any point in time, will yield a larger aggregate quantity of goods and services than any other deployment; and a major goal of social organization is and should be to approximate that optimum deployment as closely as possible. . . .

To assert that there is a pollution problem or an environmental problem is to assert, at least implicitly, that one or more resources is not being used so as to maximize human satisfactions.

NO

Lawrence E. Johnson

TOWARD THE HORIZONS OF THE MORAL UNIVERSE

Ethical criteria have been extended to many fields of conduct, with corresponding shrinkages in those judged by expediency only.

The land ethic simply enlarges the boundaries of the community to include soils, waters, plants, and animals, or collectively: the land.

A land ethic changes the role of *Homo sapiens* from conqueror of the land-community to plain member and citizen of it.

A thing is right when it tends to preserve the integrity, stability, and beauty of the biotic community. It is wrong when it tends otherwise.

Aldo Leopold, A Sand County Almanac

Galileo disturbed a great many people with his opinion that our earth was one of several planets revolving around the sun. The official view at the time was that the earth, man's home, was the center of God's creation. . . . Man, made in God's image, was the completion and moral center of the created world. It did not seem *fitting* that the moral center of creation should hold such an insignificant position in the physical universe. . . .

Astronomical fact eventually prevailed, and it was accepted that God had chosen to place his favorites on a moving planet in a less conspicuous location. The belief that humanity is the moral center of the universe has had more endurance. There have been dissenting voices, but the predominant opinion has been that humans are, rightly, of overriding or exclusive moral significance. In our actions regarding the nonhuman world we have usually been concerned only with human values. Our practical questions concerned how best to utilize the natural world to benefit humans, while our moral questions concerned the implications for other humans. . . .

In recent years there has been a revival of interest in the question of whether there are values in the nonhuman natural world. . . . On the whole . . . the Western tradition has been almost exclusively human-centered

From Lawrence E. Johnson, *A Morally Deep World: An Essay on Moral Significance and Environmental Ethics* (Cambridge University Press, 1991). Copyright © 1991 by Cambridge University Press. Reprinted by permission.

in its value schemes. These days, more and more thinkers are coming to suggest that we need a Galileo-like change in our conception of the human place in the moral universe. . . .

[M]any people . . . believe that there is intrinsic moral significance in wildernesses, ecosystems, species, and so forth, in addition to their significance for humans. . . .

I start with the assumption that humans are in the moral universe, that we humans ought to be objects of moral concern. But what qualifies us to be objects of moral concern? . . .

Moral consideration is due to us humans because we have interests. We can suffer or be happy, languish or flourish, be healthy or otherwise, whereas rocks and tractors cannot. Interests are not just something we *have*. Interests are a matter of the way we are, of the dynamic ongoing process that is a human life. Our interests are, as I shall argue, an integral feature of our life process. Those interests we have on the level of experience and desire are only the surface. We are complete beings with depth as well as surface, and we have interests to match. There is more to interests than merely favorable mental states such as pleasure or satisfaction of desire. I shall argue that favorable mental states are not the be-all and end-all, and that our (prudent) desires do not constitute, but follow from, our interests.

I am eventually led to the conclusion that animals, plants, ecosystems, and even species have interests, and that these interests are, to the extent of each interest, morally significant. . . .

It shall be presupposed throughout that there is such a thing as morality and that it does apply to humans. Given that, I shall argue that if there is a moral universe at all, it must extend beyond the human sphere. Others have differed in opinion, holding that we can draw the moral boundaries so as largely or entirely to coincide with those of the human race, or some portion of it. The burden of my argument here is that there is no plausible, nonarbitrary way of characterizing morally significant interests so as to support such a conclusion. Neither is there any plausible, nonarbitrary reason for holding that only some interests are morally significant while others are not. . . . If human interests are to have any moral weight at all, then *all* genuine interests must be recognized as having some moral weight—though some interests have more weight than others. It is a matter of degrees. In arguing that the interests of a mouse are morally considerable, I am not claiming that setting a mousetrap is on a par with the premeditated murder of a human being. Normally, a human being has more interests than does a mouse. Moreover, the interest of a mouse in continuing to live is not the same as the interest of a human in continuing to live. A mouse only has an interest in continuing a mouse life. That interest counts for what it is, but only for what it is. . . .

Some may deny that there is a moral universe at all. Perhaps moral concepts are empty, or are merely expressions of our attitudes toward things. Personally, I find it very difficult to accept that all I can say about Adolf Hitler is merely that he and I have divergent attitudes with regard to interethnic relationships. . . . [M]any people prefer to have attitudes that, at least in the area of what might be thought of as moral attitudes, are in accordance with principles that are consistent and not subject to arbitrary restriction. I shall try to persuade such people that it is purely arbitrary to restrict their moral attitudes to the human sphere or to some part of it. However, I shall not really be addressing those who believe that the moral universe has zero radius. . . .

Even if we cannot determine what all morally significant human interests are, and even if we do not know how to balance them all out properly, we do know that we ought to recognize their moral significance and take them into account as best we can. We cannot just disregard the interests of another, be it a person of another family, sex, race, religion, political persuasion, or socioeconomic group. Once we recognize that, we have come a long way, and we can at least start to learn how to act properly toward other people. So too, once we recognize that there are interests in the nonhuman world, and that they are morally significant, we will have come a long way. Then, we can at least start to learn how to act properly toward the rest of the world. . . .

ECO-INTERESTS— AND FOREST FIRES

A piece of proverbial wisdom that is actually somewhat true is that there is such a thing as the balance of nature— though we must not take that to mean anything exact or unchanging. Ecosystems display quite a high level of homeostasis. . . . Barry Commoner's "first law of ecology," that "everything is connected to everything else" (1972, 33), is particularly true of ecosystems. Not only do they maintain themselves, they do so with a very high degree of interconnection. Just as we may think of an individual organism as an ongoing life process, manifested in a continually changing combination of material elements, and a species as an ongoing process progressively

embodied in different individuals, so may we think of an ecosystem as an ongoing process taking place through a complex system of interrelationships between organisms, and between organisms and their nonliving environment. The organisms change, and the interrelationships may vary somewhat, but there is a continuity to the ecosystem, and a center of homeostasis around which the states of the ecosystem fluctuate, which defines its self-identity. Normally, an ecosystem maintains its stability through an intricately complex feedback system. One example of that is the forage-deer-mountain lion balance, which remains roughly constant through continuous oscillation. However, an ecosystem can suffer stress and be impaired. It can be degraded to lower levels of stability and interconnected complexity. It can have its self-identity ruptured. In short, an ecosystem has wellbeing interests—and therefore has moral significance.

No more than in the case of species or individual organisms are the interests of an ecosystem the aggregated interests of its components, and, as in those cases, the various interests might sometimes be in conflict. It may even be in the interests of an ecosystem for a particular species (or sometimes for particular individuals) to die off, allowing the ecosystem to develop in accordance with its inherent nature. It is often the case that a particular species is a useful component of a given ecosystem only during certain stages of the ecosystem's life cycle. In such a case, the interests of the ecosystem are still the interests of a whole life process that integrally incorporates the problematic component. In some of the valleys of California's Sierra Nevada, for instance, ecosystems often contain a high proportion of junipers, which, in the natural progression, eventually make way for the more slowly growing oaks.[1] Junipers grow rapidly and, being full of sap, are very combustible. Under natural conditions, fires caused by lightning periodically burn out the juniper, preventing it from crowding out the oaks and other plants. After a fire, not only the oaks but the smaller plants and grasses have the opportunity to flourish, and there is an attendant increase in the populations of animals, birds, and insects. If the fires do not come, the juniper, together with a few other species, largely takes over, leading to an ecosystem of reduced diversity and stability. The integrity of the complex whole and its diverse living unity is compromised in favor of an impoverished uniformity.

This is not to say that the juniper is only a weed, one that ought to be exterminated. The juniper has its role in the life of an ecosystem. There should always be a few around so that they may (re)establish themselves in that or a neighboring ecosystem if the conditions should ever become appropriate. When, for instance, there is a total burnout, completely devastating an area, the rapidly growing junipers are very useful in restoring the biotic community and maintaining it until the more slowly growing trees and the other beings of the mature ecosystem again hold sway. Most fires, though, do not devastate an area. They are generally benign. They burn through quickly, removing such things as juniper, and providing growing room for the annuals and other rapidly growing small plants. On the larger scale, they clear the way for the more slowly growing fire-resistant trees. Such trees usually sustain relatively little damage. Minor fires do not burn deeply enough to kill the living soil. When minor fires do not occur from time to time, there is a buildup of undergrowth and debris, and an overgrowth of highly flammable trees such as juniper. Then any fire will be a major one, killing everything including the soil. At certain stages, then, the juniper is helpful to the ecosystem and at others harmful to it. The ecosystem, it would be fair to say, is a life process having a self-identity distinct from that of its component entities, and which may call for juniper at some times and not at others, just as the life process of an oak calls for acorns at some times and not at others.

Homo sapiens, as so often happens, interferes to make a mess of things. When we are not making a mess of things from bad intentions, we too often make a mess of things from good intentions. When I was a boy, it was a well-known fact that forest fires were bad. Whatever our attitude toward good and bad might have been, everyone knew that forest fires were bad. The message was preached at us in school and over the media. If it was not the direct content of the message, it was a presupposition. It was drummed into us in the Boy Scouts, and Smokey Bear told us that only we could prevent forest fires. . . . [P]ublic policy was to extinguish or contain *all* fires, including those of natural origin. As a result, flammable material would accumulate to the point that a very large and very intense fire would utterly destroy an area. Where that did not happen, as in heavily protected Yosemite Valley, the resulting imbalance of species led to a weakened and impoverished ecosystem, with fewer animals, birds, and other species, less complexity and diversity, less stability and less integrity of being.

We cannot give proper recognition to the role of fires in ecosystems if we think only in terms of the welfare of individuals.

In general, we can neither understand ecosystems properly nor act properly toward them if we think only in terms of individuals. . . . In Yosemite and other areas, I am pleased to note, attempts are now being made to right past wrongs through a program of controlled burning. While I have used fires as my example, we can make similar points concerning adding or eliminating species, or other things that would affect the life process of an ecosystem. We must consider the whole not merely as a collection, but as a whole with its very own interests. Only then can we develop an adequate environmental policy. . . .

ARE WE TO POLICE OURSELVES?

[E]verything we do nevertheless affects the biosphere. If we chop a tree for firewood, if we clear a field for plowing, if we merely gather nuts from under a tree, we can never avoid affecting our environment in some way, and any course of action is bound to be injurious to some entity. . . . So, at what moral conclusions should we humans arrive?

One conclusion that might, but should not, be drawn is that we are morally at liberty to treat the environment in whatever way most suits our own convenience. . . . Since everything we might do would be injurious to some morally significant entity, we might as well do as we please. That is bad reasoning. The mere fact that no matter what we do we must harm the interests of some entities does not mean that our choices are morally indifferent. On the human level, the fact that public policies characteristically benefit some humans and injure others does not make a choice between policies morally indifferent. The logic is no better

when applied to actions affecting nonhumans. Some cost-benefit balances are better than others, some distributions are better than others, and infringing or respecting rights may or may not make a difference to a case. That any of our acts affecting the environment will have some injurious effects does not free our choice from moral assessment. . . .

Why is it that we humans, alone, ought to restrain our impact on other creatures and ecosystems? Lions are not condemned for killing other animals, nor are they to be restrained from doing so. Lions are doing what is natural for them, and taking part in natural processes. But so are we. Over thousands and millions of years we humans have evolved as exploiters of our environment, it may be argued, and what we do is natural for us. . . .

Against this sort of argument it will not do simply to point out that we are reflective moral agents, whereas lions are not. We cannot just rest on the claim that lions do not know any better, whereas we humans can work out valid moral principles and act on them. . . . Even if, miraculously, lions and other predators were transformed into rational, aware moral agents, they would be under no obligation either to become vegetarians or to starve in recognition of the interests of plants. The wellbeing of lions counts for something too. Apart from that, we have only to note that ecosystems deprived of their predators do not function nearly so well. . . .

[L]ions, left to their own devices, live in a reasonable balance with healthy ecosystems, whereas humans tend to get far out of balance with the rest of the world. . . . We act wrongly toward the biosphere if we severely disrupt it, even if it is in our nature to do so. Being natural does not imply being good, or even being morally acceptable. It is the wellbeing of morally significant entities that is the key factor, not the indiscriminate indulgence of our natural tendencies.

Cancer is a natural phenomenon. The malignant tumor arises through natural processes in the organism afflicted, and it develops in accordance with its own nature, yet it is clearly in conflict with the interests of the encompassing organism. In our unchecked drive toward proliferation, in our appropriation of all resources for our own benefit, and in our increasing incompatibility with the viability of the life processes around us, we humans in great measure resemble a cancer attacking the biosphere. Neither cancers nor we are any the less injurious for being natural. What we can say for humanity is that, unlike a cancer, it is possible in principle for us to get on in a benign way.

The conclusion so far is that we cannot defend our exploitation of the rest of the world on the grounds that it is in accordance with our nature. We cannot justify such exploitation on any grounds, since it disrupts the balance of life processes in the biosphere. . . .

The best reason for rejecting the argument that natural precedent, taking that of lions as our paradigm case, excuses human treatment of the biosphere is not just that lions are in balance with the biosphere, but that they are in quite a good balance with it. Lions enhance the quality of their ecosystems, whereas humans, at least in recent times, have tended not to. It is we who ought to mend our ways. . . . [O]n the whole, the evolutionary trend has been in the direction of greater balance, complexity, diversity, and interconnection—those things that enrich the character of ecosystems and other living things. . . . Human abuse of

the environment cannot be defended on the grounds that it is the common currency of the natural world. It is not. . . .

I do not define the good in terms of tendencies in evolution. . . . So far as I am able to define it at all, I define it in terms of wellbeing and the satisfaction of wellbeing interests. . . .

SOONER OR LATER

Wherever we draw the moral lines, we must in some way arrive at an accommodation with the world around us. . . .

The exploitation of ecosystems on a nonrenewing basis provides examples of . . . sooner-or-later cases. Cases in point are the utilization of Tasmania's temperate-zone forests for the wood-chip industry, and the clearing of tropical rain forests for wood products or to provide additional (and often soon depleted) farmland for ever expanding populations. Sooner or later we must turn to sustained yield sylvaculture for wood products, and sooner or later we must strike a balance between population and existing farmland. There is a *prima facie* case that we ought to make these shifts before we have obliterated further ecosystems and eradicated their species. We may still cut wood, and we may reduce natural ecosystems in size . . .but we ought still to preserve ecosystems and their species as living entities, unless perhaps there is very convincing reason to the contrary. . . . There can be no doubt that we must eventually stop [destroying ecosystems and their species]. The question is not whether, but when. Moreover, if we continue on to the very end, we are not doing *only* what we were doing before. We are doing something more and worse. Chopping down trees is one thing. Chopping down a forest and killing an ecosystem is quite another, even though it is the act of chopping down trees that finally does the latter. Causing the deaths of individual organisms is one thing. Causing the extinction of a species is quite another. Utilizing the biosphere is one thing. Degrading it is quite another, even though the difference may be only cumulative. . . .

BETTER OR WORSE

Not all cases are of a sooner-or-later variety. There are other cases wherein . . . we need never impose self-restraint. . . . Consider disease-causing and parasitic organisms. We have already caused the extinction, except *in vitro*, of the smallpox organism, and we may well eventually cause the extinction of other such organisms, overriding the interests of the species involved in order to improve the quality of human life. I applaud. If we can get rid of hookworm or typhoid, so much the better—though of course eliminating these pests would make it all the more necessary for us to institute our own measures for controlling our numbers. In such cases there are substantial long-term overall benefits to be gained. (Even so, there are limits. We ought not to pollute everything with DDT in order to attack malaria.) The case in favor of benefiting humans is much stronger when it comes to eradicating disease organisms and parasites than when there is only the short-term and often slight advantage of continuing somewhat longer with policies that will eventually have to be abandoned in any case. If we eradicate a disease, the benefit is considerable and, presumably, lasts as long as our own species. It certainly seems plausible that

the human interest in health outweighs that of the smallpox organism in survival. Perhaps we are biased, but certainly it seems that humans are capable of a much higher level of wellbeing than is the smallpox organism. . . . It is also relevant to the overall moral assessment that if we eliminate a species we usually weaken an ecosystem by doing so, whereas if we eradicate a disease afflicting humans, we do not necessarily weaken an ecosystem. (Of course, the result might be a human population explosion in some areas, causing havoc in ecosystems, but there are better ways of preventing that.)

I believe, then, that the eradication of disease-organisms is justified . . . and is in a different moral category from extinguishing (other) species, obliterating ecosystems, or degrading the biosphere at large. What makes the moral difference is not simply and solely that we must sooner or later desist from the later activities, while we can go on exterminating those species that specialize in humans until we have gotten rid of the lot. . . . What counts is the overall moral character of an act. It seems to me that on the whole, eradicating disease is quite a good thing to do. . . .

A MATTER OF ATTITUDE

I have not advocated any particular set of moral rules we ought to follow, or even any very complete set of principles. What I do advocate is an attitude. . . . What we need is an attitude of respect and consideration for all entities that have interests. That includes ourselves, of course, but it also includes quite a lot else. With that respectful and considerate attitude, we need an awareness that we live in a world abounding with such entities. From the ecosystem down to the lowliest microorganism, from the biosphere, to endangered species, to our next door neighbor, we live in a world of beings that count. They are not just *objects.* . . .

A MORALLY DEEP WORLD

The overall conclusion I have come to is that we live in a morally deep world. We are morally significant ourselves, and we live in a world of beings, on many different levels, that are morally significant. We do not all have the same moral significance, but if the rest of the world had absolutely no moral significance at all, then neither would we. It is not just our being rational or sentient, much less our being human, that gives us moral significance. Our interests are morally significant just because they are interests. Our wellbeing can suffer or flourish. We humans being what we are, rationality and sentience have a lot to do with our interests, yet we are beings with depth as well as rational and sentient surface. It is in those depths that our wellbeing interests have their roots. Even among humans, neither rationality nor sentience is a necessary condition for the moral significance of an interest. For us to recognize the moral standing of only those beings who are like us in being human, rational, or sentient would be arbitrary and morally unjustified.

The depth of moral significance extends at least to the depths of the living world. While individual organisms, be they humans or protozoans, have their own particular degree of moral importance, often a very high degree, it is not individual organisms alone that have moral standing. There is moral value on many different and diverse levels, levels that can be separated only artificially. Species, rain forests, ecosystems, the biosphere—all of these entities have morally significant interests to one degree or another. We live in a world of life, and all life processes, of whatever sort, define interests that count morally. It is respect for interests that is, at least, the core if not the whole of morality.

I can offer no magic formula for determining, in each instance, the morally best way to act toward those others of various sorts with whom or which we share the world. No one has ever developed an adequate and comprehensive formula for applying the principle of respect for interests to even the more restricted sphere of human affairs. . . . Whether we are dealing with our fellow humans, though, or whether we are not, the absence of an effective moral algorithm does not excuse us from our responsibility to give due consideration and respect, so far as we can do so, to the varied, and variably significant, interests of very different entities. The best we can do, which will carry us quite a long way, is to develop an awareness of other beings, and of their interests, together with an attitude of respect and consideration for their interests. . . .

To live effectively, we must fulfill our own wellbeing needs, living in harmony and balance with ourselves, and with the world around us. Morally we ought, as best we can, to allow the living world, and the entities thereof, in their diversity, to thrive in richness, harmony, and balance. In all things we must ask whether our actions are conducive to, or at least compatible with, the fullness and wellbeing of life. Thereby we may better live deep and worthwhile lives in a deep and valuable world.

NOTE

1. This material is based on public presentations at Yosemite National Park, California, and on [the author's] discussions with the staff there.

REFERENCES

Commoner, Barry. *The Closing Circle.* London: Jonathan Cape, 1972.
Leopold, Aldo, *A Sand County Almanac.* New York: Oxford University Press, 1949.

POSTSCRIPT

Should Environmental Ethics Be Human Centered?

In answering this question some people seem to be split between an approach like Baxter's and one like Johnson's. In many cases we can argue for the necessity for clean air and clean water because the condition of air and water makes a difference to *us*. Baxter's position admits this, and could even go so far as to support the protection of specific wilderness areas, *if* it were shown that human beings needed or wanted those wilderness areas for such things as recreation, as sources of inspiration, or as vacation places.

But Baxter's position seems to have left out something important. Such a position seems to imply that it does not make any difference what happens to wilderness areas. If we wish to maintain such areas in their natural state, then let us. On the other hand, if we wish to change them, then let us change them. Johnson argues that if we put out forest fires—which we might do on the grounds that the fires spoil the enjoyment of the area for us—we might actually be working against the positive development of the ecological forces that maintain a given environment. So, in his view, there *is* a right and a wrong way to treat the environment.

Many people, though, may say that we have gone too far. According to Johnson, since wilderness areas might have their own interests, we might be called on to lose (to let burn) what seems to us a significant natural area, or we might be told that we should simply stand by and allow a given set of animals to starve to death, because some larger good will come of it.

Johnson's views are based on the idea of an ecosystem having its own *interests*. But this might seem puzzling. Do all ecosystems have their own interests? Are all the interests compatible, or will one interest ever have to be promoted at the expense of another? Is the concept of *interest* even applicable here—does *interest* apply only to sentient beings, such as people?

In addition, both Baxter and Johnson seem to say very little about the future. Surely future generations of people will have interests in clean air and water, for example. Should Baxter or Johnson take the interests of future people into account?

A classic work in environmental ethics is Aldo Leopold's, *A Sand County Almanac and Sketches Here and There* (Oxford University Press, 1949). Other sources are: Donald Scherer, ed., *Upstream/Downstream: Issues in Environmental Ethics* (Temple University Press, 1990); Christopher D. Stone, *Earth and Other Ethics: The Case for Moral Pluralism* (Harper & Row, 1987); and Paul W. Taylor, *Respect for Nature: A Theory of Environmental Ethics* (Princeton University Press, 1986). The quarterly journal *Environmental Ethics* is a good source of articles that address environmental questions.

ISSUE 7

Is Feminism a Harmful Ideology?

YES: Michael Levin, from *Feminism and Freedom* (Transaction, 1987)

NO: Marilyn French, from *Beyond Power* (Summit Books, 1985)

ISSUE SUMMARY

YES: Professor of philosophy Michael Levin argues that feminism ignores innate differences between men and women. Any attempt to enforce sexual equality would violate nature and would violate liberal values.

NO: Novelist and literary critic Marilyn French argues that feminism requires a thorough change in people's attitudes. Feminism is not the simple claim that women be admitted to a previously male-only social world. It is a call to change this social world itself.

Feminism seems to be a thoroughly modern view, and, for the most part, it is. In Western societies, men have dominated over women throughout history, and the situation is even more pronounced in many Eastern societies.

From the time of the ancient Greeks (when men went to the market because respectable women stayed at home) to this century (when women in America gained the right to vote in national elections in 1920), there has been a nearly unbroken social tradition according to which men were regarded as superior in power to women. This social tradition was reflected in the intellectual tradition, so much so that the exceptions to this tradition stand out.

Two exceptional male thinkers were Plato, who held that in an ideal state the rulers would be both men and women (since there are both male and female individuals who are able to achieve wisdom and thus become good political leaders) and John Stuart Mill, who said in *The Subjection of Women* (1869), "The principle which regulates the existing social relation between the two sexes . . . is wrong in itself, and [is] now one of the chief hindrances to human improvement. . . . It ought to be replaced by a principle of perfect equality. . . ." Much more common was the view that girls should be obedient to their fathers, and women should be obedient to their husbands. Sometimes, there were even stronger misogynistic (antiwoman) views. What did the women of the past think about all this? For the most part, women did not have the education or social encouragement and standing to make their voices heard, so in many cases we simply do not know.

There has been a traditional sexual double standard for men and women, and the law has generally prescribed second-class citizenship for women. Nowadays, we call that tradition sexist, and we tell ourselves that the situation is different. But can we rightfully say that men and women have an equitable relationship in society?

Consider, for example, the fact that most secretaries are women and most executives are men, that most doctors are men and most nurses are women, and that most kindergarten teachers are women and most university professors are men. If we are asked to picture in our minds a nurse (or a professor, or a secretary), we usually picture one of the "correct" sex. Notice that in every case it is the "male" job that has the greater social prestige and the higher pay. This raises many questions. Is it that women freely prefer to be secretaries, nurses, and kindergarten teachers, and men freely prefer to be executives, doctors, and professors? Or are there some social dynamics at work here? Do women generally seek out jobs that have lower prestige, or is lower prestige attached to the jobs because women have traditionally done them? Are people socialized differently according to their sex? Are social expectations different? Social factors aside, what differences exist between males and females anyway?

In recent history, feminists have rallied against patriarchy and male power structures. The origin of some of these power structures may have been "to keep women in their place"—their place being in the home. It is one thing to challenge this power structure by placing some women in the previous power and prestige positions—there are, for example, a growing number of women executives, doctors, and professors—but it is an even greater challenge to the system to aim for the destruction of the entire power structure.

Consider this: There is no second-class citizen without a first-class citizen, and vice versa. If only some women escape second-class status and enter first-class status, there are still some women who remain in the second class. But if all women escape second-class status, then there are no first- and second-class statuses left. In the first case the structure remains the same, but in the second case it is destroyed.

In the following selections, Michael Levin argues that there are indeed natural differences between men and women and that these differences are linked to the proper social roles of men and women. Feminism, he believes, is basically a misguided view since it seeks to deny these differences. Furthermore, if the law and the government serve feminist ends, then they will end up violating the fundamental freedoms of a liberal society. Marilyn French responds that women have yet to achieve equal status with men, and feminism demands this equality. In its demand that patriarchy be destroyed, feminism is a revolutionary ideology.

YES   Michael Levin

FEMINISM AND FREEDOM

When the eighty-eight women who took the New York City Fire Department's entrance examination in 1977 failed its physical strength component, they filed a class-action sex discrimination lawsuit in federal court. The court found for the plaintiffs, agreeing in *Berkman v. NYFD* that the strength test was not job-related and therefore in violation of Title VII of the Civil Rights Act.[1] The court thereupon ordered the city to hire forty-five female firefighters and to construct a special, less demanding physical examination for female candidates, with males still to be held to the extant, more difficult—and ostensibly inappropriate—standard. In addition, the court ordered the city to provide special training to the eighty-eight female plaintiffs—but none for the 54 percent of the males who also failed the test—on the grounds that certain "tricks of the trade" available to all male candidates were not available to them.

New York declined to appeal *Berkman* and instructed its regular firemen to maintain public silence. Since *Berkman*, 38 of the original group of 145 women given special training by the NYFD have entered service as firefighters, and almost all personnel actions taken by the NYFD have required the approval of the presiding judge, Charles Sifton. Continuing litigation has resulted in further easing of the physical standards applied to female firefighting applicants.

The use of statistics in *Berkman* is particularly instructive. According to the guidelines of the Equal Employment Opportunity Commission, which are controlling in cases like *Berkman*, a test for a job is presumed to be discriminatory if the passing rate for women is less than 80 percent of that rate for men. The wider the gap, the less defeasible is the presumption. The court accordingly asked how likely it would be, in the absence of discrimination, that none of the eighty-eight women passed while 46 percent of the men did. As the court correctly noted, "the pass rates were separated by more than eight standard deviations" (1982 at 205), and the probability that this could happen is so small—less than one in 10 trillion—as to amount to virtual impossibility. The court's conclusion that discrimination must have

From Michael Levin, *Feminism and Freedom* (Transaction Books, 1987). Copyright © 1987 by Transaction, Inc. Reprinted by permission.

occurred is entirely cogent, *if strength is assumed to be uncorrelated with sex.* A difference in failure rates on a strength test is consistent with the absence of bias if it is allowed that men are on average stronger than women. The court found an outcome of fewer than thirty-seven passes unacceptably improbable because it adopted the hypothesis that gender and strength are independent variables. Rejecting the hypothesis that gender and strength are in any way connected, the court construed an observed correlation between gender and strength as an artifact to be eliminated by special treatment for one sex. Since women are the same as men, the EEOC and the court reasoned, special steps must be taken to compensate for their manifest differences.

Public reaction to *Berkman* varied. The local tabloids treated it as a joke ("Firebelles!" headlined one), while the more serious press took it, in the words of one slick magazine, as a matter of "opening the doors for women." Other commentators drew attention to the decision's conflict with common sense, public safety, the judgement of the public officials closest to the matter at hand, and the undoubted preferences of the majority. It remained for the Special Counsel for the New York City Commission on the Status of Women to draw the most appropriate connection: The NYFD's latest employees "would never have had the chance to show what [they] could do . . . were it not for the efforts of the feminists and 'women's libbers.' "[2] That is so: Were it not for the ascendancy of feminist ideas, the hypothesis that strength varies randomly with sex would have been unthinkable as the basis for a finding of fact and a guide for policy.

Berkman illustrates as well the extent to which feminism has achieved its effects

through the state, particularly unelected officials of the courts and the regulatory agencies, and those elected officials most remote from their constituencies. Gender quotas, limitations on free speech to combat "psychological damage to women" (to cite EEOC guidelines once again), among many other feminist innovations, are all state actions. What is more, the vagueness of such feminist-inspired initiatives as have been passed by elected officials—chiefly civil rights legislation governing gender, and the Equal Rights Amendments of various states—require that they be constantly interpreted, usually by unelected officials.

This, in short, is the thesis of the present book: It is not by accident that feminism has had its major impact through the necessarily coercive machinery of the state rather than through the private decisions of individuals. Although feminism speaks the language of liberation, self-fulfillment, options, and the removal of barriers, these phrases invariably mean their opposites and disguise an agenda at variance with the ideals of a free society. Feminism has been presented and widely received as a liberating force, a new view of the relations between the sexes emphasizing openness and freedom from oppressive stereotypes. The burden of the present book is to show in broad theoretical perspective and factual detail that this conventional wisdom is mistaken. Feminism is an antidemocratic, if not totalitarian, ideology.

Feminism is a program for making different beings—men and women—turn out alike, and like that other egalitarian, Procrustes, it must do a good deal of chopping to fit the real world into its ideal. More precisely, feminism is the thesis that males and females are already innately alike, with the current order of things—in which males and females appear to differ and occupy quite different social roles—being a harmful distortion of this fundamental similarity. Recognizing no innate gender differences that might explain observed gender differences and the broad structure of society, feminists are compelled to interpret these manifest differences as artifacts, judged by feminists to benefit men unfairly. Believing that overtly uncoerced behavior is the product of oppression, feminists must devise ever subtler theories about the social pressures "keeping women in their place"—pressures to be detected and cancelled.

The reader may feel an impulse to object that I am talking about radical feminism while ignoring moderate feminism, a more responsible position which concedes innate sex differences and wishes only to correct wrongs undeniably done to women. . . . [But] I believe . . . that complete environmentalism—the denial that innate sex differences have anything to do with the broad structure of society—is central to feminism, and that moderate feminism is a chimera. But even the reader wishing to distinguish moderate from radical feminism must concede that *Berkman* is radical by any standards, and that if radical feminism is sufficiently influential to sway the federal judiciary, its credentials and implications deserve close scrutiny.

The second major contention of this book complements the first. If, as I argue, . . . those broad features of society attributed by feminism to discriminatory socialization are in fact produced by innate gender differences, efforts to eradicate those features must be futile and never-ending. Reforms designed to end when sexism disappears will have to be retained indefinitely, imposing increas-

ingly heavy costs on their nonmalleable subjects. Since innate gender differences express themselves as differences in the typical preferences of men and women, so that people will never freely act in ways which produce a world devoid of sexism, the equalization of the sexes in personal behavior and in the work world demands implacable surveillance and interference. In the end it is impossible to overcome the biological inevitability of sex roles, but it is possible to try—and to violate liberal values in the process. A good summary of my main thesis might run: equality of outcome entails inequality of opportunity.

Akin to the idea that radical feminism exaggerates a more tenable moderate position is the idea that, whatever its exaggerations, the radical feminism that emerged in the 1960s was a response to genuine injustices. This claim collapses under the demand for a specification of these injustices. The denial of the vote to women and long-void laws against the possession of property by women are patently irrelevant, since the issue raised here is the character of *contemporary* society. Indeed, it is a serious distortion of history to view the suffragettes of a century ago as forerunners of today's feminists. In addition to being concerned with well-defined legal reforms, nineteenth-century feminists were if anything more convinced than anyone is today not only of innate sex differences, but of the innate superiority of women. The old feminists hoped that greater female participation in public life would raise the moral tone of society, and, in particular, by reducing drunkenness and allowing a woman to be more confident of a sober husband's income, make it easier for her to stay home and raise her children. (The suffragettes were a major force behind the prohibition movement.) Contemporary feminism, by contrast, is best viewed as an extension of the racial civil rights movement, which emphasizes the similarity of populations.

Feminists themselves are strikingly ready to dismiss as superficial the reforms won by their nineteenth-century predecessors. Kate Millett admits that "the male's *de jure* property has recently been modified through the granting of divorce, protection, citizenship, and property to women. [However,] their chattel status continues."[3] She goes on to chide early feminist "concentration on suffrage" for "its failure to challenge patriarchal ideology at a sufficiently deep and radical level." Despite the propensity of feminists and their commentators to frame issues in terms of the "politics" of women's status, legal reform is of interest to most feminists mainly as an instrument for working wholesale changes on society. Indifference to legal reform is in any case forced on feminists by the absence of anything to reform. Private discrimination against women has been illegal since 1964, and public discrimination at the state and municipal levels has been illegal since 1972. When at the behest of President Ronald Reagan the State of Georgia reviewed its statutes for possible discrimination, it reported that the most serious inequity in the state code was the occurrence of 10,000 "he's" as against 150 "she's." Popular discourse continues to allude to "much outright sex discrimination,"[4] but the examples of discrimination cited invariably concern the use of criteria in various activities that men are more likely to meet. Without some showing that these criteria are deployed *for the purpose* of excluding women, or that the discrepant effects of these criteria are *caused by* arbitrary so-cialization, these effects are not "discriminatory." The actual state of affairs is well illustrated by *Berkman:* extensive institutionalized preference favoring women over men. Feminists who explain their grievance in terms of laws against women driving buses may have a legitimate case, but it is one against Edwardian England, not a society in which female bus drivers are promoted over males with greater seniority.

To be sure, the claim that women do not yet enjoy equal opportunity is most frequently made not in connection with legal barriers but in terms of the tendency of people to think sex-stereotypically and to communicate sex-typed norms to the young. This claim will be considered in due course, but it suffices for now to reflect that, if the formation of stereotypic beliefs is a spontaneous response to perceptions of the world, altering these possibly oppressive beliefs will require manipulation of both the average person's spontaneous tendency to form beliefs and the social environment which prompts them. If the social environment is itself a spontaneous expression of innate sex differences, attempting (and inevitably failing) to alter this environment will require yet further intrusion.

Shifting the locus of unfairness from the realm of law to that of sex role stereotyping involves a shift from what can reasonably be called "political" to the entire range of extra-political institutions and behavior. Most of society's institutions emerge from the myriad uncoordinated decisions of individuals; to call these practices and institutions "political" suggests a disregard for the distinction between public and private and disdain for the private realm itself. It is not surprising that feminists who use the word "political" so expansively also speak as if they believe in an actual worldwide conspiracy against women.[5] Once this usage is adopted, everything from office flirtation to children's horseplay becomes assessable for its tendency to abet the political decision about women's condition. Erstwhile private matters become questions of socially determined rights, and are pulled within the authority of the state.

To deny that women are victims of systematic discrimination is not to assert that contemporary Western civilization is perfect. . . .

The reader may be anxious to inform me of cases known to him of a competent woman being denied a desirable position just because she is a woman. I do not deny that such cases exist, but I ask the reader to remember three points. First, no accumulation of anecdotes can demonstrate an intrinsic societal bias against women. Second, a social arrangement can do no more than treat people better than other possible arrangements; perfect justice is unattainable. Third, the wrongs with which the reader is acquainted must be kept in perspective. Can being denied a merited promotion honestly be compared to being beaten for drinking from a Whites-only fountain, the sort of treatment Blacks experienced two generations ago?

A sense of history is too often absent from discussions of the relative positions of men and women in contemporary society. Women in past eras suffered indignities that would be considered intolerable today, but so did most men. If women did not vote until the twentieth century, it must be recalled that *nobody* voted prior to the eighteenth. Far older than the franchise and the notion of universal rights is the idea that men must protect women, a duty in whose

service men have endured enormous hardships. If sex roles are to be regarded as the outcome of bargaining in which men received dominance in exchange for the risk of violent death, it is hardly clear that they got the better deal.

As groundless as the idea that feminism is a movement of liberal reform is the idea that it is passé. The immoderate language of twenty years ago is encountered less frequently today, but no doctrine is more influential in shaping institutional and public life than feminism. Under current federal law, a prospective employer is forbidden to ask a female job applicant if she plans to have children. The Supreme Court has outlawed pension plans that use the greater longevity of women as a factor in computing premiums.[6] Public speakers can no longer use "he" or "man" comfortably. Critics reflexively apologize before praising books, movies, or ideas that might displease feminists. Newspaper reports on menstrual disorders note that feminists do not like the idea that there are such things, as if nature were obliged not to mark sex distinctions, or as if citing facts at odds with feminism were intrinsically presumptuous. The navy retains the present design for the cockpits of its combat aircraft because women have difficulty fitting into the new, more efficient designs—even though women are presently barred from flying such aircraft.

Political leaders of every persuasion reflexively employ gender quotas. The liberal governor of New York State reprimanded a selection committee for not including a female among its candidates for the state's Supreme Court while simultaneously praising all the candidates as "first-rate." A conservative president highly critical of quotas as a private citizen decided that his first Supreme Court appointment had to be a woman. . . . [T]he quota mentality now dominates all phases of employment.

. . . The courts have involved themselves in university tenure decisions involving women, and have heavily penalized organizations for failing to pay women what the courts deem they deserve. I have confirmed in correspondence with the responsible executives that the national television networks instruct their writers to include nontraditional women in every script. (That they do so is in any case evident from the casting of network television programs.) The advertising industry has plainly adopted similar protocols: An advertisement for New York Life Insurance shows the "1981 woman," attaché case in hand, boarding a helicopter while her children are left "to the sharing concern of her husband." The director of the Project on the Status and Education of Women, funded by the Ford Foundation and Carnegie Corporation, boasts that "the most comprehensive national policy in the world regarding discrimination against women and girls in the schoolroom is now in place. . . . [I]t is unlikely that Congress would ever overturn the legislation."[7] The National Education Association advocates the pursuit of "psychological androgyny" as far as is "consistent with democracy."

The popular press continues to suggest that wanting to marry and raise children is a curious goal for a woman. It is becoming somewhat more acceptable for a woman to find parenting important, but it is still unacceptable to assert that it is more important for a woman than for a man. Typical of this genre is an article entitled "What Does a Woman Need? Not to Depend on a Man," which ap-

peared in *People*,[8] a periodical widely thought to be devoid of ideological content. In this article, a psychologist advises that 95 percent of all women are "desperately dependent" on men and that a too-devoted wife is apt to lose her husband to a mistress. *Parents*, another ostensibly conventional publication, runs a bulletin entitled "Are Parents Sexist?" They are, it turns out, especially fathers, and *Parents* instructs working women consciously to emulate the "ruthlessness" of men.[9] . . .

Gender differences will emerge in any human social organization. Since every human activity is either the province of one sex or a joint endeavor of both in which these differences manifest themselves, it is possible to find sexism everywhere. While in that sense feminism conflicts with every human activity, the present book concentrates on the conflict between feminism and those institutions central to a free society. Among the most important are the free market and education. The only way to stifle, or try to stifle, the manifestation of gender differences in people's working lives is through a rigid program of job quotas and pay scales. . . . The only way to stifle, or try to stifle, the manifestation of gender differences in children's perceptions of each other is through a rigid program of exhorting them to disregard their senses. . . .

Free societies like all others must use force to preserve order; the primary institutions by which they do so are the police and the military. The maintenance of order has always been a male function, as have similar functions with similar requirements of strength and audacity, like firefighting. . . .

Because feminism is regularly called the "women's movement," any criticism of feminism is apt to be viewed as an attack on women. It is a measure of the ability of slogans to paralyze thought that any writer should have to explicitly disavow the patent absurdity that men are better than women, but I shall enter one such disavowal here.[10] Men are not better than women and women are not better than men; men and women differ. Feminists may describe their opponents as those who think that "men are better than women," but it is not clear who in Western society holds such a view or what it might mean. "Better" is ill-defined in isolation—one thing being better than another only in some specific respect. To say, as the evidence suggests, that men are better than women at mathematics while women are better than men at caring for children is not to say that mathematics is more important than caring for children or vice versa. Anyone who insists that merely asserting these facts amounts to insulting women must himself believe that male talents are self-evidently more important than female talents. It is this sort of advocate of the cause of women who believes women to be inferior.

Nor do I embrace the view that men are morally better than women. No one has ever dreamed of claiming that men are kinder, more generous, and less prone to aggression. To the contrary, the received stereotype is that women are incapable of the satanic excesses which men have reached. Yet, while the moral superiority of males is a straw man not worth attacking, feminists often put themselves in the perverse position of *defending* this straw man. Feminists characteristically explain the greater person-orientedness of women in environmentalist terms extremely unflattering to women themselves.[11] More recently, the discovery of

rivalry among certain primate females has encouraged speculation that human females may happily prove to be as nasty as human males. (Rivalry among primate females generally concerns resources for offspring, while male primate rivalry concerns group dominance; nothing in recent primatology challenges standard views about sex differences.)

It should go without saying that innate sex differences are statistical. Some women are better at mathematics than most men. Neither sex monopolizes any nonanatomical trait. It should also go without saying that the within-sex variance for nonanatomical traits exceeds mean sex differences; the gap in mathematical ability between Gauss and Casey Stengel doubtless exceeds that between the average man and the average woman. I have been unable to find anyone who denies these truisms, which are irrelevant to the existence and consequences of mean gender differences.

I am willing to endorse the treatment of people as "individuals," but it is pointless to expect society to ignore inescapably obvious inductive generalizations which are, on the evidence, rooted in biology. Women with unusual traits have had to face extra difficulties just because they were women (as have men with unusual traits), and these difficulties are due to the currency of expectations based on the majority of cases. But such instances do not show that the broad structure of society inherently thwarts the desires of the great majority of women.

NOTES

1. *Berkman v. NYFD*, 536 FSupp 177 (1982); 580 FSupp 226 (1983).
2. Lynn Hecht Schafran, letter, *New York* (January 31, 1983): 5.
3. Kate Millett, *Sexual Politics* (New York: Doubleday, 1970), p. 34.

4. Lori Andrews, "Learning the Rules of the Game," *Parents* (January 1982): 34.

5. "The political nature of woman's condition has rarely been recognized. . . . [W]oman's condition, here and now, is the result of a slowly formed, deeply entrenched, extraordinarily pervasive cultural and therefore political decision." Vivian Gornick and Barbara Moran, "Introduction," in *Woman in Sexist Society,* ed. idem (New York: Mentor, 1971), p. xv.

6. *Manhart v. Los Angeles,* 403 US 702 (1978). See also "Equal Rights Ruling for Auto Insurance Expected to Spread," *New York Times* (October 23, 1984): A18.

7. Bernice Sandler, *On Campus with Women* 26 (Spring 1980): 3.

8. "What Does a Woman Need? Not to Depend on a Man," *People* (September 13, 1982): 75–79.

9. See Andrews.

10. Not that such disavowals are effective. A recent book asserts that the present author disapproves of affirmative action because of the "inferiority" of women (Anne Fausto-Sterling, *Myths of Gender* [New York: Basic Books, 1986], p. 6). No doubt this book will be similarly misread.

11. Doris Gold explains that women volunteer for charitable activities as a result of "powerful social disapproval, coupled with their own psychological conditioning of self-negation and ambivalent self-recognition." Doris Gold, "Women and Volunteerism," in Gornick and Moran, p. 534.

NO

Marilyn French

FEMINISM

Feminism is the only serious, coherent, and universal philosophy that offers an alternative to patriarchal thinking and structures. Feminists believe in a few simple tenets. They believe that women are human beings, that the two sexes are (at least) equal in all significant ways, and that this equality must be publicly recognized. They believe that qualities traditionally associated with women—the feminine principle—are (at least) equal in value to those traditionally associated with men—the masculine principle—and that this equality must be publicly recognized. (I modify these statements with *at least* because some feminists believe in the superiority of women and "feminine" qualities. Indeed, it is difficult not to stress the value of the "feminine" in our culture because it is so pervasively debased and diminished.) Finally, feminists believe the personal is the political—that is, that the value structure of a culture is identical in both public and private areas, that what happens in the bedroom has everything to do with what happens in the boardroom, and vice versa, and that, mythology notwithstanding, at present the same sex is in control in both places.

There are also those who believe they consider women equal to men, but see women as fettered by their traditional socialization and by the expectations of the larger world. These people see women as large children who have talent and energy, but who need training in male modes, male language, and an area of expertise in order to "fit in" in the male world. One philosopher, for example, has commented that women are *not yet ready* for top government posts. This is not just patronizing; it shows a lack of comprehension of feminism. For although feminists do indeed want women to become part of the structure, participants in public institutions; although they want access for women to decision-making posts, and a voice in how society is managed, *they do not want women to assimilate to society as it presently exists but to change it.* Feminism is not yet one more of a series of political movements demanding for their adherents access to existing structures and their rewards. This is how many people see it, however: as a strictly political movement through which women demand entry into the "male" world,

From Marilyn French, *Beyond Power* (Summit Books, 1985). Copyright © 1985 by Belles-Lettres, Inc. Reprinted by permission of Summit Books, a division of Simon & Schuster, Inc. Notes Omitted.

a share of male prerogatives, and the chance to be like men. This perception of feminism alienates many nonfeminist women.

Feminism is a political movement demanding access to the rewards and responsibilities of the "male" world, but it is more: it is a revolutionary moral movement, intending to use political power to transform society, to "feminize" it. For such a movement, assimilation is death. The assimilation of women to society as it presently exists would lead simply to the inclusion of certain women (not all, because society as it presently exists is highly stratified) along with certain men in its higher echelons. It would mean continued stratification and continued contempt for "feminine" values. Assimilation would be the cooption of feminism. Yet it must be admitted that the major success of the movement in the past twenty years has been to increase the assimilation of women into the existing structure. This is not to be deplored, but it is only a necessary first step.

There have been many revolutions against various patriarchal forms over the past three or four thousand years, but in each case, what has succeeded an oppressive structure is another oppressive structure. This is inevitable because, regardless of the initial ideas and ideals of rebellious groups, they come to worship power above all: only power, they believe, can overwhelm power; only their greater power can bring them victory over an "enemy" that is the Father. But each victory has increased the power of the *idea* of power, thus each victory has increased human oppression. . . .

If women and men were seen as equal, if male self-definition no longer depended upon an inferior group, other stratifications would also become unnecessary. Legitimacy (which has no meaning without the idea of illegitimacy) would no longer be a useful concept, and its disappearance from human minds would lead to the establishment of new structures for social organization. These structures would blur the distinction between public and private spheres, a distinction that was originally created not only to exclude women from a male (public) arena, but to permit discourse which ignored and effectively eliminated from existence the parts of all lives that are bound to nature, that are necessary and nonvolitional. If public and private life were integrated, it would no longer seem incongruous to discuss procreation and weapons systems in the same paragraph. Since pleasure would be the primary value of both personal and public life, harmony (which produces pleasure) would be a universal societal goal, and would no longer have to be manufactured in the ersatz form of coerced uniformity, conformity. Love too would regain its innocence, since it would not be coerced into playing a role within a power structure and thus functioning as an oppression—as it often does in our world.

The foregoing is a sketch of feminist beliefs. It is difficult at present to provide more than a sketch, for to create truly feminist programs we must rid our heads of the power notions that fill them, and that cannot be done in a generation, or even several generations. The sketch may sound utopian: I think it is not. That is, I believe such a world is possible for humans to maintain, to live within, once it is achieved. What may be utopian is the idea that we can achieve it. For to displace power as the highest human value means to supersede patriarchal modes while eschewing traditional power maneuvers as a means. But it is impossible to function in the public world without using power maneuvers; and revolution does imply overthrow of current systems.

Two elements cast a friendly light on feminist goals. One is that the movement is not aimed at overthrow of any particular government or structure, but at the displacement of one way of thinking by another. The other is that feminism offers desirable goals. The first means that the tools of feminism are naturally nonviolent: it moves and will continue to move by influencing people, by offering a vision, by providing an alternative to the cul-de-sacs of patriarchy. The second means that feminism is in a state I call blessed: its ends and its means are identical. Feminism increases the well-being of its adherents, and so can appeal to others on grounds of the possibility of greater felicity. Integration of the self, which means using the full range of one's gifts, increases one's sense of well-being; if integration of one's entire life is not always possible because of the nature of the public world, it is a desirable goal. Patriarchy, which in all its forms requires some kind of self-sacrifice, denial, or repression in the name of some higher good which is rarely (if ever) achieved on earth, stresses nobility, superiority, and victory, the satisfaction of a final triumph. Feminism requires use of the entire self in the name of present well-being, and stresses integrity, community, and the *jouissance* of present experience. . . .

It was probably Betty Friedan's *The Feminine Mystique*, published in 1963, that first galvanized American women into action. Women legislators had seen to it that laws passed to redress wrongs done to blacks were expanded to include women. The Equal Pay Act was passed in 1963; the Civil Rights Act in 1965. Title VII of the latter prohibited discrimination on grounds of sex, race, color, religion, or national origin. The word *sex* was included as a result of maneuvers by Representative Martha Griffiths, Senator Margaret Chase Smith, and a reporter, Mae Craig. In 1965 the Supreme Court held that laws banning contraceptives were unconstitutional, and in 1966 a federal court declared that an Alabama law barring women from juries violated the Fourteenth Amendment (guaranteeing equal protection under the law). In that year too, the National Organization for Woman was founded. . . .

The decade that followed was enormously fertile; the seeds planted then are still bearing fruit. Women scholars began to delve into women's history, to break away from male interpretations and lay the groundwork for an alternative view of anthropology, psychology, sociology, philosophy, and language. Politically oriented groups pressed for legislation granting women equality in education, housing, credit, and promotion and hiring. Other women established feminist magazines, journals, publishing houses, and bookstores. Some strove for political office; some entered the newly open "male" world of business and industry. In the exhilaration of that period, women who had felt crippled found limbs, women who had felt marginal found a center, women who had felt alone found sisters.

It is now less than twenty years since the rising of the "second wave." The difference is astonishing. Women are now working in hundreds of jobs that were closed to them in the past. Women can sign leases, buy cars and houses, obtain credit; they cannot be denied telephone service because they are divorced. They can be seated in restaurants although they are dining without a man. Although some women's fashions still inhibit mobility, they are no longer *de riguer*. Women are no longer expected to produce elaborate entertainments: life can be easier, more leisurely, for both sexes.

Most important of all, women now possess reproductive freedom. Although men have long had access to condoms, which were and are sold over the counter in every drugstore, women needed doctors' prescriptions to purchase diaphragms and, later, the birth control pill. This is still true, but such prescriptions are widely available now, and women do not have to be married to obtain them. (In France, where men can also obtain condoms easily, women could not purchase contraceptive devices in drugstores until 1967, and such purchases still require the authorization of the minister of social affairs.) Clearly, it is not birth control—or, more accurately, the prevention of conception—per se that is offensive to patriarchal culture, but the placing of that control in the hands of women. Despite continuing attempts to wrest it from them, American women are likely to hold on to this right over their own bodies. But in some Western nations—Ireland, for example—they still do not possess it.

The difference is great for a huge number of women, and because the difference permeates their lives, change may seem complete. But in the scale of things, the change is minimal. Capitalism, under great pressure for almost a hundred and fifty years, has yielded women about what socialism yielded them immediately. But it has managed—as has socialism—to retain its essential character. Capitalism has assimilated women, it has not broadened itself; it has swallowed women rather than alter itself. And it has done this in accordance with

its traditional structures. Thus the women who have benefited most from the changes are well-educated, white, middle-class women, often without children. Thus the divisiveness of racism has pervaded the women's movement itself. Thus women have by and large been kept out of the most sensitive and powerful areas of business and government, so that they have not achieved a voice in the running of our society. And thus women who have not managed to live like men, or with them, have been condemned to the lowest rank in our society: women are the new poor. It is not an exaggeration to say that although feminism in capitalist states has freed many women and improved the lives of others, it has had little effect on the patriarchy, which has simply absorbed a few women who appear acceptable to its purposes, and barred the door for the rest. . . .

. . . [T]he gap between male and female earnings has increased. According to the last census, the mean income of white females was $10,244 (59 cents of a white male dollar), of black females $9,476 (54 cents of a white male dollar), and of Hispanic females $8,466 (49 cents of a white male dollar). Despite differences in the concerns and approaches of women of color and white women, in the realm of economics, women as a caste comprise a lower class.

The poor of America are women: the poor of the world are women. In 1980, in America, the median adjusted income for men was $12,530, for women it was $4,920. In 1980 the poverty level was $8,414 for a nonfarm family of four, and nearly thirty million Americans live beneath it. Seventy percent of these are white, 30 percent black—and we may note that only 12 percent of the population is black—two thirds of them women and children. If we limit these figures to adults, two out of every three poor adults are female. If present trends continue, by the year 2000 the poor of America will be entirely its women.

There are a number of reasons for this. A presidential report published in 1981 claims that women are "systematically underpaid," that "women's work" pays about four thousand dollars a year less than men's work, and that occupational segregation is more pronounced by sex than by race: 70 percent of men and 54 percent of women are concentrated in jobs done only by those of their own sex.

Because women are still held responsible—by themselves and by men—for raising the children, they are forced to take jobs that are close to home, that offer flexible hours (like waitressing), or are part-time; jobs that do not require extended traveling or long hours. They are not able to "compete" in a job market that demands single-minded devotion to work, fast running on a narrow track. For some this is a tolerable situation: some women are not notably ambitious, prefer a balanced life, and have working husbands. But this is not the case for all, or even most, women.

More women than ever in the period covered by American record keeping on this point are living without men: they are single mothers, divorced mothers, and widows, as well as single working women. The reasons for this are complex. Two major reasons, however, are the movement for "sexual liberation" and the feminist movement.

The movement for "sexual liberation" begun in the 1950s was a male campaign, rooted in ideas that seem for the most part honest and beneficial: that sex was good, the body was good; that trading sexual access for financial support de-graded sex and the body; that virginity was a questionable good in women and not at all necessary in men; and that the requirement of sexual fidelity in marriage was an oppression. However, the campaign was also extremely self-serving: it was not based on a philosophy that saw a joyous sex life as one element in a life concerned with the pleasure and the good of self and others. It was not a responsible movement: in fact it "masculinized" sex by making it a commodity and by isolating sex from other elements intrinsic to it—affection, connection, and the potential for procreation. To speak lightly, what the sexual revolution accomplished was to change the price of sexual access to a woman from marriage to a dinner.

At the same time, the ties of marriage lost their force—for men. As of 1963, almost all divorces sought in America were initiated (whether openly or not) by men. Divorce—like marriage—is morally neutral. Insofar as it ends a relationship of misery, it is a good; insofar as it ends a long-term intimacy, it is to be lamented. Even when a marriage involves children, it cannot be pre-judged: divorce may be better for the children than the marriage was. It seems reasonable to assume that if one party to a marriage wants a divorce, divorce should occur. But marriage and divorce are both tied to responsibility, and it was this tie that was broken by the "sexual liberation" movement.

If a man—and society in general—requires a woman to set aside ideas of an individual life, and to accept the role of functionary—wife, mother, housekeeper—without payment, then that role must be structured to guarantee that woman a secure life despite her unpaid labor. In cognizance of this contract, traditional divorce laws stipulated alimony. Laws did not, of course, prevent men from abandoning their families completely, or failing in alimony payments. But the new sexual morality was growing in the sixties, a period when feminists were struggling to gain the right to paid employment above the national level, and when many women who had gained such work were initiating divorce themselves. The thinking of legislators and judges underwent an amazing swift change. The new assumption was that women worked, that they earned as much as men, and thus that they did not require alimony—which is rarely granted now, and even more rarely paid. In 1979, only 14 percent of all divorced or separated women were granted alimony or child support, and of those at least 30 percent did not receive what they were awarded.

This situation is unjust to women who have accepted lesser jobs to help their husbands through school, or given up fellowships or promotions to accompany a husband to his new job. It is appallingly unjust to women who have neglected their own potential careers to care for husbands and children. But it becomes outrageous when we consider the statistics (if we need statistics, many women are too well acquainted with the reality behind them) on men's support of their children after divorce.

Although some very rich men use the power of their wealth to take the children away from their mothers after divorce, most men who divorce leave not just a marriage but a family. Men father children; although the degree to which they participate in childraising varies, it seems likely that they have some love and concern for those children. Nevertheless, after divorce they often disappear: they contribute neither emotion, time, nor money to the care of their own children. More than 90 percent of children who live with one parent live with their mothers; in 1978 there were 7.1 million single mothers with custody of their children in the United States. The number of men raising children on their own declined in the decade of the seventies. "The result of divorce, in an overwhelming number of cases, is that men become singles and women become single mothers." Women's incomes decline by 73 percent in the first year after divorce; men's incomes *increase* by 42 percent. The father is better off, the children are often hungry.

In recent years judges have tended not to award child support to mothers with custody; they have denied it to 41 percent of such mothers. Studies of the amounts awarded vary, ranging from as low as an average of $539 per year to an average of $2,110. But over 50 percent of custodial mothers never receive the amounts due them. Lenore Weitzman's research in California shows that only 13 percent of women with custody of preschool children receive alimony; child support payments (even when they are made) are almost never enough to cover the cost of raising small children. . . .

The women's movement under capitalism has worked almost unbelievably hard and made large gains. Those gains are changes in law and custom, and they affect all women, although they have their greatest effect on middle-class educated women. But feminism has not been able to budge an intransigent establishment bent on destroying the globe; it has not moved us one inch closer to the feminization of society. Indeed, it seems to lose ground with every decade, as the nourishing, procreative, communal, emotional dimensions of experience are increasingly ground into dust, as high technology and more intense pursuit of power are increasingly exalted.

This situation constitutes a quandary for feminists. Only by bringing great numbers of women with feminist values into the institutional structure of the nation can women achieve a voice in the way this country is run. Only by unified political action can women influence the course of the future. But at present, and for the foreseeable future, women are carefully screened, hired in small numbers, and watched for deviance. Women hired by institutions are far more likely to be coopted by institutional policy than to change it; they will assimilate or be fired or quit. Some feminist groups oppose women's efforts to enter the establishment on the ground that women should not contribute to a structure that is sexist, racist, and dedicated to profit and power. On the other hand, to refuse to enter the establishment is to refuse even to try to change it from within and thus to accept the marginal position women have traditionally held. To refuse to enter American institutions may also be to doom oneself to poverty, and poverty is silent and invisible. It has no voice and no face.

For this problem, as for so many others, there is no clear right answer.

POSTSCRIPT

Is Feminism a Harmful Ideology?

Levin argues strenuously against feminism, but he seems to assume that feminism requires androgyny—the idea that there are no (or should not be any) differences between men and women. But this idea is not necessarily tied to feminism.

Janet Radcliffe Richards, an English feminist, takes a very different approach in *The Sceptical Feminist: A Philosophical Enquiry* (Routledge & Kegan Paul, 1980). She defines feminism as the view that "women suffer from systematic social injustice because of their sex." This definition is more inclusive than Levin's, and many more people qualify as feminists by this definition. Moreover, Richards does not tie her notion of feminism to any particular policies or politics. That is, in her view, feminism is the recognition that there are problems (of social justice for women), but her view allows different people to have different ideas about how those problems might be solved.

Levin speaks of "innate sex differences." He seems to think that feminism requires the belief that there are no such differences. It is true that in many cases in the past innate sex differences were simply made up in order to support certain ideologies and existing power structures. But it is *not* the case that we now know that there are no such differences. Rather, we should first of all be suspicious of people who make extravagant claims about the existence of such differences, since the historical record of such claims is so poor. We should also ask what if any difference would or should any such innate differences make? What impact would it have for male-female relations? Suppose such differences are statistical, like the statistical fact that women are shorter than men. This does not rule out the existence of women who are taller than many men. Even if the difference is absolute—such as the fact that women can bear babies and men cannot—what are the implications for social policy?

Further readings that give a historical overview of feminism, its varieties, and its social context are Rosemarie Tong, *Feminist Thought: A Comprehensive Introduction* (Westview, 1989); Susan Moller Okin, *Women in Western Political Thought* (Princeton University Press, 1979); Rosalind Rosenberg, *Beyond Separate Spheres: Intellectual Roots of Modern Feminism* (Yale University Press, 1982); and Alison Jaggar, *Feminist Politics and Human Nature* (Rowman & Allanheld, 1983).

Books critical of feminism include Steven Goldberg, *The Inevitability of Patriarchy* (William Morrow & Company, 1973), and Nicholas Davidson, *The Failure of Feminism* (Prometheus Books, 1978).

Relevant quarterly journals are: *Hypatia: A Journal of Feminist Philosophy; Signs: A Journal of Culture and Society*, and *Feminist Studies*.

ISSUE 8

Does Morality Require a Vegetarian Way of Life?

YES: Tom Regan, from *The Thee Generation: Reflections on the Coming Revolution* (Temple University Press, 1991)

NO: Philip E. Devine, from "The Moral Basis of Vegetarianism," *Philosophy* (1978)

ISSUE SUMMARY

YES: Professor of philosophy Tom Regan addresses the morality of raising animals for food. He considers the situation from three different points of view, which he calls the utilitarian, holist, and rights views, and concludes that all three points of view support the practice of vegetarianism.

NO: Professor of philosophy Philip E. Devine takes the view that the defenses of vegetarianism that have been offered by utilitarians and others fail to establish what they set out to prove. In light of this failure, eating meat remains a strong option for human beings.

Human relationships with animals have varied greatly from culture to culture. For example, in some Native American tribes, when an animal was killed, rituals were offered in apology to the animal's spirit.

Some religions maintain a belief in reincarnation, according to which souls that once inhabited human bodies come to inhabit animal bodies, and vice versa. Such a point of view is generally accompanied by vegetarianism, since to eat animal meat may be thought to be a form of cannibalism.

In the history of Western thought, one view has considered animals as purely physical beings, like plants and minerals, with no inner feelings. This is a view that has been attributed to the French mathematician and philosopher René Descartes (1596–1650). Related to this mechanistic view of animals are certain biblical views. According to these views, human beings have divine souls but animals do not. Moreover, it is part of the biblical message that God put animals on the Earth in order to be used by human beings, as food, for example. What follows from this is that human beings have a divinely given right to make use of animals in whatever way they wish.

There is a tendency in contemporary Western society to think of animals in terms of these views. For example, when we think of cows, we often see only milk- and meat-producing machines; when we think of lobsters, we usually think of seafood. We generally ignore the question of whether the animals can feel anything when they are slaughtered or cooked alive. In this way we avoid having to make a choice between Descartes and the biblical view. Or, if we admit that animals really do feel, we may say that their feelings are outweighed by our desire for hamburgers or boiled lobster meat.

Historically, the earliest opposition to such views probably came from English philosopher Jeremy Bentham (1748–1832). As an early utilitarian, Bentham believed that we should act in such a way as to promote the greatest happiness for the greatest possible number. Bentham made the point that, since animals can experience pleasure and pain and thus can be made worse off or better off, moral evaluation of human action must include reference to its impact on the pleasure and pain of animals (in addition, of course, to its impact on the pleasure and pain of people).

Another source of objection to the biblical view is the rights view. If we believe that there are animal rights, we will generally believe that animals have a right not to suffer and not to have their lives taken in order to be eaten by human beings. On the other hand, some people combine a rights view with a biblical view and maintain that we human beings are special and have human rights, while animals have no rights at all. But the nature of this specialness must be explained. Some people feel that such a claim to specialness is suspiciously similar to claims made by racists and sexists.

A third source of opposition to the traditional Western treatment of animals can be called holist. It takes this name because it focuses on the large-scale whole, rather than on individual animals or human beings. Such a view rejects the individualism of both utilitarianism and the rights view. It says, for example, that we should pay attention not to particular individual living things, but rather to whole ecological systems.

Concerning the commercial production of animal meat, the utilitarians would ask, "Do the animals suffer more than the people gain?" The rights theorists would ask "Are the animals' rights violated?" And the holist would ask "Does this tend to do ecological damage? Is this bad for the planet?"

In the following selections, Tom Regan argues that morality does indeed require a vegetarian life-style for people. The book from which the following passage is taken, *The Thee Generation*, takes its title from a play on the phrase "The Me Generation." Regan believes that we are moving away from self-centeredness and toward care for others. One of the ways that such a change can manifest itself is for people to embrace vegetarianism and reject meat-eating. Philip E. Devine subjects the supposed moral basis of vegetarianism to careful scrutiny. He considers both utilitarian and what he calls deontological arguments. (Deontological arguments make the point that something is absolutely forbidden, no matter how utilitarian calculations of pleasure and pain might turn out.) Unconvinced, Devine defends meat-eating.

YES

Tom Regan

ABOLISHING ANIMAL AGRICULTURE

I shall limit myself to three of the challenges being raised against moral anthropocentrism. The first comes from *utilitarians;* the second from proponents of *animal rights;* and the third from those who advocate a *holistic ethic.* This chapter offers brief summaries of each position with special reference to how they answer two questions: (1) Is vegetarianism required on ethical grounds? (2) Judged ethically, what should we say, and what should we do about, commercial animal agriculture? To ask whether vegetarianism is required on ethical grounds is to ask whether there are reasons other than those of self-interest (for example, other than those that relate to one's own health or financial well-being) that call for leading a vegetarian way of life. As for the expression "commercial animal agriculture," this refers to the practice of raising animals to be sold for food. The ethics of other practices that routinely kill other animals (for example, hunting and trapping) will not be considered except in passing, not because they are immune to moral criticism but because space and time preclude my offering it here. Space and time also preclude my offering sustained critical assessments of the views I discuss.

MORAL ANTHROPOCENTRISM

Aquinas and Kant speak for the anthropocentric tradition. This tradition does not issue a blank check when it comes to how humans may treat other animals. Positively, we are enjoined to be kind to them; negatively, we are prohibited from being cruel. But we are not enjoined to be the one and prohibited from being the other because we owe such treatment to these animals *themselves.* For we have no duties *to other animals,* according to the anthropocentric tradition; rather, it is because of *human* interests that we have those duties we do. "So far as animals are concerned," writes Kant, "we have no direct duties. . . . Our duties to animals are merely indirect duties to mankind." "He who is cruel to animals becomes hard also in his dealings with men," writes Kant. *That* is why cruelty to animals is wrong. As for kindness, Kant observes that "tender feelings towards dumb animals develop humane feelings towards mankind." And *that* is why we have a duty to be kind to animals.[1]

So reasons Kant. Aquinas predictably adds theistic considerations but the main story line is the same, as witness the following representative passage from his *Summa Contra Gentiles.*

> Hereby is refuted the error of those who said it is sinful for a man to kill dumb animals: for by divine providence they are intended for man's use in the natural order. Hence it is not wrong for man to make use of them, either by killing, or in any other way whatever. . . . And if any passages of Holy Writ seem to forbid us to be cruel to dumb animals, for instance to kill a bird with its young: this is either to remove men's thoughts from being cruel to other men, and lest through being cruel to animals one becomes cruel to human beings: or because injury to an animal leads to the temporal hurt of man, either of the doer of the deed, or of another: or on account of some [religious] signification: thus the Apostle expounds the prohibition against *muzzling the ox that treadeth the corn.*[2]

To borrow a phrase from the twentieth-century British philosopher Sir W. D. Ross, our treatment of animals for both Kant and Aquinas is "a practice ground for moral virtue." The *moral game* is played between human players or, on the theistic view, human players plus God. The way we treat other animals is a sort of moral warm-up—character calisthenics, as it were—for the real game in which these animals themselves play no part.

UTILITARIANISM

The first fairly recent spark of revolt against moral anthropocentrism comes, as do other recent protests against institutionalized prejudice, from the pens of the nineteenth-century utilitarians Jeremy Bentham and John Stuart Mill. In an oft-quoted passage Bentham enfranchises sentient animals in the utilitarian moral community by declaring, "The question is not, Can they *talk?*, or Can they *reason?*, but, Can they *suffer?*"[3] . . .

Some of our duties are *direct duties to other animals*, not indirect duties to humanity. For utilitarians, these animals are themselves involved in the moral game.

Viewed against this historical backdrop the position of the influential contemporary moral philosopher Peter Singer can be seen to be an extension of the utilitarian critique of moral anthropocentrism. In Singer's hands utilitarianism requires that we consider the interests of everyone affected by what we do, and also that we weigh equal interests equally.[4] We must not refuse to consider the interests of some people because they are Catholic, or female, or black, for example. *Everyone's* interests must be considered. And we must not discount the importance of equal interests because of whose interests they are. Everyone's interests must be weighed *equitably.* Now, to ignore or discount the importance of a woman's interests *because she is a woman* is an obvious example of the moral prejudice we call sexism, just as to ignore or discount the importance of the interests of blacks (or Native Americans, Chicanos, etc.) are obvious forms of racism. It remained for Singer to argue, which he does with great vigor, passion, and skill, that a similar moral prejudice lies at the heart of moral anthropocentrism, a prejudice that Singer, borrowing a term coined by the English author and animal activist Richard Ryder, denominates *speciesism*.[5]

Like Bentham and Mill before him, therefore, Singer denies that humans are obliged to treat other animals equitably in the name of the betterment of humanity and also denies that acting dutifully toward these animals is a warm-up for the real moral game played between humans or, as theists would add, between humans-and-humans-and-God. *We owe it to those animals who have interests to take their interests into account, just as we also owe it to them to count their interests equitably.* In these respects we have *direct* duties to them, not indirect duties to humanity. To think otherwise is to give sorry testimony to the very prejudice—speciesism—Singer is intent upon silencing.

ANIMAL AGRICULTURE TODAY

Singer believes that one of speciesism's most obvious symptoms is that we eat other animals, and his utilitarian case for vegetarianism gains strength from the radical changes that recently have taken place in commercial animal agriculture. Increasingly animals raised for food never see or smell the earth. Instead they are raised permanently indoors in unnatural, crowded conditions—raised "intensively," to use the jargon of the animal industry—in structures that look for all the world like factories. Indeed, it is now common to refer to such commercial ventures as *factory farms*. The inhabitants of these "farms" are closely confined in cages, or stalls, or pens, living out their abbreviated lives in a technologically created and sustained environment: automated feeding, automated watering, automated light cycles, automated waste removal, automated whatnot. And the crowding: as many as nine hens in cages that measure 18 by 24 inches, veal calves confined to 22-inch-wide stalls, pregnant hogs confined in tiers of cages, sometimes two, three, or four tiers high. Many of the animals' most basic interests are ignored, and most are undervalued.

Add to this sorry tale of speciesism on today's factory farms the enormous waste that characterizes the animal industry, waste to the tune of six or seven pounds of vegetable protein to produce a single pound of animal protein in the case of beef cattle, for example; and add to the accumulated waste of nutritious food the chronic need for just such food throughout the countries of the Third World, whose populations characteristically are malnourished at best and literally starving to death at worst; add all these factors together and we have the basis on which utilitarians can answer our two questions. In response to the first question, Is vegetarianism required on ethical grounds? utilitarians can reply that it is, noting that it is not for self-interested reasons alone that we should stop eating the flesh of dead animals (what we call "meat") but for reasons that count the interests of *other* humans and *other* animals. And as for our second question, the one that asks what we should think and do about commercial animal agriculture as it exists today, utilitarians can use these same considerations to support their moral condemnation.

SOME PROBLEMS FOR UTILITARIANISM

Some utilitarians, then, offer an important critique of commercial animal agriculture and, allied with this, an impassioned defense of ethical vegetarianism. . . .

As powerful and plausible as utilitarianism is, however, it does not seem to be an altogether satisfactory moral position. Because it is a future-oriented ethic, one that requires that we act now to bring about the best results in the future, it seems to undervalue obligations we have acquired in the past. The obligation to keep a promise is a case in point. We are relieved of this obligation, according to utilitarians, if the results of breaking our word to one person will cause better consequences for others. . . .

This is not the only difficulty utilitarians must face. Consider flat-out lying, or even murder. If others will gain more than you would lose if I lie to you, or if I deliberately end your life, then utilitarianism implies that I would do no wrong in either case. And this seems as plainly false as any moral claim can be.

Utilitarianism also is open to the objection that it could sanction the worst kinds of oppression, including a system of indentured slavery. Of course, the theory will not allow us to ignore the interests of slaves, or to count their interests for less than the equal interests of their owners. Having abided by these rules, however, we still need to ask about the consequences: *Would it be better* to permit enslaving a few so that the many might prosper? . . .

Utilitarians have responses to these and related objections. Most moral philosophers find some or all of them unconvincing. Most moral philosophers, that is, are not utilitarians. But whatever the merits of utilitarianism, considered in general, its particular critique of anthropocentrism deserves our lasting applause. Some of our duties are *direct duties to other animals*. Utilitarians have shown that the anthropocentric emperor has no clothes. This much is clear. And it is also clear that commercial animal agriculture must be wrong if it systematically fails to consider the interests of nonhuman animals or fails to count their interests equitably. If this much can be shown—and Singer prosecutes this case persuasively—then the utilitarian case for vegetarianism, as well as its case against commercial animal agriculture, are strong indeed, even if the theory in general is weak.

THE RIGHTS VIEW

An alternative to the utilitarian attack on anthropocentrism, and one that also issues its own severe critique of commercial animal agriculture, is the rights view. Those who accept this view hold that (1) certain individuals have moral rights, and (2) these individuals have these rights independently of considerations about the value of the consequences. The rights view, then, is strongly opposed to utilitarianism. As such, it is not open to the most telling objections raised against this latter view. It matters not, for example, how much the many benefit from oppressing the few. Such oppression is and must be wrong, according to the rights view, because it systematically violates the basic rights of the oppressed.

For reasons given elsewhere in this volume I believe that many nonhuman animals are subjects of a life, have inherent value, and thus share with us an equal right to be treated with respect.[6] Morally important questions about line drawing must be addressed in this quarter just as in other morally troubling contexts. But wherever one draws the line with reason, the animals raised for human consumption are on "our" side of it. They are, that is, individuals with a biography, not merely a biology. Those who advocate the rights view, therefore, believe that these animals possess the fundamental moral right to be treated with respect.

ANIMAL RIGHTS AND ETHICAL VEGETARIANISM

. . . [T]he rights view calls for the total dissolution of commercial animal agriculture. . . . The *basic* wrong is that animals raised to be eaten are treated disrespectfully, as if they were "commodities," "economic units," "investments," "a renewable resource," and so on. In fact, they are biographical individuals and so, like us, are owed treatment that accords with the right to be treated with respect, a respect we fail to show when we end their life so that we might eat them.

Some people think the rights view is too "radical" or "extreme," calling as it does for the total abolition of a culturally accepted institution. But when an institution is grounded in injustice, as animal agriculture, according to the rights view, is, then there is no room for internal house cleaning. Morality will not be satisfied with anything less than its total abolition. And that, for the reasons given, is the rights view's verdict regarding commercial animal agriculture.

SOME PROBLEMS FOR THE RIGHTS VIEW

. . . Like utilitarianism, . . . the rights view is not free of problems. One concerns possible conflicts of rights, cases, for example, where in the nature of the case we cannot avoid harming someone. Whatever we do, *some* evil will result. What ought we to do in such cases? And how can we decide this without having

recourse to utilitarian considerations? It is not easy for advocates of the rights view to answer these questions, though answer them they must. If the moral life were void of such conflicts, moral theory would be vastly simpler. But the moral life is not free of such conflicts, which in part is why moral theory is so difficult. One thing is clear: We do not solve these difficulties just by appealing to "the rights of the individual," as if this venerable idea were a magic wand.[7]

A different challenge probes the meaning of respect. For the most part advocates of the rights view interpret this idea negatively. If we are to show respect for the individual, we must not treat the individual as a resource, must not treat the individual as a commodity, and so on. Is there a positive side to this idea? . . .

To some degree the rights view already has answered this question. When individuals are the victims of *human injustice*, we have a duty to help the victims. This is well and good, as far as it goes. But is that all there is? Do we owe nothing more? What of cases where the victims are not harmed because of human injustice but because of natural catastrophes—earthquakes, floods, and tornadoes, for example? Do we have a duty to help these human beings? If we do, is it possible for the rights view to explain this duty without having recourse to (what for them are forbidden) utilitarian considerations?

A more difficult question changes the plot only slightly. Suppose *some nonhuman animals* are being harmed by *other nonhuman animals* (for example, in predator-prey relationships). Do we have a duty to help? If so, which ones? The predators? Or the prey? Clearly, even if it is true, as I believe it is, that the rights view has answered some basic moral questions both correctly and decisively, there are many other important questions its advocates must address, and address fairly. Otherwise this philosophy, like any other, runs the risk of reducing itself to flag-waving propaganda.

HOLISM

The abolitionist implications of both the utilitarian and the rights view's critique of commercial animal agriculture suggest how far some philosophers have moved from the anthropocentric traditions of theism and humanism. . . .

[Yet, b]ecause both [utilitarianism and the rights view] use major ethical categories handed down by our predecessors, some influential thinkers argue that these positions, despite all appearances to the contrary, remain in bondage to anthropocentric prejudices. What is needed, these thinkers believe, is not a broader interpretation of traditional categories (for example, the category of "the rights of the individual"), but the overthrow of these very categories themselves. Only then will we have a new vision, one that liberates us from the last vestiges of anthropocentrism.

Among those whose thought moves in this direction none is more influential than Aldo Leopold's.[8] Leopold rejects the individualism so dear to the hearts of those who build their moral thinking on "the value (or rights) of the individual." What has ultimate value is not the individual but the collective, not the part but the whole, meaning the entire biosphere and its constituent ecosystems. Acts are right, Leopold believes, if they promote the integrity, beauty, diversity, and harmony of the biotic community;

they are wrong if they work against these values. . . .

HOLISM AND INDIVIDUAL ANIMALS

Holists face daunting challenges when it comes to determining what is right and wrong. These are to be determined by calculating the effects of our actions on the life community. Such calculations will not always be easy. Utilitarians . . . encounter a serious problem when they are asked to say what the consequences will be if we act in one way rather than another. And this problem arises for them despite the fact that they restrict their calculations to sentient life. How much more difficult it must be, then, to calculate the consequences for the entire *biosphere!*

But perhaps the situation for holists is not as dire as I have suggested. While it is true that we often lack detailed knowledge about how the biosphere is affected by human acts and practices, we sometimes know enough to say that some of the things we are doing are unhealthy for the larger community of life. For example, we do not know exactly how much we are contaminating the water of the earth by using rivers and oceans as garbage dumps for toxic wastes, or exactly how much protection afforded by the ozone layer is being compromised by our profligate use of chlorofluorocarbons. But we do know enough to realize that neither situation bodes well for marine and other life forms as we know them. . . .

Let us assume . . . that we sometimes are wise enough to understand that the effects of some human practices act like insatiable cancers eating away at the life community. From the perspective of holism, these practices are wrong, and they are wrong because of their detrimental effects on the interrelated systems of biological life.

It is important to realize that holists are aware of the catastrophic consequences toxic dumping and the ever-widening hole in the ozone layer are having on individual biographical beings—on seals and dolphins, for example. . . . What is fair and important to note, however, is that the suffering and death of these animals are not morally significant according to these thinkers. Morally, what matters is how the diversity, sustainability, and harmony of the larger community of life are affected, not what happens to individuals.

To make the holists' position clearer, consider the practice of trapping fur-bearing animals for commercial profit. Holists find nothing wrong with this economic venture so long as it does not disrupt the integrity, diversity, and sustainability of the ecosystem. Trappers cause such disruptions when they over-trap a particular species. . . . The over-trapping (and hunting) of wolves and other predatory animals in the north-eastern United States often is cited as a case in point, though not very convincingly in my view.[9] Once these natural predators were removed, other species of wildlife—deer in particular—are said to have overpopulated, so that today these animals actually imperil the very ecosystem that supports them. All this could have been avoided if, instead of rendering local populations of natural predators extinct by overtrapping and overhunting, they had been trapped or hunted more judiciously, with an eye to sustainable yield. Although a significant number of individual animals would have been killed, the integrity, harmony,

and sustainability of the ecosystem would have been preserved. When and if commercial trappers achieve these results, holists believe they do nothing wrong. From the perspective of holism, the inevitable suffering and untimely death of individual fur-bearing animals do not matter morally.

HOLISM AND ETHICAL VEGETARIANISM

Holism's position regarding the ethics of vegetarianism is analogous to its position regarding the ethics of commercial trapping. There is nothing wrong with raising animals for food if doing so is good for the larger life community. But it is wrong to do this if the community suffers. . . . If these animals are raised in an ecologically sensitive way, we do nothing wrong when we eat them.

While this may seem like good news to meat eaters, it isn't. Speaking generally, commercial animal agriculture is an ecological disaster. Or, rather, it is part of a more general ecological disaster, one that begins with grain production. Almost all the grain grown in affluent countries (over 90 percent of the oats, barley, and rye, for example) is used as animal feed. The agriculture that produces these massive amounts of animal feed is literally killing the planet. . . . Because the same crop is grown on the same land year after year after year (this is what is meant by saying the system is "monocultural"), and because of the heavy use of toxic synthetic chemicals such as herbicides, nematocides, and fungicides (this is what is meant by saying the system is "chemically intensive"), the future fertility of the land is being compromised.

And it is not just the land that is a casualty of modern agriculture. The quality of our water also is at risk. Once applied to crops, chemicals do not disappear. Often they run off into neighboring creeks or rivers, or trickle down through the earth into underground lakes only to surface again, at some other time and place. We do not speak loosely when we say that chemically intensive, monocultural agriculture is far and away the greatest single cause of the deteriorating quality of the earth's water supply. Because commercial animal agriculture is the largest consumer of a system of grain production that has these deleterious ecological consequences, holists can, and holists are, speaking out in favor of a vegetarian way of life.[10]

There is a longer story to be told about the ecological carnage attributable to commercial animal farming, a *much* longer story than can be told here, one that would detail, for example, the environmental degradation that is the *direct* result of factory farms.[11] Suffice it to say on this occasion that the more we learn about why and how commercial animal agriculture is implicated in environmental degradation, the stronger holism's case in favor of vegetarianism becomes, and this, paradoxically, despite the fact that what is done to the animals meat eaters eat is not morally relevant.

SOME PROBLEMS FOR HOLISM

. . . [H]olism goes too far when it maintains that any ecologically sensitive human practice is right. This must be false, if any moral claim is. Judged on the basis of all the available evidence, cotton production in the antebellum South was ecologically sensitive. The ecology of the area was in harmony, the agriculture was sustainable. Yet surely we are not prepared to say that the forced labor of indentured slaves was therefore quite all right. There is more to morality than asking how the life community is affected by what we do. There are also questions that concern the justice of how we do them. Because holists like Leopold look only to ecological ends and neglect the ethics of the means used to achieve them, their position is a half-truth at best, a serious threat to justice at worst.

What is true of holism's inability to criticize ecologically sensitive but unjust practices involving human beings, is no less true of similar practices involving other animals. This can be illustrated by first considering commercial trapping. It is not enough to ask whether commercial trapping is ecologically sensitive, since, like cotton produced by slaves, it might be this and *still* be wrong. We also need to ask (minimally) how this end is achieved.

Among the things we know is this. Some traps used by trappers, such as the infamous steel-jawed leghold trap, are veritable instruments of torture. Most civilized countries have outlawed the steel-jawed leghold trap because of its barbarous cruelty. Holists must find it difficult to add their voice. What matters to them is not the means, and not whether fur-bearing animals suffer, but whether trapping is sustainable. Surely this cannot be right. Quite aside from questions of sustainable populations, the suffering of individual trapped animals matters morally, just as, quite aside from questions about sustainable agriculture, the suffering of human slaves matters morally, too.

An analogous argument can be given in the case of commercial animal agriculture. Even when this form of agriculture is ecologically sensitive (increasingly rare in this day of factory farms), it does not follow that it is right. We must also ask, How is this end achieved? What are the means? The means, in the simplest terms, are: by bringing about the untimely death of biographical animals. Does this matter morally? Not to holists. But, then, neither does the untimely death of human beings who, by their forced labors, contribute, like the good "team members" they are, to ecological sustainability. On a previous occasion I characterized the sort of holism we find in Leopold as "environmental fascism."[12] This indictment remains. Like political fascism, where the individual is made to serve the interests of the larger political community, an unbridled ecological holism, where it is permissible to force the individual to serve the interests of the larger life community, is fascistic too. . . .

SAMENESS AMONG THE DIFFERENCES

. . . Most people who read this . . . , and who still eat meat, will buy the meat they eat at nationally franchised food stores. This meat is therefore the end product of factory farms. How we know this is simple. It's a matter of economics. Wholesalers and retailers buy as cheap as they can, which means—in the case of meat—at the trough of factory farms. It's that simple.

Now, despite their many differences, proponents of these three philosophies— utilitarians, holists, and advocates of the rights view—can speak with one voice on some occasions. This is one of them. All agree that factory farming is wrong: wrong because it violates the rights of individual animals (the position of the advocate of the rights view), wrong because it either does not count the interests of nonhuman animals at all or does not count them equitably (the utilitarian's position), or wrong because it is destroying the ecology of the planet (the holist's position). Cut it any way you wish, these influential philosophies agree: This form of animal agriculture is wrong.

If the system of supply is wrong, what about individual consumers? Can these three views, despite their many differences, reach the same conclusion here too? They can. Viewed against the backdrop of factory farming, each can say the same thing (though for different reasons): *Vegetarianism is ethically required.* And that is enough for the rest of us to digest today. More than enough, really, since to unburden one's self of the weight of culturally conditioned prejudices (and a culturally encouraged palate) is not easy. For a while, then, it is enough to act on the conclusion these philosophers have put on our plates: Give up eating meat. After some good vegetarian food we can ask which one of these three philosophies has the right reasons. There is time enough to ask many interesting questions with our words, but limited time to answer some of the more important ones with our deeds.

NOTES

1. Kant's views are set forth in a short section of his *Lectures on Ethics*, trans. Louis Infield (New York: Harper and Row, 1963), pp. 239–41. They are included in *Animal Rights and Human Obligations*, ed. Tom Regan and Peter Singer (Englewood Cliffs, N.J.: Prentice-Hall, 1976, 1st ed., pp. 122–23; and 1989, 2d ed., pp. 23–24).

2. Thomas Aquinas, *Summa Contra Gentiles*, literally translated by the English Dominican Fathers (Benziger Brothers, 1928), Book 3, pt. 2, chap. 112. For a more readily available source, see Regan and Singer, *Animal Rights and Human Obligations*, 1st ed., pp. 58–59; and 2d ed., pp. 8–9.

3. Jeremy Bentham, *The Principles of Morals and Legislation* (1789), chap. 17, sec. 1. Reprinted in

Regan and Singer, *Animal Rights and Human Obligations*, 1st ed., p. 130; and 2d ed., p. 26.

4. See, in particular, Peter Singer, *Animal Liberation*, 2d ed. (New York: Random House, 1990).

5. Richard Ryder, *Speciesism: The Ethics of Vivisection* (Edinburgh: Scottish Society for the Prevention of Vivisection, 1974). See also his *Victims of Science* (Fontwell, England: Centaur Press, 1983).

6. See, in particular, [*The Thee Generation* (Philadelphia: Temple University Press, 1991)] Chapter 3, "Ill-Gotten Gains."

7. For my responses to the problems raised against the rights view, see *The Case for Animal Rights* (Berkeley: University of California Press; London: Routledge and Kegan Paul, 1983).

8. See, in particular, Aldo Leopold, *A Sand County Almanac* (New York: Baltimore Books, 1970).

9. For a compelling response to this view, see Ron Baker, *The American Hunting Myth* (New York: Vantage Press, 1987).

10. See, for example, J. Baird Callicott, "In Search of an Environmental Ethic," in *Matters of Life and Death*, 2d ed., ed. Tom Regan, pp. 381–424 (New York: McGraw-Hill, 1986).

11. The best account of these results is found in Jim Mason and Peter Singer, *Animal Factories* (New York: Crown, 1980).

12. Regan, *The Case for Animal Rights*, esp. chaps. 7 and 8.

NO

Philip E. Devine

THE MORAL BASIS OF VEGETARIANISM

If someone abstains from meat-eating for reasons of taste or personal economics, no moral or philosophical question arises. But when a vegetarian attempts to persuade others that they, too, should adopt his diet, then what he says requires philosophical attention.[1] While a vegetarian might argue in any number of ways, this essay will be concerned only with the argument for a vegetarian diet resting on a moral objection to the rearing and killing of animals[2] for the human table. The vegetarian, in this sense, does not merely require us to change or justify our eating habits, but to reconsider our attitudes and behaviour towards members of other species across a wide range of practices. . . .

I

There are two approaches a vegetarian might take in arguing that rearing and killing animals for food is morally offensive. He might argue that eating animals is morally bad because of the pain inflicted on animals in rearing and killing them to be eaten. Or he could object to the killing itself.

These two kinds of argument support rather different conclusions. A vegetarian of the first sort has no grounds for objecting to the eating of animals—molluscs for example—too rudimentary in their development to feel pain. Nor could he object to meat-eating if the slaughter were completely painless and the raising of animals at least as comfortable as life in the wild. Nor could he object to the painless killing of wild animals. Such a vegetarian will, however, object to the drinking of milk, since the production of milk requires a painful separation between cow and calf. He will also object to the eating of eggs laid by hens which did not have scope for normal activity. (He will not, however, object to the eating of fertile eggs as such.) To that extent, he will be not only a vegetarian, but also a vegan, one who abstains not only from meat but also from animal products.

One might of course defend the consumption of animal products, while opposing the eating of meat, on the ground that killing a steer, say, produces

From Philip E. Devine, "The Moral Basis of Vegetarianism," *Philosophy*, vol. 53 (1978). Copyright © 1978 by The Royal Institute of Philosophy. Reprinted by permission of Cambridge University Press.

more suffering than separating a cow from her calf. The argument seems to me a chancy one, but an intermediate kind of vegetarian on this kind of ground does seem possible.

In contrast, a vegetarian who has objections only to the killing of animals will object to all forms of meat, but he will not object to milk or eggs, so long as the eggs are not fertile. For such a vegetarian, a borderline case would be the consumption of animal products not, in the ordinary course of nature, produced by the animal; for instance the drinking of cattle blood as practised by the Masai. Of course one could be a vegetarian on both grounds, and object to anything either kind of vegetarian objects to.

There is an important difference between the two kinds of vegetarian in the casuistry of diet. For one who objects to the killing of animals, the moral question will be straightforward. A meat diet requires that animals be killed, and to demand that animals be killed—whether by buying meat from the butcher, ordering a meat dish in a restaurant, or accepting an invitation to dinner in the expectation that meat will be served—will be wrong if killing animals for food is wrong. But if what one objects to is animal pain, the moral situation is cloudier. One might argue that more pain is inflicted on animals on factory farms than is morally acceptable, while still holding that animals could be killed for food with a morally acceptable degree of pain if the imperative to do so were recognized. And so, unless there is a moral objection to consuming a product which has an injustice in its history, the eating of meat might be legitimate though the way animals are reared and killed is not.

The premise that it is in general wrong to benefit from another's wrong-doing cannot be accepted. A child conceived in rape is obliged neither to kill himself nor to lament his own existence. If we live in the United States, the land on which we live, and on which our bread is grown, is land unjustly taken from the Indians. And yet it is difficult to argue that we have an obligation to leave the country or abstain from all products grown here. A similar point can be made for the inhabitants of most other parts of the world. I am not defending indifference to the injustices taking place in one's world, only maintaining that while a person might have an obligation to protest against the injustices from which he benefits, he does not have an obligation to refuse to consume the products of injustice. There has been so much injustice in human history that untainted merchandise is not available. . . .

[V]egetarians on strictly moral grounds fall into two classes: those who object to the infliction of suffering on animals, and those who object to killing them. . . . While a vegetarian of the second sort can appeal to a highly plausible moral principle to support the claim that one ought to abstain entirely from meat-eating, no such principle is available for a vegetarian of the first sort. It is possible in good conscience to consume meat and other animal products while regretting and even opposing the suffering imposed on animals in producing these items. Let us examine the credentials of each of the two kinds of vegetarian argument.

II

The first argument starts with the fact that animals are capable of suffering pain, and do in fact suffer pain in being reared and slaughtered for food. To this fact it adds the widely shared ethical premise that pain is an intrinsic evil. Since it seems self-evident that it is wrong to produce an intrinsic evil for no reason at all, it follows that it is wrong to produce pain, including animal pain, for no reason at all. In other words, to cause animal pain is *prima facie* wrong.

But of course no one defends inflicting pain on animals for no reason at all. Practices entailing pain for animals are defended by the benefits they produce for human beings. In particular, the practice of killing and rearing animals for food is justified as necessary to provide for human beings the kind of food that they want. The question at issue is whether this benefit is a sufficient justification for the rearing and killing of animals. . . .

'Pain' and 'suffering' are . . . words in human language. The ascription of these experiences to ourselves and other human beings is part of a complex mode of human life, including the making of statements like 'I am in pain' as well as inarticulate expressions of pain, the noticing of damage to the body, and various forms of care for those in distress. Now in the case of animals one crucial element is lacking—animals are permanently and by their nature[3] incapable of telling that they are in pain, as distinct from (say) moaning. That this is the case does not mean that we should, like Descartes, refuse to ascribe pain of any sort to non-human animals. But it may well justify ascribing to them pains of much less intensity than those we ascribe to human beings. And it is this that from a utilitarian standpoint should be the crucial issue. . . .

Pain involves elements both of emotion and sensation—both of distress and of a particular kind of feeling which char-acteristically (but not invariably) produces such distress.[4] Now it is the capacity for pain as a sensation which chiefly unites human beings with other animals. But a credible hedonist theory of the good cannot maintain that only painful sensation is bad, but must instead take as its intrinsic evil suffering and distress. And it is highly plausible to maintain that non-human animals—even supposing that they experience pain as a sensation as intensely as human beings do—experience far less suffering. It would, however, be more accurate to speak here, not of more or less intense sufferings, but of sufferings of greater or lesser conceptual richness. A cow may experience some distress at losing her calf, but it makes little sense to speak of her grief.

The vegetarian may reply that animals still suffer intensely enough to warrant his conclusions. And it is easy enough to describe the suffering of animals in vivid terms while deprecating the 'trivial desires' of the human palate. But the question is whether such rhetoric is appropriate: whether for example it is appropriate to compare the sufferings of a cow separated from her calf with the feelings of a human mother in a similar situation, or the feelings of a dying fish with those of a dying human being. Everything seems to depend on how we perceive animals: if we see birds as winged people and cattle as our four-footed cousins, then we will be disposed to take their sufferings very seriously; if not, we will not be so disposed.

A second vegetarian strategy is simply to reject as immoral the balancing of animal pains against human pleasures. Thus John Harris's reply to the Benthamite defence of meat-eating [based on the idea that animal suffering is outweighed by human pleasure] is quite simply: 'Those who use it are saying that they think more about their stomach than their morals, and so a moral argument will probably not affect them'.[5] We can call this move the deontological stop.

Deontological stops are not uncommon in philosophical discussions of moral questions. Perhaps the best known is in G. E. M. Anscombe's outburst: 'If anyone really thinks, *in advance*, that it is open to question whether such an action as procuring the judicial execution of the innocent should be excluded from consideration—I do not want to argue with him; he shows a corrupt mind'.[6] And it may not be possible to avoid them without giving up the discussion of practical issues altogether or claiming, implausibly, that our arguments could have convinced Hitler or Stalin. But Anscombe could at least count on a certain aversion to judicial murder on the part of her audience. For a vegetarian to employ a deontological stop against those who defend the eating of meat would be to guarantee that vegetarian views will remain, and deserve to remain, the exclusive property of a sect.

A third vegetarian strategy is the formulation of a plausible nonutilitarian principle, . . . One such principle has been formulated in the following terms by Tom Regan: 'No practice which causes undeserved non-trivial pain can be justified solely on the ground of the amount of pleasure it brings about for others'.[7] This principle is acceptable (I should hope) to nearly everyone when the pain in question is inflicted on human beings or persons. Whether it applies to pain inflicted on animals, however, is another matter altogether.

One indication that this principle should not be applied to pains inflicted on the animals is the word 'undeserved'.

While it is not strictly speaking false to say that an animal experiences undeserved pains, such a statement is surely misleading. Non-human animals—and vegetarians insist on this point as much as anyone—are not moral agents and thus can neither deserve to suffer nor, in a significant sense, suffer undeservedly. (They may of course still suffer in ways they ought not to.) A wolf which eats a lamb and a female hamster which eats her young are not guilty: neither are they, in a significant sense, innocent. Considerations of retributive justice, whether they are thought to warrant the infliction of deserved suffering or only to forbid the infliction of undeserved suffering, are irrelevant to the treatment of animals. . . .

A final vegetarian strategy goes as follows. Granted, the vegetarian might say, that if we take our present tastes in food as immutable we get more pleasure out of eating meat (or would suffer more from abandoning the habit) than animals suffer pain by being killed and reared for our table. But our tastes in food are not immutable. If we come to adopt a vegetarian regimen, we will find that we enjoy a vegetarian diet as much as we enjoy a meat one, and the sum of happiness prevailing in the universe will thus be increased. Perhaps the recipes and so on which Singer appends to his book are not merely helps to virtuous and happy living, but essential parts of his argument.

The problem is how the vegetarian knows that his meat-eating associates would enjoy a vegetarian (or vegan) diet as much as one containing meat, or that they could successfully free themselves of their desire for this form of food. The question would seem altogether to be one of individual psychology. Moreover, the prospect of guilt-feelings experienced by backsliding vegetarians, and of the harmful effects of repressing desires for meat (kinds of considerations utilitarians are ready enough to emphasize in other contexts) make the arguments from mutable habits an extremely unattractive one.

The sum of the matter is as follows. Either the vegetarian argues on utilitarian premises, or he tries to supplement or replace his utilitarianism with some plausible non-utilitarian principles implying the wrongfulness of rearing and killing animals for food. In the first case, there is no way around the suggestion, which many people appear to believe, that animal experience is so lacking in intensity that the pains of animals are overridden by the pleasures experienced by human beings. That the argument may appear cynical is no concern of the utilitarian, who is forced by his moral theory to admit the relevance of even the most cynical-seeming arguments. On the other hand, all the non-utilitarian principles which have been put forward turn out on inspection to have reference only to human beings. If they were to be abandoned, the practical result would be more likely to be that human beings would be treated as we now treat animals rather than animals as we now treat (or believe that we should treat) human beings.

III

At least such is the result of taking seriously only the pains suffered by animals in being reared and killed for food. Perhaps a different result will be reached by taking into account the value of the animals' existence. . . .

As Robert Nozick has observed, we should not conclude that an animal's existence is not important to it until we have a better idea of how our existence is important to us. And, as Roslind Godlovitch has observed, it seems absurd to kill a healthy animal 'to prevent cruelty', but such killing seems to be what is required if we wish only to avoid animal pain and care nothing for animal existence.[8]

Animal shelters often seem to act on this assumption, for instance by destroying unwanted kittens; but one suspects that what is really at work here, as in the practice of spaying or neutering pets, is an interest of human beings in keeping down the pet population. *Prima facie*, it would seem that sexual (and in the case of a female animal, reproductive) satisfactions are more important in the life of an animal than they are in that of a human being. Likewise, quite arguably the existence of an animal is more important relative to its other interests than is the case with a human being, since animals lack the various ways that human beings have of transcending their own deaths.

But none of this establishes how important animal existence is when it conflicts with human desires. In rough terms, animal life may be lived at such a low level of intensity that its value provides no serious competition with human gastronomic interests. . . .

There are . . . specific considerations of moral importance on the side of meat-eating. There are forms of human solidarity expressed by eating together, and the effect of food prohibitions will be to break up these forms, or at least to make them more difficult.

At another level, while priority arguments are notoriously slippery, it remains the case that the energies available for moral and social reform or revolution, including the reform of one's own habits, are not unlimited. And there is evidence among vegetarians of a turning away from human problems to the question of animal liberation. Singer for instance observes:

> All reasonable people want to prevent war, racial inequality, inflation, and unemployment; the problem is that we have been trying to prevent these things for years, and now we have to admit that we do not really know how to do it. By comparison, the reduction of the sufferings of non-human animals at the hands of humans will be relatively easy, once human beings set themselves to do it.[9]

But the only reason why the task of animal liberation might look easy is that it is so far from success.

More subtly, vegetarianism might actually interfere with the attempt to improve the lot of human beings. A radical moral position has its costs, since it makes it easier for one's opponents to dismiss one as an eccentric. So that someone who wishes to change society should not be in a hurry to accept every radical moral position that looks vaguely attractive.[10]

None of this would matter, perhaps, were the vegetarian clearly right in his central contentions. But since he is not, since what we have here is a question of balancing values of very different sorts in a way of whose outcome we can never be really confident, considerations of the above sort do seem to bear very heavily towards the rejection of the vegetarian moral position.

[Another vegetarian argument] is the argument from moral progress. One way moral progress takes place is by extending the scope of moral concern from the tribe to the nation, from the nation to the world, and so on. And so we should take the next step and extend our moral concern to animals. Once having done so, we will be unable to justify eating meat any longer.

I am not sure that everyone accepts the characterization of moral progress just offered. . . .

Moral progress consists, it would seem, in discovering what the requirements of morality are and learning to keep them. So that whether a given change in our opinions constitutes moral progress depends entirely on whether it constitutes movement towards, or away from, the correct moral opinions. Hence one cannot argue for a change in moral belief as progressive without first arguing that it is (at least) a movement towards moral truth, in other words without having already decided the crucial question at issue.

Perhaps the progressive argument could be made like this. To an unknown extent, the moral requirements binding upon us are a function of the contingencies of our society, including its conventions. If a society improves or degenerates, these requirements change—in the one case we have moral progress, in the other moral retreat. And the changes which would produce a duty to stop rearing and killing animals for food would be desirable ones. But, supposing this to be so, it is still the case that a possible and desirable future in which a change in our mode of life would become morally required does not of itself establish that such a change is morally required now. Thus the upshot of the discussion . . . is that it is morally legitimate (at least in the present world) to rear and kill non-human animals for the human table.

NOTES

1. Pride of place among contemporary philosophical vegetarians probably belongs to Peter Singer. Singer's contribution includes an article (in *Moral Problems*, James Rachels (ed.), 2nd ed. (New York: 1975)) and a book (*New York Review*, 1975), both sharing the title 'Animal Liberation'.

Singer's essay started life as a review (in *The New York Review of Books*) of *Animals, Man and Morals*, Stanley and Roslind Godlovitch and John Harris (eds), (New York: Grove, n.d.). Another anthology is *Animal Rights and Human Obligations*, Peter Singer and Tom Regan (eds), (Englewood Cliffs, New Jersey: Prentice-Hall, 1976).

Also worthy of mention are Tom Regan, 'The Moral Basis of Vegetarianism', *Canadian Journal of Philosophy*, V, No. 2 (October, 1975) and the discussion in Robert Nozick, *Anarchy, State, and Utopia* (Oxford: Blackwell, n.d.), 35 ff. Stephen R. L. Clark, *The Moral Status of Animals* (Oxford, 1977), is of special interest as a Christian vegetarian, but does not contribute much to the vegetarian argument. See also A. M. MacIver, 'Ethics and the Beetle', in *Ethics*, Judith J. Thomson and Gerald Dworkin (eds), (New York: Harper & Row, 1968).

Useful critical discussions include Kevin Donaghy, 'Singer on Speciesism', *Philosophic Exchange* (Summer, 1974); Bonnie Steinbock, 'Speciesism and the Idea of Equality', American Philosophical Association (Eastern Division), 1975 (published in *Philosophy*, April, 1978); and Ronald DeSousa's comments on Steinbock's paper.

I am also indebted to the following for criticisms and suggestions: Merritt Abrash, Albert Flores, Roger Guttentag, James Hanink, John Koller, Joseph Ryshpan and David Wieck.

I discuss the issues concerning the killing of human beings touched on in this paper in *The Ethics of Homicide* (Cornell University Press, 1978).

2. One might object to the use of the word 'animal' in this context, as concealing the fact that human beings are also a kind of animal. But while this objection has greater merit than most ideological objections to common usage, it would be pedantic to attempt a greater revolutionary purity than that achieved by the revolutionaries themselves.

3. The phrase 'permanently and by their nature' distinguishes animal pain from that of human infants for example.

4. For an attempt to sort out these elements, see Roger Trigg, *Pain and Emotion* (Oxford: 1970).

5. John Harris, 'Killing for Food', *Animals, Men and Morals*, op. cit., n. I, p. 99.

6. G. E. M. Anscombe, 'Modern Moral Philosophy', in Thomson and Dworkin (eds), op. cit., n. I, 206–207.

7. Regan, op. cit., n. I, 199.

8. Roslind Godlovitch, 'Animals and Morals', in *Animals, Men and Morals*, op. cit., n. I.

9. *Animal Liberation*, op. cit., n. I, 245–246.

10. This is the point of George Orwell's discussion (*The Road to Wigan Pier* (New York: 1958), pp. 173–175).

POSTSCRIPT

Does Morality Require a Vegetarian Way of Life?

Devine claims that the demands of those who support vegetarianism are revolutionary. Regan would probably agree. The demands are revolutionary in that they are part of a change in our attitudes toward animals and in our eating habits. But they are not revolutionary in the sense that they are totally disconnected from our moral traditions. Regan argues that utilitarian theory, the rights view, and the holist approach all support vegetarianism.

Revolutionary ideas always have a danger of initially seeming unsound, though, and one claim that Regan makes that might sound ridiculous is that animals share with us an equal right to be treated with respect. This does not mean that if part of the respectful treatment of people is to offer them a chair when they enter a room, then we should offer animals a chair too. Chickens, for example, do not sit in chairs, so it is no mark of respect to provide them with one. But it does offend against their rights—a rights theorist like Regan would say—to crowd them into cages, cut off their beaks, and raise them for food.

Utilitarians who support vegetarianism would want to look into the positive and negative consequences of meat-eating. A useful book here is C. David Coats, *Old MacDonald's Factory Farm: The Myth of the Traditional Farm and the Shocking Truth About Animal Suffering in Today's Agribusiness* (Continuum, 1989). Here we find out that the serene images many people have of a peaceful and pleasant barnyard do not correspond at all to the big business of raising animals for food.

James Rachels, in "Vegetarianism and 'The Other Weight Problem,' " in Aiken and La Follette, eds., *World Hunger and Moral Obligation* (Prentice Hall, 1977), points out that much of the protein that we produce in this country (in plant form) is wastefully transformed into animal protein, resulting in less available protein for people. The "other weight problem" has to do with people who suffer from malnutrition or die of starvation.

Perhaps the strongest spokesman on this whole topic is Peter Singer, who edited *In Defense of Animals* (Basil Blackwell, 1985) and authored *Animal Liberation: A New Ethics for Our Treatment of Animals*, 2d ed. (Random House, 1990). One answer to Singer's idea of animal liberation is Michael Leahy's *Against Liberation: Putting Animals in Perspective* (Routledge, 1991).

Further sources are Tom Regan, *The Case For Animal Rights* (University of California Press, 1983); Cora Diamond, "Eating Meat and Eating People," *Philosophy* (1978); R. G. Frey, *Rights, Killing, and Suffering* (Basil Blackwell, 1983); S. F. Sapontzis, *Morals, Reason, and Animals* (Temple University Press, 1987); and the quarterly journals *Ethics & Animals* and *Between the Species*. See also the January 1987 issue of *The Monist*, which is devoted to the discussion of animal rights.

ISSUE 9

Does Society Have an Obligation to Care for the Less Well Off?

YES: Trudy Govier, from "The Right to Eat and the Duty to Work," *Philosophy of the Social Sciences* (June 1975)

NO: Irving Kristol, from *Two Cheers for Capitalism* (Basic Books, 1978)

ISSUE SUMMARY

YES: Canadian philosopher Trudy Govier argues that society does have an obligation to care for the less well off, and that welfare should be provided without being made contingent upon something (a willingness to work, for example).

NO: Author and social critic Irving Kristol argues that society should not redistribute wealth to the less well off but should promote economic growth in general.

The first question that might be asked about the "less well off" is, how desperate are they? If it is the case that income and wealth simply vary, so that some people have more and some less, then, unless we favor some strict form of egalitarianism, this economic discrepancy alone need not present a problem. But how should we respond if those who are less well off are unable to provide for themselves even basic needs, such as food, shelter, and medicine? There are social critics who argue that a rich society that does not provide all members with the basic necessities is failing at a most fundamental level.

It is clear that some people in the United States (and in other similarly wealthy industrial nations) do not have even their basic needs met. In any large city we can see people sleeping on sidewalks, next to subway grates, or under bridges. Moreover, the ranks of the homeless now include not only single men but also women, children, and families. If you live in a small town or in a place where the homeless are not visible, the plight of the homeless may not be familiar to you firsthand. But it should be familiar from newspaper stories, magazine articles, and television reports. There is even a danger that we have been overexposed to the homeless and have consequently become callous to them and insensitive to their problems.

Government statistics show that poverty and unemployment rates are particularly high among young urban minorities and for families headed by single women. Poor people in the United States are more likely to be victims of violent crimes, have higher infant mortality rates, and are less healthy than the general population.

In our society, which is predominantly capitalistic, people fulfill needs, including basic needs, through the mechanism of the marketplace—we purchase the goods and services we require. But the market does not provide for the needs of those who simply do not have the money to purchase basic goods.

How should we respond? One might argue that society has an obligation to meet the basic needs of its less fortunate citizens, whether those people can afford goods or not, and whether those people are willing to contribute to a free enterprise system or not. A second approach is to argue that the economic system should be made so prosperous that everyone could afford any good they really want.

In the following selections, Trudy Govier argues that society has a direct obligation to meet the fundamental needs of its members and to do so unconditionally (and not, for example, only on the condition that people are willing to work). Irving Kristol argues that society should not provide welfare programs in order to meet citizens' basic needs, but should promote general economic growth that will raise everyone's standard of living.

YES

Trudy Govier

THE RIGHT TO EAT
AND THE DUTY TO WORK

Although the topic of welfare is not one with which philosophers have often concerned themselves, it is a topic which gives rise to many complex and fascinating questions—some in the area of political philosophy, some in the area of ethics, and some of a more practical kind. The variety of issues related to the subject of welfare makes it particularly necessary to be clear just which issue one is examining in a discussion of welfare. In a recent book on the subject, Nicholas Rescher asks:

> In what respects and to what extent is society, working through the instrumentality of the state, responsible for the welfare of its members? What demands for the promotion of his welfare can an individual reasonably make upon his society? These are questions to which no answer can be given in terms of some *a priori* approach with reference to universal ultimates. Whatever answer can appropriately be given will depend, in the final analysis, on what the society decides it should be.[1]

Rescher raises this question only to avoid it. His response to his own question is that a society has all and only those responsibilities for its members that it thinks it has. Although this claim is trivially true as regards legal responsibilities, it is inadequate from a moral perspective. If one imagines the case of an affluent society which leaves the blind, the disabled, and the needy to die of starvation, the incompleteness of Rescher's account becomes obvious. In this imagined case one is naturally led to raise the question as to whether those in power ought to supply those in need with the necessities of life. Though the needy have no legal right to welfare benefits of any kind, one might very well say that they ought to have such a right. It is this claim which I propose to discuss here.

I shall approach this issue by examining three positions which may be adopted in response to it. These are:

(1) *The Individualist Position:* Even in an affluent society, one ought not to have any legal right to state-supplied welfare benefits.

From Trudy Govier, "The Right to Eat and the Duty to Work," *Philosophy of the Social Sciences*, vol. 5 (1975). Copyright © 1975 by *Philosophy of the Social Sciences*. Reprinted by permission of Wilfrid Laurier University Press.

(2) *The Permissive Position:* In a society with sufficient resources, one ought to have an unconditional legal right to receive state-supplied welfare benefits. (That is, one's right to receive such benefits ought not to depend on one's behaviour; it should be guaranteed.)

(3) *The Puritan Position:* In a society with sufficient resources one ought to have a legal right to state-supplied welfare benefits; this right ought to be conditional, however, on one's willingness to work. . . .

1. The Individualist View

It might be maintained that a person in need has no legitimate moral claim on those around him and that the hypothetical inattentive society which left its blind citizens to beg or starve cannot rightly be censured for doing so. This view is vividly portrayed in the writings of Ayn Rand and her followers.[2] The Individualist sets a high value on uncoerced personal choice. He sees each person as a responsible agent who is able to make his own decisions and to plan his own life. He insists that with the freedom to make decisions goes responsibility for the consequences of those decisions. A person has every right, for example, to spend ten years of his life studying Sanskrit—but if, as a result of this choice, he is unemployable, he ought not to expect others to labour on his behalf. No one has a proper claim on the labour of another, or on the income ensuing from that labour, unless he can repay the labourer in a way acceptable to that labourer himself. Government welfare schemes provide benefits from funds gained largely by taxing earned income. One cannot "opt out" of such schemes. To the Individualist, this means that a person is forced to work part of his time for others.

Suppose that a man works forty hours and earns two hundred dollars. Under modern-day taxation, it may well be that he can spend only two-thirds of that money as he chooses. The rest is taken by government and goes to support programmes which the working individual may not himself endorse. The beneficiaries of such programmes—those beneficiaries who do not work themselves—are as though they have slaves working for them. Backed by the force which government authorities can command, they are able to exist on the earnings of others. Those who support them do not do so voluntarily, out of charity; they do so on government command.

Someone across the street is unemployed. Should you be taxed extra to pay for his expenses? Not at all. You have not injured him, you are not responsible for the fact that he is unemployed (unless you are a senator or bureaucrat who agitated for further curtailing of business which legislation passed, with the result that your neighbour was laid off by the curtailed business). You may voluntarily wish to help him out, or better still, try to get him a job to put him on his feet again; but since you have initiated no aggressive act against him, and neither purposefully nor accidentally injured him in any way, you should not be legally penalized for the fact of his unemployment.[3]

The Individualist need not lack concern for those in need. He may give generously to charity; he might give more generously still, if his whole income were his to use, as he would like it to be. He may also believe that, as a matter of empirical fact, existing government programmes do not actually help the poor. They support a cumbersome bureaucracy and they use financial resources which, if untaxed, might be used by those with initiative to pursue job-creating endeavours. The thrust of the Individualist's position is that each person owns his own body and his own labour; thus each person is taken to have a virtually unconditional right to the income which that labour can earn him in a free market place. For anyone to pre-empt part of a worker's earnings without that worker's voluntary consent is tantamount to robbery. And the fact that the government is the intermediary through which this deed is committed does not change its moral status one iota.

On an Individualist's view, those in need should be cared for by charities or through other schemes to which contributions are voluntary. Many people may wish to insure themselves against unforeseen calamities and they should be free to do so. But there is no justification for non-optional government schemes financed by taxpayers money. . . .

2. The Permissive View

Directly contrary to the Individualist view of welfare is what I have termed the Permissive view. According to this view, in a society which has sufficient resources so that everyone could be supplied with the necessities of life, every individual ought to be given the legal right to social security, and this right ought not to be conditional in any way upon an individual's behaviour. *Ex hypothesi* the society which we are discussing has sufficient goods to provide everyone with food, clothing, shelter and other necessities. Someone who does without these basic goods is scarcely living at all, and a society which takes no steps to change this state of affairs implies by its inaction that the life

of such a person is without value. It does not execute him; but it may allow him to die. It does not put him in prison; but it may leave him with a life of lower quality than that of some prison inmates. A society which can rectify these circumstances and does not can justly be accused of imposing upon the needy either death or lifelong deprivation. And those characteristics which make a person needy—whether they be illness, old age, insanity, feeblemindedness, inability to find paid work, or even poor moral character—are insufficient to make him deserve the fate to which an inactive society would in effect condemn him. One would not be executed for inability or failure to find paid work; neither should one be allowed to die for this misfortune or failing. . . .

The adoption of a Permissive view of welfare would have significant practical implications. If there were a legal right, unconditional upon behaviour, to a specified level of state-supplied benefits, then state investigation of the prospective welfare recipient could be kept to a minimum. Why he is in need, whether he can work, whether he is willing to work, and what he does while receiving welfare benefits are on this view quite irrelevant to his right to receive those benefits. . . . If the Permissive view of welfare were widely believed, then there would be no social stigma attached to being on welfare. There is such a stigma, and many long-term welfare recipients are considerably demoralized by their dependent status.[4] These facts suggest that the Permissive view of welfare is not widely held in our society.

3. The Puritan View

This view of welfare rather naturally emerges when we consider that no one can have a right to something without someone else's, or some group of other persons', having responsibilities correlative to this right. In the case in which the right in question is a legal right to social security, the correlative responsibilities may be rather extensive. They have been deemed responsibilities of "the state." The state will require resources and funds to meet these responsibilities, and these do not emerge from the sky miraculously, or zip into existence as a consequence of virtually effortless acts of will. They are taken by the state from its citizens, often in the form of taxation on earned income. The funds given to the welfare recipient and many of the goods which he purchases with these funds are produced by other members of society, many of whom give a considerable portion of their time and their energy to this end. If a state has the moral responsibility to ensure the social security of its citizens then all the citizens of that state have the responsibility to provide state agencies with the means to carry out their duties. This responsibility, in our present contingent circumstances, seems to generate an obligation to *work*.

A person who works helps to produce the goods which all use in daily living and, when paid, contributes through taxation to government endeavours. The person who does not work, even though able to work, does not make his contribution to social efforts towards obtaining the means of life. He is not entitled to a share of the goods produced by others if he chooses not to take part in their labours. Unless he can show that there is a moral justification for his not making the sacrifice of time and energy which others make, he has no legitimate claim to welfare benefits. If he is disabled or unable to obtain work, he cannot work; hence

he has no need to justify his failure to work. But if he does choose not to work, he would have to justify his choice by saying "others should sacrifice their time and energy for me; I have no need to sacrifice time and energy for them." This principle, a version of what Rawls refers to as a free-rider's principle, simply will not stand up to criticism.[5] To deliberately avoid working and benefit from the labours of others is morally indefensible.

Within a welfare system erected on these principles, the right to welfare is conditional upon one's satisfactorily accounting for his failure to obtain the necessities of life by his own efforts. Someone who is severely disabled mentally or physically, or who for some other reason cannot work, is morally entitled to receive welfare benefits. Someone who chooses not to work is not. The Puritan view of welfare is a kind of compromise between the Individualist view and the Permissive view. . . .

The Puritan view of welfare, based as it is on the inter-relation between welfare and work, provides a rationale for two connected principles which those establishing welfare schemes in Canada and in the United States seem to endorse. First of all, those on welfare should never receive a higher income than the working poor. Secondly, a welfare scheme should, in some way or other, incorporate incentives to work. These principles, which presuppose that it is better to work than not to work, emerge rather naturally from the contingency which is at the basis of the Puritan view: the goods essential for social security are products of the labour of some members of society. If we wish to have a continued supply of such goods, we must encourage those who work to produce them. . . .

APPRAISAL OF POLICIES: SOCIAL CONSEQUENCES AND SOCIAL JUSTICE . . .

1. Consequences of Welfare Schemes

First, let us consider the consequences of the non-scheme advocated by the Individualist. He would have us abolish all non-optional government programmes which have as their goal the improvement of anyone's personal welfare. This rejection extends to health schemes, pension plans and education, as well as to welfare and unemployment insurance. So following the Individualist would lead to very sweeping changes.

The Individualist will claim (as do Hospers and Ayn Rand) that on the whole his non-scheme will bring beneficial consequences. He will admit, as he must, that there are people who would suffer tremendously if welfare and other social security programmes were simply terminated. Some would even die as a result. We cannot assume that spontaneously developing charities would cover every case of dire need. Nevertheless the Individualist wants to point to benefits which would accrue to businessmen and to working people and their families if taxation were drastically cut. It is his claim that consumption would rise, hence production would rise, job opportunities would be extended, and there would be an economic boom, if people could only spend all their earned income as they wished. This boom would benefit both rich and poor.

There are significant omissions which are necessary in order to render the Individualist's optimism plausible. Either workers and businessmen would have insurance of various kinds, or they would be insecure in their prosperity. If they did have insurance to cover health prob-

lems, old age and possible job loss, then they would pay for it; hence they would not be spending their whole earned income on consumer goods. Those who run the insurance schemes could, of course, put this money back into the economy—but government schemes already do this. The economic boom under Individualism would not be as loud as originally expected. Furthermore the goal of increased consumption-increased productivity must be questioned from an ecological viewpoint: many necessary materials are available only in limited quantities.

Finally, a word about charity. It is not to be expected that those who are at the mercy of charities will benefit from this state, either materially or psychologically. Those who prosper will be able to choose between giving a great deal to charity and suffering from the very real insecurity and guilt which would accompany the existence of starvation and grim poverty outside their padlocked doors. It is to be hoped that they would opt for the first alternative. But, if they did, this might be every bit as expensive for them as government-supported benefit schemes are now. If they did not give generously to charity, violence might result. However one looks at it, the consequences of individualism are unlikely to be good.

Welfare schemes operating in Canada today (1976) are almost without exception based upon the principles of the Puritan view. . . .

Both the Special Senate Committee Report on Poverty and the Real Poverty Report criticize our present system of welfare for its demoralization of recipients, who often must deal with several levels of government and are vulnerable to arbitrary interference on the part of administering officials. Welfare officials have the power to check on welfare recipients and cut off or limit their benefits under a large number of circumstances. The dangers to welfare recipients in terms of anxiety, threats to privacy and loss of dignity are obvious. According to the Senate Report, the single aspect shared by all Canada's welfare systems is "a record of failure and insufficiency, of bureaucratic rigidities that often result in the degradation, humiliation and alienation of recipients."[6] The writers of this report cite many instances of humiliation, leaving the impression that these are too easily found to be "incidental aberrations."[7] Concern that a welfare recipient either be unable to work or be willing to work (if unemployed) can easily turn into concern about how he spends the income supplied him, what his plans for the future are, where he lives, how many children he has. . . .

In fairness, it must be noted here that bureaucratic checks and controls are not a feature only of Puritan welfare systems. To a limited extent, Permissive systems would have to incorporate them too. Within those systems, welfare benefits would be given only to those whose income was inadequate to meet basic needs. However, there would be no checks on "willingness to work," and there would be no need for welfare workers to evaluate the merits of the daily activities of recipients. If a Permissive guaranteed income system were administered through income tax returns, everyone receiving the basic income and those not needing it paying it back in taxes, then the special status of welfare recipients would fade. They would no longer be singled out as a special group within the population. It is to be expected that living solely on government-supplied benefits would be psychologically easier in that type of situation.

Thus it can be argued that for the recipients of welfare, a Permissive scheme has more advantages than a Puritan one. This is not a very surprising conclusion. . . . The concern which most people have regarding the Permissive scheme relates to its costs and its dangers to the "work ethic." It is commonly thought that people work only because they have to work to survive in a tolerable style. If a guaranteed income scheme were adopted by the government, this incentive to work would disappear. No one would be faced with the choice between a nasty and boring job and starvation. Who would do the nasty and boring jobs then? Many of them are not eliminable and they have to be done somehow, by someone. Puritans fear that a great many people—even some with relatively pleasant jobs—might simply cease to work if they could receive non-stigmatized government money to live on. If this were to happen, the permissive society would simply grind to a halt.

In addressing these anxieties about the consequences of Permissive welfare schemes, we must recall that welfare benefits are set to ensure only that those who do not work have a bearable existence, with an income sufficient for basic needs, and that they have this income regardless of why they fail to work. Welfare benefits will not finance luxury living for a family of five! If jobs are adequately paid so that workers receive more than the minimum welfare income in an earned salary, then there will still be a financial incentive to take jobs. What guaranteed income schemes will do is to raise the salary floor. . . .

Furthermore it is unlikely that people work solely due to (i) the desire for money and the things it can buy and (ii) belief in the Puritan work ethic. There are many other reasons for working, some of which would persist in a society which had adopted a Permissive welfare system. Most people are happier when their time is structured in some way, when they are active outside their own homes, when they feel themselves part of an endeavour whose purposes transcend their particular egoistic ones. Women often choose to work outside the home for these reasons as much as for financial ones. With these and other factors operating I cannot see that the adoption of a Permissive welfare scheme would be followed by a level of slothfulness which would jeopardize human well-being.

Another worry about the Permissive scheme concerns cost. It is difficult to comment on this in a general way, since it would vary so much from case to case. Of Canada at the present it has been said that a guaranteed income scheme administered through income tax would cost less than social security payments administered through the present bureaucracies. It is thought that this saving would result from a drastic cut in administrative costs. . . .

In summary, we can appraise Individualism, Puritanism and Permissivism with respect to their anticipated consequences, as follows: Individualism is unacceptable; Puritanism is tolerable, but has some undesirable consequences for welfare recipients; Permissivism appears to be the winner. Worries about bad effects which Permissive welfare schemes might have due to high costs and (alleged) reduced work-incentives appear to be without solid basis.

2. Social Justice under Proposed Welfare Schemes

We must now try to consider the merits of Individualism, Puritanism and Permissivism with regard to their impact on the distribution of the goods necessary for well-being. Nozick has argued against the whole conception of a distributive justice on the grounds that it presupposes that goods are like manna from heaven: we simply get them and then have a problem—to whom to give them. According to Nozick we know where things come from and we do not have the problem of to whom to give them. There is not really a problem of distributive justice, for there is no central distributor giving out manna from heaven! It is necessary to counter Nozick on this point since his reaction to the (purported) problems of distributive justice would undercut much of what follows.[8]

There is a level at which Nozick's point is obviously valid. If A discovers a cure for cancer, then it is A and not B or C who is responsible for this discovery. On Nozick's view this is taken to imply that A should reap any monetary profits which are forthcoming; other people will benefit from the cure itself. Now although it cannot be doubted that A is a bright and hardworking person, neither can it be denied that A and his circumstances are the product of many co-operative endeavours: schools and laboratories, for instance. Because this is so, I find Nozick's claim that "we know where things come from" unconvincing at a deeper level. Since achievements like A's presuppose extensive social cooperation, it is morally permissible to regard even the monetary profits accruing from them as shareable by the "owner" and society at large.

Laws support existing income levels in many ways. Governments specify taxation so as to further determine net income. Property ownership is a legal matter. In all these ways people's incomes and possibilities for obtaining income are affected by deliberate state action. It is always possible to raise questions about the moral desirability of actual conventional arrangements. Should university professors earn less than lawyers? More than waitresses? Why? Why not? Anyone who gives an account of distributive justice is trying to specify principles which will make it possible to answer questions such as these, and nothing in Nozick's argument suffices to show that the questions are meaningless or unimportant.

Any human distribution of anything is unjust insofar as differences exist for no good reason. If goods did come like manna from heaven and the Central Distributor gave A ten times more than B, we should want to know why. The skewed distribution might be deemed a just one if A's needs were objectively ten times greater than B's, or if B refused to accept more than his small portion of goods. But if no reason at all could be given for it, or if only an irrelevant reason could be given (e.g., A is blue-eyed and B is not), then it is an unjust distribution. All the views we have expounded concerning welfare permit differences in income level. . . . But we . . . deal here solely with the question of whether everyone should receive a floor level of income; decisions on this matter are independent of decisions on overall equality or principles of variation among incomes above the floor. The Permissivist contends that all should receive at least the floor income; the Individualist and the Puritan deny this. All would claim justice for their side.

The Individualist attempts to justify extreme variations in income, with some people below the level where they can fulfill their basic needs, with reference to the fact of people's actual accomplishments. This approach to the question is open to the same objections as those which have already been raised against Nozick's non-manna-from-heaven argument, and I shall not repeat them here. Let us move on to the Puritan account. It is because goods emerge from human efforts that the Puritan advances his view of welfare. He stresses the unfairness of a system which would permit some people to take advantage of others. A Permissive welfare system would do this, as it makes no attempt to distinguish between those who choose not to work and those who cannot work. No one should be able to take advantage of another under the auspices of a government institution. The Puritan scheme seeks to eliminate this possibility, and for that reason, Puritans would allege, it is a more just scheme than the Permissive one.

Permissivists can best reply to this contention by acknowledging that any instance of free-riding would be an instance where those working were done an injustice, but by showing that any justice which the Puritan preserves by eliminating free-riding is outweighted by *injustice* perpetrated elsewhere. Consider the children of the Puritan's free-riders. They will suffer greatly for the "sins" of their parents. Within the institution of the family, the Puritan cannot suitably hurt the guilty without cruelly depriving the innocent. There is a sense, too, in which Puritanism does injustice to the many people on welfare who are not free-riders. It perpetuates the opinion that they are non-contributors to society and this doctrine, which is over-simplified if not downright false, has a harmful effect upon welfare recipients.

Social justice is not simply a matter of the distribution of goods, or the income with which goods are to be purchased. It is also a matter of the protection of rights. Western societies claim to give their citizens equal rights in political and legal contexts; they also claim to endorse the larger conception of a right to life. Now it is possible to interpret these rights in a limited and formalistic way, so that the duties correlative to them are minimal. On the limited, or negative, interpretation, to say that A has a right to life is simply to say that others have a duty not to interfere with A's attempts to keep himself alive. This interpretation of the right to life is compatible with Individualism as well as with Puritanism. But it is an inadequate interpretation of the right to life and of other rights. A right to vote is meaningless if one is starving and unable to get to the polls; a right to equality before the law is meaningless if one cannot afford to hire a lawyer. And so on.

Even a Permissive welfare scheme will go only a very small way towards protecting people's rights. It will amount to a meaningful acknowledgement of a right to life, by ensuring income adequate to purchase food, clothing and shelter—at the very least. These minimum necessities are presupposed by all other rights a society may endorse in that their possession is a precondition of being able to exercise these other rights. Because it protects the rights of all within a society better than do Puritanism and Individualism, the Permissive view can rightly claim superiority over the others with regard to justice.

NOTES

1. Nicholas Rescher, *Welfare: Social Issues in Philosophical·Perspective*, p. 114.

2. See, for example, Ayn Rand's *Atlas Shrugged*, *The Virtue of Selfishness*, and *Capitalism: The Unknown Ideal*.

3. John Hospers, *Libertarianism: A Political Philosophy for Tomorrow*, p. 67.

4. Ian Adams, William Cameron, Brian Hill,and Peter Penz, *The Real Poverty Report*, pp. 167–187.

5. See *A Theory of Justice*, p. 124, 136. Rawls defines the free-rider as one who relies on the principle "everyone is to act justly except for myself, if I choose not to," and says that his position is a version of egoism which is eliminated as a morally acceptable principle by formal constraints. This conclusion regarding the tenability of egoism is one which I accept and which is taken for granted in the present context.

6. *Senate Report on Poverty*, p. 73.

7. The Hamilton Public Welfare Department takes automobile license plates from recipients, making them available again only to those whose needs meet with the Department's approval. (*Real Poverty Report*, p. 186.) The *Globe and Mail* for 12 January 1974 reported that welfare recipients in the city of Toronto are to be subjected to computerized budgeting. In the summer of 1973, the two young daughters of an Alabama man on welfare were sterilized against their own wishes and without their parents' informed consent. (See *Time*, 23 July 1973.)

8. Robert Nozick, "Distributive Justice," *Philosophy and Public Affairs*, Fall 1973.

NO

Irving Kristol

"SOCIAL JUSTICE" AND
THE POVERTY OF REDISTRIBUTION

I recently received a letter from a magazine which is preparing a special issue on the distribution of income in the United States. The letter asked for my thoughts on such questions as: "How should a society determine wages and salaries? Does our society do a fair job of distributing income?" And so on.

The issue to which these questions are addressed is certainly a crucial one. It is nothing less than the issue of "social justice"—or what used to be known, among political philosophers, as "distributive justice." The change in terminology, as it happens, has its own significance; in politics, the language we use to ask questions is always more important than any particular answer. "Distributive justice" is a neutral phrase; it points to a problem without suggesting any particular solution. "Social justice," however, is a loaded phrase: it blithely suggests that "society" ought to determine the distribution of income. This assumption is now so common that few people realize how controversial its implications are.

The social order we call "capitalism," constructed on the basis of a market economy, does *not* believe that "society" ought to prescribe a "fair" distribution of income. "Society," in this context, means government; "society" is voiceless until the political authorities speak. And the kind of liberal society historically associated with capitalism was, from its very beginnings, hostile to any political or "social" definition of distributive justice.

It is the basic premise of a liberal-capitalist society that a "fair" distribution of income is determined by the productive input—"productive" as determined by the market—of individuals into the economy. Such productivity is determined by specific talents, general traits of character, and just plain luck (being at the right place at the right time). This market-based distribution of income will create economic incentives and thereby encourage economic growth. As a result of such economic growth, everyone will be better off (though not necessarily equally better off). The economic growth that ensues may itself shape society in ways not everyone might like. But a liberal-capitalist order does not—except in extraordinary circumstances—concede to any authority the right to overrule the aggregate of individual preferences on this matter.

In contrast, non-capitalist societies—whether pre-capitalist or post-capitalist—have a very different conception of "fairness," based on one's contribution *to the society*, not merely to the economy. In such non-capitalist societies, economic rewards are "socially" justified, as distinct from being economically justified. Thus, in the Middle Ages it was thought to be fair to compel ordinary people to support the church and the clergy, whose activities were deemed to be of major social significance and social value. Similarly, in the Soviet Union today, the Communist Party does not have to defend its budget on any economic grounds: the value of its contribution to the polity as a whole is put beyond question. Such societies, of course, place no high valuation on individual liberty.

NO "PURE" TYPES OF SOCIETY

Obviously, there is no such pure type as "a capitalist society" or "a non-capitalist society." All non-capitalist societies recognize, to one degree or another, the importance of economic activity and material welfare. They therefore will allow differential rewards—again, to one degree or another—based on one's skill at such activity.

Similarly, all capitalist societies recognize, to one degree or another, that there is more to life than economic growth or material welfare, and they therefore make some provision for differential rewards based on one's skill at literary criticism, music, and philosophy. Ohio State University, for example, is exactly such a provision.

Still, though "pure" types may not exist, the types themselves do, in however impure a form. And there are three important points to be made about these different conceptions of a good society and the principles of "fairness" in income distribution by which they operate.

(1) There is no rational method which permits us to determine, *in the abstract*, which principle of distribution is superior. It is absurd to claim that capitalism, anywhere, at any time, is superior to non-capitalism, or vice versa. Any such judgment is bound to be contingent, i.e., based on the particular society's history and traditions, on the attitudes and social habits of its citizenry, and the like. There is no point in arguing that a particular society "ought" to be capitalist or socialist if the overwhelming majority of the people are not of a mind to be bound by the different kinds of self-discipline that these different political philosophies require, if they are to work. And this, of course, holds true for all large political ideals. Which is why Jefferson, living in Paris before the French Revolution, could write—in all good republican conscience—that the French people were not "ready" for republican self-government, and that it would be a mistake for them to try to establish it immediately.

(2) A distribution of income according to one's contribution to the society—to the "common good"—requires that this society have a powerful consensus as to what the "common good" is, and that it also have institutions with the authority to give specific meaning and application to this consensus on all occasions. Now, when you have such a consensus, and such authoritative institutions, you do not have—cannot have—a liberal society as we understand it. It can certainly be a good society (if the values behind the

consensus are good); but it will not be a liberal society. The authorities which represent the "common good," and which distribute income in accordance with their conception of the common good, will—with a clear conscience—surely discriminate against those who are subversive of this "common good." They may, if they are broad-minded, tolerate dissidents, but they will never concede to them equal rights—even if equality is a prime social value. The dissidents, after all, may be those who believe in inequality.

(3) A liberal society is one that is based on a *weak* consensus. There is nothing like near-unanimity on what the "common good" is, who contributes to it, or how. There is not utter disagreement, of course; a liberal society is not—no society can be—in a condition of perpetual moral and political chaos. But the liberty of a liberal society derives from a prevalent skepticism as to anyone's ability to know the "common good" with certainty, and from the conviction that the authorities should not try to define this "common good" in any but a minimal way. That minimal definition, in a liberal society, will naturally tend to emphasize the improvement of the material conditions of life—something that very few people are actually against. A liberal society, therefore, will be very tolerant of capitalist transactions between consenting adults because such transactions are for mutual advantage, and the sum of such transactions is to everyone's material advantage. And, consequently, a liberal society will think it reasonable and "fair" that income should, on the whole, be distributed according to one's productive input into the economy, as this is measured by the marketplace and the transactions which occur there.

LIBERTY AS A VALUE

In sum, the distribution of income under liberal capitalism is "fair" if, and only if, you think that liberty is, or ought to be, the most important political value. If not, then not. This distribution of income under capitalism is an expression of the general belief that it is better for society to be shaped by the interplay of people's free opinions and free preferences than by the enforcement of any one set of values by government.

But there have always been many people in this world who do not believe that liberty is the most important political value. These people are sincere dogmatists. They believe they know *the* truth about a good society; they believe they possess *the* true definition of distributive justice; and they inevitably wish to see society shaped in the image of these true beliefs. Sometimes they have prized religious truth more than liberty; sometimes they have prized philosophic truth more than liberty (e.g., the Marxist philosophy); and sometimes they have prized equality more than liberty. It is this last point of view that is especially popular in some circles—mainly academic circles—in the United States today.

Thus professor Ronald Dworkin, one of our most distinguished liberal legal philosophers, has recently written that *"a more equal society is a better society even if its citizens prefer inequality."* (Italics mine.) From which it follows that "social justice" may require a people, whose preferences are corrupt (in that they prefer liberty to equality), to be coerced into equality. It is precisely because they define "social justice" and "fairness" in terms of equality that so many liberal thinkers find it so difficult genuinely to detest left-wing (i.e., egalitarian) authoritarian or totalitarian regimes. And, similarly, it is precisely because they are true believers in justice-as-equality that they dislike a free society, with all its inevitable inequalities.

As one who does like a free society, I have to concede to these people the right to hold and freely express such opinions. But I do find it ironical that their conception of "social justice" should be generally designated as the "liberal" one. Whatever its other merits, an authentic attachment to liberty is not one of them. . . .

Is there a "problem" in the distribution of income in the United States today? We are frequently assured that there is, and are confronted with Census Bureau statistics to prove it. Those statistics, widely quoted, show that the top 20 percent of American families get 40 percent of the national income, while the lowest 20 percent of the population get only 5 percent. The statistics are accurate enough, but they are also wildly misleading.

One reason they are misleading is that they refer only to *cash* income. They omit in-kind transfers (e.g., Medicare, Medicaid, food stamps, subsidized housing, etc.), and it is precisely such in-kind transfers that have mushroomed during the past 15 years. Edgar K. Browning (*The Public Interest*, Spring 1976) has shown that, once such in-kind transfers are included, the lowest fifth gets almost 12 percent of the national income, the top fifth about 33 percent.

Moreover, even this revised picture grossly exaggerates the degree of income inequality. That is because the statistics are not corrected for age. Clearly, young people who have recently entered the labor force, and old people who have left it, will have significantly lower incomes than those in mid-career. Even in a strictly egalitarian society, where everyone's lifetime income is equal, a cross-cut statistical snapshot at any one moment will show substantial inequality.

The statistical problems involved in correcting the picture of income distribution for age are formidable, and there are no meaningful percentages to be quoted. But where statistical precision is lacking, common sense will take us at least part of the way. Let us assume that any revision which takes account of age has only modest effects—that perhaps it will show the top 20 percent of the population to receive 28 percent to 30 percent of the national income. Does this degree of inequality represent an "inequity"? Is it a "problem"?

Obviously, it is for those who believe in the ideal of absolute equality for all. But most Americans who express concern about inequality have no such extreme thoughts. Indeed, most of their interest in inequality arises from the very reasonable desire to eradicate, or at least alleviate, poverty. And this confusion between the issue of inequality and the issue of poverty is indeed a very serious problem.

The notion that income redistribution is the effective means to end poverty is age-old: one finds it expressed in the civil strife of the Greek city-states, the medieval peasant rebellions, and the socialist movements of the past 200 years. But if the modern science of economics has taught us anything, it is that the connection is usually spurious.

The redistribution impulse is most powerful today in those poor countries, the so-called less-developed countries, where it makes the least sense. In such countries, the alleviation of poverty is utterly dependent on economic growth.

There never is enough money among the small number of wealthy citizens to make a significant dent in the poverty of the masses. When the rich are expropriated in such countries, everyone becomes equal in poverty—though the political authorities who do the expropriating usually end up being more equal than the rest.

Even in affluent, developed societies, where the poor are a minority, the alleviation of poverty is mainly dependent on economic growth. (The one instance where it makes sense to think of income redistribution as a cure for poverty involves the aged and infirm, that portion of the population who are not in the labor force because they are by nature dependent.) The experience of the United States over these past 15 years demonstrates how the idea of "abolishing poverty" through income redistribution turns out to be a will-o'-the-wisp.

POVERTY AND PATHOLOGY

Let us draw the poverty line at a fairly high level—at one half the median income. (This is the level preferred by most liberal reformers, as distinct from the official "subsistence" level fixed by government.) Well, in New York City, where our politicians are notoriously compassionate, we have achieved even that high level. A family of four on welfare receives in cash and kind, between $7,000 and $7,500 a year. (The median household income in the United States is about $12,500 annually.) *We have abolished poverty in New York City!*

So why hasn't anyone noticed?

The reason is that, for the non-aged and non-infirm, poverty turns out to be more than a simple shortage of money. Poverty as a human condition, as distinct from a statistical condition, is defined to a substantial degree by the ways in which one copes with poverty. A visitor to the Greek islands, or to an Italian village, is impressed first of all, not by the poverty of the people there—which is acute—but by their determination to make the best of things and their extraordinary ability to do so.

And what is true for the way one copes with poverty is also true for the way one goes about abolishing poverty. For the way in which poverty is abolished turns out to be more important than the statistical abolition itself. In New York, we have tried to abolish poverty through a generous welfare program, and have therewith rediscovered the truth of an old adage: dependency tends to corrupt and absolute dependency corrupts absolutely. Our welfare population, statistically lifted out of poverty, has actually and simultaneously sunk to various depths of social pathology. It is largely a demoralized population, with higher rates of crime, juvenile delinquency, drug addiction, teenage pregnancy, and alcoholism, than when the welfare checks were less generous.

The reason for this demoralization is obvious enough, though scholars with a middle-class background have difficulty in perceiving it. Being a "breadwinner" is the major source of self-respect for a man or woman working at a tedious, low-paying job that offers few prospects for advancement. It is also the major source of such respect as he (or she) receives from family, friends, and neighbors. When welfare provides more generously for a family than a breadwinner can, he becomes a superfluous human being. Both self-respect and respect soon crumble, family ties unravel, and a "culture of poverty" sets in that has more to do with the welfare system than with poverty itself.

Meanwhile, there are many poor people (including, of course, poor blacks) in this country who are too proud to go on welfare, who prefer to work hard at low-paying jobs, earning less than if they had gone on welfare, whose spirits are undestroyed, whose lives are less afflicted, and whose children are less likely "to get into trouble." It would be instructive to see a comparative study of those two groups of poor people. But when the state of California tried to sponsor one, liberal academe and the liberal media—committed to reform-through-redistribution—denounced and killed the idea.

WHATEVER HAPPENED TO . . .

So the evidence is clear that trying to abolish poverty through income distribution does nothing of the sort. The evidence is also clear that when poverty is abolished through economic growth, something real and desirable has occurred. The history of the United States since 1940 testifies to the truth of this latter proposition. What happened to the "Okies" whom Steinbeck and others wrote so poignantly about? What happened to the poor whites who, in most American cities (and all American movies), lived on "the other side of the tracks"? And what is happening to Appalachia today, where a boom in coal mining is accomplishing what a dozen government programs failed to do?

But, ironically, efforts to redistribute income by governmental fiat have the precise effect of impairing economic efficiency and growth—and therefore of preserving poverty in the name of equality. All such schemes of income distribution imply higher rates of marginal taxation for the productive population, with a consequent diminution of work incentives and a shrinking of capital available for reinvestment. When this happens on a sufficiently large scale, the results become disastrous for everyone.

This is evidently the case in the United Kingdom today, where a massive redistribution has indeed taken place, and where the society as a whole is getting poorer with every passing year. Twenty years ago, there was no noteworthy "poverty problem" in Britain. As things are now going, however, there will surely be one tomorrow. Egalitarianism may be motivated by a sincere desire to abolish poverty, but it is one of the most efficient poverty-creating ideologies of our century.

POSTSCRIPT

Does Society Have an Obligation to Care for the Less Well Off?

Govier and Kristol agree that it is not right for people to die homeless in the streets or to starve, but this is not a significant point of agreement since no one is likely to take issue with that.

At issue between Govier and Kristol is whether the state has an obligation to care for needy and poor individuals by providing them with what would fulfill their needs: food, shelter, medicine. To this question Govier responds with an unconditional *yes*. Kristol's position is that society's care and concern should *not* be directed toward needy people, to whom society does not have obligations, but rather toward economic growth and development in general. One ultimate result of this economic growth is (presumably) that the needy will have their needs met. Of course, this is not a result that society has an obligation to produce; it would come about as a by-product of favorable economic conditions. Govier, on the other hand, would have the state simply give these people the food and shelter they need, at the expense of tax-paying people—that is, individuals who do have incomes and resources.

In addition to considering financial and economic factors, both Govier and Kristol draw attention to psychological factors involved with meeting the needs of the poor and needy. Govier is concerned that the state might infringe on a potential welfare recipient's private life, or subject the person to demeaning and prying questions (about why the person does not have a job, about how a welfare check would be spent, and so on), which could be humiliating. These psychological considerations are introduced by Govier in order to support a no-questions-asked approach to welfare. Kristol, on the other hand, points out that people on the low rungs of the economic ladder derive much of their sense of identity and self-respect from their status as breadwinners. If that status is taken away from them by the state, and they are simply given handouts, they will suffer psychological damage at the hand of the state.

A classic work in this field is Michael Harrington, *The Other America* (Macmillan, 1962). Further sources are Virginia Held, ed., *Property, Profits, and Economic Justice* (Wadsworth, 1980); Peter G. Brown, Conrad Johnson, and Paul Vernier, eds., *Income Support: Conceptual and Policy Issues* (Rowman & Allanheld, 1981); George Gilder, *Wealth and Poverty* (Basic Books, 1981); Ellen F. Paul, Fred D. Miller, Jr., and Jeffrey Paul, eds., *Liberty and Equality* (Blackwell, 1985); and Kenneth Kipnis and Diane T. Meyers, eds., *Economic Justice: Private Rights and Public Responsibilities* (Rowman & Littlefield, 1985).

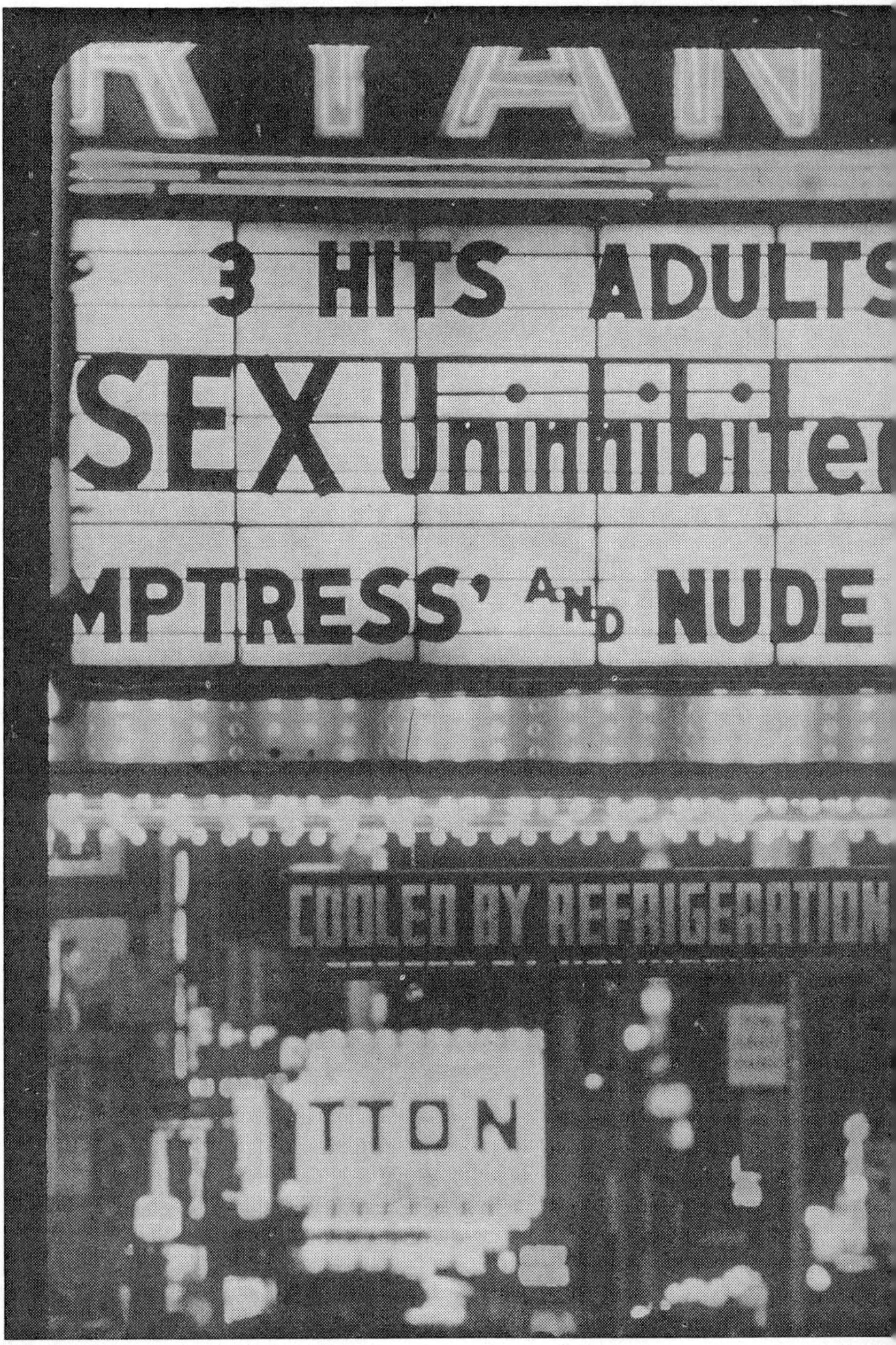
3 HITS ADULTS
SEX Uninhibite
MPTRESS' AND NUDE
COOLED BY REFRIGERATION
TTON

PART 3

Morality, Sex, and Reproduction

The issues in this section specifically address matters of sexuality and reproduction. Since we are sexual and reproductive beings, and since human beings are social and naturally interact with each other, it is imperative to have some idea of what is allowable and what is not, with respect to sexual and reproductive matters.

The issues in this section do not presuppose that there is anything morally questionable about sex itself, but they do raise questions about how, in today's world, we should regard certain matters of sex and reproduction.

Should Homosexuality Be Accepted by Society?

_____

Is Pornography Immoral?

_____

Is Abortion Immoral?

_____

Is Surrogate Motherhood Wrong?

ISSUE 10

Should Homosexuality Be Accepted by Society?

YES: Richard D. Mohr, from "Gay Basics: Some Questions, Facts, and Values," in James Rachels, ed., *The Right Thing to Do* (Random House, 1989)

NO: Paul Cameron, from "A Case Against Homosexuality," *The Human Life Review* (1978)

ISSUE SUMMARY

YES: Professor of philosophy Richard D. Mohr argues that homosexuals suffer from unjust discrimination and defends homosexuality against charges that it is immoral and unnatural.

NO: Psychologist Paul Cameron claims that homosexuality is associated with many negative personal traits and argues that society would be making a mistake to allow homosexuality equal status with heterosexuality.

For many people in our society, homosexuality is a difficult subject to discuss. We can usually talk about such subjects as teenage pregnancy, rape, incest, premarital sex, and sexual fantasies without the difficulties that often attend discussions of homosexuality. Why is this so?

Part of the problem might be that we are just more certain about what to think about other sexual topics. Consider rape, for instance. We are reasonably clear on certain facts about it: it occurs every day in the United States but is underreported and underprosecuted. We are also reasonably clear about its moral status: we generally agree that the victim *is* a victim and the rapist is in the moral (and legal) wrong. With homosexuality, there is less agreement both on the facts associated with it and on its moral status. In this age of information and sexual frankness, why is there a knowledge vacuum about homosexuality?

One reason might be tied to some people's belief that a homosexual perspective is a "perverted" one. Is this reasonable? Is it presumptuous for heterosexuals to say that they already understand sexuality enough (from their own perspective) to be able to make judgments about homosexuality?

Another reason to explain the knowledge vacuum stems from a traditional rejection of homosexuality. Some people may think that even to talk about the subject may raise issues or challenges as to their own sexual orientation. Suppose a person suggests that in order to achieve understanding of homosexuality, we might try viewing things from a homosexual perspective.

The listener may then conclude that the speaker is homosexual. (As a contrast, note that those who suggest that some insight into rape can be gained by seeing things from the rapist's point of view probably are not similarly suspected of being rapists.) This idea is perhaps even stronger (and possibly more hostile) if one uses a term like "gay," because this is a term that homosexuals have accepted for themselves and rallied behind.

For these and other reasons, homosexuality remains a sensitive topic. Many people who are not homosexual are reluctant to discuss the subject; so too are many homosexuals, especially those who fear hostility or those who do not wish to "come out of the closet," or to have their homosexuality made public knowledge.

In the readings that follow, Richard D. Mohr and Paul Cameron approach the knowledge-gathering task quite differently. Mohr cites some statistics but puts emphasis on general considerations, such as the idea that society has predesigned gender roles that homosexuals reject (which in turn causes society to reject homosexuals). He uses some specific events as clues to larger social realities. For example, Mohr cites the case of Dan White, who shot and killed both the mayor of San Francisco and openly gay councilman Harvey Milk. The defense, which managed to sustain a plea of "diminished capacity" (and thus bring what would probably have been a first- or second-degree murder charge down to a charge of voluntary manslaughter), rested on the fact that Dan White, who was depressed, consumed a quantity of Twinkies. The claim was made (and, complains Mohr, the court was apparently convinced) that eating junk food such as Twinkies caused Dan White's rational capacity to become diminished. Mohr claims that gay people do not receive the same protection of the law that others receive.

Cameron's approach is more grounded in surveys and data collection, but he also discusses some general conceptions and looks for clues. Cameron asserts that sexual orientation is completely learned; Mohr claims that it is discovered within each individual. The differences between Mohr and Cameron over this one question—whether one's sexual orientation is discovered or learned—are a source of many of the further distinctions between these writers.

YES
Richard D. Mohr

GAY BASICS: SOME QUESTIONS, FACTS, AND VALUES

I. WHO ARE GAYS ANYWAY?

A recent Gallup poll found that only one in five Americans reports having a gay or lesbian acquaintance.[1] This finding is extraordinary given the number of practicing homosexuals in America. Alfred Kinsey's 1948 study of the sex lives of 12,000 white males shocked the nation: 37 percent had at least one homosexual experience to orgasm in their adult lives; an additional 13 percent had homosexual fantasies to orgasm; 4 percent were exclusively homosexual in their practices; another 5 percent had virtually no heterosexual experience and nearly 20 percent had at least as many homosexual as heterosexual experiences.[2]

Two out of five men one passes on the street have had orgasmic sex with men. Every second family in the country has a member who is essentially homosexual and many more people regularly have homosexual experiences. Who are homosexuals? They are your friends, your minister, your teacher, your bank teller, your doctor, your mail carrier, your officemate, your roommate, your congressional representative, your sibling, parent, and spouse. They are everywhere, virtually all ordinary, virtually all unknown.

Several important consequences follow. First, the country is profoundly ignorant of the actual experience of gay people. Second, social attitudes and practices that are harmful to gays have a much greater overall harmful impact on society than is usually realized. Third, most gay people live in hiding—in the closet—making the "coming out" experience the central fixture of gay consciousness and invisibility the chief characteristic of the gay community.

II. IGNORANCE, STEREOTYPE, AND MORALITY

Ignorance about gays, however, has not stopped people from having strong opinions about them. The void which ignorance leaves has been filled with stereotypes. Society holds chiefly two groups of anti-gay stereotypes; the two are an oddly contradictory lot. One set of stereotypes revolves around alleged mistakes in an individual's gender identity: lesbians are women that want to be, or at least look and act like, men—bull dykes, diesel dykes; while gay men are those who want to be, or at least look and act like, women—queens, fairies, limp-wrists, nellies. These stereotypes of mismatched genders provide the materials through which gays and lesbians become the butts of ethniclike jokes. These stereotypes and jokes, though derisive, basically view gays and lesbians as ridiculous.

Another set of stereotypes revolves around gays as a pervasive, sinister, conspiratorial threat. The core stereotype here is the gay person as child molester, and more generally as sex-crazed maniac. These stereotypes carry with them fears of the very destruction of family and civilization itself. . . .

[A]nti-gay stereotypes surrounding gender identification are chiefly means of reinforcing still powerful gender roles in society. If, as this stereotype presumes and condemns, one is free to choose one's social roles independently of gender, many guiding social divisions, both domestic and commercial, might be threatened. The socially gender-linked distinctions between breadwinner and homemaker, boss and secretary, doctor and nurse, protector and protected would blur. The accusations "dyke" and "fag" exist in significant part to keep women in their place and to prevent men from breaking ranks and ceding away theirs.

The stereotypes of gays as child molesters, sex-crazed maniacs, and civilization destroyers function to displace (socially irresolvable) problems from their actual source to a foreign (and so, it is thought, manageable) one. Thus the stereotype of child molester functions to give the family unit a false sheen of absolute innocence. It keeps the unit from being examined too closely for incest, child abuse, wife-battering, and the terrorism of constant threats. The stereotype teaches that the problems of the family are not internal to it, but external.[3]

One can see these cultural forces at work in society's and the media's treatment of current reports of violence, especially domestic violence. When a mother kills her child or a father rapes his daughter—regular Section B fare even in major urban papers—this is never taken by reporters, columnists, or pundits as evidence that there is something wrong with heterosexuality or with traditional families. These issues are not even raised. But when a homosexual child molestation is reported it is taken as confirming evidence of the way homosexuals are. One never hears of heterosexual murders, but one regularly hears of "homosexual" ones. Compare the social treatment of Richard Speck's sexually motivated mass murder of Chicago nurses with that of John Wayne Gacy's murders of Chicago youths. Gacy was in the culture's mind taken as symbolic of gay men in general. To prevent the possibility that The Family was viewed as anything but an innocent victim in this affair, the mainstream press knowingly failed to mention that most of Gacy's adolescent victims were homeless hustlers. That knowledge would be too much for the six o'clock news and for cherished beliefs. . . .

III. ARE GAYS DISCRIMINATED AGAINST? DOES IT MATTER?

Partly because lots of people suppose they don't know any gay people and partly through willful ignorance of its own workings, society at large is unaware of the many ways in which gays are subject to discrimination in consequence of widespread fear and hatred. Contributing to this social ignorance of discrimination is the difficulty for gay people, as an invisible minority, even to complain of discrimination. For if one is gay, to register a complaint would suddenly target one as a stigmatized person, and so in the absence of any protections against discrimination, would simply invite additional discrimination. . . .

[G]ays are subject to violence and harassment based simply on their perceived status rather than because of any actions they have performed. A recent extensive study by the National Gay Task Force found that over 90 percent of gays and lesbians had been victimized in some form on the basis of their sexual orientation.[4] Greater than one in five gay men and nearly one in ten lesbians had been punched, hit, or kicked; a quarter of all gays had had objects thrown at them; a third had been chased; a third had been sexually harassed; and 14 percent had been spit on—all just for being perceived as gay.

The most extreme form of anti-gay violence is "queerbashing"—where groups of young men target a person who they suppose is a gay man and beat and kick him unconscious and sometimes to death amid a torrent of taunts and slurs. Such seemingly random but in reality socially encouraged violence has the same origin and function as lynchings of blacks—to keep a whole stigmatized group in line. As with lynchings of the recent past, the police and courts have routinely averted their eyes, giving their implicit approval to the practice.

Few such cases with gay victims reach the courts. Those that do are marked by inequitable procedures and results. Frequently judges will describe "queerbashers" as "just all-American boys." Recently a District of Columbia judge handed suspended sentences to queerbashers whose victim had been stalked, beaten, stripped at knife point, slashed, kicked, threatened with castration, and pissed on, because the judge thought the bashers were good boys at heart—after all, they went to a religious prep school.[5]

Police and juries will simply discount testimony from gays; they typically construe assaults on and murders of gays as "justified" self-defense—the killer need only claim his act was a panicked response to a sexual overture. Alternatively, when guilt seems patent, juries will accept highly implausible "diminished capacity" defenses, as in the case of Dan White's 1978 assassination of openly gay San Francisco city councilman Harvey Milk: Hostess Twinkies made him do it. . . .[6]

Gays are subject to widespread discrimination in employment—the very means by which one puts bread on one's table and one of the chief means by which individuals identify themselves to themselves and achieve personal dignity. Governments are leading offenders here. They do a lot of discriminating themselves, require that others do it (e.g., government contractors), and set precedents favoring discrimination in the private sector. The federal government explicitly discriminates against gays in the armed forces, the CIA, FBI, National Security Agency, and the state department. The federal government refuses to give security clearances to gays and so forces the country's considerable private sector military and aerospace contractors to fire known gay employees. State and local governments regularly fire gay teachers, policemen, firemen, social workers, and anyone who has contact with the public. Further, through licensing laws states officially bar gays from a vast array of occupations and professions—everything from doctors, lawyers, accountants, and nurses to hairdressers, morticians, and used car dealers. The American Civil Liberties Union's handbook *The Rights of Gay People* lists 307 such prohibited occupations.[7]

Gays are subject to discrimination in a wide variety of other ways, including private-sector employment, public accommodations, housing, immigration and naturalization, insurance of all types, custody and adoption, and zoning regulations that bar "singles" or "nonrelated" couples. All of these discriminations affect central components of a meaningful life; some even reach to the means by which life itself is sustained. In half the states, where gay sex is illegal, the central role of sex to meaningful life is officially denied to gays. . . .

IV. BUT AREN'T THEY IMMORAL?

Many people think society's treatment of gays is justified because they think gays are extremely immoral. To evaluate this claim, different senses of "moral" must be distinguished. Sometimes by "morality" is meant the overall beliefs affecting behavior in the society—its mores, norms, and customs. On this understanding, gays certainly are not moral: lots of people hate them and social customs are designed to register widespread disapproval of gays. The problem here is that this sense of morality is merely a *descriptive* one. On this understanding *every* society has a morality—even Nazi society, which had racism and mob rule as central features of its "morality," understood in this sense. What is needed in order to use the notion of morality to praise or condemn behavior is a sense of morality that is *prescriptive* or *normative*— a sense of morality whereby, for instance, the descriptive morality of the Nazis is found wanting. . . .

Furthermore, recent historical and anthropological research has shown that opinion about gays has been by no means universally negative. Historically, it has varied widely even within the larger part of the Christian era and even within the church itself.[8] There are even societies— current ones—where homosexuality is not only tolerated but a universal compulsory part of social maturation.[9] . . .

If popular opinion and custom are not enough to ground moral condemnation of homosexuality, perhaps religion can. . . .

One of the more remarkable discoveries of recent gay research is that the Bible may not be as univocal in its condemnation of homosexuality as has been usually believed.[10] Christ never mentions homosexuality. Recent interpreters of the Old Testament have pointed out that the story of Lot at Sodom is probably intended to condemn inhospitality rather than homosexuality. Further, some of the Old Testament condemnations of homosexuality seem simply to be ways of tarring those of the Israelites' opponents who happened to accept homosexual practices when the Israelites themselves did not. If so, the condemnation is merely a quirk of history and rhetoric rather than a moral precept.

What does seem clear is that those who regularly cite the Bible to condemn an activity like homosexuality do so by reading it selectively. Do ministers who cite what they take to be condemnations of homosexuality in Leviticus maintain in their lives all the hygienic and dietary laws of Leviticus? If they cite the story of Lot at Sodom to condemn homosexuality, do they also cite the story of Lot in the cave to praise incestuous rape? It seems then not that the Bible is being used to ground condemnations of homosexuality as much as society's dislike of homosexuality is being used to interpret the Bible.[11]

Even if a consistent portrait of condemnation could be gleaned from the Bible, what social significance should it be given? One of the guiding principles of society, enshrined in the Constitution as a check against the government, is that decisions affecting social policy are not made on religious grounds. If the real ground of the alleged immorality invoked by governments to discriminate against gays is religious (as it has explicitly been even in some recent court cases involving teachers and guardians), then one of the major commitments of our nation is violated.

V. BUT AREN'T THEY UNNATURAL?

. . . Though the accusation of unnaturalness looks whimsical, in actual ordinary discourse when applied to homosexuality, it is usually delivered with venom aforethought. It carries a high emotional charge, usually expressing disgust and evincing queasiness. Probably it is nothing but an emotional charge. For people get equally disgusted and queasy at all sorts of things that are perfectly natural—to be expected in nature apart from artifice—and that could hardly be fit subjects for moral condemnation. Two typical examples in current American culture are some people's responses to mothers'

suckling in public and to women who do not shave body hair. When people have strong emotional reactions, as they do in these cases, without being able to give good reasons for them, we think of them not as operating morally, but rather as being obsessed and manic. So the feelings of disgust that some people have to gays will hardly ground a charge of immorality. People fling the term "unnatural" against gays in the same breath and with the same force as when they call gays "sick" and "gross." When they do this, they give every appearance of being neurotically fearful and incapable of reasoned discourse.

When "nature" is taken in *technical* rather than ordinary usages, it looks like the notion also will not ground a charge of homosexual immorality. When unnatural means "by artifice" or "made by humans," it need only be pointed out that virtually everything that is good about life is unnatural in this sense, that the chief feature that distinguishes people from other animals is their very ability to make over the world to meet their needs and desires, and that their well-being depends upon these departures from nature. On this understanding of human nature and the natural, homosexuality is perfectly unobjectionable.

Another technical sense of natural is that something is natural and so, good, if it fulfills some function in nature. Homosexuality on this view is unnatural because it allegedly violates the function of genitals, which is to produce babies. One problem with this view is that lots of bodily parts have lots of functions and just because some one activity can be fulfilled by only one organ (say, the mouth for eating) this activity does not condemn other functions of the organ to immorality (say the mouth for talking, licking stamps, blowing bubbles, or having sex). So the possible use of the genitals to produce children does not, without more, condemn the use of the genitals for other purposes, say, achieving ecstasy and intimacy. . . .

Further, ordinary moral attitudes about childbearing will not provide the needed supplement which in conjunction with the natural function view of bodily parts would produce a positive obligation to use the genitals for procreation. Society's attitude toward a childless couple is that of pity not censure—even if the couple could have children. . . . The couple who discovers they cannot have children are viewed not as having thereby had a debt canceled, but rather as having to forgo some of the richness of life, just as a quadriplegic is viewed not as absolved from some moral obligation to hop, skip, jump, but as missing some of the richness of life. Consistency requires then that, at most, gays who do not or cannot have children are to be pitied rather than condemned. What *is* immoral is the willful preventing of people from achieving the richness of life. Immorality in this regard lies with those social customs, regulations, and statutes that prevent lesbians and gay men from establishing blood or adoptive families, not with gays themselves. . . .

If one looks to people . . . for a model—and looks hard enough—one finds amazing variety, including homosexuality as a social ideal (upper-class fifth-century Athens) and even as socially mandatory (Melanesia today). When one looks to people, one is simply unable to strip away the layers of social custom, history, and taboo in order to see what's really there to any degree more specific than that people are the creatures that make over their world and are capable of ab-

stract thought. That this is so should raise doubts that neutral principles are to be found in human nature that will condemn homosexuality.

On the other hand, if one looks to nature apart from people for models, the possibilities are staggering. There are fish that change gender over their lifetimes: should we "follow nature" and be operative transsexuals? Orangutans, genetically our next of kin, live completely solitary lives without social organization of any kind: ought we to "follow nature" and be hermits? There are many species where only two members per generation reproduce: should we be bees? The search in nature for people's purpose, far from finding sure models for action, is likely to leave one morally rudderless.

VI. BUT AREN'T GAYS WILLFULLY THE WAY THEY ARE?

It is generally conceded that if sexual orientation is something over which an individual—for whatever reason—has virtually no control, then discrimination against gays is especially deplorable, as it is against racial and ethnic classes, because it holds people accountable without regard for anything they themselves have done. And to hold a person accountable for that over which the person has no control is a central form of prejudice.

Attempts to answer the question whether or not sexual orientation is something that is reasonably thought to be within one's own control usually appeal simply to various claims of the biological or "mental" sciences. But the ensuing debate over genes, hormones, twins, early childhood development, and the like, is as unnecessary as it is currently inconclusive.[12] All that is needed to answer the question is to look at the actual experience of gays in current society and it becomes fairly clear that sexual orientation is not likely a matter of choice. For coming to have a homosexual identity simply does not have the same sort of structure that decision making has.

On the one hand, the "choice" of the gender of a sexual partner does not seem to express a trivial desire that might be as easily well fulfilled by a simple substitution of the desired object. Picking the gender of a sex partner is decidedly dissimilar, that is, to such activities as picking a flavor of ice cream. If an ice-cream parlor is out of one's flavor, one simply picks another. And if people were persecuted, threatened with jail terms, shattered careers, loss of family and housing, and the like, for eating, say, rocky road ice cream, no one would ever eat it; everyone would pick another easily available flavor. That gay people abide in being gay even in the face of persecution shows that being gay is not a matter of easy choice.

On the other hand, even if establishing a sexual orientation is not like making a relatively trivial choice, perhaps it is nevertheless relevantly like making the central and serious life choices by which individuals try to establish themselves as being of some type. Again, if one examines gay experience, this seems not to be the case. For one never sees anyone setting out to become a homosexual, in the way one does see people setting out to become doctors, lawyers, and bricklayers. One does not find "gays-to-be" picking some end—"At some point in the future, I want to become a homosexual"—and then setting about planning and acquiring the ways and means to that end, in the way one does see people deciding that they want to become lawyers, and then sees them plan what courses to take and what sort of temperaments, habits, and skills to develop in order to become lawyers. Typically gays-to-be simply find themselves having homosexual encounters and yet at least initially resisting quite strongly the identification of being homosexual. . . . Only with time, luck, and great personal effort, but sometimes never, does the person gradually come to accept her or his orientation, to view it as a given material condition of life, coming as materials do with certain capacities and limitations. The person begins to act in accordance with his or her orientation and its capacities, seeing its actualization as a requisite for an integrated personality and as a central component of personal well-being. As a result, the experience of coming out to oneself has for gays the basic structure of a discovery, not the structure of a choice. . . .

VII. HOW WOULD SOCIETY AT LARGE BE CHANGED IF GAYS WERE SOCIALLY ACCEPTED?

Suggestions to change social policy with regard to gays are invariably met with claims that to do so would invite the destruction of civilization itself: after all, isn't that what did Rome in? Actually Rome's decay paralleled not the flourishing of homosexuality but its repression under the later Christianized emperors.[13] Predictions of American civilization's imminent demise have been as premature as they have been frequent. Civilization has shown itself rather resilient here, in large part because of the country's traditional commitments to a respect for privacy, to individual liberties, and especially to people minding their own business. . . .

Half the states have decriminalized homosexual acts. Can you guess which of the following states still have sodomy laws: Wisconsin, Minnesota; New Mexico, Arizona; Vermont, New Hampshire; Nebraska, Kansas. One from each pair does and one does not have sodomy laws. And yet one would be hard pressed to point out any substantial difference between the members of each pair. (If you're interested, it is the second of each pair with them.) Empirical studies have shown that there is no increase in other crimes in states that have decriminalized.[14] Further, sodomy laws are virtually never enforced. They remain on the books not to "protect society" but to insult gays, and for that reason need to be removed.

Neither has the passage of legislation barring discrimination against gays ushered in the end of civilization. Some 50 counties and municipalities, including some of the country's largest cities (like Los Angeles and Boston), have passed such statutes and among the states and colonies Wisconsin and the District of Columbia have model protective codes. Again, no more brimstone has fallen in these places than elsewhere. Staunchly anti-gay cities, like Miami and Houston, have not been spared the AIDS crisis.

Berkeley, California, has even passed domestic partner legislation giving gay couples the same rights to city benefits as married couples, and yet Berkeley has not become more weird than it already was.

Seemingly hysterical predictions that the American family would collapse if such reforms would pass proved false, just as the same dire predictions that the availability of divorce would lessen the ideal and desirability of marriage proved completely unfounded. Indeed if current discriminations, which drive gays into hiding and into anonymous relations, were lifted, far from seeing gays raze American families, one would see gays forming them.

Virtually all gays express a desire to have a permanent lover. Many would like to raise or foster children—perhaps those alarming numbers of gay kids who have been beaten up and thrown out of their "families" for being gay. But currently society makes gay coupling very difficult. A life of hiding is a pressure-cooker existence not easily shared with another. Members of non-gay couples are here asked to imagine what it would take to erase every trace of their own sexual orientation for even just a week. . . .

Finally . . . , in extending to gays the rights and benefits it has reserved for its dominant culture, America would confirm its deeply held vision of itself as a morally progressing nation, a nation itself advancing and serving as a beacon for others—especially with regard to human rights. The words with which our national pledge ends—"with liberty and justice for all"— are not a description of the present but a call for the future. Ours is a nation given to a prophetic political rhetoric which acknowledges that morality is not arbitrary and that justice is not merely the expression of the current collective will. It is this vision that led the black civil rights movement to its successes. Those congressmen who opposed that movement and its centerpiece, the 1964 Civil Rights Act, on obscurantist grounds, but who lived long enough and were noble enough, came in time to express their heartfelt regret and shame at what they had done. It is to be hoped and someday to be expected that those who now grasp at anything to oppose the extension of that which is best about America to gays will one day feel the same.

NOTES

1. "Public Fears—And Sympathies," *Newsweek*, August 12, 1985, p. 23.

2. Alfred C. Kinsey, *Sexual Behavior in the Human Male* (Philadelphia: Saunders, 1948), pp. 650–51. On the somewhat lower incidences of lesbianism, see Alfred C. Kinsey, *Sexual Behavior in the Human Female* (Philadelphia: Saunders, 1953), pp. 472–475.

3. For studies showing that gay men are no more likely—indeed, are less likely—than heterosexuals to be child molesters and that the largest groups of sexual abusers of children and the people most persistent in their molestation of children are the children's fathers or stepfathers or mother's boyfriends, see Vincent De Francis, *Protecting the Child Victim of Sex Crimes Committed by Adults* (Denver: The American Humane Association, 1969), pp. vii, 38, 69–70; A. Nicholas Groth, "Adult Sexual Orientation and Attraction to Underage Persons," *Archives of Sexual Behavior* 7 (1978): 175–181; Mary J. Spencer, "Sexual Abuse of Boys," *Pediatrics* 78, no. 1 (July 1986): 133–138.

4. See National Gay Task Force, *Anti-Gay/Lesbian Victimization* (New York: NGTF, 1984).

5. "2 St. John's Students Given Probation in Assault on Gay," *The Washington Post*, May 15, 1984, p. 1.

6. See Randy Shilts, *The Mayor of Castro Street: The Life and Times of Harvey Milk* (New York: St. Martin's, 1982). pp. 308–325.

7. E. Carrington Boggan, *The Rights of Gay People: The Basic ACLU Guide to a Gay Person's Rights* (New York: Avon, 1975), pp. 211–235.

8. John Boswell, *Christianity, Social Tolerance and Homosexuality: Gay People in Western Europe from the Beginning of the Christian Era to the Fourteenth Century* (Chicago: University of Chicago Press, 1980).

9. See Gilbert Herdt, *Guardians of the Flute: Idioms of Masculinity* (New York: McGraw-Hill, 1981), pp. 232–239, 284–288; and see generally Gilbert Herdt, ed., *Ritualized Homosexuality in Melanesia* (Berkeley: University of California Press, 1984). For another eye-opener, see Walter L. Williams, *The Spirit and the Flesh: Sexual Diversity in American Indian Culture* (Boston: Beacon, 1986).

10. See especially Boswell, *Christianity*, ch. 4.

11. For Old Testament condemnations of homosexual acts, see Leviticus 18:22, 21:3. For hygienic and dietary codes, see, for example, Leviticus 15:19–27 (on the uncleanliness of women) and Leviticus 11:1–47 (on not eating rabbits, pigs, bats, finless water creatures, legless creeping creatures, etc.). For Lot at Sodom, see Genesis 19:1–25. For Lot in the cave, see Genesis 19:30–38.

12. The preponderance of the scientific evidence supports the view that homosexuality is either genetically determined or a permanent result of early childhood development. See the Kinsey Institute's study by Alan Bell, Martin Weinberg, and Sue Hammersmith, *Sexual Preference: Its Development in Men and Women* (Bloomington: Indiana University Press, 1981); Frederick Whitam and Robin Mathy, *Male Homosexuality in Four Societies* (New York: Praeger, 1986), ch. 7.

13. See Boswell, *Christianity*, ch. 3.

14. See Gilbert Geis, "Reported Consequences of Decriminalization of Consensual Adult Homosexuality in Seven American States," *Journal of Homosexuality* 1, no. 4 (1976): 419–426; Ken Sinclair and Michael Ross, "Consequences of Decriminalization of Homosexuality: A Study of Two Australian States," *Journal of Homosexuality* 12, no. 1 (1985); 119–127.

NO
Paul Cameron

A CASE AGAINST HOMOSEXUALITY

In some segments of the mass media, the homosexuality issue takes on the appearance of a struggle between orange juice peddlers and bathhouse owners. At a different level individual rights vs. the interests of society provide the conflict. Some argue that adult homosexuals ought to be allowed to do what they want behind closed doors. Others, often seeing the issue in terms of rights, honesty, and overpopulation, seek to grant homosexuality equal status with heterosexuality. The school system of San Francisco, apparently resonating with the latter tack, is offering a course including "homosexual life-styles." Liberals attempt to shame as unenlightened all who oppose complete equality as vigorously as conservative Bible-thumpers threaten wrath from above.

No known human society has ever granted equal status to homo- and heterosexuality. What information do those who desire social equivalence for these two sexual orientations possess that assures them that this new venture in human social organization is called for at this time? Have the cultures of the past practiced discrimination against homosexuality out of a mere prejudice, or was there substance to their bias? At the risk of seeming rather out of step with the academic community, no new information has surfaced that would lead me to discount the social policies of the past. On the contrary, the policies of the past in regard to homosexuality appear generally wise, and considerable discrimination against homosexuality and for heterosexuality, marriage and parenthood appears needful for the social good.

DISCRIMINATION

Discrimination is something all humans, and all human communities do. Individually we discriminate for certain things and against others, e.g., movies over T.V. Collectively we discriminate for and against selected: 1) acts (pleasantries, sharing vs. murder, robbery) 2) traits (generous, kind vs. whiny, hostile) and 3) life-styles (independent, productive vs. gambling, indolent). Prejudice is unwarranted discrimination. The issue is not whether

From Paul Cameron, "A Case Against Homosexuality," *The Human Life Review,* vol. 4 (1978).

discrimination should exist—for human society to exist, it must. The issues are always: 1) is discrimination called for? and 2) how much is necessary? Reasonable people can and do disagree on what ought to be discriminated for and against, to what degree, and even if discrimination is prejudicial rather than called for. But reasoned opinion *can* hold that homosexuality and homosexuals ought to be discriminated against. . . .

THE CASE AGAINST HOMOSEXUALITY/WISDOM OF THE AGES

No contemporary society accords homosexuality equivalent status with heterosexuality. No known society has accorded equivalent status in the past (Karlen, 1971). No current or ancient religion of any consequence has failed to teach discrimination against homosexuality. The Judeo-Christian tradition is no exception to this rule. The Old Testament made homosexuality a capital offense, and while the New Testament writers failed to invoke capital punishment for any offense, they did manage to consign homosexuals to eternal hell for the practice. Church fathers and traditions have stayed in line with this position until recently. To the degree that tradition and agreed-upon social policy ought to carry weight in our thinking about issues, the weight of tradition is preponderately on the side of discrimination. . . .

While one cannot carry the "wisdom of the ages" argument too far—just because all peoples up to a certain point in time believed something does not necessarily mean that it was so—yet it appears more than a little injudicious to cast it aside as merely "quaint." Probably no

issue has occupied man's collective attentions more than successful living together. That such unanimity of opinion and practice should exist must give one pause. Certainly such congruence "puts the ball in the changer's court." As in so many spheres of human endeavor, when we know that we can get on in a particular way, the burden of proof that we can get on as well or better by following a different custom falls upon those seeking the change. . . .

To date, those seeking change have not been flush with scientific evidence that homosexuality is not socially disruptive. On the contrary, the arguments that have been advanced have been little more than "people ought not to be discriminated against; homosexuals are people; ergo homosexuals ought not to be discriminated against" shouted larger and louder. No one to my knowledge has ever claimed that homosexuals were not people, and one would have to be a dunce to believe that being a person qualifies one, *ipso facto*, for nondiscrimination. Aside from this argument repeated in endless variations and *ad nauseam*, the evidence is simply not there. . . .

Homosociality Coupled With Increasing Self-Centeredness Could Lead to Widespread Homosexuality
. . . Jimmy Carter said: "I don't see homosexuality as a threat to the family" (Washington *Post*, June 19, 1977). His sentiments probably echo those of the educated class of our society. They trust that "only deviants" are really into homosexuality anyway, and, more importantly, that "mother nature" will come through in the last analysis. Biology, they assume, has a great deal to do with sexuality and sexual attraction, and mil-

lions of years of heterosexuality has firmly engraved itself on the genetic code.

Such thinking betrays a lack of appreciation of the enormous component of learning that goes into human sexuality. The point that anthropology has made over the past hundred years is the *tremendous diversity of human social organization*. . . . While the onset of the events of puberty vary relatively little from one society to another, the onset of copulation varies over a full quarter of the life-span—from 5 or 6 years of age to mid-20s. . . . Many mammals practice sex for only a few days or weeks in the year, but man varies from untrammeled lust to studied virginity. While I have enumerated my reasons more fully elsewhere (Cameron, 1977), I believe that the most reasonable construal of the evidence to date suggests that *human sexuality is totally learned*. . . .

Because human sexuality is totally learned, humans must be pointed in the "right" direction, and taught how and with whom to perform. And there's the rub. Homosexuality and heterosexuality do not start off on the same footing. *Au contraire*, one gets a number of important boosts in the scheme of things. In our society the developmental process is decidedly *tilted toward the adoption of homosexuality!*

Part of the homosexual tilt is the extreme homosociality of children starting around the age of 5. As everyone is aware, boys want to play with boys and girls with girls, and they do so with a vengeance. It's quite reasonable, on their part. First, boys' and girls' bodies are different and they are aware that their bodies-to-be will differ still more. In part because of this the games, sports and skills they practice differ. As if in antici-

pation of the differing roles they will have, their interests and proclivities differ. Even if they try, few girls can do as well as most boys at "boy things" and few boys can do as well as girls at "girl things." They almost inhabit different worlds. Not surprisingly for members of two different "races," poles apart psychologically, socially, and physically, they "stick to their own kind." . . .

There are three other components that contribute to the homosexual tilt. First, on the average in our society, males are considerably more taken with sex than females are. In my 1975 survey of 818 persons on the east coast of the U.S., respondents were asked to rate the degree of pleasure they obtained from 22 activities including "being with one's family," "listening to music," "being out in nature," "housework," and "sexual activity." Between the late teens through middle age, sexual activity topped the male list as the "most pleasurable activity." It did manage to rank as high as fifth place for young adult women (aged 18 to 25), but, overall for the female life span, was outscored by almost everything including "housework" (which, incidentally, ranked dead last among males). . . .

How well suited are "hot" males to "cool" females? Not very. One of (if not the) most common problems in marital counseling is sexual incompatibility. *Females pay sex as the price of love/companionship and males pay love for sex.* While this is rather too aphoristic to capture all that goes on in the male-female struggle, there is a great deal of truth to it. Even among homosexuals, the males probably out sex lesbians by a factor of 5 to 1 (see Tripp's sympathetic treatment for elaboration on this theme). Where is a male most apt to find his counterpart, among maledom or femaledom? If he wants hot, dripping sex, what better place to find it than with another of similar bent? If she wants tender companionship, which sex is most apt to provide the partner? The answers are obvious.

The second part of the homosexual tilt derives from the fact that *homosexual encounter offers better sex,* on the average, *than heterosexual sex.* If pleasure is what you are after, who better to fulfill you than a partner who has a body and predilections like yours? One of the things that both the male homosexual and lesbian societies advertise is that "they satisfy.". . . From a sexual standpoint, a female can offer little extra orifice as compensation for her: ignorance, timidity, desire for companionship first, etc. Further, sex between members of a sex assures that there will be no pregnancy problems further on down the line.

Another developmental boost for homosexuality comes from the self-servingness/egocentricity of the young. Humans are born with, at best, rudimentary consciousness. Then, over time and experience, they learn to differentiate themselves from the environment. From about the age of 5 or 6 onward for the next decade or so for life, they are engrossed in themselves, in the service of them-selves, their pleasures, their interests, their ways. Reciprocity of interaction is rendered begrudgingly, certainly far from spontaneously. My research, involving the interviewing of over 8,000 respondents from the U.S. and five other nations, in which we asked persons to tell us: 1) whose interests they had just been thinking about serving—their own or another's or others' and 2) whether they had just been thinking about themselves, things, or other people, indicated that younger persons more frequently reported themselves in a self-serving attitude and thinking about themselves than adults did. In the U.S., adults of both sexes typically reported themselves in an other-serving attitude. But U.S. males "switched" from self-servingness to other-servingness around age 26 while for females the switch occurred in the middle teens. If one is after self-fulfillment, pleasure for self, which sexual orientation "fits" better? Homosexuality, obviously. One can have his homosociality and sex too. One can comfortably neglect the painful transformation from self-interest to other-interest. Me and mine to the fore.

Which kind of sexuality is the more compelling? The one that can say "come, sex my way and I will show you a life of complexity. Of children and responsibility. Of getting on with 'that other kind.' I will offer you poorer sex initially, and, who knows, perhaps you will just have to satisfy yourself with poorer sex permanently. But you will be able to 'glimpse immortality in your children' (Plato)." Or "come, sex my way and I will give it to you straight and hot. Pleasures of the best quality, almost on demand, with persons with whom you already share a great deal, and I will enable you to share more. It will not be difficult, in fact, it will be fun. You will not have to change or adapt your personality style or your egocentric orientation. You'll fit right in immediately. None of this hemming and hawing—you'll get what you want when you want it. Motto? Pleasure—now. The future? Who knows, but the present is going to be a dilly." Which kind of sexuality is the more compelling? Does anyone doubt which way most youth would turn if equivalent social status attended homosexuality and heterosexuality? . . .

A Cluster of Undesirable Traits Is Disproportionately Associated with Homosexuality

Though some may shriek that "my personality traits are my business," let us acknowledge that some traits are society's business. A person's traits can lead to actions which affect the collectivity. Megalomania often proves socially disruptive, and sometimes, as in the case of Hitler, leads to incredible human destruction. It is obviously in society's interest to encourage those social roles and traits that tend to social cohesion and betterment. Similarly, it is in the social interest to discourage those that tend to produce disruption and harm. . . .

It would be as silly to contend that each of the following traits is associated with each homosexual as to argue that none of these appear in heterosexuals (or even worse, that the obverse of these traits always accompanies heterosexuality). However, for social policy formulation, it is enough to demonstrate disproportionate "loading" of undesirable traits within a given subgroup or subculture to justify social discrimination.

THE EGOCENTRIC/SUPERCILIOUS/ NARCISSISTIC/SELF-ORIENTED/ HOSTILE COMPLEX

This cluster of traits appears to "go together" with homosexuality. . . . A person who, in part, seeks more of himself in his lover, is more apt to remain in the egocentric/self-centered orientation of youth. Such a person is more apt to gravitate toward those kinds of professions in which he can be a "star" and be noticed. . . .

The "star" lives for gratification of self. *My* way is his motto. . . . The star need not accommodate himself to the needs of others to the same degree as most folk. If a current love is "not working out" he can be discarded and a more suitable one found. . . .

Superciliousness—an attitude of aloof, hostile disdain—is also consonant with the egocentric person. If you will not realize his marvelous qualities and pay homage, he still has you one down. After all he treated you with contempt *first*. Even if you become hostile, his preceded yours. . . .

The greater component of the childish "I want it my way" associated with homosexuality stems, in part, from the greater ease connected with homosexual attachments. Developmentally, both hetero- and homosexuals want things "their way." But the kinds of accommodations and adjustments necessary for successful heterosexuality assure participants that it won't be all their way. Just because so much of the time things don't work out perfectly in the face of such effort helps wean one from the coddled security of childhood. Parents and the rest of society work to "make the world nice" for children. Every childhood painting is worthy of note, as is every musical note. But adulthood is strewn with disappointments. Heterosexuality is a "maturing" sexual orientation. . . .

It appears to me that homosexuality leads to a shallower commitment to society and its betterment. Such shallowness comes about both because of a lack of children and the ease of sexual gratification. The *effort* involved in being heterosexual, the *effort* expended in being a parent—these are denied the homosexual. As he *has* less responsibility and commitment, so he *is* or becomes less responsible and committed. It is difficult to develop personality characteristics that fail to resonate with one's environment. While we are not totally creatures of our environment, it is far easier to "swim with the tide."

It is difficult to find anything like "hard" scientific evidence to substantiate the notion that homosexuals are on the average, less responsible/trustworthy than heterosexuals. The Weinberg and Williams sample of homosexuals was asked a question that bears upon the issue. Do you agree or disagree with the statement "most people can be trusted"? To a degree, since a person cannot know "most people" it appears reasonable to assume that he might project his own personality onto "most people" and/or assume that those people with whom he comes in contact are like "most people." While 77% of a reasonably representative sample of the U.S. population chose "agree," only 47% of the homosexuals ticked the same response. Because of the ambiguity of such items, I would not make too much of the difference. But it could suggest that homosexuals are less trustworthy.

HOMOSEXUALITY IS ASSOCIATED WITH PERSONAL LETHALITY

One of the more troubling traits associated with homosexuality is personal lethality. Extending back in time to classical Greece, a lethal theme shines through. In Greece, if historical sources are to be believed, companies of homosexual warriors were assembled because it was believed that they made better killers. The same pattern appears to be repeated in history. . . .

In our society the childless are more apt to suicide and childless couples are more apt to be involved in homicide. Further, both suicide and homicide accompany divorce and separation disproportionately frequently. Social cohesion needs to be developed and maintained for optimum personal and social health. . . .

HETEROSEXUALITY PROVIDES THE MOST DESIRABLE MODEL OF LOVE

Myths are created not only by storytellers but by people living within the myths. Almost all (95% or so) heterosexuals get married, and 75%–80% stay married to their original partner till death. To be sure, there are marriage "hogs" within the heterosexual camp who play serial monogamy and assure that a third of all marriages end in divorce. Further, about half of all married men and about a third of all married women admit to one or more infidelities over the duration of their marriage (probably the greater bulk of the "cheaters" come from the serial monogamy camp). While heterosexuality's colors are far from simon pure, the relationship heterosexuality spawns is among, if not *the*, most enduring of human bonds. . . .

Homosexuality offers no comparison in durability. While "slam, bam, thank you ma'am" occurs in heterosexuality, few heterosexuals could more than fantasize about what occurs in homosexual bathhouses or tearooms. As Weinberg and Williams note, the homosexual community typically features "sex for sex's sake." Their survey in which two thirds of their respondents chose to respond "no" to whether they had limited their " . . . sexual relationships primarily to (another)" is telling. Names and banter are typically neglected in bathhouses. . . .

When people are merely "getting their jollies," and fantasizing perfection while doing so, reduced communication is an asset. If you discover that your beautiful lover holds political views antithetical to your own, how can you really enjoy him/her? The "less known the better" is fantasy sex. Communicating, mutually knowledgeable people often have to "work it out" before attempts at sex can even occur. But while typically short on durability, some homosexual relationships are more lasting. The quality of even these is often questionably desirable. Part of the problem lies in the lack of commitment that follows lower effort in the homosexual pairing. Tripp, for instance, opines that part " . . . of the reason many homosexual relationships do not survive the first serious quarrel is that one or both partners simply find it much easier to remarket themselves than work out conflicts (p. 155)." In heterosexuality, no matter how similar the participants, there is always a considerable gap between them. To stay together takes great effort, and the expenditure of this effort prompts both personal and social commitment to the partner. . . .

Because the heterosexual partners are so dissimilar, accommodation and adjustment are their key strategies. Because mutually satisfying heterosexual sexing takes so long and so much effort, both participants have to "hang in there" long after "sane people" would have toddled off in frustration. *We become the way we act. The heterosexual relationship places a premium on "getting on" and thus provides a model to smooth countless other human interactions.* The homosexual model is a considerably less satisfactory one upon which to build a civilization. Note Tripp again (p. 167): " . . .the problems encountered in balancing heterosexual and homosexual relationships are strikingly different. *The heterosexual blend tends to be rich in stimulating contrasts and short on support*—so much so that popular marriage counseling literature incessantly hammers home the advice that couples should develop common interests and dissolve their conflicts by increasing their 'communication.' By comparison, homosexual relationships are overclose, fatigue-prone, and are often adjusted to such narrow, trigger-sensitive tolerances that a mere whisper of disrapport can jolt the partners into making repairs, or into conflict." . . .

Our social system also features large components of delay of gratification. The heterosexual "carrot" is hard to get and requires a lot of input before successful outcome is achieved. The homosexual model is too immediate and influences people to expect instant results. . . .

In short, heterosexuality is effortful, durable, and demands delay of gratification. While any human relationship takes effort, homosexuality pales in comparison to heterosexuality on each count. . . .

From the prudent standpoint, homosexuality is an obstacle in the pursuit of happiness. . . .

Does homosexuality make being happy more difficult? In the Weinberg and Williams study, homosexuals were asked to respond "yes" or "no" to the statement "no one cares what happens to you." While a general population sample had chosen "yes" 23% of the time, 34% of homosexuals chose "yes." . . . Homosexuality, with its emphasis upon self-gratification, does little to generate others who care about you. . . . *In the long run,* heterosexuality has a lot more to offer as a life-style than homosexuality. . . .

SUMMARY

In sum, there are a number of reasons why homosexuality is best treated as a deviant sexual mode. I do not believe that homosexuality ought to be placed on an even-keel with heterosexuality. Further, homosexuals ought not, in my opinion, to be permitted to openly ply their sexual orientation and retain influential positions in the social system. Thus teachers, or pastors who "come out," ought, in my opinion, to lose their claim to the roles they occupy. . . .

REFERENCES

Allport, G. W. The Person in Psychology. NY: Beacon, 1961.

Atkins, J. Sex in Literature. NY: Grove Press, 1970.

Bergler, E. Homosexuality: Disease or Way of Life? NY: Macmillan, 1956.

Bieber, I. Homosexuality: A Psychoanalytic Study. NY: Basic Books, 1962.

Cameron, P. "Immolations to the Juggernaut," Linacre Quarterly, 1977, 44, 64–74.

Cameron, P. The Life-Cycle: Perspectives and Commentary. NY: General Health, 1977.

Cameron, P. & Oeschger, D. "Homosexuality in the Mass Media as Indexed by Magazine Literature over the Past Half Century in the U.S." Paper presented at Eastern Psychological Association Convention, New York, April 4, 1975.

Davis, N. & Graubert, J. Heterosexual. NY: Vantage Press, 1975.

Freud, S. "Three Contributions to Sexual Theory," Nervous and Mental Disease Monograph Series, 1925, 7.

Gubrium, J. F. "Being Single in Old Age," International Journal of Aging and Human Development, 1975, 6, 29–41.

Hunt, M. Sexual Behavior in the 1970s, Chicago: Playboy Press, 1974.

Karlen, A. Sexuality and Homosexuality. NY: Norton, 1971.

Kastenbaum, R. J. & Costa, P. T. "Psychological Perspectives on Death," Annual Review of Psychology, 1977, 28, 225–49.

Maugham, S. El Greco. NY: Doubleday, 1950.

Sears, R. R. "Sources of Life Satisfactions of the Terman Gifted Man," American Psychologist, 1977, 32, 119–128.

Tripp, C. A. The Homosexual Matrix. NY: McGraw-Hill, 1975.

Weinberg, M. S. & Williams, C. J. Male Homosexuals: Their Problems and Adaptations. NY: Oxford University Press, 1974.

POSTSCRIPT

Should Homosexuality Be Accepted by Society?

In the introduction to this issue, attention was drawn to the fact that there is a lack of clear knowledge about homosexuality, which makes this issue somewhat more complicated than many others. It should also be noticed that Cameron's title is "A Case Against Homosexuality"; he doesn't claim that he has the best case or even a representative case, but only that he has *a* case.

On both sides of this question, there is bound to be some selective presentation of "the facts." Often, writers will present as facts many things that are simply regarded by them (but not necessarily by many others) as facts. Mohr and Cameron, for example, seem to disagree about the anthropological facts concerning the role of homosexuality in other societies (particularly in American Indian societies) and its level of acceptance. They also conflict in their account of the history of Judeo-Christian views about homosexuality and its moral status.

Other items are mutually agreed upon, but *interpreted* differently. Cameron, for instance, has some data to support the idea that homosexuals in our society are not happy; but Mohr could use the same data to point out the fact that society has failed these people. (Mohr mentions the victims of "queer-bashing"; how would we expect them to answer the question of whether they were happy?) Cameron also mentions that there are ancient sources that speak of companies of homosexual soldiers being assembled. He suggests that homosexuals have a trait that leads them to be "killers," and thus good soldiers. But the ancients who believed that homosexual soldiers fought bravely and well did not base this belief on the idea that homosexuals were "killers"; they believed that homosexual men fought well because they fought side by side with their lovers. These points bring us to the common problem that much of what we think is the result of what is filtered through our own culture, attitudes, and stereotypes. We cannot take everything that we read at strict face value, and perhaps we should try to overcome some of the difficulties that come with the discussion of homosexuality.

A good scientific account of all aspects of human sexuality is Gary F. Kelly, *Sexuality Today: The Human Perspective*, 3rd ed. (Dushkin Publishing Group, 1992). For a history of Christianity and homosexuality, see J. Boswell, *Christianity, Social Tolerance, and Homosexuality: Gay People in Western Europe from the Beginning of the Christian Era to the Fourteenth Century* (University of Chicago Press, 1980).

Books that discuss homosexuality in America today are Neil Miller, *In Search of Gay America: Women and Men in a Time of Change* (Atlantic Monthly Press, 1989) and Marshall Kirk and Hunter Madsen, *After the Ball: How America Will Conquer Its Fear and Hatred of Gays in the 90s* (Doubleday, 1989).

ISSUE 11

Is Pornography Immoral?

YES: Ann Garry, from "Pornography and Respect for Women," *Social Theory and Practice* (Summer 1978)

NO: G. L. Simons, from *Pornography Without Prejudice* (Abelard-Schuman, 1972)

ISSUE SUMMARY

YES: Professor of philosophy Ann Garry argues that pornography—as it exists today—degrades women and therefore is immoral. Pornographic materials violate principles of respect, and they send a message that calls for the violation of respect for women.

NO: G. L. Simons, a British writer on sex and social issues, claims that while it would be almost impossible to show that pornography (or anything else) is totally harm-free, some people do enjoy pornography and some even learn from it. There is no evidence to show some great harm that would outweigh these acknowledged goods.

Pornography is somewhat difficult to define, and one might well sympathize with the judge who said, "I can't define pornography, but I know it when I see it!" Assuming that we do have some idea about what pornography is, let us hazard the following suggestions: pornography is sexually explicit; it is intended to cause sexual arousal; and pornographic items are generally for sale, or at least are very closely related to commercial operations.

It has sometimes been claimed—especially in the past—that pornography is inherently immoral because it is so clearly focused on sex and sexual arousal, and that these in themselves are bad. Another claim that has been made is that pornography has undesirable consequences, such as violence and crime. We could consider these ideas to be part of the traditional negative view of pornography.

A modern positive view, in answer to these objections, affirms, first, that since sex and sexual arousal are not bad, pornography is not bad; and second, pornography simply does not have the dire consequences that traditional moralists have warned against. The modern positive view often presents itself as a liberation from the old-fashioned narrowness and oppressiveness of the negative view.

Is this positive view simply part of the more liberal and enlightened modern approach to sexual matters? If so, why has it come under attack by many feminists and by those who support sexual liberation?

For the sake of convenience, we will refer to this new attack as "the feminist view"; but although the view stems from feminism, feminism is not one hundred percent behind it, and some feminists would not support it.

We can gain some understanding of the feminist view by comparing it to the traditional negative view. The traditional negative view disapproves of pornography for two main reasons. First, pornography is sexually oriented and sexually explicit. This is seen as a problem because of the traditional view's negative attitude toward sexual matters in general. This is not a problem for the feminist view; subscribers to this view object not to the portrayal of sex but to the portrayal of the degradation of women and of the use of women as sex objects. They object to women being portrayed as *things* used by men for their own sexual purposes. The naked bodies are not the problem, whereas they might be in the traditional view, which is sensitive to nudity; the problem is in the exploitation and degradation of women. We may thus conclude that both the traditional and the feminist critiques of pornography would agree that the content of pornography is offensive, but for different reasons.

The second objection of the traditional negative view is that pornography leads to sexual violence, crimes, and other forms of antisocial behavior. Many would agree that this is indeed the case and that it is one of the many problems with pornography. Others might be more hesitant to agree; perhaps they would regard the data on this as unclear. But many people would want to point out that the important causal connection here might be the other way around. That is, the interesting question might not be whether pornography is a *cause* of sexual and social problems, but whether it is an *effect*; whether it is one of the many results of widespread social injustice and sexism that women suffer from in contemporary society.

The modern view can attempt to meet this criticism of pornography, but it cannot ignore it. Can the modern view assert that "anything goes, now that we are not prudes" if part of this "anything" will include degradation and exploitation? Or will the modern view have some way of showing that degradation and exploitation do not play a part in pornography anyway?

In the following selections, Ann Garry develops one kind of feminist criticism of pornography, while G. L. Simons argues in defense of pornography.

YES

Ann Garry

PORNOGRAPHY AND RESPECT
FOR WOMEN

Pornography, like rape, is a male invention, designed to dehumanize women, to reduce the female to an object of sexual access, not to free sensuality from moralistic or parental inhibition. . . . Pornography is the undiluted essence of anti-female propaganda.

Susan Brownmiller
Against Our Will: Men, Women and Rape[1]

It is often asserted that a distinguishing characteristic of sexually explicit material is the degrading and demeaning portrayal of the role and status of the human female. It has been argued that erotic materials describe the female as a mere sexual object to be exploited and manipulated sexually. . . . A recent survey shows that 41 percent of American males and 46 percent of the females believe that "sexual materials lead people to lose respect for women." . . . Recent experiments suggest that such fears are probably unwarranted.

Presidential Commission on Obscenity and Pornography[2]

The kind of apparent conflict illustrated in these passages is easy to find in one's own thinking as well. For example, I have been inclined to think that pornography is innocuous and to dismiss "moral" arguments for censoring it because many such arguments rest on an assumption I do not share—that sex is an evil to be controlled. At the same time I believe that it is wrong to exploit or degrade human beings, particularly women and others who are especially susceptible. So if pornography degrades human beings, then even if I would oppose its censorship I surely cannot find it morally innocuous.

In an attempt to resolve this apparent conflict I discuss three questions: Does pornography degrade (or exploit or dehumanize) human beings? If so, does it degrade women in ways or to an extent that it does not degrade men? If so, must pornography degrade women, as Brownmiller thinks, or could genuinely innocuous, nonsexist pornography exist? Although much current pornography does degrade women, I will argue that it is possible to have nondegrading, nonsexist pornography. However, this possibility rests on our making certain fundamental changes in our conceptions of sex and sex roles. . . .

From Ann Garry, "Pornography and Respect for Women," *Social Theory and Practice*, vol. 4 (Summer 1978). Copyright © 1978 by Ann Garry. Reprinted by permission of the author.

The . . . argument I will consider is that pornography is morally objectionable, not because it leads people to show disrespect for women, but because pornography itself exemplifies and recommends behavior that violates the moral principle to respect persons. The content of pornography is what one objects to. It treats women as mere sex objects "to be exploited and manipulated" and degrades the role and status of women. In order to evaluate this argument, I will first clarify what it would mean for pornography itself to treat someone as a sex object in a degrading manner. I will then deal with three issues central to the discussion of pornography and respect for women: how "losing respect" for a woman is connected with treating her as a sex object; what is wrong with treating someone as a sex object; and why it is worse to treat women rather than men as sex objects. I will argue that the current content of pornography sometimes violates the moral principle to respect persons. Then . . . I will suggest that pornography need not violate this principle if certain fundamental changes were to occur in attitudes about sex. . . .

First, is it permissible to say that either the content of pornography or pornography itself degrades people or treats people as sex objects? It is not difficult to find examples of degrading content in which women are treated as sex objects. Some pornographic films convey the message that all women really want to be raped, that their resisting struggle is not to be believed. By portraying women in this manner, the content of the movie degrades women. Degrading women is morally objectionable. While seeing the movie need not cause anyone to imitate the behavior shown, we can call the content degrading to women because of the

character of the behavior and attitudes it recommends. The same kind of point can be made about films (or books or TV commercials) with other kinds of degrading, thus morally objectionable, content— for example, racist messages.[3]

The next step in the argument is to infer that, because the content or message of pornography is morally objectionable, we can call pornography itself morally objectionable. Support for this step can be found in an analogy. If a person takes every opportunity to recommend that men rape women, we would think not only that his recommendation is immoral but that he is immoral too. In the case of pornography, the objection to making an inference from recommended behavior to the person who recommends is that we ascribe predicates such as "immoral" differently to people than to films or books. A film vehicle for an objectionable message is still an object independent of its message, its director, its producer, those who act in it, and those who respond to it. Hence one cannot make an unsupported inference from "the content of the film is morally objectionable" to "the film is morally objectionable." Because the central points in this paper do not depend on whether pornography itself (in addition to its content) is morally objectionable, I will not try to support this inference. (The question about the relation of content to the work itself is, of course, extremely interesting; but in part because I cannot decide which side of the argument is more persuasive, I will pass.[4]) Certainly one appropriate way to evaluate pornography is in terms of the moral features of its content. If a pornographic film exemplifies and recommends morally objectionable attitudes or behavior, then its content is morally objectionable.

Let us now turn to the first of our three questions about respect and sex objects: What is the connection between losing respect for a woman and treating her as a sex object? Some people who have lived through the era in which women were taught to worry about men "losing respect" for them if they engaged in sex in inappropriate circumstances find it troublesome (or at least amusing) that feminists—supposedly "liberated" women—are outraged at being treated as sex objects, either by pornography or in any other way. The apparent alignment between feminists and traditionally "proper" women need not surprise us when we look at it more closely.

The "respect" that men have traditionally believed they have for women—hence a respect they can lose—is not a general respect for persons as autonomous beings; nor is it respect that is earned because of one's personal merits or achievements. It is respect that is an outgrowth of the "double standard." Women are to be respected because they are more pure, delicate, and fragile than men, have more refined sensibilities, and so on. Because some women clearly do not have these qualities, thus do not deserve respect, women must be divided into two groups—the good ones on the pedestal and the bad ones who have fallen from it. One's mother, grandmother, Sunday School teacher, and usually one's wife are "good" women. The appropriate behavior by which to express respect for good women would be, for example, not swearing or telling dirty jokes in front of them, giving them seats on buses, and other "chivalrous" acts. This kind of "respect" for good women is the same sort that adolescent boys in the back seats of cars used to "promise" not to lose. Note that men define, dis-

play, and lose this kind of respect. If women lose respect for women, it is not typically a loss of respect for (other) women as a class but a loss of self-respect. . . .

If a person makes two traditional assumptions—that (at least some) sex is dirty and that women fall into two classes, good and bad—it is easy to see how that person might think that pornography could lead people to lose respect for women or that pornography is itself disrespectful to women.[5] Pornography describes or shows women engaging in activities inappropriate for good women to engage in—or at least inappropriate for them to be seen by strangers engaging in. If one sees these women as symbolic representatives of all women, then all women fall from grace with these women. This fall is possible, I believe, because the traditional "respect" that men have had for women is not genuine, wholehearted respect for full-fledged human beings but half-hearted respect for lesser beings, some of whom they feel the need to glorify and purify.[6] It is easy to fall from a pedestal. Can we imagine 41 percent of men and 46 percent of women answering "yes" to the question, "Do movies showing men engaging in violent acts lead people to lose respect for men?"

Two interesting asymmetries appear. The first is that losing respect for men as a class (men with power, typically Anglo men) is more difficult than losing respect for women or ethnic minorities as a class. Anglo men whose behavior warrants disrespect are more likely to be seen as exceptional cases than are women or minorities (whose "transgressions" may be far less serious). Think of the following: women are temptresses; Blacks cheat the welfare system: Italians are gangsters; but the men of the Nixon administration are exceptions—Anglo men as a class did not lose respect because of Watergate and related scandals.

The second asymmetry concerns the active and passive roles of the sexes. Men are seen in the active role. If men lose respect for women because of something "evil" done by women (such as appearing in pornography), the fear is that men will then do harm to women—not that women will do harm to men. Whereas if women lose respect for male politicians because of Watergate, the fear is still that male politicians will do harm, not that women will do harm to male politicians. This asymmetry might be a result of one way in which our society thinks of sex as bad—as harm that men do to women (or to the person playing a female role, as in a homosexual rape) . . . Our slang words for sexual intercourse . . . or older words such as 'take' or 'have'—not only can mean harm but have traditionally taken a male subject and a female object. The active male screws (harms) the passive female. A "bad" woman only tempts men to hurt her further.

It is easy to understand why one's proper grandmother would not want men to see pornography or lose respect for women. But feminists reject these "proper" assumptions: good and bad classes of women do not exist; and sex is not dirty (though many people believe it is). Why then are feminists angry at the treatment of women as sex objects, and why are some feminists opposed to pornography?

The answer is that feminists as well as proper grandparents are concerned with respect. However, there are differences. A feminist's distinction between treating a woman as a full-fledged person and treating her as merely a sex object does not correspond to the good-bad woman distinction. In the latter distinction, "good" and "bad" are properties applicable to groups of women. In the feminist view, all women are full-fledged people—some, however, are treated as sex objects and perhaps think of themselves as sex objects. A further difference is that, although "bad" women correspond to those thought to deserve treatment as sex objects, good women have not corresponded to full-fledged people; only men have been full-fledged people. Given the feminist's distinction, she has no difficulty whatever in saying that pornography treats women as sex objects, not as full-fledged people. She can morally object to pornography or anything else that treats women as sex objects.

One might wonder whether any objection to treatment as a sex object implies that the person objecting still believes, deep down, that sex is dirty. I don't think so. Several other possibilities emerge. First, even if I believe intellectually and emotionally that sex is healthy, I might object to being treated *only* as a sex object. In the same spirit, I would object to being treated *only* as a maker of chocolate chip cookies or *only* as a tennis partner, because only one of my talents is being valued. Second, perhaps I feel that sex is healthy, but it is apparent to me that you think sex is dirty; so I don't want you to treat me as a sex object. Third, being treated as any kind of object, not just as a sex object, is unappealing. I would rather be a partner (sexual or otherwise) than an object. Fourth, and more plausible than the first three possibilities, is [the] view mentioned above [that sex is a harm men do to women]. Both (i) our traditional double standard of sexual behavior for men and women and (ii) the linguistic evidence that we connect the concept of sex with the concept of harm point to what is wrong with treating women as sex objects. . . . Because in our culture we connect sex with harm that men do to women, and because we think of the female role in sex as that of harmed object, we can see that to treat a woman as a sex object is automatically to treat her as less than fully human. To say this does not imply that no healthy sexual relationships exist; nor does it say anything about individual men's conscious intentions to degrade women by desiring them sexually (though no doubt some men have these intentions). It is merely to make a point about the concepts embodied in our language. . . .

Thinking of sex objects as harmed objects enables us to explain some of the first three reasons why one wouldn't want to be treated as a sex object: (1) I may object to being treated only as a tennis partner, but being a tennis partner is not connected in our culture with being a harmed object; and (2) I may not think that sex is dirty and that I would be a harmed object; I may not know what your view is; but what bothers me is that this is the view embodied in our language and culture.

Awareness of the connection between sex and harm helps explain other interesting points. Women are angry about being treated as sex objects in situations or roles in which they do not intend to be regarded in that manner—for example, while serving on a committee or attending a discussion. It is not merely that a sexual role is inappropriate for the circumstances; it is thought to be a less fully human role than the one in which they intended to function.

Finally, the sex-harm connection makes clear why it is worse to treat women as sex objects than to treat men as sex objects, and why some men have had difficulty understanding women's anger about the matter. It is more difficult for heterosexual men than for women to assume the role of "harmed object" in sex; for men have the self-concept of sexual agents, not of passive objects. This is also related to my earlier point concerning the difference in the solidity of respect for men and for women; respect for women is more fragile. Despite exceptions, it is generally harder for people to degrade men, either sexually or nonsexually, than to degrade women. Men and women have grown up with different patterns of self-respect and expectations regarding the extent to which they deserve and will receive respect or degradation. The man who doesn't understand why women do not want to be treated as sex objects (because he'd sure like to be) would not think of himself as being harmed by that treatment; a woman might.[7] Pornography, probably more than any other contemporary institution, succeeds in treating men as sex objects.

Having seen that the connection between sex and harm helps explain both what is wrong with treating someone as a sex object and why it is worse to treat a woman in this way, I want to use the sex-harm connection to try to resolve a dispute about pornography and women. Brownmiller's view, remember, was that pornography is "the undiluted essence of antifemale propaganda" whose purpose is to degrade women.[8] Some people object to Brownmiller's view by saying that, since pornography treats both men and women as sex objects for the purpose of arousing the viewer, it is neither sexist, antifemale, nor designed to degrade women; it just happens that degrading of women arouses some men. How can this dispute be resolved?

Suppose we were to rate the content of all pornography from most morally objectionable to least morally objectionable. Among the most objectionable would be the most degrading—for example, "snuff" films and movies which recommend that men rape women, molest children and puppies, and treat nonmasochists very sadistically.

Next we would find a large amount of material (probably most pornography) not quite so blatantly offensive. With this material it is relevant to use the analysis of sex objects given above. As long as sex is connected with harm done to women, it will be very difficult not to see pornography as degrading to women. We can agree with Brownmiller's opponent that pornography treats men as sex objects, too, but we maintain that this is only pseudoequality; such treatment is still more degrading to women.[9]

In addition, pornography often exemplifies the active/passive, harmer/harmed object roles in a very obvious way. Because pornography today is male-oriented and is supposed to make a profit, the content is designed to appeal to male fantasies. If we judge from the content of the most popular legally available pornography, male fantasies still run along the lines of stereotypical sex roles— . . . [possibly including] elements of hostility. In much pornography the woman's purpose is to cater to male desires, to service the man or men. Her own pleasure is rarely emphasized for its own sake; she is merely allowed a little heavy breathing, perhaps in order to show her dependence on the great male "lover" who produces her pleasure. . . .

What would cases toward the least objectionable end of the spectrum be like? They would be increasingly less degrading and sexist. The genuinely nonobjectionable cases would be nonsexist and nondegrading; but commercial examples do not readily spring to mind.[10] The question is: Does or could any pornography have nonsexist, nondegrading content?

I want to start with the easier question: Is it possible for pornography to have nonsexist, morally acceptable content? Then I will consider whether any pornography of this sort currently exists.

Imagine the following situation, which exists only rarely today: Two fairly conventional people who love each other enjoy playing tennis and bridge together, cooking good food together, and having sex together. In all these activities they are free from hang-ups, guilt, and tendencies to dominate or objectify each other. These two people like to watch tennis matches and old romantic movies on TV, like to watch Julia Child cook, like to read the bridge column in the newspaper, and like to watch pornographic movies. Imagine further that this couple is not at all uncommon in society and that nonsexist pornography is as common as this kind of nonsexist sexual relationship. This situation sounds fine and healthy to me. I see no reason to think that an interest in pornography would disappear in these circumstances. . . . People seem to enjoy watching others experience or do (especially do well) what they enjoy experiencing, doing, or wish they could do themselves. We do not morally object to people watching tennis on TV; why would we object to these hypothetical people watching pornography?

Can we go from the situation today to the situation just imagined? In much current pornography, people are treated in morally objectionable ways. In the scene just imagined, however, pornography would be nonsexist, nondegrading, morally acceptable. The key to making the change is to break the connection between sex and harm. . . . But . . . the sex-harm connection is deeply entrenched and has widespread implications. What is needed is a thorough change in people's deepseated attitudes and feelings about sex roles in general, as well as about sex and roles in sex (sexual roles). Although I cannot even sketch a general outline of such changes here, changes in pornography should be part of a comprehensive program. Television, children's educational material, and nonpornographic movies and novels may be far better avenues for attempting to change attitudes; but one does not want to take the chance that pornography is working against one.

What can be done about pornography in particular? If one wanted to work within the current institutions, one's attempt to use pornography as a tool for the education of male pornography audiences would have to be fairly subtle at first; nonsexist pornography must become familiar enough to sell and be watched. One should realize too that any positive educational value that nonsexist pornography might have may well be as short-lived as most of the effects of pornography. But given these limitations, what could one do?

Two kinds of films must be considered. First is the short film with no plot or character development, just depicted sexual activity in which nonsexist pornography would treat men and women as equal sex partners.[11] The man would not control the circumstances in which the partners had sex or the choice of positions or acts; the woman's preference would be counted equally. There would be no suggestion of a power play or

conquest on the man's part, no suggestion that "she likes it when I hurt her." Sexual intercourse would not be portrayed as primarily for the purpose of male ejaculation—his orgasm is not "the best part" of the movie. In addition, both the man and woman would express their enjoyment; the man need not be cool and detached.

The film with a plot provides even more opportunity for nonsexist education. Today's pornography often portrays the female characters as playthings even when not engaging in sexual activity. Nonsexist pornography could show women and men in roles equally valued by society, and sex equality would amount to more than possession of equally functional genitalia. Characters would customarily treat each other with respect and consideration, with no attempt to treat men or women brutally or thoughtlessly. The local Pussycat Theater showed a film written and directed by a woman (*The Passions of Carol*), which exhibited a few of the features just mentioned. The main female character in it was the editor of a magazine parody of *Viva*. The fact that some of the characters treated each other very nicely, warmly, and tenderly did not detract from the pornographic features of the movie. This should not surprise us, for even in traditional male-oriented films, lesbian scenes usually exhibit tenderness and kindness.

Plots for nonsexist films could include women in traditionally male jobs (e.g., long-distance truckdriver) or in positions usually held in respect by pornography audiences. For example, a high-ranking female Army officer, treated with respect by men and women alike, could be shown not only in various sexual encounters with other people but also carrying out her job in a humane manner.[12]

Or perhaps the main character could be a female urologist. She could interact with nurses and other medical personnel, diagnose illnesses brilliantly, and treat patients with great sympathy as well as have sex with them. When the Army officer or the urologist engage in sexual activities, they will treat their partners and be treated by them in some of the considerate ways described above. . . .

Of course, I could not deny that anyone who tries to change an institution from within faces serious difficulties. This is particularly evident when one is trying to change both pornography and a whole set of related attitudes, feelings, and institutions concerning sex and sex roles. But in conjunction with other attempts to change this set of attitudes, it seems preferable to try to change pornography instead of closing one's eyes in the hope that it will go away. For I suspect that pornography is here to stay.

NOTES

This article first appeared in *Social Theory and Practice*, 4(Summer 1978). It is reprinted here as it appears in Sharon Bishop and Marjorie Weinzweig, eds. *Philosophy and Women* (Wadsworth, 1979). Reprinted by permission of the author.

1. (New York: Simon and Schuster, 1975), p. 394.

2. *The Report of the Commission on Obscenity and Pornography* (Washington, D.C., 1970), p. 201. Hereinafter, *Report*.

3. Two further points need to be mentioned here. Sharon Bishop pointed out to me one reason why we might object to either a racist or rapist mentality in film: it might be difficult for a Black or a woman not to identify with the degraded person. A second point concerns different uses of the phrase "treats women as sex objects." A film treats a subject—the meaninglessness of contemporary life, women as sex objects, and so on—and this use of "treats" is unproblematic. But one should not suppose that this is the same use of "treats women as sex objects" that is found in the sentence "David treats women as sex objects." David is not treating the *subject* of women as sex objects.

4. In order to help one determine which position one feels inclined to take, consider the following statement: It is morally objectionable to write, make, sell, act in, use, and enjoy pornography; in addition, the content of pornography is immoral; however, pornography itself is not morally objectionable. If this statement seems extremely problematic, then one might well be satisfied with the claim that pornography is degrading because its content is.

5. The traditional meaning of "lose respect for women" was evidently the one assumed in the Abelson survey cited by the Presidential Commission. No explanation of its meaning is given in the report of the study. See H. Abelson et al., "National Survey of Public Attitudes Toward and Experience with Erotic Materials." *Tech. Report*, vol. 6, pp. 1–137.

6. Many feminists point this out. One of the most accessible references is Shulamith Firestone, *The Dialectic of Sex: The Case for the Feminist Revolution* (New York: Bantam, 1970), especially pp. 128–32.

7. Men seem to be developing more sensitivity to being treated as sex objects. Many homosexual men have long understood the problem. As women become more sexually aggressive, some heterosexual men I know are beginning to feel treated as sex objects. A man can feel that he is not being taken seriously if a woman looks lustfully at him while he is holding forth about the French judicial system or the failure of liberal politics. Some of his most important talents are not being properly valued.

8. Brownmiller, *Against Our Will*, p. 394.

9. I don't agree with Brownmiller that the purpose of pornography is to dehumanize women; rather it is to arouse the audience. The differences between our views can be explained, in part, by the points from which we begin. She is writing about rape; her views about pornography grow out of her views about rape. I begin by thinking of pornography as merely depicted sexual activity, though I am well aware of the male hostility and contempt for women that it often expresses. That pornography degrades women and excites men is an illustration of this contempt.

10. Virginia Wright Wexman uses the film *Group Marriage* (Stephanie Rothman, 1973) as an example of "more enlightened erotica." Wexman also asks the following questions in an attempt to point out sexism in pornographic films:

Does it [the film] portray rape as pleasurable to women? Does it consistently show females nude but present men fully clothed? Does it present women as childlike creatures whose sexual interests must be guided by knowing experienced men? Does it show sexually aggressive women as castrating viragos? Does it pretend that sex is exclusively the prerogative of women under twenty-five? Does it focus on the physical aspects of lovemaking rather than the emotional ones? Does it portray women as purely sexual beings? ("Sexism of X-rated Films," *Chicago Sun-Times*, 28 March 1976.)

11. If it is a lesbian or male homosexual film, no one would play a caricatured male or female role. The reader has probably noticed that I have limited my discussion to heterosexual pornography, but there are many interesting analogies to be drawn with male homosexual pornography. Very little lesbian pornography exists, though lesbian scenes are commonly found in male-oriented pornography.

12. One should note that behavior of this kind is still considered unacceptable by the military. A female officer resigned from the U.S. Navy recently rather than be court-martialed for having sex with several enlisted men whom she met in a class of interpersonal relations.

NO

G. L. Simons

PORNOGRAPHY WITHOUT PREJUDICE

It is not sufficient, for the objectors' case, that they demonstrate that some harm has flowed from pornography. It would be extremely difficult to show that pornography had *never* had unfortunate consequences, but we should not make too much of this. Harm has flowed from religion, patriotism, alcohol and cigarettes without this fact impelling people to demand abolition. The harm, if established, has to be weighed against a variety of considerations before a decision can be reached as to the propriety of certain laws. Of the British Obscenity Laws the Arts Council Report comments[1] that "the harm would need to be both indisputable and very dire indeed before it could be judged to outweigh the evils and anomalies inherent in the Acts we have been asked to examine."

The onus therefore is upon the anti-pornographers to demonstrate not only that harm is caused by certain types of sexual material but that the harm is considerable: if the first is difficult the second is necessarily more so, and the attempts to date have not been impressive. It is even possible to argue that easily available pornography has a number of benefits. Many people will be familiar with the *catharsis* argument whereby pornography is said to cut down on delinquency by providing would-be criminals with substitute satisfactions. This is considered later but we mention it here to indicate that access to pornography may be socially beneficial in certain instances, and that where this is possible the requirement for anti-pornographers to *justify* their objections must be stressed.

The general conclusion[2] of the U.S. Commission was that no adequate proof had been provided that pornography was harmful to individual or society—"if a case is to be made out against 'pornography' [in 1970] it will have to be made on the grounds other than demonstrated effects of a damaging personal or social nature." . . .

The heresy (to some ears) that pornography is harmless is compounded by the even greater impiety that it may be beneficial. Some of us are managing to adjust to the notion that pornography is unlikely to bring down the world in moral ruin, but the idea that it may actually do good is altogether

From G. L. Simons, *Pornography Without Prejudice* (Blackie & Son, 1972). Copyright © 1972 by G. L. Simons. Reprinted by permission of Blackie & Son, Ltd.

another thing. When we read of Professor Emeritus E. T. Rasmussen, a pioneer of psychological studies in Denmark, a government adviser, saying that there is a possibility "that pornography can be beneficial," many of us are likely to have *mixed* reactions, to say the least. In fact this thesis can be argued in a number of ways.

The simplest approach is to remark that people enjoy it. This can be seen to be true whether we rely on personal testimony or the most respectable index of all in capitalist society—"preparedness to pay." The appeal that pornography has for many people is hardly in dispute, and in a more sober social climate that would be justification enough. Today we are not quite puritan enough to deny that *pleasure* has a worthwhile place in human life: not many of us object to our food being tasty or our clothes being attractive. It was not always like this. In sterner times it was *de rigueur* to prepare food without spices and to wear the plainest clothes. The cult of puritanism reached its apotheosis in the most fanatical asceticism, where it was fashionable for holy men to wander off into a convenient desert and neglect the body to the point of cultivating its lice as "pearls of God." In such a bizarre philosophy pleasure was not only condemned in its sexual manifestations but in all areas where the body could conceivably take satisfaction. These days we are able to countenance pleasure in most fields but in many instances still the case for *sexual* pleasure has to be argued.

Pleasure is not of course its own justification. If it clearly leads to serious malaise, early death, or the *dis*pleasure of others, then there is something to be said against it. But the serious consequences have to be demonstrated: it is not enough to condemn certain forms of pleasurable experience on the grounds of *possible* ill effect. With such an approach *any* human activity could be censured and freedom would have no place. In short, if something is pleasurable and its bad effects are small or nonexistent then it is to be encouraged: opposition to such a creed should be recognized as an unwholesome antipathy to human potential. Pleasure is a good except where it is harmful (and where the harmfulness is *significant*). . . .

That pornography is enjoyable to many people is the first of the arguments in its favour. In any other field this would be argument enough. It is certainly sufficient to justify many activities that have—unlike a taste for pornography—demonstrably harmful consequences. Only in a sexually neurotic society could a tool for heightening sexual enjoyment be regarded as reprehensible and such as to warrant suppression by law. The position is well summarized[3] in the *first* of the Arts Council's twelve reasons for advocating the repeal of the Obscenity Publications Acts:

> It is not for the State to prohibit private citizens from choosing what they may or may not enjoy in literature or art unless there were incontrovertible evidence that the result would be injurious to society. There is no such evidence.

A further point is that availability of pornography may *aid*, rather than frustrate normal sexual development. Thus in 1966, for example, the New Jersey Committee for the Right to Read presented the findings of a survey conducted among nearly a thousand psychiatrists and psychologists of that state. Amongst the various personal statements included was the view that "sexually stimulating materials" might help particular people develop a normal sex drive.[4] In similar spirit, Dr. John Money writes[5] that pornography "may encourage normal sexual development and broadmindedness," a view that may not sound well to the anti-pornographers. And even in circumstances where possible dangers of pornography are pointed out conceivable good effects are sometimes acknowledged. In a paper issued[6] by The Danish Forensic Medicine Council it is pointed out that neurotic and sexually shy people may, by reading pornographic descriptions of normal sexual activity, be freed from some of their apprehension regarding sex and may thereby attain a freer and less frustrated attitude to the sexual side of life. . . .

One argument in favour of pornography is that it can serve as a substitute for actual sexual activity involving another person or other people. This argument has two parts, relating as it does to (1) people who fantasize over *socially acceptable* modes of sexual involvement, and (2) people who fantasize over types of sexual activity that would be regarded as illegal or at least immoral. The first type relates to lonely and deprived people who for one reason or another have been unable to form "normal" sexual contacts with other people; the second type are instances of the much quoted *catharsis* argument.

One writer notes[7] that pornography can serve as a substitute for both the knowledge of which some people have been deprived and the pleasure in sexual experience which they have not enjoyed. One can well imagine men or women too inhibited to secure sexual satisfaction with other adults and where explicit sexual material can alleviate some of their misery. It is facile to remark that such people should seek psychiatric assistance

or even "make an effort": the factors that prevent the forming of effective sexual liaisons are just as likely to inhibit any efforts to seek medical or other assistance. Pornography provides *sex by proxy,* and in such usage it can have a clear justification.

It is also possible to imagine circumstances in which men or women—for reasons of illness, travel or bereavement—are unable to seek sexual satisfaction with spouse or other loved one. Pornography can help here too. Again it is easy to suggest that a person abstain from sexual experience, or, if having *permanently* lost a spouse, seek out another partner. Needless to say such advice is often quite impractical—and the alternative to pornography may be prostitution or adultery. Montagu notes that pornography can serve the same purpose as "dirty jokes," allowing a person to discharge harmlessly repressed and unsatisfied sexual desires.

In this spirit, Mercier (1970) is quoted by the U.S. Commission:

. . . it is in periods of sexual deprivation—to which the young and the old are far more subject than those in their prime—that males, at any rate, are likely to reap psychological benefit from pornography.

And also Kenneth Tynan (1970):

For men on long journeys, geographically cut off from wives and mistresses, pornography can act as a portable memory, a welcome shortcut to remembered bliss, relieving tension without involving disloyalty.

It is difficult to see how anyone could object to the use of pornography in such circumstances, other than on the grounds of a morbid anti-sexuality.

The *catharsis argument* has long been put forward to suggest the availability of pornography will neutralize "aberrant" sexual tendencies and so reduce the incidence of sex crime or clearly immoral behaviour in related fields. (Before evidence is put forward for this thesis it is worth remarking that it should not be necessary to demonstrate a *reduction* in sex crime to justify repeal of the Obscenity Laws. It should be quite sufficient to show that an *increase* in crime will not ensue following repeal. We may even argue that a small increase may be tolerable if other benefits from easy access to pornography could be shown: but it is no part of the present argument to put this latter contention.)

Many psychiatrists and psychologists have favoured the catharsis argument. Chesser, for instance, sees[8] pornography as a form of voyeurism in which—as with sado-masochistic material—the desire to hurt is satisfied passively. If this is so and the analogy can be extended we have only to look at the character of the voyeur—generally furtive and clandestine—to realize that we have little to fear from the pornography addict. Where consumers are preoccupied with fantasy there is little danger to the rest of us. Karpman (1959), quoted by the U.S. Commission, notes that people reading "salacious literature" are less likely to become sexual offenders than those who do not since the reading often neutralizes "aberrant sexual interests." Similarly the Kronhausens have argued that "these 'unholy' instruments" may be a safety-valve for the sexual deviate and potential sex offender. And Cairns, Paul and Wishner (1962) have remarked that *obscene materials* provide a way of releasing strong sexual urges without doing harm to others.

It is easy to see the plausibility of this argument. The popularity of all forms of sexual literature—from the superficial, *sexless*, sentimentality of the popular women's magazine to the clearest "hardcore" porn—has demonstrated over the ages the perennial appetite that people have for fantasy. To an extent, a great extent with many single people and frustrated married ones, the fantasy constitutes an important part of the sex-life. The experience may be vicarious and sterile but it self-evidently fills a need for many individuals. If literature, as a *symbol* of reality, can so involve human sensitivities it is highly likely that when the sensitivities are *distorted* for one reason or another the same sublimatory function can occur: the "perverted" or potentially criminal mentality can gain satisfaction, as does the lonely unfortunate, in *sex by proxy*. If we wanted to force the potential sex criminal on to the streets in search of a human victim perhaps we would do well to deny him his sublimatory substitutes: deny him fantasy and he will be forced to go after the real thing. . . .

The importance of this possibility should be fully faced. If a causal connection *does* exist between availability of pornographic material and a *reduction* in the amount of sex crime—and the evidence is wholly consistent with this possibility rather than its converse—then people who deliberately restrict pornography by supporting repressive legislation are prime architects of sexual offences against the individual. The anti-pornographers would do well to note that their anxieties may be driving them into a position the exact opposite of the one they explicitly maintain—their commitment to reduce the amount of sexual delinquency in society.

The most that the anti-pornographers can argue is that at present the evidence is inconclusive. . . . But if the inconclusive character of the data is once admitted then the case for repressive legislation falls at once. For in a *free* society, or one supposedly aiming after freedom, social phenomena are, like individuals, innocent until proven guilty—and an activity will be permitted unless there is clear evidence of its harmful consequences. This point was well put—in the specific connection with pornography—by Bertrand Russell, talking[9] when he was well over 90 to Rupert Crawshay-Williams.

After noting how people beg the question of causation in instances such as the Moors murders (where the murders and the reading of de Sade *may* have a common cause), Russell ("Bertie") said that on the whole he disapproved of sadistic pornography being available. But when Crawshay-Williams put the catharsis view, that such material might provide a harmless release for individuals who otherwise may be dangerous, Russell said at once—"Oh, well, if that's true, then I don't see that there is anything against sadistic pornography. In fact it should be encouraged . . ." When it was stressed that there was no preponderating evidence either way Russell argued that we should fall back on an overriding principle—"in this case the principle of free speech."

Thus in the absence of evidence of harm we should be permissive. Any other view is totalitarian. . . .

If human enjoyment *per se* is not to be condemned then it is not too rash to say that we *know* pornography does good. We can easily produce our witnesses to testify to experiencing pleasure. If in the face of this—and no other favourable argument—we are unable to demonstrate a countervailing harm, then the case for easy availability of pornography is unassailable. If, in such circumstances,

we find some people unconvinced it is futile to seek out further empirical data. Once we commit ourselves to the notion that the evil nature of something is axiomatic we tacitly concede that evidence is largely irrelevant to our position. If pornography never fails to fill us with predictable loathing then statistics on crime, or measured statements by careful specialists, will not be useful: our reactions will stay the same. But in this event we would do well to reflect on what our emotions tell us of our own mentality.

NOTES

1. *The Obscenity Laws*, André Deutsch, 1969, p. 33.

2. *The Report of the Commission on Obscenity and Pornography*, Part Three, II, Bantam Books, 1970, p. 169.

3. *The Obscenity Laws*, André Deutsch, 1969, p. 35.

4. Quoted by Isadore Rubin, "What Should Parents Do About Pornography?" *Sex in the Adolescent Years*, Fontana, 1969, p. 202.

5. John Money, contribution to "Is Pornography Harmful to Young Children?" *Sex in the Childhood Years*, Fontana, 1971, pp. 181-5.

6. Paper from The Danish Forensic Medicine Council to The Danish Penal Code Council, published in The Penal Code Council Report on Penalty for Pornography, Report No. 435, Copenhagen, 1966, pp. 78-80, and as appendix to *The Obscenity Laws*, pp. 120-4.

7. Ashley Montagu, "Is Pornography Harmful to Young Children?" *Sex in the Childhood Years*, Fontana, 1971, p. 1982.

8. Eustace Chesser, *The Human Aspects of Sexual Deviation*, Arrow Books, 1971, p. 39.

9. Rupert Crawshay-Williams, *Russell Remembered*, Oxford University Press, 1970, p. 144.

POSTSCRIPT

Is Pornography Immoral?

The feminist view admits a possibility that the traditional, negative view of pornography would never allow: that nonsexist, nondegrading pornography might appear in the future. According to the feminist view, it is possible to remove the offending elements from pornography and still have pornography. With the traditional view, to remove the "offending" elements would require removal of the sexual elements—then you would no longer have pornography.

Here are some further questions to consider about the validity of Simons's catharsis argument. Suppose, for example, that some parents could be prevented from committing child abuse by working off their pent-up feelings in a harmless, cathartic way through the viewing of films in which children were portrayed as being the objects of hostility and abuse. If this were true, should these films be made available to parents? Would the films be a reasonable short-term as well as long-term solution to child abuse? Does this example suggest that the cathartic argument is as strong as Simons believes?

One reply to this line of thought might be that child abuse is a bad thing but that the sex that is portrayed in pornography (and the sexual feelings that are released through the catharsis) is not bad. This might be where the feminist could reenter the argument and assert that in most present-day pornography, the feelings that are aroused (and, according to Simons, purged) are bad: they focus on the dehumanization of women.

Many questions remain unanswered. First, it is unclear when we say "pornography" whether we are talking about violent pornography, child pornography, heterosexual pornography, novels, videotapes, stories involving rapes, stories involving mutually enjoyable sex, all of the above, some of the above, or more than the above. Second, some questions might be explored by some empirical research, such as: Does a given type of pornography have a detrimental impact on behavior and attitudes? There are also legal and constitutional questions concerning what the law is (or what it ought to be) with respect to the censorship or protection of pornographic materials.

These issues are treated further in Laura Lederer, ed., *Take Back the Night: Women on Pornography* (Morrow, 1980); Alan Soble, "Pornography: Defamation and the Endorsement of Degradation," *Social Theory and Practice* (1985); Varda Burstyn, ed., *Women Against Censorship* (Douglas & McIntyre, 1985); David Copp and Susan Wendell, eds., *Pornography and Censorship* (Prometheus Books, 1983); Andrea Dworkin, *Pornography: Men Possessing Women* (Putnam, 1981); Edward Donnerstein, Daniel Linz, and Steven Penrop, *The Question of Pornography: Research Findings and Policy Implications* (Free Press, 1987); Ronald Dworkin, "Liberty and Pornography," in *New York Review of Books* (August 15, 1991); also his *A Matter of Principle* (Harvard University Press, 1985); Catharine MacKinnon, "Pornography, Civil Rights, and Speech," *Harvard Civil Rights-Civil Liberties Law Review* (Winter 1985); also her "Sexuality, Pornography, and Method: 'Pleasure under Patriarchy,' " *Ethics* (1989),; and F. M. Christensen, *Pornography: The Other Side* (Praeger, 1990).

Relevant government reports recently published in the United States, Canada, and Great Britain include the Attorney General's Commission on Pornography, *Final Report* (U.S. Department of Justice, 1986); Special Committee on Pornography and Prostitution, *Pornography and Prostitution Issues Paper* (Minister of Supply and Services, Canada, 1983); and Bernard Williams, *Report of the Committee on Obscenity and Film Censorship* (Her Majesty's Stationery Office, 1979), abridged in Bernard Williams, ed., *Obscenity and Film Censorship* (Cambridge University Press, 1981).

ISSUE 12

Is Abortion Immoral?

YES: Don Marquis, from "Why Abortion Is Immoral," *The Journal of Philosophy* (1989)

NO: Jane English, from "Abortion and the Concept of a Person," *Canadian Journal of Philosophy* (October 1975)

ISSUE SUMMARY

YES: Professor of philosophy Don Marquis argues that abortion is generally wrong for the same reason that killing an innocent adult human being is generally wrong: we deprive the individual of a future that he or she would otherwise have.

NO: Philosopher Jane English (1947–1978) argues that there is no well-defined line dividing persons from nonpersons. She claims that both the conservative and the liberal positions are too extreme and that some abortions are morally justifiable and some are not.

Abortion is a divisive topic, and discussions can easily become polarized. Here we will briefly consider some of the biological facts associated with abortion; then we will review relevant historical and legal matters; and finally the articles themselves will look at the moral issues raised by abortion.

Conception occurs when the spermatozoon of a male unites with the ovum of a female. The single cell thus formed is called a zygote. In a normal pregnancy, this zygote will multiply into several cells, travel through the fallopian tube, enter the uterus, and implant itself in the uterine wall. When implantation is complete, one to two weeks after fertilization, as the original conception is also called, we can say that the pregnancy is established and that the zygote has become an embryo. (Between the second and fourth week after conception, it is thought that it is possible for the embryo to divide into two, which could later result in the birth of identical twins.) Once the placenta and umbilical cord are established, the embryo takes nourishment by means of these from the blood of the pregnant woman and grows primitive limbs and organs rather quickly. At eight weeks from conception, the first brain waves can be detected and the embryo is now called a fetus. So-called quickening, the first felt spontaneous movement of the fetus, occurs at around 14 or 15 weeks. The threshhold of viability (the point at which the fetus can be kept alive outside the uterus) is dependent upon many factors, especially the development of the cardiopulmonary system. Depending on the level of available medical technology, viability can be reached sometime between about 20 to 28 weeks. Birth generally takes place about 38 to 40 weeks after conception, although here too there is significant variation.

There are other possibilities once the spermatozoon and ovum unite. The fertilized ovum, for example, might never be implanted in the wall of the uterus and might be expelled uneventfully, and even without notice, from the body. Or the zygote might implant itself somewhere other than inside the uterus, resulting in an ectopic pregnancy. The embryo will not grow properly and this kind of pregnancy can be dangerous. (In the case of an ectopic pregnancy, the Roman Catholic Church will permit an abortion to save the pregnant woman's life.) Another possibility is that the pregnancy will develop normally for a while but then end in miscarriage; this is sometimes called a spontaneous abortion.

The historic *Roe v. Wade* case, decided in 1973 by the U.S. Supreme Court in a split decision of 7-2, ruled that the nineteenth-century Texas statutes against abortion were unconstitutional. The Court divided the normal pregnancy into three trimesters, and ruled as follows.

For the stage prior to approximately the end of the first trimester, the abortion decision and its effectuation must be left to the medical judgment of the pregnant woman's attending physician. For the stage subsequent to approximately the end of the first trimester, the State, in promoting its interest in the health of the mother, may, if it chooses, regulate the abortion procedure in ways that are reasonably related to maternal health. For the stages subsequent to viability, the State, in promoting its interest in the potentiality of human life, may, if it chooses, regulate, and even proscribe, abortion except where it is necessary, in appropriate medical judgment, for the preservation of the life or health of the mother. (410 U.S. 113, 93 S.Ct. 705 [1973])

Before *Roe v. Wade*, some states, like Texas, permitted abortion only if a woman's *life* was in danger; abortion for any other reason or consideration was illegal and punishable by law. *Roe v. Wade* ruled that states do not have the right to regulate abortion procedures in any way during the first trimester of pregnancy. It is important to note that neither the Supreme Court nor the Texas statutes said anything about the relation of the woman to the fetus (or embryo) or about the reasons a woman might have for seeking an abortion.

In the following selections, Don Marquis constructs a secular argument that aims to show that abortion is immoral. He addresses a question that is not considered by the Texas courts or the U.S. Supreme Court, but is nevertheless thought by many people to be absolutely central here: when does the fetus become a human being (or person)? Jane English argues that this question is *not* decisive and in any case has no determinate answer. In her view, neither the standard conservative position nor the standard liberal position adequately address what she feels are the circumstances that surround a permissible abortion.

207

YES
Don Marquis

WHY ABORTION IS IMMORAL

The view that abortion is, with rare exceptions, seriously immoral has received little support in the recent philosophical literature. No doubt most philosophers affiliated with secular institutions of higher education believe that the anti-abortion position is either a symptom of irrational religious dogma or a conclusion generated by seriously confused philosophical argument. The purpose of this essay is to undermine this general belief. This essay sets out an argument that purports to show, as well as any argument in ethics can show, that abortion is, except possibly in rare cases, seriously immoral, that it is in the same moral category as killing an innocent adult human being.

The argument is based on a major assumption. Many of the most insightful and careful writers on the ethics of abortion—such as Joel Feinberg, Michael Tooley, Mary Anne Warren, H. Tristram Engelhardt, Jr., L. W. Sumner, John T. Noonan, Jr., and Philip Devine[1]—believe that whether or not abortion is morally permissible stands or falls on whether or not a fetus is the sort of being whose life it is seriously wrong to end. The argument of this essay will assume, but not argue, that they are correct.

Also, this essay will neglect issues of great importance to a complete ethics of abortion. Some anti-abortionists will allow that certain abortions, such as abortion before implantation or abortion when the life of a woman is threatened by a pregnancy or abortion after rape, may be morally permissible. This essay will not explore the casuistry of these hard cases. The purpose of this essay is to develop a general argument for the claim that the overwhelming majority of deliberate abortions are seriously immoral.

I.

A sketch of standard anti-abortion and pro-choice arguments exhibits how those arguments possess certain symmetries that explain why partisans of those positions are so convinced of the correctness of their own positions,

From Don Marquis, "Why Abortion Is Immoral," *The Journal of Philosophy*, vol. 86, no. 4 (April 1989). Copyright © 1989 by The Journal of Philosophy, Inc. Reprinted by permission why they are not successful in convincing their opponents, and why, to others, this issue seems to be unresolvable. An analysis of the nature of this standoff suggests a strategy for surmounting it.

Consider the way a typical anti-abortionist argues. She will argue or assert that life is present from the moment of conception or that fetuses look like babies or that fetuses possess a characteristic such as a genetic code that is both necessary and sufficient for being human. Anti-abortionists seem to believe that (1) the truth of all of these claims is quite obvious, and (2) establishing any of these claims is sufficient to show that abortion is morally akin to murder.

A standard pro-choice strategy exhibits similarities. The pro-choicer will argue or assert that fetuses are not persons or that fetuses are not rational agents or that fetuses are not social beings. Pro-choicers seem to believe that (1) the truth of any of these claims is quite obvious, and (2) establishing any of these claims is sufficient to show that an abortion is not a wrongful killing.

In fact, both the pro-choice and the anti-abortion claims do seem to be true, although the "it looks like a baby" claim is more difficult to establish the earlier the pregnancy. We seem to have a standoff. How can it be resolved?

As everyone who has taken a bit of logic knows, if any of these arguments concerning abortion is a good argument, it requires not only some claim characterizing fetuses, but also some general moral principle that ties a characteristic of fetuses to having or not having the right to life or to some other moral characteristic that will generate the obligation or the lack of obligation not to end the life of a fetus. Accordingly, the arguments of the anti-abortionist and the pro-choicer need a bit of filling in to be regarded as adequate.

Note what each partisan will say. The anti-abortionist will claim that her position is supported by such generally accepted moral principles as "It is always prima facie seriously wrong to take a human life" or "It is always prima facie seriously wrong to end the life of a baby." Since these are generally accepted moral principles, her position is certainly not obviously wrong. The pro-choicer will claim that her position is supported by such plausible moral principles as "Being a person is what gives an individual intrinsic moral worth" or "It is only seriously prima facie wrong to take the life of a member of the human community." Since these are generally accepted moral principles, the pro-choice position is certainly not obviously wrong. Unfortunately, we have again arrived at a standoff.

Now, how might one deal with this standoff? The standard approach is to try to show how the moral principles of one's opponent lose their plausibility under analysis. It is easy to see how this is possible. On the one hand, the anti-abortionist will defend a moral principle concerning the wrongness of killing which tends to be broad in scope in order that even fetuses at an early stage of pregnancy will fall under it. The problem with broad principles is that they often embrace too much. In this particular instance, the principle "It is always prima facie wrong to take a human life" seems to entail that it is wrong to end the existence of a living human cancer-cell culture, on the grounds that the culture is both living and human. Therefore, it seems that the anti-abortionist's favored principle is too broad.

On the other hand, the pro-choicer wants to find a moral principle concerning the wrongness of killing which tends to be narrow in scope in order that fetuses will *not* fall under it. The problem with narrow principles is that they often do not embrace enough. Hence, the needed principles such as "It is prima facie seriously wrong to kill only persons" or "It is prima facie wrong to kill only rational agents" do not explain why it is wrong to kill infants or young children or the severely retarded or even perhaps the severely mentally ill. Therefore, we seem again to have a standoff. The anti-abortionist charges, not unreasonably, that pro-choice principles concerning killing are too narrow to be acceptable; the pro-choicer charges, not unreasonably, that anti-abortionist principles concerning killing are too broad to be acceptable.

Attempts by both sides to patch up the difficulties in their positions run into further difficulties. The anti-abortionist will try to remove the problem in her position by reformulating her principle concerning killing in terms of human beings. Now we end up with: "It is always prima facie seriously wrong to end the life of a human being." This principle has the advantage of avoiding the problem of the human cancer-cell culture counterexample. But this advantage is purchased at a high price. For although it is clear that a fetus is both human and alive, it is not at all clear that a fetus is a human *being*. There is at least something to be said for the view that something becomes a human being only after a process of development, and that therefore first trimester fetuses and perhaps all fetuses are not yet human beings. Hence, the anti-abortionist, by this move, has merely exchanged one problem for another.[2]

The pro-choicer fares no better. She may attempt to find reasons why killing infants, young children, and the severely retarded is wrong which are independent of her major principle that is supposed to explain the wrongness of taking human life, but which will not also make abortion immoral. This is no easy task. Appeals to social utility will seem satisfactory only to those who resolve not to think of the enormous difficulties with a utilitarian account of the wrongness of killing and the significant social costs of preserving the lives of the unproductive.[3] A pro-choice strategy that extends the definition of 'person' to infants or even to young children seems just as arbitrary as an anti-abortion strategy that extends the definition of 'human being' to fetuses. Again, we find symmetries in the two positions and we arrive at a standoff.

There are even further problems that reflect symmetries in the two positions. In addition to counterexample problems, or the arbitrary application problems that can be exchanged for them, the standard anti-abortionist principle "It is prima facie seriously wrong to kill a human being," or one of its variants, can be objected to on the grounds of ambiguity. If 'human being' is taken to be a *biological* category, then the anti-abortionist is left with the problem of explaining why a merely biological category should make a moral difference. Why, it is asked, is it any more reasonable to base a moral conclusion on the number of chromosomes in one's cells than on the color of one's skin?[4] If 'human being', on the other hand, is taken to be a *moral* category, then the claim that a fetus is a human being cannot be taken to be a premise in the anti-abortion argument, for it is precisely what needs to be established. Hence, either the anti-abortionist's main category is a morally irrelevant, merely biological category, or it is of no use to the anti-abortionist in establishing (noncircularly, of course) that abortion is wrong.

Although this problem with the anti-abortionist position is often noticed, it is less often noticed that the pro-choice position suffers from an analogous problem. The principle "Only persons have the right to life" also suffers from an ambiguity. The term 'person' is typically defined in terms of psychological characteristics, although there will certainly be disagreement concerning which characteristics are most important. Supposing that this matter can be settled, the pro-choicer is left with the problem of explaining why *psychological* characteristics should make a *moral* difference. If the pro-choicer should attempt to deal with this problem by claiming that an explanation is not necessary, that in fact we do treat such a cluster of psychological properties as having moral significance, the sharp-witted anti-abortionist should have a ready response. We do treat being both living and human as having moral significance. If it is legitimate for the pro-choicer to demand that the anti-abortionist provide an explanation of the connection between the biological character of being a human being and the wrongness of being killed (even though people accept this connection), then it is legitimate for the anti-abortionist to demand that the pro-choicer provide an explanation of the connection between psychological criteria for being a person and the wrongness of being killed (even though that connection is accepted).[5] . . .

[T]he pro-choicer cannot any more escape her problem by making person a purely moral category than the anti-abor-tionist could escape by the analogous move. For if person is a moral category, then the pro-choicer is left without the resources for establishing (noncircularly, of course) the claim that a fetus is not a person, which is an essential premise in her argument. Again, we have both a symmetry and a standoff between pro-choice and anti-abortion views.

Passions in the abortion debate run high. There are both plausibilities and difficulties with the standard positions. Accordingly, it is hardly surprising that partisans of either side embrace with fervor the moral generalizations that support the conclusions they preanalytically favor, and reject with disdain the moral generalizations of their opponents as being subject to inescapable difficulties. It is easy to believe that the counterexamples to one's own moral principles are merely temporary difficulties that will dissolve in the wake of further philosophical research, and that the counterexamples to the principles of one's opponents are . . . straightforward. . . . This might suggest to an impartial observer (if there are any) that the abortion issue is unresolvable.

There is a way out of this apparent dialectical quandary. The moral generalizations of both sides are not quite correct. The generalizations hold for the most part, for the usual cases. This suggests that they are all *accidental* generalizations, that the moral claims made by those on both sides of the dispute do not touch on the *essence* of the matter.

This use of the distinction between essence and accident is not meant to invoke obscure metaphysical categories. Rather, it is intended to reflect the rather atheoretical nature of the abortion discussion. If the generalization a partisan in the abortion dispute adopts were derived from the reason why ending the life of a human being is wrong, then there could not be exceptions to that generalization unless some special case obtains in which there are even more powerful countervailing reasons. Such generalizations would not be merely accidental generalizations; they would point to, or be based upon, the essence of the wrongness of killing, what it is that makes killing wrong. All this suggests that a necessary condition of resolving the abortion controversy is a more theoretical account of the wrongness of killing. After all, if we merely believe, but do not understand, why killing adult human beings such as ourselves is wrong, how could we conceivably show that abortion is either immoral or permissible?

II.

In order to develop such an account, we can start from the following unproblematic assumption concerning our own case: it is wrong to kill *us*. Why is it wrong? . . .

What primarily makes killing wrong is neither its effect on the murderer nor its effect on the victim's friends and relatives, but its effect on the victim. The loss of one's life is one of the greatest losses one can suffer. The loss of one's life deprives one of all the experiences, activities, projects, and enjoyments that would otherwise have constituted one's future. Therefore, killing someone is wrong, primarily because the killing inflicts (one of) the greatest possible losses on the victim. To describe this as the loss of life can be misleading, however. The change in my biological state does not by itself make killing me wrong. The effect of the loss of my biological life is the loss to me of all those activities, projects, experiences, and enjoyments which would otherwise have constituted my future personal life. These

activities, projects, experiences, and enjoyments are either valuable for their own sakes or are means to something else that is valuable for its own sake. Some parts of my future are not valued by me now, but will come to be valued by me as I grow older and as my values and capacities change. When I am killed, I am deprived both of what I now value which would have been part of my future personal life, but also what I would come to value. Therefore, when I die, I am deprived of all of the value of my future. Inflicting this loss on me is ultimately what makes killing me wrong. This being the case, it would seem that what makes killing *any* adult human being prima facie seriously wrong is the loss of his or her future.[6] . . .

The claim that what makes killing wrong is the loss of the victim's future is directly supported by two considerations. In the first place, this theory explains why we regard killing as one of the worst of crimes. Killing is especially wrong, because it deprives the victim of more than perhaps any other crime. In the second place, people with AIDS or cancer who know they are dying believe, of course, that dying is a very bad thing for them. They believe that the loss of a future to them that they would otherwise have experienced is what makes their premature death a very bad thing for them. A better theory of the wrongness of killing would require a different natural property associated with killing which better fits with the attitudes of the dying. What could it be?

The view that what makes killing wrong is the loss to the victim of the value of the victim's future gains additional support when some of its implications are examined. In the first place, it is incompatible with the view that it is wrong to kill only beings who are biologically human. It is possible that there exists a different species from another planet whose members have a future like ours. Since having a future like that is what makes killing someone wrong, this theory entails that it would be wrong to kill members of such a species. Hence, this theory is opposed to the claim that only life that is biologically human has great moral worth, a claim which many anti-abortionists have seemed to adopt. This opposition, which this theory has in common with personhood theories, seems to be a merit of the theory.

In the second place, the claim that the loss of one's future is the wrong-making feature of one's being killed entails the possibility that the futures of some actual nonhuman mammals on our own planet are sufficiently like ours that it is seriously wrong to kill them also. Whether some animals do have the same right to life as human beings depends on adding to the account of the wrongness of killing some additional account of just what it is about my future or the futures of other adult human beings which makes it wrong to kill us. No such additional account will be offered in this essay. Undoubtedly, the provision of such an account would be a very difficult matter. Undoubtedly, any such account would be quite controversial. Hence, it surely should not reflect badly on this sketch of an elementary theory of the wrongness of killing that it is indeterminate with respect to some very difficult issues regarding animal rights.

In the third place, the claim that the loss of one's future is the wrong-making feature of one's being killed does not entail, as sanctity of human life theories do, that active euthanasia is wrong. Persons who are severely and incurably ill, who face a future of pain and despair, and who wish to die will not have suffered a loss if they are killed. It is, strictly speaking, the value of a human's future which makes killing wrong in this theory. This being so, killing does not necessarily wrong some persons who are sick and dying. Of course, there may be other reasons for a prohibition of active euthanasia, but that is another matter. Sanctity-of-human-life theories seem to hold that active euthanasia is seriously wrong even in an individual case where there seems to be good reason for it independently of public policy considerations. This consequence is most implausible, and it is a plus for the claim that the loss of a future of value is what makes killing wrong that it does not share this consequence.

In the fourth place, the account of the wrongness of killing defended in this essay does straightforwardly entail that it is prima facie seriously wrong to kill children and infants, for we do presume that they have futures of value. Since we do believe that it is wrong to kill defenseless little babies, it is important that a theory of the wrongness of killing easily account for this. Personhood theories of the wrongness of killing, on the other hand, cannot straightforwardly account for the wrongness of killing infants and young children.[7] Hence, such theories must add special ad hoc accounts of the wrongness of killing the young. The plausibility of such ad hoc theories seems to be a function of how desperately one wants such theories to work. The claim that the primary wrong-making feature of a killing is the loss to the victim of the value of its future accounts for the wrongness of killing young children and infants directly; it makes the wrongness of such acts as obvious as we actually think it is.

This is a further merit of this theory. Accordingly, it seems that this value of a future-like-ours theory of the wrongness of killing shares strengths of both sanctity-of-life and personhood accounts while avoiding weaknesses of both. In addition, it meshes with a central intuition concerning what makes killing wrong.

The claim that the primary wrong-making feature of a killing is the loss to the victim of the value of its future has obvious consequences for the ethics of abortion. The future of a standard fetus includes a set of experiences, projects, activities, and such which are identical with the futures of adult human beings and are identical with the futures of young children. Since the reason that is sufficient to explain why it is wrong to kill human beings after the time of birth is a reason that also applies to fetuses, it follows that abortion is prima facie seriously morally wrong. . . .

III.

How complete an account of the wrongness of killing does the value of a future-like-ours account have to be in order that the wrongness of abortion is a consequence? This account does not have to be an account of the necessary conditions for the wrongness of killing. Some persons in nursing homes may lack valuable human futures, yet it may be wrong to kill them for other reasons. Furthermore, this account does not obviously have to be the sole reason killing is wrong where the victim did have a valuable future. This analysis claims only that, for any killing where the victim did have a valuable future like ours, having that future by itself is sufficient to create the strong presumption that the killing is seriously wrong. . . .

IV.

In this essay, it has been argued that the correct ethic of the wrongness of killing can be extended to fetal life and used to show that there is a strong presumption that any abortion is morally impermissible. If the ethic of killing adopted here entails, however, that contraception is also seriously immoral, then there would appear to be a difficulty with the analysis of this essay.

But this analysis does not entail that contraception is wrong. Of course, contraception prevents the actualization of a possible future of value. Hence, it follows from the claim that futures of value should be maximized that contraception is prima facie immoral. This obligation to maximize does not exist, however; furthermore, nothing in the ethics of killing in this paper entails that it does. The ethics of killing in this essay would entail that contraception is wrong only if something were denied a human future of value by contraception. Nothing at all is denied such a future by contraception, however. . . .

At the time of contraception, there are hundreds of millions of sperm, one (released) ovum and millions of possible combinations of all of these. There is no actual combination at all. Is the subject of the loss to be a merely possible combination? Which one? This alternative does not yield an actual subject of harm either. Accordingly, the immorality of contraception is not entailed by the loss of a future-like-ours argument simply because there is no nonarbitrarily identifiable subject of the loss in the case of contraception.

V.

The purpose of this essay has been to set out an argument for the serious presumptive wrongness of abortion subject to the assumption that the moral permissibility of abortion stands or falls on the moral status of the fetus. Since a fetus possesses a property, the possession of which in adult human beings is sufficient to make killing an adult human being wrong, abortion is wrong. This way of dealing with the problem of abortion seems superior to other approaches to the ethics of abortion, because it rests on an ethics of killing which is close to self-evident, because the crucial morally relevant property clearly applies to fetuses, and because the argument avoids the usual equivocations on 'human life', 'human being', or 'person'. The argument rests neither on religious claims nor on Papal dogma. It is not subject to the objection of "speciesism." Its soundness is compatible with the moral permissibility of euthanasia and contraception. It deals with our intuitions concerning young children.

Finally, this analysis can be viewed as resolving a standard problem—indeed, *the* standard problem—concerning the ethics of abortion. Clearly, it is wrong to kill adult human beings. Clearly, it is not wrong to end the life of some arbitrarily chosen single human cell. Fetuses seem to be like arbitrarily chosen human cells in some respects and like adult humans in other respects. The problem of the ethics of abortion is the problem of determining the fetal property that settles this moral controversy. The thesis of this essay is that the problem of the ethics of abortion, so understood, is solvable.

NOTES

1. Feinberg, "Abortion," in *Matters of Life and Death: New Introductory Essays in Moral Philosophy*, Tom Regan, ed. (New York: Random House, 1986), pp. 256–293; Tooley, "Abortion and Infanticide," *Philosophy and Public Affairs*, ii, 1 (1972): 37–65; Tooley, *Abortion and Infanticide* (New York: Oxford, 1984); Warren, "On the Moral and Legal Status of Abortion," *The Monist*, i.vii, 1 (1973): 43–61; Engelhardt, "The Ontology of Abortion," *Ethics*, i.xxxiv, 3 (1974):217–234; Sumner, *Abortion and Moral Theory* (Princeton: University Press, 1981); Noonan, "An Almost Absolute Value in History," in *The Morality of Abortion: Legal and Historical Perspectives*, Noonan, ed. (Cambridge: Harvard, 1970); and Devine, *The Ethics of Homicide* (Ithaca: Cornell, 1978).

2. For interesting discussions of this issue, see Warren Quinn, "Abortion: Identity and Loss," *Philosophy and Public Affairs*, xiii, 1 (1984):24–54; and Lawrence C. Becker, "Human Being: The Boundaries of the Concept," *Philosophy and Public Affairs*, iv, 4 (1975):334–359.

3. For example, see my "Ethics and the Elderly: Some Problems," in Stuart Spicker, Kathleen Woodward, and David Van Tassel, eds., *Aging and the Elderly: Humanistic Perspectives in Gerontology* (Atlantic Highlands, NJ: Humanities, 1978), pp. 341–355.

4. See Warren, *op. cit.*, and Tooley, "Abortion and Infanticide."

5. This seems to be the fatal flaw in Warren's treatment of this issue.

6. I have been most influenced on this matter by Jonathan Glover, *Causing Death and Saving Lives* (New York: Penguin, 1977), ch. 3; and Robert Young, "What Is So Wrong with Killing People?" *Philosophy*, liv 210 (1979):515–528.

7. Feinberg, Tooley, Warren, and Engelhardt have all dealt with this problem.

NO   Jane English

ABORTION AND THE
CONCEPT OF A PERSON

The abortion debate rages on. Yet the two most popular positions seem to be clearly mistaken. Conservatives maintain that a human life begins at conception and that therefore abortion must be wrong because it is murder. But not all killings of humans are murders. Most notably, self-defense may justify even the killing of an innocent person.

Liberals, on the other hand, are just as mistaken in their argument that since a fetus does not become a person until birth, a woman may do whatever she pleases in and to her own body. First, you cannot do to as you please with your own body if it affects other people adversely.[1] Second, if a fetus is not a person, that does not imply that you can do to it anything you wish. Animals, for example, are not persons, yet to kill or torture them for no reason at all is wrong.

At the center of the storm has been the issue of just when it is between ovulation and adulthood that a person appears on the scene. Conservatives draw the line at conception, liberals at birth. In this paper I first examine our concept of a person and conclude that no single criterion can capture the concept of a person and no sharp line can be drawn. Next I argue that if a fetus is a person, abortion is still justifiable in many cases; and if a fetus is not a person, killing it is still wrong in many cases. To a large extent, these two solutions are in agreement. I conclude that our concept of a person cannot and need not bear the weight that the abortion controversy has thrust upon it.

The several factions in the abortion argument have drawn battle lines around various proposed criteria for determining what is and what is not a person. For example, Mary Anne Warren[2] lists five features (capacities for reasoning, self-awareness, complex communication, etc.) as her criteria for personhood and argues for the permissibility of abortion because a fetus falls outside this concept. Baruch Brody[3] uses brain waves. Michael Tooley[4] picks having-a-concept-of-self as his criterion and concludes that infanticide and

From Jane English, "Abortion and the Concept of a Person," *Canadian Journal of Philosophy*, vol. 5, no. 2 (October 1975), pp. 233–243. Copyright © 1975 by the *Canadian Journal of Philosophy*. Reprinted by permission.

abortion are justifiable, while the killing of adult animals is not. On the other side, Paul Ramsey[5] claims a certain gene structure is the defining characteristic. John Noonan[6] prefers conceived-of-humans and presents counterexamples to various other candidate criteria. For instance, he argues against viability as the criterion because the newborn and infirm would then be nonpersons, since they cannot live without the aid of others. He rejects any criterion that calls upon the sorts of sentiments a being can evoke in adults on the grounds that this would allow us to exclude other races as nonpersons if we could just view them sufficiently unsentimentally.

These approaches are typical: foes of abortion propose sufficient conditions for personhood which fetuses satisfy, while friends of abortion counter with necessary conditions for personhood which fetuses lack. But these both presuppose that the concept of a person can be captured in a strait jacket of necessary and/or sufficient conditions.[7] Rather, "person" is a cluster of features, of which rationality, having a self concept and being conceived of humans are only part.

What is typical of persons? Within our concept of a person we include, first, certain biological factors: descended from humans, having a certain genetic makeup, having a head, hands, arms, eyes, capable of locomotion, breathing, eating, sleeping. There are psychological factors: sentience, perception, having a concept of self and of one's own interests and desires, the ability to use tools, the ability to use language or symbol systems, the ability to joke, to be angry, to doubt. There are rationality factors: the ability to reason and draw conclusions, the ability to generalize and to learn from past experience, the ability to sacrifice present interests for greater gains in the future. There are social factors: the ability to work in groups and respond to peer pressure, the ability to recognize and consider as valuable the interests of others, seeing oneself as one among "other minds," the ability to sympathize, encourage, love, the ability to evoke from others the responses of sympathy, encouragement, love, the ability to work with others for mutual advantage. Then there are legal factors: being subject to the law and protected by it, having the ability to sue and enter contracts, being counted in the census, having a name and citizenship, the ability to own property, inherit, and so forth.

Now the point is not that this list is incomplete, or that you can find counterinstances to each of its points. People typically exhibit rationality, for instance, but someone who was irrational would not thereby fail to qualify as a person. On the other hand, something could exhibit the majority of these features and still fail to be a person, as an advanced robot might. There is no single core of necessary and sufficient features which we can draw upon with the assurance that they constitute what really makes a person; there are only features that are more or less typical.

This is not to say that no necessary or sufficient conditions can be given. Being alive is a necessary condition for being a person, and being a U.S. Senator is sufficient. But rather than falling inside a sufficient condition or outside a necessary one, a fetus lies in the penumbra region where our concept of a person is not so simple. For this reason I think a conclusive answer to the question whether a fetus is a person is unattainable.

Here we might note a family of simple fallacies that proceed by stating a necessary condition for personhood and showing that a fetus has that characteristic. This is a form of the fallacy of affirming the consequent. For example, some have mistakenly reasoned from the premise that a fetus is human (after all, it is a human fetus rather than, say, a canine fetus), to the conclusion that it is a human. Adding an equivocation on "being," we get the fallacious argument that since a fetus is something both living and human, it is a human being.

Nonetheless, it does seem clear that a fetus has very few of the above family of characteristics, whereas a newborn baby exhibits a much larger proportion of them—and a two-year-old has even more. Note that one traditional antiabortion argument has centered on pointing out the many ways in which a fetus resembles a baby. They emphasize its development ("It already has ten fingers . . .") without mentioning its dissimilarities to adults (it still has gills and a tail). They also try to evoke the sort of sympathy on our part that we only feel toward other persons ("Never to laugh . . . or feel the sunshine?"). This all seems to be a relevant way to argue, since its purpose is to persuade us that a fetus satisfies so many of the important features on the list that it ought to be treated as a person. Also note that a fetus near the time of birth satisfies many more of these factors than a fetus in the early months of development. This could provide reason for making distinctions among the different stages of pregnancy, as the U.S. Supreme Court has done.[8]

Historically, the time at which a person has been said to come into existence has varied widely. Muslims date personhood from fourteen days after conception. Some medievals followed Aristotle in placing ensoulment at forty days after conception for a male fetus and eighty days for a female fetus.[9] In European common law since the seventeenth century, abortion was considered the killing of a person only after quickening, the time when a pregnant woman first feels the fetus move on its own. Nor is this variety of opinions surprising. Biologically, a human being develops gradually. We shouldn't expect there to be any specific time or sharp dividing point when a person appears on the scene.

For these reasons I believe our concept of a person is not sharp or decisive enough to bear the weight of a solution to the abortion controversy. To use it to solve that problem is to clarify *obscurum per obscurius.**

Next let us consider what follows if a fetus is a person after all. Judith Jarvis Thomson's landmark article, "A Defense of Abortion,"[10] correctly points out that some additional argumentation is needed at this point in the conservative argument to bridge the gap between the premise that a fetus is an innocent person and the conclusion that killing it is always wrong. To arrive at this conclusion, we would need the additional premise that killing an innocent person is always wrong. But killing an innocent person is sometimes permissible, most notably in self-defense. Some examples may help draw out our intuitions or ordinary judgments about self-defense.

Suppose a mad scientist, for instance, hypnotized innocent people to jump out of the bushes and attack innocent passers-by with knives. If you are so attacked, we agree you have a right to kill the attacker in self-defense, if killing him is the only way to protect your life or

*To clarify what is obscure by what is more obscure—ED.

to save yourself from serious injury. It does not seem to matter here that the attacker is not malicious but himself an innocent pawn, for your killing of him is not done in a spirit of retribution but only in self-defense.

How severe an injury may you inflict in self-defense? In part this depends upon the severity of the injury to be avoided: you may not shoot someone merely to avoid having your clothes torn. This might lead one to the mistaken conclusion that the defense may only equal the threatened injury in severity; that to avoid death you may kill, but to avoid a black eye you may only inflict a black eye or the equivalent. Rather, our laws and customs seem to say that you may create an injury somewhat, but not enormously, greater than the injury to be avoided. To fend off an attack whose outcome would be as serious as rape, a severe beating or the loss of a finger, you may shoot; to avoid having your clothes torn, you may blacken an eye. . . .

Some cases of pregnancy present a parallel situation. Though the fetus is itself innocent, it may pose a threat to the pregnant woman's well-being, life prospects or health, mental or physical. If the pregnancy presents a slight threat to her interests, it seems self-defense cannot justify abortion. But if the threat is on a par with a serious beating or the loss of a finger, she may kill the fetus that poses such a threat, even if it is an innocent person. If a lesser harm to the fetus could have the same defensive effect, killing it would not be justified. It is unfortunate that the only way to free the woman from the pregnancy entails the death of the fetus (except in very late stages of pregnancy). Thus a self-defense model supports Thomson's point that the woman has a right only to be freed from the fetus, not a right to demand its death.[11] . . .

Thanks to modern technology, the cases are rare in which pregnancy poses as clear a threat to a woman's bodily health as an attacker brandishing a switchblade. How does self-defense fare when more subtle, complex and long-range harms are involved?

To consider a somewhat fanciful example, suppose you are a highly trained surgeon when you are kidnapped by the hypnotic attacker. He says he does not intend to harm you but to take you back to the mad scientist who, it turns out, plans to hypnotize you to have a permanent mental block against all your knowledge of medicine. This would automatically destroy your career which would in turn have a serious adverse impact on your family, your personal relationships and your happiness. It seems to me that if the only way you can avoid this outcome is to shoot the innocent attacker, you are justified in so doing. You are defending yourself from a drastic injury to your life prospects. I think it is no exaggeration to claim that unwanted pregnancies (most obviously among teenagers) often have such adverse life-long consequences as the surgeon's loss of livelihood.

Several parallels arise between various views on abortion and the self-defense model. Let's suppose further that these hypnotized attackers only operate at night, so that it is well known that they can be avoided completely by the considerable inconvenience of never leaving your house after dark. One view is that since you could stay home at night, therefore if you go out and are selected by one of these hypnotized people, you have no right to defend yourself. This parallels the view that abstinence is the only acceptable way to avoid pregnancy. Others might hold that you ought to take along some defense such as Mace which will deter the hypnotized person without killing him, but that if this defense fails, you are obliged to submit to the resulting injury, no matter how severe it is. This parallels the view that contraception is all right but abortion is always wrong, even in cases of contraceptive failure.

A third view is that you may kill the hypnotized person only if he will actually kill you, but not if he will only injure you. This is like the position that abortion is permissible only if it is required to save a woman's life. Finally we have the view that it is all right to kill the attacker, even if only to avoid a very slight inconvenience to yourself and even if you knowingly walked down the very street where all these incidents have been taking place without taking along any Mace or protective escort. If we assume that a fetus is a person, this is the analogue of the view that abortion is always justifiable, "on demand."

The self-defense model allows us to see an important difference that exists between abortion and infanticide, even if a fetus is a person from conception. Many have argued that the only way to justify abortion without justifying infanticide would be to find some characteristic of personhood that is acquired at birth. Michael Tooley, for one, claims infanticide is justifiable because the really significant characteristics of person[hood] are acquired some time after birth. But all such approaches look to characteristics of the developing human and ignore the relation between the fetus and the woman. What if, after birth, the presence of an infant or the need to support it posed a grave threat to the woman's sanity or life prospects? She could es-

cape this threat by the simple expedient of running away. So a solution that does not entail the death of the infant is available. Before birth, such solutions are not available because of the biological dependence of the fetus on the woman. Birth is the crucial point not because of any characteristics the fetus gains, but because after birth the woman can defend herself by a means less drastic than killing the infant. Hence self-defense can only be used to justify abortion without necessarily thereby justifying infanticide.

On the other hand, supposing a fetus is not after all a person, would abortion always be morally permissible? Some opponents of abortion seem worried that if a fetus is not a full-fledged person, then we are justified in treating it in any way at all. However, this does not follow. Nonpersons do get some consideration in our moral code, though of course they do not have the same rights as persons have (and in general they do not have moral responsibilities), and though their interests may be overridden by the interests of persons. Still, we cannot just treat them in any way at all.

Treatment of animals is a case in point. It is wrong to torture dogs for fun or to kill wild birds for no reason at all. It is wrong Period, even though dogs and birds do not have the same rights persons do. However, few people think it is wrong to use dogs as experimental animals, causing them considerable suffering in some cases, provided that the resulting research will probably bring discoveries of great benefit to people. And most of us think it all right to kill birds for food or to protect our crops. People's rights are different from the consideration we give to animals, then, for it is wrong to experiment on people, even if others might later benefit a great deal as a result of their suffering. You might volunteer to be a subject, but this would be supererogatory; you certainly have a right to refuse to be a medical guinea pig.

But how do we decide what you may or may not do to nonpersons? This is a difficult problem, one for which I believe no adequate account exists. You do not want to say, for instance, that torturing dogs is all right whenever the sum of its effects on people is good—when it doesn't warp the sensibilities of the torturer so much that he mistreats people. If that were the case, it would be all right to torture dogs if you did it in private, or if the torturer lived on a desert island or died soon afterward, so that his actions had no effect on people. This is an inadequate account, because whatever moral consideration animals get, it has to be indefeasible, too. It will have to be a general proscription of certain actions, not merely a weighing of the impact on people on a case-by-case basis. . . .

An ethical theory must operate by generating a set of sympathies and attitudes toward others which reinforces the functioning of . . . moral principles. Our prohibition against killing people operates by means of certain moral sentiments including sympathy, compassion and guilt. But if these attitudes are to form a coherent set, they carry us further; we tend to perform supererogatory actions, and we tend to feel similar compassion toward person-like nonpersons.

It is crucial that psychological facts play a role here. Our psychological constitution makes it the case that for our ethical theory to work, it must prohibit certain treatment of nonpersons which are significantly person-like. If our moral rules allowed people to treat some person-like nonpersons in ways we do not want people to be treated, this would undermine the system of sympathies and attitudes that makes the ethical system work. . . . Thus it makes sense that it is those animals whose appearance and behavior are most like those people that get the most consideration in our moral scheme.

It is because of "coherence of attitudes," I think, that the similarity of a fetus to a baby is very significant. A fetus one week before birth is so much like a newborn baby in our psychological space that we cannot allow any cavalier treatment of the former while expecting full sympathy and nurturative support for the latter. Thus, I think that antiabortion forces are indeed giving their strongest arguments when they point to the similarities between a fetus and a baby, and when they try to evoke our emotional attachment to and sympathy for the fetus. An early horror story from New York about nurses who were expected to alternate between caring for six-week premature infants and disposing of viable 24-week aborted fetuses is just that— a horror story. These beings are so much alike that no one can be asked to draw a distinction and treat them so very differently.

Remember, however, that in the early weeks after conception, a fetus is very much unlike a person. It is hard to develop these feelings for a set of genes which doesn't yet have a head, hands, beating heart, response to touch or the ability to move by itself. Thus it seems to me that the alleged "slippery slope" between conception and birth is not so very slippery. In the early stages of pregnancy, abortion can hardly be compared to murder for psychological reasons, but in the latest stages it is psychologically akin to murder.

Another source of similarity is the bodily continuity between fetus and adult. Bodies play a surprisingly central role in our attitudes toward persons. One has only to think of the philosophical literature on how far physical identity suffices for personal identity or Wittgenstein's remark that the best picture of the human soul is the human body. Even after death, when all agree the body is no longer a person, we will observe elaborate customs of respect for the human body; like people who torture dogs, necrophiliacs are not to be trusted with people.[12] So it is appropriate that we show respect to a fetus as the body continuous with the body of the person. This is a degree of resemblance to persons that animals cannot rival. . . .

. . . Even if a fetus is not a person, abortion is not always permissible, because of the resemblance of a fetus to a person. I agree with Thomson that it would be wrong for a woman who is seven months pregnant to have an abortion just to avoid having to postpone a trip to Europe. In the early months of pregnancy when the fetus hardly resembles a baby at all, then, abortion is permissible whenever it is in the interests of the pregnant woman or her family. The reasons would only need to outweigh the pain and inconvenience of the abortion itself. In the middle months, when the fetus comes to resemble a person, abortion would be justifiable only when the continuation of the pregnancy or the birth of the child would cause harms— physical, psychological, economic or social—to the woman. In the late months of pregnancy, even on our current assumption that a fetus is not a person, abortion seems to be wrong except to save a woman from significant injury or death.

The Supreme Court has recognized similar gradations in the alleged slippery slope stretching between conception and birth. To this point, the present paper has been a discussion of the moral status of abortion only, not its legal status. In view of the great physical, financial and sometimes psychological costs of abortion, perhaps the legal arrangement most compatible with the proposed moral solution would be the absence of restrictions, that is, so-called abortion "on demand."

So I conclude, first, that application of our concept of a person will not suffice to settle the abortion issue. After all, the biological development of a human being is gradual. Second, whether a fetus is a person or not, abortion is justifiable early in pregnancy to avoid modest harms and seldom justifiable late in pregnancy except to avoid significant injury or death.[13]

NOTES

1. We also have paternalistic laws which keep us from harming our own bodies even when no one else is affected. Ironically, antiabortion laws were originally designed to protect pregnant women from a dangerous but tempting procedure.

2. Mary Anne Warren, "On the Moral and Legal Status of Abortion," *Monist* 57 (1973), p. 55.

3. Baruch Brody, "Fetal Humanity and the Theory of Essentialism," in Robert Baker and Frederick Elliston, eds., *Philosophy and Sex* (Buffalo, N.Y., 1975).

4. Michael Tolley, "Abortion and Infanticide," *Philosophy and Public Affairs* 2 (1982).

5. Paul Ramsey, "The Morality of Abortion," in James Rachels, ed., *Moral Problems* (New York, 1971).

6. John Noonan, "Abortion and the Catholic Church. A Summary History," *Natural Law Forum* 12 (1967), pp. 125-131.

7. Wittgenstein has argued against the possibility of so capturing the concept of a game, *Philosophical Investigations* (New York, 1958), § 66.

8. Not because the fetus is partly a person and so has some of the rights of persons, but rather because of the rights of person-like nonpersons. This I discuss . . . below.

9. Aristotle himself was concerned, however, with the different question of when the soul takes form. For historical data, see Jimmye Kimmey, "How the Abortion Laws Happened," Ms. 1 (April 1973), pp. 48ff, and John Noonan, *loc. cit.*

10. J. J. Thomson, "A Defense of Abortion," *Philosophy and Public Affairs* 1 (1971).

11. *Ibid.*, p. 62.

12. On the other hand, if they can be trusted with people, then our moral customs are mistaken. It all depends on the facts of psychology.

13. I am deeply indebted to Larry Crocker and Arthur Kuflik for their constructive comments.

POSTSCRIPT

Is Abortion Immoral?

Whether or not a fetus can be considered to be a person is often at the center of the abortion issue. Marquis, however, dismisses the angle of fetal person-hood as impossible to argue in either direction because the biological definitions of human and nonhuman are too broad. Instead he cites the effect of aborting a fetus, which is the loss of that fetus's future experiences, as the reason why abortion is immoral. Marquis considers this loss to be the reason why killing adult human beings is wrong, and he carries the logic over to fetuses.

English also does not think that the question "Is it a person?" is a key one. It is not decisive because, first, even if the fetus is *not* a person, this does not imply that we may do anything to it that we like. Second, even if it *is* a person, this does not mean that abortion is always ruled out. Not only is the question not decisive, English claims, but it has no *right* answer. She does not mean that there really is a right answer but that we don't know it; she argues instead that our concepts (including the concept of a person) do not have clear boundaries. Likewise, we might ask, when does a baby become a child? Again, there is no right answer. The problem is not that babies turn into children without our being able to catch them in the act. There is no right answer because the concepts in our language (such as *baby* and *child*) do not have sharply defined boundaries. Thus, when we ask whether a fetus is a person, instead of finding out that it is or that it isn't, we find out that it has some of the features of a person but lacks other features.

Judith Jarvis Thomson, in her ground-breaking article "In Defense of Abortion," *Philosophy and Public Affairs* (Fall 1971), argued that, from the premise that the fetus is a person with a right to life, it does not follow that a woman cannot disconnect herself from it and terminate an unwanted pregnancy. Suppose, she says, that you wake up one day to find yourself medically attached to a famous violinist who would die if you detached yourself. A violinist is a person and has a right to life. Does it then follow, asks Thomson, that you may not detach yourself from this unwanted arrangement?

An excellent collection of articles on abortion is found in Joel Feinberg, ed., *The Problem of Abortion*, 2d ed. (Wadsworth, 1984). See also Joel Feinberg's essay "Abortion," in Tom Regan, ed., *Matters of Life and Death*, 2d ed. (Random House, 1986).

ISSUE 13

Is Surrogate Motherhood Wrong?

YES: Herbert T. Krimmel, from "The Case Against Surrogate Parenting," *Hastings Center Report* (October 1983)

NO: Ruth Macklin, from "Is There Anything Wrong With Surrogate Motherhood? An Ethical Analysis," *Law, Medicine and Health Care* (Spring 1988)

ISSUE SUMMARY

YES: Professor of law Herbert T. Krimmel argues that the fundamental wrong in surrogate motherhood lies in a woman's intention to have a baby not because she wants it but because she wants to give it away. In addition, numerous practical problems arise from surrogate arrangements.

NO: Philosopher Ruth Macklin argues that once we put purely emotional responses and "gut reactions" aside—and that is indeed necessary—the only thing wrong with the current practice of surrogate motherhood is the commercial aspect.

The usual practice of surrogate motherhood involves a married couple who cannot produce a child together and another woman who is able to do so, if her ovum is fertilized. This fertilization is usually accomplished by artifical insemination (that is, by the introduction of the sperm of the man into the uterus of the surrogate mother by other than natural means). If everything goes according to plan, the surrogate mother carries the fetus to term, delivers the baby, and gives it to the couple, who legally adopt it as their own. Thus, the man is the biological father of the child, the surrogate mother is the biological mother, and the wife of the man is the adoptive mother. The usual practice also involves a cash payment from the couple to the surrogate mother in compensation for her services and to cover the medical costs that accompany the pregnancy. Lawyers, too, are involved in this practice. They usually draw up the surrogate motherhood contract and receive a cash payment for doing so. (But we will follow the lead of the writers of the following selections, both of whom are careful to separate the commercial or business aspect of this from the essential practice itself.)

It should be noted that the term "surrogate mother" is somewhat inaccurate, since the woman who is called the surrogate mother *is* the mother of the baby: she supplies the ovum, she carries the fetus, and she gives birth. In fact, if she finds herself psychologically unable to hand over the child to the couple, she would be a "regular" mother. Her position is in some ways similar to that of any woman who gives birth and then surrenders her baby for adoption by others. (One reason for the use of the term "surrogate mother" might be to enforce the thought that she is not going to be the "real" mother and should not make a claim on the baby once it is born, but rather should surrender it to the couple as agreed in the contract.)

The situation of the surrogate mother is *not* analogous to that of any other woman who would give up a baby for adoption in that the surrogate mother gives the baby to the baby's father (and his wife). Also, the surrogate mother's whole purpose in bringing this baby into the world is to give it to a specific couple, but a woman who gives up a baby for adoption does not usually become pregnant specifically for adoptive purposes.

These complications are part of what is so new and controversial about the practice of surrogate motherhood. In an effort to understand the practice, we ask ourselves whether it is analogous to adoption, baby selling, "normal" reproduction, or some other model with which we are familiar. If the practice is seen to fit our model of baby selling, for example, we would tend to think more negatively about it. If it is seen to fit our model of adoption or "normal" reproduction (aided by technology in the form of artificial insemination), we would tend to think better of it. The problem is that the practice has some of the features of some of the models but doesn't fit neatly into any one particular model.

Let's go back to the original motivation behind the idea. Consider a married couple who want to have a baby. The wife (for some reason) cannot have a child, although the husband is capable of fathering one. They could remain childless; they could separate; they could adopt a child; or they could have a child by means of a surrogate mother. They find the first option (childlessness) unacceptable; they *want* to have a child. Separation is also out of the question; they want to maintain their marriage. It seems to them that adoption has a number of drawbacks: there may be a long wait to adopt a baby; the baby might develop some undesirable features, or perhaps it would develop medical problems, inherited from its unknown background; and the baby would be completely unrelated to them. The option of surrogate motherhood would go a long way toward answering these concerns.

But is this something that society should support? Not everything that technology makes possible (in this case, artificial insemination) is a good thing to do.

In the following selections, Herbert T. Krimmel argues against surrogate motherhood. He emphasizes the importance of the motive behind the surrogate mother's desire to have a baby and give it up, and he discusses some of the social implications and unwelcome possibilities that surround surrogate motherhood. Ruth Macklin argues that, from a moral point of view, there is nothing wrong with surrogate motherhood.

YES

Herbert T. Krimmel

THE CASE AGAINST
SURROGATE PARENTING

Is it ethical for someone to create a human life with the intention of giving it up? This seems to be the primary question for both surrogate mother arrangements and artificial insemination by donor (AID), since in both situations a person who is providing germinal material does so only upon the assurance that someone else will assume full responsibility for the child he or she helps to create.

THE ETHICAL ISSUE

In analyzing the ethics of surrogate mother arrangements, it is helpful to begin by examining the roles the surrogate mother performs. First, she acts as a procreator in providing an ovum to be fertilized. Second, after her ovum has been fertilized by the sperm of the man who wishes to parent the child, she acts as host to the fetus, providing nurture and protection while the newly conceived individual develops.

I see no insurmountable moral objections to the functions the mother performs in this second role as host. Her actions are analogous to those of a foster mother or of a wet-nurse who cares for a child when the natural mother cannot or does not do so. Using a surrogate mother as a host for the fetus when the biological mother cannot bear the child is no more morally objectionable than employing others to help educate, train, or otherwise care for a child. Except in extremes, where the parent relinquishes or delegates responsibilities for a child for trivial reasons, the practice would not seem to raise a serious moral issue.

I would argue, however, that the first role that the surrogate mother performs—providing germinal material to be fertilized—does pose a major ethical problem. The surrogate mother provides her ovum, and enters into a surrogate mother arrangement, with the clear understanding that she is to avoid responsibility for the life she creates. Surrogate mother arrangements are designed to separate in the mind of the surrogate mother the decision to

From Herbert T. Krimmel, "The Case Against Surrogate Parenting," *Hastings Center Report*, vol. 13, no. 5 (October 1983). Copyright © 1983 by the Hastings Center. Reprinted by permission.

create a child from the decision to have and raise that child. The cause of this dissociation is some other benefit she will receive, most often money.[1] In other words, her desire to create a child is born of some motive other than the desire to be a parent. This separation of the decision to create a child from the decision to parent it is ethically suspect. The child is conceived not because he is wanted by his biological mother, but because he can be useful to someone else. He is conceived in order to be given away.

At their deepest level, surrogate mother arrangements involve a change in motive for creating children: from a desire to have them for their own sake, to a desire to have them because they can provide some other benefit. The surrogate mother creates a child with the intention to abdicate parental responsibilities. Can we view this as ethical? My answer is no. I will explain why by analyzing various situations in which surrogate mother arrangements might be used.

WHY MOTIVE MATTERS

Let's begin with the single parent. A single woman might use AID, or a single man might use a surrogate mother arrangement, if she or he wanted a child but did not want to be burdened with a spouse.[2] Either practice would intentionally deprive the child of a mother or a father. This, I assert, is fundamentally unfair to the child.

Those who disagree might point to divorce or to the death of a parent as situations in which a child is deprived of one parent and must rely solely or primarily upon the other. The comparison, however, is inapt. After divorce or the death of a parent, a child may find herself with a single parent due to circumstances that were unfortunate, unintended, and undesired. But when surrogate mother arrangements are used by a single parent, depriving the child of a second parent is one of the intended and desired effects. It is one thing to ask how to make the best of a bad situation when it is thrust upon a person. It is different altogether to ask whether one may intentionally set out to achieve the same result. The morality of identical results (for example, killings) will oftentimes differ depending upon whether the situation is invited by, or involuntarily thrust upon, the actor. Legal distinctions following and based upon this ethical distinction are abundant. The law of self-defense provides a notable example.[3]

Since a woman can get pregnant if she wishes whether or not she is married, and since there is little that society can do to prevent women from creating children even if their intention is to deprive the children of a father, why should we be so concerned about single men using surrogate mother arrangements if they too want a child but not a spouse? To say that women can intentionally plan to be unwed mothers is not to condone the practice. Besides, society will hold the father liable in a paternity action if he can be found and identified, which indicates some social concern that people should not be able to abdicate the responsibilities that they incur in generating children. Otherwise, why do we condemn the proverbial sailor with a pregnant girlfriend in every port?

In many surrogate mother arrangements, or course, the surrogate mother will not be transferring custody of the child to a single man, but to a couple: the child's biological father and a stepmother, his wife. What are the ethics of surrogate mother arrangements when the child is taken into a two-parent family? Again, surrogate mother arrangements and AID pose similar ethical questions: The surrogate mother transfers her parental responsibilities to the wife of the biological father, while with AID the sperm donor relinquishes his interest in the child to the husband of the biological mother. In both cases the child is created with the intention of transferring the responsibility for its care to a new set of parents. The surrogate mother situation is more dramatic than AID since the transfer occurs after the child is born, while in the case of AID the transfer takes place at the time of the insemination. Nevertheless, the ethical point is the same: creating children for the purpose of transferring them. For a surrogate mother the question remains: Is it ethical to create a child for the purpose of transferring it to the wife of the biological father?

At first blush this looks to be little different from the typical adoption, for what is an adoption other than a transfer of responsibility from one set of parents to another? The analogy is misleading, however, for two reasons. First, it is difficult to imagine anyone conceiving children for the purpose of putting them up for adoption. And, if such a bizarre event were to occur, I doubt that we would look upon it with moral approval. Most adoptions arise either because an undesired conception is brought to term, or because the parents wanted to have the child, but find that they are unable to provide for it because of some unfortunate circumstances that develop after conception.

Second, even if surrogate mother arrangements were to be classified as a type of adoption, not all offerings of children for adoption are necessarily moral. For example, would it be moral for parents to offer their three-year-old for adoption because they are bored with the child? Would it be moral for a couple to offer for adoption their newborn female baby because they wanted a boy?

Therefore, even though surrogate mother arrangements may in some superficial ways be likened to adoption, one must still ask whether it is ethical to separate the decision to create children from the desire to have them. I would answer no. The procreator should desire the child for its own sake, and not as a means to attaining some other end. Even though one of the ends may be stated altruistically as an attempt to bring happiness to an infertile couple, the child is still being used by the surrogate. She creates it not because she desires it, but because she desires something from it.

To sanction the use and treatment of human beings as means to the achievement of other goals instead of as ends in themselves is to accept an ethic with a tragic past, and to establish a precedent with a dangerous future. Already the press has reported the decision of one couple to conceive a child for the purpose of using it as a bone marrow donor for its sibling (*Los Angeles Times*, April 17, 1979, p. I-2). And the bioethics literature contains articles seriously considering whether we should clone human beings to serve as an inventory of spare parts for organ transplants[4] and articles that foresee the use of comatose human beings as self-replenishing blood banks and manufacturing plants for human hormones.[5] How far our society is willing to proceed down this road is uncertain, but it is clear that the first step to all these practices is the acceptance of the same principle that the Nazis attempted to use to justify their medical experiments at the Nuremberg War Crimes Trials: that human beings may be used as means to the achievement of other goals, and need not be treated as ends in themselves.[6]

But why, it might be asked, is it so terrible if the surrogate mother does not desire the child for its own sake, when under the proposed surrogate mother arrangements there will be a couple eagerly desiring to have the child and to be its parents? That this argument may not be entirely accurate will be illustrated in the following section, but the basic reply is that creating a child without desiring it fundamentally changes the way we look at children—instead of viewing them as unique individual personalities to be desired in their own right, we may come to view them as commodities or items of manufacture to be desired because of their utility. A recent newspaper account describes the business of an agency that matches surrogate mothers with barren couples as follows:

Its first product is due for delivery today. Twelve others are on the way and an additional 20 have been ordered. The "company" is Surrogate Mothering Ltd. and the "product" is babies.[7]

The dangers of this view are best illustrated by examining what might go wrong in a surrogate mother arrangement, and most important, by viewing how the various parties to the contract may react to the disappointment.

WHAT MIGHT GO WRONG

Ninety-nine percent of the surrogate mother arrangements may work out just fine; the child will be born normal, and the adopting parents (that is, the biological father and his wife) will want it. But, what happens when, unforeseeably, the child is born deformed? Since many defects cannot be discovered prenatally by amniocentesis or other means, the situation is bound to arise.[8] Similarly, consider what would happen if the biological father were to die before the birth of the child. Or if the "child" turns out to be twins or triplets. Each of these instances poses an inevitable situation where the adopting parents may be unhappy with the prospect of getting the child or children. Although legislation can mandate that the adopting parents take the child or children in whatever condition they come or whatever the situation, provided the surrogate mother has abided by all the contractual provisions of the surrogate mother arrangement, the important point for our discussion is the attitude that the surrogate mother or the adopting parent might have. Consider the example of the deformed child.

When I participated in the Surrogate Parent Foundation's inaugural symposium in November 1981, I was struck by the attitude of both the surrogate mothers and the adopting parents to these problems. The adopting parents worried, "Do we have to take such a child?" and the surrogate mothers said in response, "Well, we don't want to be stuck with it." Clearly, both groups were anxious not be responsible for the "undesirable child" born of the surrogate mother arrangement. What does this portend?

It is human nature that when one pays money, one expects value. Things that one pays for have a way of being seen as commodities. Unavoidable in surrogate mother arrangements are questions such as: "Did I get a good one?" We see similar behavior with respect to the adoption of children: comparatively speaking, there is no shortage of black, Mexican-American, mentally retarded, or older children seeking homes; the shortage is in attractive, intelligent-looking Caucasian babies.[9] Similarly, surrogate mother arrangements involve more than just the desire to have a child. The desire is for a certain type of child.

But, it may be objected, don't all parents voice these same concerns in the normal course of having children? Not exactly. No one doubts or minimizes the pain and disappointment parents feel when they learn that their child is born with some genetic or congenital birth defect. But this is different from the surrogate mother situation, where neither the surrogate mother nor the adopting parents may feel responsible, and both sides may feel that they have a legitimate excuse not to assume responsibility for the child. The surrogate mother might blame the biological father for having "defective sperm," as the adopting parents might blame the surrogate mother for a "defective ovum" or for improper care of the fetus during pregnancy. The adopting parents desire a normal child, not *this* child in any condition, and the surrogate mother doesn't want it in any event. So both sides will feel threatened by the birth of an "undesirable child." Like bruised fruit in the produce bin of a supermarket, this child is likely to become an object of avoidance.

Certainly, in the natural course of having children a mother may doubt whether she wants a child if the father has died before its birth; parents may shy away from a defective infant, or be distressed at the thought of multiple births. Nevertheless, I believe they are more likely to accept these contingencies as a matter of fate. I do not think this is the case with surrogate mother arrangements. After all, in the surrogate mother arrangement the adopting parents can blame someone outside the marital relationship. The surrogate mother has been

hosting this child all along, and she is delivering it. It certainly *looks* far more like a commodity than the child that arrives in the natural course within the family unit.

A DANGEROUS AGENDA

Another social problem, which arises out of the first, is the fear that surrogate mother arrangements will fall prey to eugenic concerns.[10] Surrogate mother contracts typically have clauses requiring genetic tests of the fetus and stating that the surrogate mother must have an abortion (or keep the child herself) if the child does not pass these tests.[11]

In the last decade we have witnessed a renaissance of interest in eugenics. This, coupled with advances in biomedical technology, has created a host of abuses and new moral problems. For example, genetic counseling clinics now face a dilemma: amniocentesis, the same procedure that identifies whether a fetus suffers from certain genetic defects, also discloses the sex of a fetus. Genetic counseling clinics have reported that even when the fetus is normal, a disproportionate number of mothers abort female children.[12] Aborting normal fetuses simply because the prospective parents desire children of a certain sex is one result of viewing children as commodities. The recent scandal at the Repository for Germinal Choice, the so-called "Nobel Sperm Bank," provides another chilling example. Their first "customer" was, unbeknownst to the staff, a woman who "had lost custody of two other children because they were abused in an effort to 'make them smart.' "[13] Of course, these and similar evils may occur whether or not surrogate mother arrangements are allowed by law. But to the extent that they promote the view of children as commodities, these arrangements contribute to these problems. There is nothing wrong with striving for betterment, as long as it does not result in intolerance to that which is not perfect. But I fear that the latter attitude will become prevalent.

Sanctioning surrogate mother arrangements can also exert pressures upon the family structure. First, as was noted earlier, there is nothing technically to prevent the use of surrogate mother arrangements by single males desiring to become parents. Indeed, single females can already do this with AID or even without it. But even if legislation were to limit the use of the surrogate mother arrangement to infertile couples, other pressures would occur: namely the intrusion of a third adult into the marital community.[14] I do not think that society is ready to accept either single parenting or quasi-adulterous arrangements as normal.

Another stress on the family structure arises within the family of the surrogate mother. When the child is surrendered to the adopting parents it is removed not only from the surrogate mother, but also from her family. They too have interests to be considered. Do not the siblings of that child have an interest in the fact that their little baby brother has been "given" away?[15] One woman, the mother of a medical student who had often donated sperm for artificial insemination, expressed her feelings to me eloquently. She asked, "I wonder how many grandchildren I have that I have never seen and never been able to hold or cuddle." Intrafamily tensions can also be expected to result in the family of the adopting parents due to the asymmetry of relationship the adopting parents will have toward the child. The adopting mother has no biological relationship to the child, whereas the adopting father is also the child's biological father. Won't this unequal biological claim on the child be used as a wedge in child-rearing arguments? Can't we imagine the father saying, "Well, he is my son, not yours"? What if the couple eventually gets divorced? Should custody in a subsequent divorce between the adopting mother and the biological father be treated simply as a normal child custody dispute? Or should the biological relationship between father and child weigh more heavily? These questions do not arise in typical adoption situations since both parents are equally unrelated biologically to the child. Indeed, in adoption there is symmetry. The surrogate mother situation is more analogous to second marriages, where the children of one party by a prior marriage are adopted by the new spouse. Since asymmetry in second marriage situations causes problems, we can anticipate similar difficulties arising from surrogate mother arrangements.

There is also the worry that the offspring of a surrogate mother arrangement will be deprived of important information about his or her heritage. This also happens with adopted children or children conceived by AID,[16] who lack information about their biological parents, which could be important to them medically. Another less popularly recognized problem is the danger of half-sibling marriages,[17] where the child of the surrogate mother unwittingly falls in love with a half sister or brother. The only way to avoid these problems is to dispense with the confidentiality of parental records; however, the natural parents may not always want their identity disclosed.

The legalization of surrogate mother arrangements may also put undue pressure upon poor women to use their bodies in this way to support themselves and their families. Analogous problems have arisen in the past with the use of paid blood donors.[18] And occasionally the press reports someone desperate enough to offer to sell an eye or some other organ.[19] I believe that certain things should be viewed as too important to be sold as commodities, and I hope that we have advanced from the time when parents raised children for profitable labor, or found themselves forced to sell their children.

While many of the social dilemmas I have outlined here have their analogies in other present-day occurrences such as divorced families or in adoption, every addition is hurtful. Legalizing surrogate mother arrangements will increase the frequency of these problems, and put more stress on our society's shared moral values.[20]

A TALE FOR OUR TIME

An infertile couple might prefer to raise a child with a biological relationship to the husband, rather than to raise an adopted child who has no biological relationship to either the husband or the wife. But does the marginal increase in joy that they might therefore experience outweigh the potential pain that they, or the child conceived in such arrangements, or others might suffer? Does their preference outweigh the social costs and problems that the legalization of surrogate mothering might well engender? I honestly do not know. I don't even know on what hypothetical scale such interests could be weighed and balanced. But even if we could weigh such interests, and even if

personal preference outweighed the costs, I still would not be able to say that we could justify achieving those ends by these means; that ethically it would be permissible for a person to create a child, not because she desired it, but because it could be useful to her.

REFERENCES

1. See Philip J. Parker, "Motivation of Surrogate Mothers: Initial Findings," *American Journal of Psychiatry* 140:1 (January 1983), 117–18; see also Doe v. Kelley, Circuit Court of Wayne County, Michigan (1980) reported in 1980 Rep. on Human Reproduction and Law II-A-1.

2. See, e.g., C.M. v. C.C., 152 N.J. Supp. 160, 377 A.2d 821 (1977); "Why She Went to 'Nobel Sperm Bank' for Child," *Los Angeles Herald Examiner*, Aug. 6, 1982, p. A9; "Womb for Rent," *Los Angeles Herald Examiner*, Sept. 21, 1981, p. A3.

3. See also Richard McCormick, "Reproductive Technologies: Ethical Issues" in *Encyclopedia of Bioethics*, edited by Walter Reich, Vol. 4 (New York: The Free Press, 1978) pp. 1454, 1459; Robert Snowden and G. D. Mitchell, *The Artificial Family* (London: George Allen & Unwin, 1981), p. 71.

4. See, e.g., Alexander Peters, "The Brave New World: Can the Law Bring Order Within Traditional Concepts of Due Process?" *Suffolk Law Review* 4 (1970), 894, 901–02; Roderic Gorney, "The New Biology and the Future of Man," *UCLA Law Review* 15 (1968), 273, 302; J. G. Castel, "Legal Implications of Biomedical Science and Technology in the Twenty-First Century," *Canadian Bar Review* 51 (1973), 119, 127.

5. See Harry Nelson, "Maintaining Dead to Serve as Blood Makers Proposed: Logical, Sociologist Says," *Los Angeles Times*, February 26, 1974 p. II-1; Hans Jonas, "Against the Stream: Comments on the Definition and Redefinition of Death," in *Philosophical Essays: From Ancient Creed to Technological Man* (Chicago: University of Chicago Press, 1974), pp. 132–40.

6. See Leo Alexander, "Medical Science under Dictatorship," *New England Journal of Medicine* 241:2 (1949), 39; United States v. Brandt, Trial of the Major War Criminals, International Military Tribunal: Nuremberg, 14 November 1945–1 October 1946.

7. Bob Dvorchak, "Surrogate Mothers: Pregnant Idea Now a Pregnant Business," *Los Angeles Herald Examiner*, December 27, 1983, p. A1.

8. "Surrogate's Baby Born with Deformities Rejected by All," *Los Angeles Times*, January 22, 1983, p. I-17; "Man Who Hired Surrogate Did Not

Father Ailing Baby," *Los Angeles Herald Examiner*, February 3, 1983, p. A-6.

9. See, e.g., Adoption in America, Hearing before the Subcommittee on Aging, Family and Human Services of the Senate Committee on Labor and Human Resources, 97th Congress. 1st Session (1981), p. 3 (comments of Senator Jeremiah Denton) and pp. 16–17 (statement of Warren Master, Acting Commissioner of Administration for Children, Youth and Families, HHS).

10. Cf. "Discussion: Moral, Social and Ethical Issues," in *Law and Ethics of A.I.D. and Embryo Transfer* (1973) (comments of Himmelweit); reprinted in Michael Shapiro and Roy Spece, *Bioethics and Law* (St. Paul: West Publishing Company, 1981), p. 548.

11. See, e.g., Lane (Newsday), "Womb for Rent," *Tucson Citizen* (Weekender), June 7, 1980, p. 3; Susan Lewis, "Baby Bartering? Surrogate Mothers Pose Issues for Lawyers, Courts," *The Los Angeles Daily Journal*, April 20, 1981; see also Elaine Markoutsas, "Women Who Have Babies for Other Women," *Good Housekeeping* 96 (April 1981), 104.

12. See Morton A. Stenchever, "An Abuse of Prenatal Diagnosis," *Journal of the American Medical Association* 221 (1972), 408; Charles Westoff and Ronald R. Rindfus, "Sex Preselection in the United States: Some Implications," *Science* 184 (1974), 633, 636; see also Phyllis Battelle, "Is It a Boy or a Girl?" *Los Angeles Herald Examiner*, Oct. 8, 1981, p. A17.

13. "2 Children Taken from Sperm Bank Mother," *Los Angeles Times*, July 14, 1982; p. I-3; "The Sperm-Bank Scandal," *Newsweek* 24 (July 26, 1982).

14. See Helmut Thielicke, *The Ethics of Sex*, John W. Doberstein, trans. (New York: Harper & Row, 1964).

15. According to one newspaper account, when a surrogate mother informed her nine-year-old daughter that the new baby would be given away, the daughter replied: "Oh, good. If it's a girl we can keep it and give Jeffrey [her two-year-old half brother] away." "Womb for Rent," *Los Angeles Herald Examiner*, Sept. 21, 1981, p. A3.

16. See, e.g., Lorraine Dusky, "Brave New Babies?" *Newsweek* 30 (December 6, 1982). Also testimony of Suzanne Rubin before the California Assembly Committee on Judiciary, Surrogate Parenting Contracts, Assembly Publication No. 962, pp. 72–75 (November 19, 1982).

17. This has posed an increasing problem for children conceived through AID. See, e.g., Martin Curie-Cohen, et al., "Current Practice of Artificial Insemination by Donor in the United States," *New England Journal of Medicine* 300 (1979), 585–89.

18. See e.g., Richard M. Titmuss, *The Gift Relationship: From Human Blood to Social Policy* (New York: Random House, 1971).

19. See, e.g., "Man Desperate for Funds: Eye for Sale at $35,000," *Los Angeles Times*, February 1, 1975, p. II-1; "100 Answer Man's Ad for New Kidney," *Los Angeles Times*, September 12, 1974, p. I-4.

20. See generally Guido Calabresi, "Reflections on Medical Experimentation in Humans," *Daedalus* 98 (1969), 387–93; also see Michael Shapiro and Roy Spece, "On Being 'Unprincipled on Principle': The Limits of Decision Making 'On the Merits,' " in *Bioethics and Law*, pp. 67–71.

NO
Ruth Macklin

IS THERE ANYTHING WRONG WITH SURROGATE MOTHERHOOD? AN ETHICAL ANALYSIS

THE EMOTIONAL RESPONSE

Is there anything ethically wrong with surrogate motherhood? Many people confess their inability to articulate their opposition in rational terms, yet they feel uneasy. The practice arouses negative emotions ranging from mild distaste to revulsion. Others say there is nothing wrong, in principle, with surrogate motherhood. It is a way of helping infertile women fulfill a fundamental human longing and, therefore, should be permitted and even facilitated. Many who are not fundamentally opposed to surrogacy nonetheless maintain that the practice ought to be regulated, in order to prevent abuses and to provide a mechanism for resolving conflicts that may develop in particular cases.

Surrogacy arrangements have been condemned by Roman Catholic spokesmen, in a legal brief by a conference of bishops in New Jersey,[1] and by the Vatican in a statement issued by the Pope in March 1987. Feminists have denounced the practice, using rhetoric rather than argument, with the slogan "woman as vessel." A group of women who agreed to bear children under surrogacy contracts has convened to speak out against such arrangements. A number of them, like Mary Beth Whitehead, the surrogate mother in the Baby M case, were seeking to get their babies back.[2]

Some critics charge that surrogacy exploits women, particularly those from lower economic classes, thus constituting a new form of "slavery."[3] Others contend that it dehumanizes babies, amounting to a new variety of "baby selling." The lawyer for Mary Beth Whitehead argued that surrogacy contracts are "against public policy" and ought to be outlawed, and called the idea of paying surrogate mothers to bear and surrender infants "repulsive and repugnant."[4]

From Ruth Macklin, "Is There Anything Wrong With Surrogate Motherhood? An Ethical Analysis," *Law, Medicine & Health Care*, vol. 16 (1988). Copyright © 1988 by the American Society of Law and Medicine. Reprinted by permission.

Yet others disagree. Some, consistent with the feminist stance that women should be allowed to control their own bodies, insist that being a surrogate mother is just another reproductive choice, which ought to remain open to women. It is also pointed out that surrogacy fulfills an important biological and emotional need: couples in which the wife is infertile are often desperate to have a child with the father's genetic inheritance, and look to surrogacy as the only way to make this possible. And Noel P. Keane, the Detroit lawyer and founder of the Infertility Center in Manhattan, which arranged the contract between Mary Beth Whitehead and William Stern, Baby M's father, has argued that surrogacy permits "the furtherance of [a couple's] constitutionally protected right to procreation."[5]

The most striking feature of the controversy over surrogacy is the level of emotional response. Few people are neutral on the issue. Newspaper reports of the seven-week Baby M trial remarked on the "many basic emotions" touched by the legal proceedings.[6] An account of legislative hearings on a bill to regulate surrogacy in New York State described the proceedings as "an emotional State Senate committee hearing."[7] Many health professionals and academics confess to having strong feelings against surrogacy, but remain unable to come up with a rational position in defense in their view.

Not long ago, new accounts of a novel surrogacy arrangement stirred even deeper feelings. A forty-eight-year-old South African grandmother, Pat Anthony, served as a surrogate mother for her own daughter's biological infants. Ms. Anthony was implanted with four embryos resulting from ova produced by her daughter and fertilized in vitro with her son-in-law's sperm. On October 1, 1987, she gave birth to triplets. Reactions to this story ranged from astonishment to repugnance. The trenchant comment of one biology professor was, "Yuk!"

UNDERSTANDING ETHICAL CONFLICTS

Many ethical conflicts are soluble, while others are doomed never to be resolved. In the field of biomedical ethics, examples of both types of ethical conflicts exist.

An example of a basically resolvable ethical controversy is in vitro fertilization, the technique of fertilizing a female egg with a male sperm outside the human body. Although legal and regulatory details still need to be worked out, the ethical acceptability of in vitro fertilization is widely acknowledged. . . .

In contrast to reactions stemming from gut feelings, a reasoned approach to the ethics of surrogacy can proceed by using either of two well-known ethical perspectives. The first perspective examines the good and bad consequences of an action or practice as a means of determining its moral rightness or wrongness, while the second tries to determine whether an act or practice is inherently or intrinsically wrong.

According to the first ethical perspective—consequentialism—if the good consequences outweigh the bad, the action or practice is ethically acceptable. If, on the other hand, there is a balance of bad consequences over good ones, then the action or practice is morally wrong. The best-known version of a consequentialist ethical theory is utilitarianism, but that is only one among several ways of articulating the details of this moral perspective.

Although a consequentialist mode of conducting an ethical analysis is basically sound, it is fraught with both theoretical and practical difficulties. Not only is it difficult to predict good and bad results; it is also hard to weigh consequences, even those that have already come about. Moreover, reasonable people frequently disagree over what should count as good and bad consequences, and how much weight should be assigned to each.

It is worth noting that hundreds of surrogacy arrangements have been successfully completed, with a distinct minority resulting in regrets by the surrogate mother and only a few leading to the sorts of devastating consequences exemplified by the Baby M case. If applying the utilitarian principle were simply a matter of subtracting the number of individuals who experienced bad consequences from the number of those who experienced good consequences, it would be an easy matter to determine the rightness or wrongness of surrogacy. But a proper application of the principle is methodologically much more complex. It requires assessing the magnitude of the good and bad consequences for every individual affected by the action or practice, a task that is fraught with problems of measurement and interpersonal comparisons.

The competing approach to ethics rejects as morally irrelevant the consequences of actions or practices. Sometimes known as formalism, this approach holds that certain actions are wrong because of the very type of action they are. It is the "form" the action takes that makes it right or wrong, not its consequences. Examples include killing innocent human beings, enslaving individuals or groups, the economic or social exploitation of persons or classes, and physical or mental torture. Debates erupt over just which human beings should be considered "innocent"; over whether some living entities, such as fetuses, should be considered human beings; and over just what should count as economic or social exploitation. But such debates do not detract from the respectability of formalism as a leading approach to ethics. A notable feature of this perspective is that it generates the morally important concept of rights.

ETHICAL ANALYSIS

In tackling the broader issue of surrogacy, the first and most fundamental ethical question is whether there is something intrinsically wrong with surrogacy arrangements. Couched in the language of ethical formalism, is this a practice whose very form makes it immoral? Does surrogate motherhood violate some basic ethical principle? Those who believe it does argue that surrogacy ought to be outlawed, not simply regulated. They contend that the practice of surrogacy is morally flawed, in principle, and that erecting safeguards cannot erase the fundamental ethical wrong of the practice. Within this category fall the objections of the Roman Catholic church and some feminist groups.

In a brief filed with the New Jersey Supreme Court prior to the appeal in the Baby M case, the New Jersey Catholic Conference, composed of the state's fourteen Roman Catholic bishops, argued that surrogate motherhood "promotes the exploitation of women and infertile couples and the dehumanization of babies." The bishops' brief focused largely (but not entirely) on the commercial aspects of surrogacy. . . . But in trying to determine whether surrogacy is intrinsically immoral, it is necessary to separate the commercial aspects from the practice itself. In fact, just that separation is evident from developments in Britain. The Surrogacy Arrangements Act passed in 1985 bans commercial surrogacy and advertising of and for surrogacy services. But the act does not ban surrogacy itself.[8]

The Catholic bishops in New Jersey did not limit their criticism of surrogacy to its commercial aspects. Their brief also referred to the best interests of children born under such arrangements:

> In surrogacy, a child is conceived precisely in order to be abandoned to others and his or her best interests are the last factors to be considered. . . . There is great potential for psychological injury to the child when he realizes that he was born, not of a loving relationship, but from a cold, usually financial relationship.[9]

A similar position is argued by a feminist psychologist, who asserts that "no child wants to live in a womb for hire."[10]

When we begin to contemplate the possible consequences for the child born of surrogacy arrangements, and what is in the child's best interests, a new set of questions arises. Should the child be told, when old enough, the pertinent details about his or her conception and birth? Should the identity of the surrogate mother routinely be disclosed? What if the surrogate mother wants to be known to the child? What if she does not? What if she insists on visitation rights or other ongoing involvement with the child?

Such questions are identical to those that have been posed about adoption and about artificial insemination using the sperm of an anonymous donor. It is instructive that replies to these questions have changed over the years, and that even today there are no settled, universally accepted answers. In fact, some recent proposals mark a radical shift from earlier practices. Some people are now urging that the identity of birth mothers and fathers be disclosed to adoptive parents and, eventually, the child, and that the long-established practice of anonymous donor insemination be eliminated. These suggestions arise partly out of increasing efforts by many adopted children to discover the identity of their biological parents, and also from an assessment of the negative consequences for the children of secrecy surrounding the men who have anonymously donated their sperm for artificial insemination.

As important as these issues are, they are questions that pertain to the consequences of surrogate arrangements. They become pertinent only when the formalist approach to the morality of surrogacy has been rejected, or when it has been determined that the practice does not violate a prohibition against actions of an unacceptable type.

While some critics of surrogate motherhood base their opposition on the best interests of the children or on the motives of the surrogates, others oppose it as exploitative of women. This makes it appear that surrogacy is unethical because of the type of practice it is, namely, a form of exploitation. According to one writer: "When a woman provides womb service, the feminist issue surfaces. Women object to being baby factories or sex objects because it offends their human dignity."[11] And further: "This is going to end up as the final exploitation of women. It is always going to be poor women who have the babies and rich women who get them."[12]

These statements confuse two distinct issues: first, the exploitation of individual women, if that is indeed what really happens in surrogacy arrangements; and second, a form of class exploitation, since poorer women will be the ones serving as surrogates for the more well-to-do. My own view is that these would be sound, principled objections if it were clear that exploitation in some form actually occurs.

The feminist charge that the practice of surrogacy exploits women is paternalistic. It questions women's ability to know their own interests and to enter into a contractual arrangement knowingly and competently. There may well be a coercive aspect to commercial surrogacy, since money—especially a large enough sum—can serve as a coercive inducement to do something a person might not otherwise do voluntarily. But that speaks more to the exploitation of poorer classes of women, which I think is a genuine moral worry, than it does to the exploitation of women generally. Feminists who oppose surrogacy presume to speak for all women. But what they are really saying is that those who elect to enter surrogacy arrangements are incompetent to choose and stand in need of protection.

The charge of "exploitation" contradicts the moral stance that women have the ability and the right to control their own bodies. If that right grants women reproductive freedoms of other sorts, such as the right to abortion or to control the number and spacing of their children, why does it not similarly apply to the informed, voluntary choice to serve as a surrogate? Some feminists draw an analogy with prostitution, another practice believed to constitute exploitation of women. But the chief feminist complaint about prostitution pertains to its commercial aspect, the feature that transforms women's bodies into a commodity. Feminists who see nothing wrong with

women engaging in sexual intercourse outside of marriage (in today's terms—as long as they practice safer sex) are inconsistent if they contend that noncommercial surrogacy arrangements are demeaning to women.

Still, it could be argued, to treat one's body as a mere means to the ends of others is degrading. It could be viewed as a violation of Kant's supreme moral principle, the categorical imperative, which prohibits treating persons merely as a means. But according to that interpretation, other acts and practices typically considered altruistic or even noble would similarly have to be viewed as degrading. A normal, healthy volunteer for biomedical or behavioral research is also acting as a "mere means" to the ends of others—of either the researchers, or future generations, or both. Monetary payments to research subjects would surely have to be outlawed, if it is exploitation to pay people for the use of their bodies or for services that use their bodies. And in the therapeutic context, requests for bone marrow donations would have to be considered suspect.

These analogies serve as a reminder that surrogate motherhood is a biomedical as well as a social practice, as it involves either artificial insemination or embryo transfer, then pregnancy and childbirth. It leads naturally to a consideration of informed consent.

Is Informed Consent Possible?

Although surrogacy arrangements are typically governed by a legal contract, the concept of informed consent is still applicable. Yet it has been argued that no one is capable of granting truly informed consent to be a surrogate mother. This argument contends that even if a woman has already borne children, she cannot know what it is like to have to give them up after birth. In fact, most surrogacy arrangements do require that women who offer to be surrogates already have children. This would seem to meet the objection that surrogate mothers cannot possibly know what it is like to go through pregnancy and childbirth. Yet according to those who say genuine informed consent to be a surrogate mother is impossible, it is the feature of having to give up the child that cannot be known in advance.

There is some merit to that argument. Yet as an argument against the very possibility of informed consent, it is too strong. If it holds for surrogate motherhood, it would seem to apply, as well, to a wide variety of other biomedical treatments and research maneuvers that people have never before experienced. . . . It is unrealistic to maintain that the only way to gain [the necessary] understanding is to have had the actual experience, along with the accompanying feelings.

So, either the meaning of informed consent to become a surrogate mother is the same as that of informed consent to medical treatment, or it is different. If it should be understood in the usual sense, then women should be as capable of granting informed consent to carry a baby to term and then relinquish it as they are to grant consent for removal of a breast when they have breast cancer, or removal of their uterus if they develop a tumor, or for an operation to reduce or enlarge their breasts.

However, if a different, higher standard of informed consent is to be used, then the only women who could qualify would be those who had already undergone the experience of having had a baby and lost it. But that would surely be a bizarre requirement, and probably a cruel one, as well. Having experienced the loss of an infant, such women would be the only ones judged able to consent to enter a surrogacy agreement.

Additional Ethical Concerns

I believe it is not the element of understanding that poses the problem for the possibility of informed consent but, rather, the element of voluntariness when the arrangement is a commercial one and the surrogate is a person with limited financial assets. A fee of $10,000 paid to a woman of low income may well be an offer she cannot refuse. The remedy for this problem is to pay nothing at all, and to allow surrogacy arrangements only as purely altruistic acts on the part of the surrogate mother.

But is that fair? Is it reasonable? After all, the surrogate mother does have to undergo the inconvenience of pregnancy, with its possible discomforts, as well as take the time for prenatal visits to the obstetrician, and then undergo the risks and rigors of childbirth. Shouldn't she be paid for her time and inconvenience?

A physician colleague of mine has argued that she should. He said:

> If I wanted to hire a surrogate mother to bear my child, I'd want her to be adequately taken care of financially. I wouldn't want her to have to work at a grueling job. I'd want her to keep from exhausting herself, from being forced to go to work where she may be exposed to environmental hazards to the fetus. In short, I'd want her to be as comfortable and as free from stress as possible during the entire pregnancy.

I find this argument persuasive, but only to a point. For one thing, there is just so much that money can do to alleviate stress. And even if a woman is not exposed to the hazards of toxic fumes in a factory or to a video display terminal in an office, there is no way to eliminate entirely her exposure to potentially damaging substances, and surely no way to protect her from the emotional upset of daily life. It would take more evidence than is now available to conclude that monetary payments to surrogate mothers are likely to decrease the risks of harm to the fetus.

It is true, however, that contracts for surrogate arrangements impose obligations and restrictions on the woman during pregnancy. Most surrogacy contracts include prohibitions against smoking, drinking, and the use of prescription as well as recreational drugs. In the contract signed by Mary Beth Whitehead, the mother of Baby M, clause 15 required her "to adhere to all medical instructions given to her by the inseminating physician as well as her independent obstetrician." She had to agree "not to smoke cigarettes, drink alcoholic beverages, use illegal drugs, or take nonprescription medication or prescribed medications without written consent from her physician." She also had to agree to follow a prenatal medical examination schedule.[13]

These contractual provisions create a different sort of ethical problem: How can it be known whether the surrogate mother is adhering to the restrictions? How can such provisions be enforced? Should monitoring be permitted—for example, screening urine for drug use during pregnancy, installing cigarette smoke detectors in the home or in the car, doing random breathalyzer tests for alcohol? These questions might seem far-fetched were it not for the fact that such tests are already in use in some places and for some purposes in our society, and have been recommended in many other settings. Would it be reasonable to require surrogate mothers to give up a substantial amount of privacy for the purpose of detecting violations of the surrogacy contract?

The discussion has now shifted to the provisions of surrogacy contracts, and away from the question with which we began: an ethical assessment of the practice of surrogacy itself. Yet a thorough evaluation of this new reproductive practice requires an examination of relevant public policy concerns.

SURROGACY AND PUBLIC POLICY

A factor that complicates the debate at the policy level is the contention that surrogate motherhood is a form of "baby selling." When the attorney for Mary Beth Whitehead asserted that a contract to be a surrogate mother for money is "against public policy," he was referring to his belief that the contract violated state adoption laws and public policies against the sale of babies.

Once again, this places the assessment of surrogacy in the context of a commercial arrangement. Although I have been urging that the commercial aspects be separated from the social arrangement of surrogacy for the purpose of ethical evaluation, the underlying conceptual question remains: Is this a form of baby-selling? Or should it be considered more like a fee for services rendered? People who express a strong emotional distaste for surrogate motherhood are quick to label it "baby selling." That term has such negative connotations, and the practice is so universally disapproved, that once surrogacy is categorized as a new variety of "baby selling," its rejection is sure to follow quickly. But fairness demands an objective examination of the issue. It is an old trick of argumentation to apply a concept that already carries negative connotations to a different situation, with the aim of persuading listeners that the new situation should, like the old one, be viewed in a negative light.

A Kentucky court, holding that surrogate contracts did not violate public policy, asked how it was possible for a natural father to be accused of buying his own child.[14] My own view on this question is that paying a woman to be a surrogate mother is more like "renting a womb" than it is like buying a baby. Monetary payment is for the woman's inconvenience and possible discomfort, including the risks of any complications of pregnancy. This interpretation can be supported by looking at the features of surrogacy contracts, features that impose certain duties and obligations on the surrogate mother during pregnancy. Also, one proposed law in the state of Michigan contains the provision that the surrogate agreement may not allow for a reduction of payment if the baby is stillborn or born alive but impaired.[15]

But an opposing interpretation is supported by some existing programs and proposed laws. In many surrogacy arrangements, the bulk of the payment is made after birth, and in some cases the surrogate mother does not receive full payment if she miscarries.[16] The law proposed in South Carolina would codify that approach by a provision that the woman will receive no compensation beyond her medical expenses if she miscarries before the fifth month of pregnancy, and will receive only 10 percent of the agreed-upon fee plus medical expenses if she miscarries during or after the fifth month.[17]

Despite my conclusion that contracts for surrogacy should not be considered a form of baby-selling, and therefore in violation of laws that prohibit that activity, I believe it is morally wrong to undertake commercial surrogacy transactions. There are two arguments in support of this view.

TWO ARGUMENTS AGAINST COMMERCIAL SURROGACY

The "Exploitation" Argument

The first argument goes back to an earlier point: there is a risk of richer women exploiting those who are poorer or less advantaged. The magnitude of this danger is probably exaggerated by the opponents of surrogate motherhood. Yet it is surely true that women who are poor, uneducated, or both have fewer options than those who are better off financially. They are more likely to be unemployed, receiving welfare payments, or forced to remain at home caring for their own young children. To offer money to a woman in these circumstances to bear the child of another woman is probably to offer her an undue inducement. It is an offer that may be difficult for a person of little financial means to refuse and would, in that case, be coercive. . . .

The "Commodification" Argument

The potential for better-off women to exploit those who are less well off is the first argument against commercial surrogacy arrangements. The second is a broader argument that applies to other biomedical concerns as well. Medical and other health services are a special sort of social good, one that should not be subject to the same market forces that govern the sale of pork bellies. The human body, its parts, and its reproductive products are not "mere meat."[18] The United States Congress wisely enacted a law prohibiting commercial arrangements for procuring and distributing organs for transplantation.[19] There is sufficient evidence of greed, corruption, and duplicity on the part of persons in financial markets, among defense contractors, local and federal officials, and others in the public and private sectors to make us wary of allowing commercial practices to invade and dominate the delivery of health care.

Medical services and other health-related activities should not be treated as commodities.[20] To do so is to feed the coffers of profiteers and enrich brokers and middlemen, people eager to reap personal gain from the misfortunes of others. Commercial arrangements drain monetary resources away from providing medical services and products directly to those in need.

The standard cost of a surrogacy arrangement is a case in point. When Noel P. Keane, the Detroit lawyer, appeared on the TV program "60 Minutes," he reported the breakdown of costs as follows: a one-time fee of $10,000 to the broker; $10,000 to the surrogate mother; and $5,000 for "other costs," for a total of $25,000.

CONCLUSION

From all of the considerations enumerated here, I conclude that it is not the practice of surrogate motherhood itself that is ethically wrong, rather, its commercialization. This conclusion answers "no" to the question of whether there is something intrinsically unethical about surrogacy. It cannot be seen to violate any fundamental moral principle prohibiting certain types of action. But this conclusion does not yet answer the question of whether, on the whole, the bad consequences of allowing this practice outweigh the good ones. There is not enough evidence at this point for an empirically well-confirmed answer to that question.

But, it will be objected, if commercial surrogacy is prohibited, is that not likely to result in the disappearance of the practice? Who will come forward to serve as surrogate mothers—except for a few women who want to help their own sisters, or daughters, or even mothers, as the case may be?

My reply to this question is simple. The argument that there is nothing inherently unethical about surrogacy is not an argument that surrogacy is a good thing and that, therefore, it ought to be encouraged or promoted. It is simply an argument that noncommercial surrogacy is morally permissible and, therefore, should not be prohibited. If the practice disappears for lack of monetary incentive for women to act as surrogates, so be it. In the absence of evidence or arguments that surrogacy is such a desirable practice that its disappearance would constitute a harm or wrong to society, its loss should not be lamented.

Still, there is sufficient evidence from the Baby M case and that of other surrogate mothers who are seeking to get their babies back to suggest that even noncommercial surrogacy needs to be carefully regulated. Thought should be given to requiring the sort of provisions typical in adoption cases, which permit the birth mother to change her mind during a limited period after the baby is born. That would surely be preferable to lengthy trials, accompanied by the sensational publicity and humiliation that marked the Baby M case.

An ethical analysis of surrogate motherhood should proceed by seeking to determine the probable beneficial and harmful consequences. This requires an ongoing review of evidence as it becomes available. It brings to mind the recommendations of the Ethics Committee of the American Fertility Society noted earlier. Not only did the committee propose that surrogacy be practiced exclusively as a clinical experiment; it also recommended that clinics involved in surrogacy arrangements publish data about the process and outcomes. Some people might contend that it is too late to reverse social practices already set in motion, but that view is mistaken. Biomedical research involving human subjects was practiced for a long time before regulations and safeguards were introduced. It makes perfectly good sense to do the same for novel reproductive arrangements, in order to provide a scientific basis on which they can be evaluated for the purpose of fashioning public policy.

The argument that surrogacy is a morally flawed activity because of exploitation, dehumanization, or the base motives of the participants does not stand up to critical analysis. The moral flaws are tied to the commercial features of surrogacy, not to the arrangement itself. Although there is nothing ethically wrong, in principle, with surrogate motherhood, if it becomes evident that surrogacy arrangements result in more overall harm than benefits, we shall have to conclude that the practice is morally wrong.

REFERENCES

1. Joseph Sullivan, "Bishops File Brief Against Surrogate Motherhood," *New York Times*, July 19, 1987, 28.

2. Keith Schneider, "Mothers Urge Ban on Surrogacy as Form of 'Slavery,' " *New York Times*, Sept. 1, 1987.

3. Id.

4. Quoted in "Who's Who in the Fight for Baby M," *New York Times*, April 1, 1987, sec. B2.

5. Quoted in Schneider, supra note 2.

6. Robert Hanley, "Seven-Week Trial Touched Many Basic Emotions," *New York Times*, April 1, 1987, sec. B2.

7. James Feron, "Testimony Is Given on Surrogate Bill," *New York Times*, April 11, 1987.

8. Diana Brahams, "The Hasty British Ban on Commercial Surrogacy," *Hastings Center Report*, 17 (Feb. 1987): 16–19.

9. Sullivan, supra note 1, at 28.

10. Sidney Callahan, "No Child Wants to Live in a Womb for Hire," *National Catholic Reporter*, Oct. 11, 1985.

11. Id.

12. Sidney Callahan, as quoted in Iver Peterson, "Baby M Trial Splits Ranks of Feminists," *New York Times*, Feb. 24, 1987, sec. B1.

13. George Annas, "Baby M: Babies (and Justice) for Sale," *Hastings Center Report*, 17 (June 1987): 13–15, at 14.

14. Commonwealth of Kentucky v. Surrogate Parenting Associates, Inc. (Oct. 26, 1983), Kentucky Circuit Court, Franklin County.

15. Lori Andrews, "The Aftermath of Baby M: Proposed State Laws on Surrogate Motherhood," *Hastings Center Report*, 17 (Oct./Nov. 1987): 31–40, at 35.

16. Id.

17. Id.

18. See Leon Kass, " 'Making Babies' Revisited," *The Public Interest*, 54 (Winter 1979): 32–60.

19. National Organ Transplant Act of 1984, 42 U.S.C. Para. 274(e) (1982).

20. See, gen., Margaret Radin, "Market Inalienability," *Harvard Law Review*, 100 (June 1987): 1849–1937.

POSTSCRIPT

Is Surrogate Motherhood Wrong?

The idea of surrogate motherhood, as made possible by recently developed technology, is relatively new. As individuals, we do not already have a well-defined place for this idea. We need to relate it to ideas with which we are already familiar and consider some "worst-case scenarios" in order to evaluate what surrogate motherhood might bring.

Surrogate motherhood has been compared to adoption, baby selling, "regular" parenthood (with technological assistance), and artificial insemination by donor (AID, by which a woman conceives through the use of sperm that is usually anonymously donated). In every case, the comparison has both true and false aspects.

Worst-case scenarios are worth contemplating because while there may be cases in which all goes well and no one has a complaint, there may also be cases in which various things go wrong. Although we need to be prepared for both eventualities, we tend to think only of the more pleasant cases. This is not just a feature of surrogate motherhood. Even in natural parenthood, there are worst-case scenarios to be considered and dealt with. Suppose, for instance, that the natural parents abuse or neglect the child. We then recognize appropriate methods of dealing with this contingency: we understand that a court may make the child a ward of the state. Suppose that in a surrogate motherhood arrangement, neither the biological father nor the biological mother (the so-called surrogate mother) is willing to accept the child; suppose both the biological father and the surrogate mother want the child; suppose the father dies; suppose the child is born with a physical problem that is possibly the result of the surrogate mother's prenatal activity. The point of raising such possibilities is not to suggest that surrogate motherhood is a bad idea or that society should not support the idea. The point is that all contingencies, even unwelcome ones, need to be considered and dealt with.

Various other human factors also come into the picture. The parents of the surrogate mother become biological grandparents. Do they have some rights, too, with respect to their grandchildren? Is any consideration going to be given to any other children of the surrogate mother? If they are young, they may fear that they too might be given away, just as they saw happen to their little sibling. (Or *was* it their little sibling?) What if they want to communicate with their sibling later in life?

Surrogate motherhood presents some particular difficulties for feminism, which has traditionally supported self-determination for women with respect to reproduction and has fought against the idea of women as "baby producers." Should we think that surrogate motherhood is one way that some women are able to assume control over their bodies? Or should we think that this is one way in which some women are made into mere baby producers?

Certain cases of surrogate motherhood are particularly striking. A woman in South Dakota recently became pregnant with twins who will be her grandchildren. The woman received ova of her daughter that had been fertilized *in vitro* by the sperm of the daughter's husband. In some ways this case, although unusual, is a "best case" for surrogacy, since no money is involved and the woman (who expects to become a grandmother in November 1991, when she gives birth) did not herself provide any ova for the pregnancy.

Further sources for reading on this subject are Richard Hull, ed., *Ethical Issues in the New Reproductive Technologies* (Wadsworth, 1990); Hilde Lindemann Nelson and James Linedemann Nelson, "Cutting Motherhood in Two: Some Suspicions Concerning Surrogacy," *Hypatia* (1989); Lori Andrews, *Between Strangers: Surrogate Mothers, Expectant Fathers, and Brave New Babies* (Harper & Row, 1989); Elaine Baruch, Amadeo D'Adamo, Jr., and Joni Seager, eds., *Embryos, Ethics, and Women's Rights: Exploring the New Reproductive Technologies* (Haworth Press, 1988); Gena Corea, *The Mother Machine: Reproductive Technologies from Artificial Insemination to Artificial Wombs* (Harper & Row, 1986); Peter Singer and W. A. W. Walters, eds., *Test-Tube Babies: A Guide to Moral Questions, Present Techniques and Future Possibilities* (Oxford University Press, 1982); Gena Corea et al., eds., *Man-Made Women: How New Reproductive Technologies Affect Women* (Indiana University Press, 1987); M. Field, *Surrogate Motherhood* (Harvard University Press, 1990); and Carmel Shalev, *Birth Power: The Case for Surrogacy* (Yale University Press, 1989).

First-person accounts can be found in Mary Beth Whitehead, *A Mother's Story: The Truth About the Baby M Case* (St. Martin's, 1989); Elizabeth Kane and Loretta Schwartz-Nobel, *Birth Mother: America's First Legal Surrogate Mother Tells the Story of Her Change of Heart* (Harcourt Brace Jovanovich, 1988); and Patricia Adair, *A Surrogate Mother's Story* (Loiry Publishing House, 1987).

Government reports include: The New York State Task Force on Life and the Law, *Surrogate Parenting: Analysis and Recommendations for Public Policy* (New York State Task Force on Life and the Law, 1988), and Mary Warnock, *A Question of Life: The Warnock Report on Human Fertilisation and Embryology* (Basil Blackwell, 1985), which is the report of a British committee on many reproductive topics, including surrogate motherhood.

PART 4

Morality, Law, and Society

It is part of the social nature of human beings that we live in groups. And this requires that we have laws or rules that govern our relationships and interactions. Morality and shared values can be positive tools for social living. One presupposition in a democratic society is that social differences must be settled by open discussion and argument. The issues in this section include some of those that have strongly divided our own society and some that challenge existing social institutions and practices.

Do We Have a Moral Responsibility to Rehabilitate Criminals?

_____

Should Capital Punishment Be Abolished?

_____

Is Euthanasia Immoral?

_____

Is Affirmative Action Morally Justifiable?

ISSUE 14

Do We Have a Moral Responsibility to Rehabilitate Criminals?

YES: Karl Menninger, from "The Crime of Punishment," *Saturday Review* (1968)

NO: C. S. Lewis, from "The Humanitarian Theory of Punishment," in *God in the Dock: Essays on Theology and Ethics*, edited by Walter Hooper (reprinted by Eerdmans, 1970)

ISSUE SUMMARY

YES: Psychiatrist Karl Menninger (1893–1990) argues that people have a double attitude toward crime. We condemn crime, but we also seem to need to keep it around. We hold criminals in prison, make little or no effort to rehabilitate them, and then release them back into society. A therapeutic attitude should replace this vindictiveness, and treatment of criminals should replace punishment.

NO: Religious writer C. S. Lewis (1898–1963) argues that this so-called humanitarian approach is not really merciful and not really just. It does not consider criminals to be human beings but "cases" to be "cured." Criminals deserve, and should receive, punishment, not treatment.

Punishment is a puzzling topic. The two spheres in which punishment is most frequently administered are in families, where parents punish children, and in the larger society, where those who are convicted of crimes are punished through legislatures and courts of law. But it does not seem that the rationale for punishment in the family case can extend to the societal case.

The idea of parents punishing their children is not one that is much attacked, although some of the various methods are often criticized. The justification for punishment in the family environment is that parents have a responsibility to raise children, not just to watch them grow. In cultivating and nourishing what is best in children, there are times when the parental punishment of children is justified. Certain moral lessons must be learned, for example, and punishment shows the child where the limits of acceptability lie. It is easy to imagine that if parents did not punish, children would grow up to be spoiled, overly demanding, and totally unprepared for life. Parents who love their children have no desire for them to turn out this way. Children are punished not to do them harm, but to do them good.

What about the punishment of criminals by society? The punishment of criminals does not seem to be part of a large-scale project to turn them into respectable citizens and members of the community. In many cases, criminals are locked up for a certain period of time to "pay their debt to society" and are then released. Repeated offenses bring greater curtailment of liberty and longer prison sentences. In some extreme cases, criminals are executed. The aim of this kind of punishment does not seem to be to bring about responsible and acceptable behavior. The same concerns that justify parental punishment do not translate into social concerns that justify social punishment.

Why then does society punish criminals? One answer is that the criminal has done wrong and must be made to pay for it. But what is the purpose of this "paying"? The point seems to be that the criminal should be made to suffer. The criminal might be imprisoned for several years. After imprisonment, however, it is likely that the criminal's attitudes are unchanged, or perhaps they have become even more criminal and antisocial. Society may have "made the criminal pay," but neither seems to have benefited.

Parents punish children so that they will learn and be better for it. None of this happens in the case of societal punishment of the criminal. All that happens is that the criminal is made to suffer. What moral justification can exist for intentionally causing people to suffer and for keeping them in a state in which they are likely to later provoke even more punishment from society?

At this point the thought may arise that we should treat or rehabilitate criminals. It might even be claimed that not only would the criminal benefit from this arrangement, but, in the long run, society would as well. Supporters of this view say that we have to develop new attitudes toward criminals. They compare our current attitudes to those held by earlier unenlightened people toward the mentally ill. Treatment, rather than confinement in cruel institutions, is claimed to be the proper method of dealing with criminals.

Treatment, not punishment, is advocated by Karl Menninger in the following selection. He is answered by C. S. Lewis, who claims that such an approach leaves out the essential element of wrongdoing on the part of the criminals. Those who do wrong should be punished precisely on that account; they are not sick or ill or in need of treatment.

YES   Karl Menninger

THE CRIME OF PUNISHMENT

Few words in our language arrest our attention as do "crime," "violence," "revenge," and "injustice." We abhor crime; we adore justice; we boast that we live by the rule of law. Violence and vengefulness we repudiate as unworthy of our civilization, and we assume this sentiment to be unanimous among all human beings.

Yet crime continues to be a national disgrace and a world-wide problem. It is threatening, alarming, wasteful, expensive, abundant, and apparently increasing! In actuality it is decreasing in frequency of occurrence, but it is certainly increasing in visibility and the reactions of the public to it.

Our system for controlling crime is ineffective, unjust, expensive. Prisons seem to operate with revolving doors—the same people going in and out and in and out. *Who cares?*

Our city jails and inhuman reformatories and wretched prisons are jammed. They are known to be unhealthy, dangerous, immoral, indecent, crime-breeding dens of iniquity. Not everyone has smelled them, as some of us have. Not many have heard the groans and the curses. Not everyone has seen the hate and despair in a thousand blank, hollow faces. But, in a way, we all know how miserable prisons are. *We want them to be that way.* And they are. *Who cares?*

Professional and big-time criminals prosper as never before. Gambling syndicates flourish. White-collar crime may even exceed all others, but goes undetected in the majority of cases. We are all being robbed and we know who the robbers are. They live nearby. *Who cares?*

The public filches millions of dollars worth of food and clothing from stores, towels and sheets from hotels, jewelry and knick-knacks from shops. The public steals, and the same public pays it back in higher prices. *Who cares?*

Time and time again somebody shouts about this state of affairs, just as I am shouting now. The magazines shout. The newspapers shout. The television and radio commentators shout (or at least they "deplore").

Psychologists, sociologists, leading jurists, wardens, and intelligent police chiefs join the chorus. Governors and mayors and Congressmen are sometimes heard. They shout that the situation is bad, bad, bad, and getting worse. Some suggested that we immediately replace obsolete procedures with scientific methods. A few shout contrary sentiments. Do the clear indications derived from scientific discovery for appropriate changes continue to fall on deaf ears? Why is the public so long-suffering, so apathetic, and thereby so continuingly self-destructive? How many Presidents (and other citizens) do we have to lose before we do something?

The public behaves as a sick patient does when a dreaded treatment is proposed for his ailment. We all know how the aching tooth may suddenly quiet down in the dentist's office, or the abdominal pain disappear in the surgeon's examining room. Why should a sufferer seek relief and shun it? Is it merely the fear of the pain of the treatment? Is it the fear of unknown complications? Is it distrust of the doctor's ability? All of these, no doubt.

But, as Freud made so incontestably clear, the sufferer is always somewhat deterred by a kind of subversive, internal opposition to the work of cure. He suffers on the one hand from the pains of his affliction and yearns to get well. But he suffers at the same time from traitorous impulses that fight against the accomplishment of any change in himself, even recovery! Like Hamlet, he wonders whether it may be better after all to suffer the familiar pains and aches associated with the old method than to face the complications of a new and strange, even though possibly better, way of handling things.

The inescapable conclusion is that society *wants* crime, *needs* crime, and gains definite satisfactions from the present mishandling of it! We condemn crime; we punish offenders for it; but we need it. The crime and punishment ritual is a part of our lives. We need crimes to wonder at, to enjoy vicariously, to discuss and speculate about, and to publicly deplore. We need criminals to identify ourselves with, to envy secretly, and to punish stoutly. They do for us the forbidden, illegal things we *wish* to do, and, like scapegoats of old, they bear the burdens of our displaced guilt and punishment—"the iniquities of us all." . . .

Fifty years ago, Winston Churchill declared that the mood and temper of the public in regard to crime and criminals is one of the unfailing tests of the civilization of any country. Judged by this standard, how civilized are we?

The chairman of the President's National Crime Commission . . . declared recently that organized crime flourishes in America because enough of the public wants its services, and most citizens are apathetic about its impact. It will continue uncurbed as long as Americans accept it as inevitable and, in some instances, desirable.

Are there steps that we can take which will reduce the aggressive stabs and self-destructive lurches of our less well-managing fellow men? Are there ways to prevent and control the grosser violations, other than the clumsy traditional maneuvers which we have inherited? These depend basically upon intimidation and slow-motion torture. We call it punishment, and justify it with our "feeling." We know it doesn't work.

Yes, there *are* better ways. There are steps that could be taken; some *are* taken. But we move too slowly. Much better use, it seems to me, could be made of the members of my profession and other behavioral scientists than having them deliver courtroom pronunciamentos. The consistent use of a diagnostic clinic would enable trained workers to lay what they can learn about an offender before the judge who would know best how to implement the recommendation.

This would no doubt lead to a transformation of prisons, if not to their total disappearance in their present form and function. Temporary and permanent detention will perhaps always be necessary for a few, especially the professionals, but this could be more effectively and economically performed with new types of "facility" (that strange, awkward word for institution).

I assume it to be a matter of common and general agreement that our object in all this is to protect the community from a repetition of the offense by the most economical method consonant with our other purposes. Our "other purposes" include the desire to prevent these offenses from occurring, to reclaim offenders for social usefulness, if possible, and to detain them in protective custody, if reclamation is *not* possible. But how?

The treatment of human failure or dereliction by the infliction of pain is still used and believed in by many nonmedical people. "Spare the rod and spoil the child" is still considered wise counsel by many.

Whipping is still used by many secondary schoolmasters in England, I am informed, to stimulate study, attention, and the love of learning. Whipping was long a traditional treatment for the "crime" of disobedience on the part of children, pupils, servants, apprentices, employees. And slaves were treated for

centuries by flogging for such offenses as weariness, confusion, stupidity, exhaustion, fear, grief, and even overcheerfulness. It was assumed and stoutly defended that these "treatments" cured conditions for which they were administered.

Meanwhile, scientific medicine was acquiring many new healing methods and devices. Doctors can now transplant organs and limbs; they can remove brain tumors and cure incipient cancers; they can halt pneumonia, meningitis, and other infections; they can correct deformities and repair breaks and tears and scars. But these wonderful achievements are accomplished on *willing* subjects, people who voluntarily ask for help by even heroic measures. And the reader will be wondering, no doubt, whether doctors can do anything with or for people who *do not want* to be treated at all, in any way! Can doctors cure willful aberrant behavior? Are we to believe that crime is a *disease* that can be reached by scientific measures? Isn't it merely "natural meanness" that makes all of us do wrong things at times even when we "know better"? And are not self-control, moral stamina, and will power the things needed? Surely there is no medical treatment for the lack of those!

Let me answer this carefully, for much misunderstanding accumulates here. I would say that according to the prevalent understanding of the words, crime is *not* a disease. Neither is it an illness, although I think it *should* be! It *should* be treated, and it could be; but it mostly isn't.

These enigmatic statements are simply explained. Diseases are undesired states of being which have been described and defined by doctors, usually given Greek or Latin appellations, and treated by long-established physical and pharmacological formulae. Illness, on the other hand, is best defined as a state of impaired functioning of such a nature that the public expects the sufferer to repair to the physician for help. The illness may prove to be a disease; more often it is only vague and nameless misery, but something which doctors, not lawyers, teachers, or preachers, are supposed to be able and willing to help.

When the community begins to look upon the expression of aggressive violence as the symptom of an illness or as indicative of illness, it will be because it believes doctors can do something to correct such a condition. At present, some better-informed individuals do believe and expect this. However angry at or sorry for the offender, they want him "treated" in an effective way so that he will cease to be a danger to them. And they know that traditional punishment, "treatment-punishment," will not effect this.

What *will*? What effective treatment is there for such violence? It will surely have to begin with motivating or stimulating or arousing in a cornered individual the wish and hope and intention to change his methods of dealing with the realities of life. Can this be done by education, medication, counseling, training? I would answer *yes*. It can be done successfully in a majority of cases, if undertaken in time.

The present penal system and the existing legal philosophy do not stimulate or even expect such a change to take place in the criminal. Yet change is what medical science always aims for. The prisoner, like the doctor's other patients, should emerge from his treatment experience a different person, differently equipped, differently functioning, and headed in a different direction than when he began the treatment.

It is natural for the public to doubt that this can be accomplished with criminals. But remember that the public *used* to doubt that change could be effected in the mentally ill. No one a hundred years ago believed mental illness to be curable. Today *all* people know (or should know) that *mental illness is curable* in the great majority of instances and that the prospects and rapidity of cure are directly related to the availability and intensity of proper treatment.

The forms and techniques of psychiatric treatment used today number in the hundreds. No one patient requires or receives all forms, but each patient is studied with respect to his particular needs, his basic assets, his interests, and his special difficulties. A therapeutic team may embrace a dozen workers—as in a hospital setting—or it may narrow down to the doctor and the spouse. Clergymen, teachers, relatives, friends, and even fellow patients often participate informally but helpfully in the process of readaptation.

All of the participants in this effort to bring about a favorable change in the patient—i.e., in his vital balance and life program—are imbued with what we may call a *therapeutic attitude*. This is one in direct antithesis to attitudes of avoidance, ridicule, scorn, or punitiveness. Hostile feelings toward the subject, however justified by his unpleasant and even destructive behavior, are not in the curriculum of therapy or in the therapist. This does not mean that therapists approve of the offensive and obnoxious behavior of the patient; they distinctly disapprove of it. But they recognize it as symptomatic of continued imbalance and disorganization, which is what they are seeking to change. They distinguish between disapproval, penalty, price, and punishment.

Doctors charge fees; they impose certain "penalties" or prices, but they have long since put aside primitive attitudes of retaliation toward offensive patients. A patient may cough in the doctor's face or may vomit on the office rug; a patient may curse or scream or even struggle in the extremity of his pain. But these acts are not "punished." Doctors and nurses have no time or thought for inflicting unnecessary pain even upon patients who may be difficult, disagreeable, provocative, and even dangerous. It is their duty to care for them, to try to make them well, and to prevent them from doing themselves or others harm. This requires love, not hate. This is the deepest meaning of the therapeutic attitude. Every doctor knows this; every worker in a hospital or clinic knows it (or should).

There is another element in the therapeutic attitude. It is the quality of hopefulness. If no one believes that the patient can get well, if no one—not even the doctor—has any hope, there probably won't be any recovery. Hope is just as important as love in the therapeutic attitude.

"But you were talking about the mentally ill," readers may interject, "those poor, confused, bereft, frightened individuals who yearn for help from you doctors and nurses. Do you mean to imply that willfully perverse individuals, our criminals, can be similarly reached and rehabilitated? Do you really believe that effective treatment of the sort you visualize can be applied to people *who do not want any help*, who are so willfully vicious, so well aware of the wrongs they are doing, so lacking in penitence or even common decency that punishment seems to be the only thing left?"

Do I believe there is effective treatment for offenders, and that they *can* be changed? *Most certainly and definitely I do.* Not all cases, to be sure; there are also some physical afflictions which we cannot cure at the moment. Some provision has to be made for incurables—pending new knowledge—and these will include some offenders. But I believe the majority of them would prove to be curable. The willfulness and the viciousness of offenders are part of the thing for which they have to be treated. These must not thwart the therapeutic attitude.

It is simply not true that most of them are "fully aware" of what they are doing, nor is it true that they want no help from anyone, although some of them say so. Prisoners are individuals: Some want treatment, some do not. Some don't know what treatment is. Many are utterly despairing and hopeless. Where treatment is made available in institutions, many prisoners seek it even with the full knowledge that doing so will not lessen their sentences. In some prisons, seeking treatment by prisoners is frowned upon by the officials.

Various forms of treatment are even now being tried in some progressive courts and prisons over the country—educational, social, industrial, religious, recreational, and psychological treatments. Socially acceptable behavior, new work-play opportunities, new identity and companion patterns all help toward community reacceptance. Some parole officers and some wardens have been extremely ingenious in developing these modalities of rehabilitation and reconstruction—more than I could list here even if I knew them all. But some are trying. The secret of success in all programs, however, is the replacement of the punitive attitude with a therapeutic attitude.

Offenders with propensities for impulsive and predatory aggression should not be permitted to live among us unrestrained by some kind of social control. *But the great majority of offenders, even "criminals," should never become prisoners if we want to "cure" them.*

There are now throughout the country many citizens' action groups and programs for the prevention and control of crime and delinquency. With such attitudes of inquiry and concern, the public could acquire information (and incentive) leading to a change of feeling about crime and criminals. It will discover how unjust is much so-called "justice," how baffled and frustrated many judges are by the ossified rigidity of old-fashioned, obsolete laws and state constitutions which effectively prevent the introduction of sensible procedures to replace useless, harmful ones.

I want to proclaim to the public that things are not what it wishes them to be, and will only become so if it will take an interest in the matter and assume some responsibility for its own self-protection.

Will the public listen?

If the public does become interested, it will realize that we must have more facts, more trial projects, more checked results. It will share the dismay of the President's Commission in finding that no one knows much about even the incidence of crime with any definiteness or statistical accuracy.

The average citizen finds it difficult to see how any research would in any way change his mind about a man who brutally murders his children. But just such inconceivably awful acts most dramatically point up the need for research. Why should—how can—a man become so dreadful as that in our culture? How is such a man made? Is it comprehensible that he can be born to become so depraved?

There are thousands of questions regarding crime and public protection which deserve scientific study. What makes some individuals maintain their interior equilibrium by one kind of disturbance of the social structure rather than by another kind, one that would have landed him in a hospital? Why do some individuals specialize in certain types of crime? Why do so many young people reared in areas of delinquency and poverty and bad example never become habitual delinquents? (Perhaps this is a more important question than why some of them do.)

The public has a fascination for violence, and clings tenaciously to its yen for vengeance, blind and deaf to the expense, futility, and dangerousness of the resulting penal system. But we are bound to hope that this will yield in time to the persistent, penetrating light of intelligence and accumulating scientific knowledge. The public will grow increasingly ashamed of its cry for retaliation, its persistent demand to punish. This is its crime, *our* crime against criminals— and, incidentally, our crime against ourselves. For before we can diminish our sufferings from the ill-controlled aggressive assaults of fellow citizens, we must renounce the philosophy of punishment, the obsolete, vengeful penal attitude. In its place we would seek a comprehensive constructive social attitude—therapeutic in some instances, restraining in some instances, but preventive in its total social impact.

In the last analysis this becomes a question of personal morals and values. No matter how glorified or how piously disguised, vengeance as a human motive must be personally repudiated by each and every one of us. This is the message of old religions and new psychiatries. Unless this message is heard, unless we, the people—the man on the street, the housewife in the home—can give up our delicious satisfaction in opportunities for vengeful retaliation on scapegoats, we cannot expect to preserve our peace, our public safety, or our mental health.

NO

C. S. Lewis

THE HUMANITARIAN
THEORY OF PUNISHMENT

In England we have lately had a controversy about Capital Punishment. I do not know whether a murderer is more likely to repent and make a good end on the gallows a few weeks after his trial or in the prison infirmary thirty years later. I do not know whether the fear of death is an indispensable deterrent. I need not, for the purpose of this article, decide whether it is a morally permissible deterrent. Those are questions which I propose to leave untouched. My subject is not Capital Punishment in particular, but that theory of punishment in general which the controversy showed to be almost universal among my fellow-countrymen. It may be called the Humanitarian theory. Those who hold it think that it is mild and merciful. In this I believe that they are seriously mistaken. I believe that the 'Humanity' which it claims is a dangerous illusion and disguises the possibility of cruelty and injustice without end. I urge a return to the traditional or Retributive theory not solely, not even primarily, in the interests of society, but in the interests of the criminal.

According to the Humanitarian theory, to punish a man because he deserves it, and as much as he deserves, is mere revenge, and, therefore, barbarous and immoral. It is maintained that the only legitimate motives for punishing are the desire to deter others by example or to mend the criminal. When this theory is combined, as frequently happens, with the belief that all crime is more or less pathological, the idea of mending tails off into that of healing or curing and punishment becomes therapeutic. Thus it appears at first sight that we have passed from the harsh and self-righteous notion of giving the wicked their deserts to the charitable and enlightened one of tending the psychologically sick. What could be more amiable? One little point which is taken for granted in this theory needs, however, to be made explicit. The things done to the criminal, even if they are called cures, will be just as compulsory as they were in the old days when we called them punishments. If a tendency to steal can be cured by psychotherapy, the thief will no doubt be forced to undergo the treatment. Otherwise, society cannot continue.

My contention is that this doctrine, merciful though it appears, really means that each one of us, from the moment he breaks the law, is deprived of the rights of a human being.

The reason is this. The Humanitarian theory removes from Punishment the concept of Desert. But the concept of Desert is the only connecting link between punishment and justice. It is only as deserved or undeserved that a sentence can be just or unjust. I do not here contend that the question 'Is it deserved?' is the only one we can reasonably ask about a punishment. We may very properly ask whether it is likely to deter others and to reform the criminal. But neither of these two last questions is a question about justice. There is no sense in talking about a 'just deterrent' or a 'just cure'. We demand of a deterrent not whether it is just but whether it will deter. We demand of a cure not whether it is just but whether it succeeds. Thus when we cease to consider what the criminal deserves and consider only what will cure him or deter others, we have tacitly removed him from the sphere of justice altogether; instead of a person, a subject of rights, we now have a mere object, a patient, a 'case'.

The distinction will become clearer if we ask who will be qualified to determine sentences when sentences are no longer held to derive their propriety from the criminal's deservings. On the old view the problem of fixing the right sentence was a moral problem. Accordingly, the judge who did it was a person trained in jurisprudence; trained, that is, in a science which deals with rights and duties, and which, in origin at least, was consciously accepting guidance from the Law of Nature, and from Scripture. We must admit that in the actual penal code of most countries at most times these high originals were so much modified by local custom, class interests, and utilitarian concessions, as to be very imperfectly recognizable. But the code was never in principle, and not always in fact, beyond the control of the conscience of the society. And when (say, in eighteenth-century England) actual punishments conflicted too violently with the moral sense of the community, juries refused to convict and reform was finally brought about. This was possible because, so long as we are thinking in terms of Desert, the propriety of the penal code, being a moral question, is a question on which every man has the right to an opinion, not because he follows this or that profession, but because he is simply a man, a rational animal enjoying the Natural Light. But all this is changed when we drop the concept of Desert. The only two questions we may now ask about a punishment are whether it deters and whether it cures. But these are not questions on which anyone is entitled to have an opinion simply because he is a man. He is not entitled to an opinion even if, in addition to being a man, he should happen also to be a jurist, a Christian, and a moral theologian. For they are not questions about principle but about matter of fact; and for such *cuiquam in sua arte credendum*.[1] Only the expert 'penologist' (let barbarous things have barbarous names), in the light of previous experiment, can tell us what is likely to deter: only the psychotherapist can tell us what is likely to cure. It will be in vain for the rest of us, speaking simply as men, to say, 'but this punishment is hideously unjust, hideously disproportionate to the criminal's deserts'. The experts with perfect logic will reply, 'but nobody was talking about deserts. No one was talking about *punishment* in your archaic vindictive sense of the word. Here are the statistics proving that this treatment deters. Here are the statistics proving that this other treatment cures. What is your trouble?'

The Humanitarian theory, then, removes sentences from the hands of jurists whom the public conscience is entitled to criticize and places them in the hands of technical experts whose special sciences do not even employ such categories as rights or justice. It might be argued that since this transference results from an abandonment of the old idea of punishment, and, therefore, of all vindictive motives, it will be safe to leave our criminals in such hands. I will not pause to comment on the simple-minded view of fallen human nature which such a belief implies. Let us rather remember that the 'cure' of criminals is to be compulsory; and let us then watch how the theory actually works in the mind of the Humanitarian. The immediate starting point of this article was a letter I read in one of our Leftist weeklies. The author was pleading that a certain sin, now treated by our laws as a crime, should henceforward be treated as a disease. And he complained that under the present system the offender, after a term in gaol, was simply let out to return to his original environment where he would probably relapse. What he complained of was not the shutting up but the letting out. On his remedial view of punishment the offender should, of course, be detained until he was cured. And of course the official straighteners are the only people who can say when that is. The first result of the Humanitarian theory is, therefore, to substitute for a definite sentence (reflecting to some extent

the community's moral judgment on the degree of ill-desert involved) an indefinite sentence terminable only by the word of those experts—and they are not experts in moral theology nor even in the Law of Nature—who inflict it. Which of us, if he stood in the dock, would not prefer to be tried by the old system?

It may be said that by the continued use of the word punishment and the use of the verb 'inflict' I am misrepresenting Humanitarians. They are not punishing, not inflicting, only healing. But do not let us be deceived by a name. To be taken without consent from my home and friends; to lose my liberty; to undergo all those assaults on my personality which modern psychotherapy knows how to deliver; to be re-made after some pattern of 'normality' hatched in a Viennese laboratory to which I never professed allegiance; to know that this process will never end until either my captors have succeeded or I grown wise enough to cheat them with apparent success—who cares whether this is called Punishment or not? That it includes most of the elements for which any punishment is feared—shame, exile, bondage, and years eaten by the locust—is obvious. Only enormous ill-desert could justify it; but ill-desert is the very conception which the Humanitarian theory has thrown overboard.

If we turn from the curative to the deterrent justification of punishment we shall find the new theory even more alarming. When you punish a man *in terrorem*,[2] make of him an 'example' to others, you are admittedly using him as a means to an end; someone else's end. This, in itself, would be a very wicked thing to do. On the classical theory of Punishment it was of course justified on the ground that the man deserved it.

That was assumed to be established before any question of 'making him an example' arose. You then, as the saying is, killed two birds with one stone; in the process of giving him what he deserved you set an example to others. But take away desert and the whole morality of the punishment disappears. Why, in Heaven's name, am I to be sacrificed to the good of society in this way?—unless, of course, I deserve it.

But that is not the worst. If the justification of exemplary punishment is not to be based on desert but solely on its efficacy as a deterrent, it is not absolutely necessary that the man we punish should even have committed the crime. The deterrent effect demands that the public should draw the moral, 'If we do such an act we shall suffer like that man.' The punishment of a man actually guilty whom the public think innocent will not have the desired effect; the punishment of a man actually innocent will, provided the public think him guilty. But every modern State has powers which make it easy to fake a trial. When a victim is urgently needed for exemplary purposes and a guilty victim cannot be found, all the purposes of deterrence will be equally served by the punishment (call it 'cure' if you prefer) of an innocent victim, provided that the public can be cheated into thinking him guilty. It is no use to ask me why I assume that our rulers will be so wicked. The punishment of an innocent, that is, an undeserving, man is wicked only if we grant the traditional view that righteous punishment means deserved punishment. Once we have abandoned that criterion, all punishments have to be justified, if at all, on other grounds that have nothing to do with desert. Where the punishment of the innocent can be justified on those grounds (and it could

in some cases be justified as a deterrent) it will be no less moral than any other punishment. Any distaste for it on the part of a Humanitarian will be merely a hang-over from the Retributive theory.

It is, indeed, important to notice that my argument so far supposes no evil intentions on the part of the Humanitarian and considers only what is involved in the logic of his position. My contention is that good men (not bad men) consistently acting upon that position would act as cruelly and unjustly as the greatest tyrants. They might in some respects act even worse. Of all tyrannies a tyranny sincerely exercised for the good of its victims may be the most oppressive. It may be better to live under robber barons than under omnipotent moral busybodies. The robber baron's cruelty may sometimes sleep, his cupidity may at some point be satiated; but those who torment us for our own good will torment us without end for they do so with the approval of their own conscience. They may be more likely to go to Heaven yet at the same time likelier to make a Hell of earth. Their very kindness stings with intolerable insult. To be 'cured' against one's will and cured of states which we may not regard as disease is to be put on a level with those who have not yet reached the age of reason or those who never will; to be classed with infants, imbeciles, and domestic animals. But to be punished, however severely, because we have deserved it, because we 'ought to have known better', is to be treated as a human person made in God's image.

In reality, however, we must face the possibility of bad rulers armed with a Humanitarian theory of punishment. A great many popular blue prints for a Christian society are merely what the

Elizabethans called 'eggs in moonshine' because they assume that the whole society is Christian or that the Christians are in control. This is not so in most contemporary States. Even if it were, our rulers would still be fallen men, and, therefore, neither very wise nor very good. As it is, they will usually be unbelievers. And since wisdom and virtue are not the only or the commonest qualifications for a place in the government, they will not often be even the best unbelievers.

The practical problem of Christian politics is not that of drawing up schemes for a Christian society, but that of living as innocently as we can with unbelieving fellow-subjects under unbelieving rulers who will never be perfectly wise and good and who will sometimes be very wicked and very foolish. And when they are wicked the Humanitarian theory of punishment will put in their hands a finer instrument of tyranny than wickedness ever had before. For if crime and disease are to be regarded as the same thing, it follows that any state of mind which our masters choose to call 'disease' can be treated as crime; and compulsorily cured. It will be vain to plead that states of mind which displease government need not always involve moral turpitude and do not therefore always deserve forfeiture of liberty. For our masters will not be using the concepts of Desert and Punishment but those of disease and cure. We know that one school of psychology already regards religion as a neurosis. When this particular neurosis becomes inconvenient to government, what is to hinder government from proceeding to 'cure' it? Such 'cure' will, of course, be compulsory; but under the Humanitarian theory it will not be called by the shocking name of Persecution. No one will blame us for being Christians, no one will hate us, no one will revile us. The new Nero will approach us with the silky manners of a doctor, and though all will be in fact as compulsory as the *tunica molesta*[3] or Smithfield or Tyburn,[4] all will go on within the unemotional therapeutic sphere where words like 'right' and 'wrong' or 'freedom' and 'slavery' are never heard. And thus when the command is given, every prominent Christian in the land may vanish overnight into Institutions for the Treatment of the Ideologically Unsound, and it will rest with the expert gaolers to say when (if ever) they are to re-emerge. But it will not be persecution. Even if the treatment is painful, even if it is life-long, even if it is fatal, that will be only a regrettable accident; the intention was purely therapeutic. In ordinary medicine there were painful operations and fatal operations; so in this. But because they are 'treatment', not punishment, they can be criticized only by fellow-experts and on technical grounds, never by men as men and on grounds of justice.

This is why I think it essential to oppose the Humanitarian theory of punishment, root and branch, wherever we encounter it. It carries on its front a semblance of mercy which is wholly false. That is how it can deceive men of good will. The error began, perhaps, with Shelley's statement that the distinction between mercy and justice was invented in the courts of tyrants. It sounds noble, and was indeed the error of a noble mind. But the distinction is essential. The older view was that mercy 'tempered' justice, or (on the highest level of all) that mercy and justice had met and kissed. The essential act of mercy was to pardon; and pardon in its very essence involves the recognition of guilt and ill-desert in the recipient. If crime is only a disease which needs cure, not sin which deserves punishment, it cannot be pardoned. How can you pardon a man for having a gumboil or a club foot? But the Humanitarian theory wants simply to abolish Justice and substitute Mercy for it. This means that you start being 'kind' to people before you have considered their rights, and then force upon them supposed kindnesses which no one but you will recognize as kindnesses and which the recipient will feel as abominable cruelties. You have overshot the mark. Mercy, detached from Justice, grows unmerciful. That is the important paradox. As there are plants which will flourish only in mountain soil, so it appears that Mercy will flower only when it grows in the crannies of the rock of Justice: transplanted to the marshlands of mere Humanitarianism, it becomes a man-eating weed, all the more dangerous because it is still called by the same name as the mountain variety. But we ought long ago to have learned our lesson. We should be too old now to be deceived by those humane pretensions which have served to usher in every cruelty of the revolutionary period in which we live. These are the 'precious balms' which will 'break our heads'.[5] . . .

NOTES

1. 'We must believe the expert in his own field.'
2. 'to cause terror'.
3. Painful clothing worn as a punishment.—Ed.
4. Execution sites.—Ed.
5. Psalm cxli. 6.

POSTSCRIPT

Do We Have a Moral Responsibility to Rehabilitate Criminals?

Menninger argues that we should rehabilitate criminals if we really wish to eliminate crime. He suggests, however, that as a society we might really have hidden desires to keep the whole crime scenario going—the perpetration of crimes, the arrest and trial, and the punishment. If this suggestion is right, criminals are actually victims—victims of society's desire for the "crime ritual" to be played through again and again. Menninger tries to get us to look at crime and criminals in an entirely different way.

Menninger specifically compares our current attitudes toward criminals with previous social attitudes toward the mentally ill. Until after the turn of the century, the mentally ill were not treated; they were locked up and often chained and manacled. Menninger does not need to argue that criminals *are* mentally ill, nor does he need to argue that the mentally ill are physically ill. His basic point is this: Treatment, which was once reserved for the physically ill, was extended to the mentally ill; likewise, it could usefully be extended to the criminal. Any such extension requires a revolution in social attitudes.

Lewis believes that much more than social attitudes is at stake here. The essential point for him is that the criminal has done wrong and is guilty. The criminal *deserves* punishment. Menninger's theory might sound high-minded and humanitarian, but, Lewis claims, it would be wrong for us to drop our moral judgments and to treat the criminal as a practical problem, or a "case" that must be met somehow with therapy. Lewis indicates several specific difficulties that would exist if the rehabilitative theory were actually put into practice. As it is now, for example, criminals can "pay their debt to society" by serving more or less determinate sentences. Under rehabilitation, they would be put into the hands of therapists for indefinite periods—perhaps, if the therapy were ineffective, for the rest of their lives.

These and other issues are discussed further in Martin Perlmutter, "Punishment and Desert," in John Arthur, ed., *Morality and Moral Controversies*, 2d ed. (Prentice Hall, 1986); American Friends Service Committee, *Struggle for Justice* (Hill and Wang, 1971); Herbert Morris, *On Guilt and Innocence: Essays in Legal Philosophy and Moral Psychology* (University of California Press, 1974); and George Sher, *Desert* (Princeton University Press, 1989). For a provocative history of punishment and changing attitudes toward those convicted of crime, see Michel Foucault, *Discipline and Punish: The Birth of the Prison*, translated by Alan Sheridan (Random House, 1979).

ISSUE 15

Should Capital Punishment Be Abolished?

YES: Hugo Adam Bedau, from "Capital Punishment," in Tom Regan, ed., *Matters of Life and Death*, 2d ed. (Random House, 1986)

NO: Ernest van den Haag, from "The Ultimate Punishment: A Defense," *Harvard Law Review* (1986)

ISSUE SUMMARY

YES: Professor of philosophy Hugo Adam Bedau argues that the idea of "an eye for an eye" (of retribution in kind) has not historically supported capital punishment; in actuality, a wide variety of offenses have been punished by death. The death penalty claims the lives of the least well defended (including some innocent people) rather than the most serious criminals.

NO: Ernest van den Haag, legal professor and social critic, argues that capital punishment is a fitting punishment for murder and that there are some crimes that are so terrible that the most appropriate response is the death penalty.

Since punishment involves the intentional infliction of harm upon another person, and since intentional infliction of harm is generally wrong, the idea of punishment itself is somewhat problematic. Punishment requires some strong rationale behind it if it is not to be just another form of wrongdoing, and capital punishment requires an especially strong rationale.

Consider some actual cases of capital punishment. Socrates was tried in ancient Athens and condemned to die (by drinking poison) for not believing in the gods of the state and for corrupting young people. In 1977 a princess and her lover were executed (by firing squad and beheading, respectively) in Saudi Arabia for adultery. Also in 1977 Gary Gilmore insisted that he receive the death penalty and was executed by a firing squad in Utah for murder.

Justification for capital punishment usually comes down to one of two different lines of reasoning. One is based on the idea of justice, the other on the idea of deterrence.

Justice, it is said, demands that certain criminal acts be paid for by death. The idea is that some people deserve death and have to pay for their criminal acts with their lives.

There are several objections to this view. One of the most important of these focuses on the idea of a person "paying" for a crime by death (or even in some other way). What concept of "paying" is being used here? It does not seem like an ordinary case of paying a debt. It seems to be a kind of vengeance, as when one person says to another "I'll make you pay for that," meaning "I'll make you suffer for that." Yet one of the ideas behind state-inflicted punishment is that it is supposed to be very official, even bureaucratic, and it is designed to eliminate private vendettas and personal vindictiveness. The state, in a civilized society, is not supposed to be motivated by revenge or vindictiveness. The state's only intent is to support law and order and to protect its citizens from coming to harm at the hands of wrongdoers.

The other major line of reasoning in support of capital punishment is based on the idea of deterrence. According to this view, capital punishment must be retained in order to deter criminals and potential criminals from committing capital crimes. An old joke reflects this view: A Texan tells a visitor that in the old days the local punishment for horse-stealing was hanging. The visitor is shocked. "You used to hang people just for taking horses?" "Nope," says the Texan, "horses never got stolen."

Unlike the argument about "paying," the logic behind deterrence is supposed to be intuitively easy to understand, and to be borne out by actual statistics and empirical evidence. However, the statistics and evidence are ambiguous and subject to alternative explanations.

Your intuition may support the judgment that the death penalty deters crime, but the empirical evidence is not similarly uniform and clear, and in some cases even points to the opposite conclusion. (For example, some people may be more likely to murder an innocent victim if they are reasonably certain of achieving their own death and perhaps some notoriety.) Or consider the example of the failure of deterrence that occurred in England when public hanging was the punishment given for the crime of pickpocketing. Professional pickpockets, undeterred by the activity on the gallows, circulated among the crowd of spectators, aware that a good time to pick pockets was when everyone's attention was focused on something else—in this case, when the rope tightened around the neck of the convicted pickpocket.

Further thought about this matter of deterrence raises more questions. Consider this scenario. Two men get into an argument while drinking, and one pulls a gun and shoots the other, who dies. Do we suppose that this killer is even aware of the punishment for murder when he acts? Would he have been deterred by the prospect of capital punishment but willing to shoot if the punishment were only 20 years or life in prison?

In the following selections, Hugo Adam Bedau makes the case for the abolition of capital punishment, while Ernest van den Haag argues for its retention. Both authors base their claims on what they think justice requires.

YES

Hugo Adam Bedau

CAPITAL PUNISHMENT

CAPITAL PUNISHMENT AND RETRIBUTIVE JUSTICE

[T]here are two leading principles of retributive justice relevant to the capital punishment controversy. One is the principle that crimes should be punished. The other is the principle that the severity of a punishment should be proportional to the gravity of the offense. They are moral principles of recognized weight. No discussion of the morality of punishment would be complete without taking them into account. Leaving aside all questions of social defense, how strong a case for capital punishment can be made on their basis? How reliable and persuasive are these principles themselves?

Crime Must Be Punished

Given [a] general rationale for punishment . . . there cannot be any dispute over this principle. In embracing it, of course, we are not automatically making a fetish of "law and order," in the sense that we would be if we thought that the most important single thing to do with social resources is to punish crimes. In addition, this principle need not be in dispute between proponents and opponents of the death penalty. Only those who completely oppose punishment for murder and other erstwhile capital crimes would appear to disregard this principle. Even defenders of the death penalty must admit that putting a convicted murderer in prison for years is a punishment of that criminal. The principle that crime must be punished is neutral to our controversy, because both sides acknowledge it.

It is the other principle of retributive justice that seems to be a decisive one. Under the principle of retaliation, *lex talionis*, it must always have seemed that murderers ought to be put to death. Proponents of the death penalty, with rare exceptions, have insisted on this point, and it seems that even opponents of the death penalty must give it grudging assent. The strategy for opponents of the death penalty is to argue either that (1) this principle is not really a principle of justice after all, or that (2) to the extent it is, it does not require death for murderers, or that (3) in any case it is not the only principle of punitive justice. As we shall see, all these objections have merit.

Is Murder Alone to Be Punished by Death?

Let us recall, first, that not even the Biblical world limited the death penalty to the punishment of murder. Many other nonhomicidal crimes also carried this penalty (e.g., kidnapping, witchcraft, cursing one's parents). In our own nation's recent history, persons have been executed for aggravated assault, rape, kidnapping, armed robbery, sabotage, and espionage. It is not possible to defend *any* of these executions (not to mention some of the more bizarre capital statutes, like the one in Georgia that used to provide an optional death penalty for desecration of a grave) on grounds of just retribution. This entails that either such executions are not justified or that they are justified on some ground other than retribution. In actual practice, few if any defenders of the death penalty have ever been willing to rest their case entirely on the moral principle of just retribution as formulated in terms of "a life for a life." (Kant seems to have been a conspicuous exception.) Most defenders of the death penalty have implied by their willingness to use executions to defend not only life but limb and property as well, that they did not place much value on the lives of criminals when compared to the value of both lives and things belonging to innocent citizens.

Are All Murders to Be Punished by Death?

European civilization for several centuries has tended to limit the variety of criminal homicides punishable by death.

Even Kant took a casual attitude toward a mother's killing of her illegitimate child ("A child born into the world outside marriage is outside the law . . ., and consequently it is also outside the protection of the law.")[1] In our society, the development nearly two hundred years ago of the distinction between first- and second-degree murder was an attempt to narrow the class of criminal homicides deserving the death penalty. Yet those dead owing to manslaughter, or to any kind of unintentional, accidental, unpremeditated, unavoidable, unmalicious killing are just as dead as the victims of the most ghastly murder. Both the law in practice and moral reflection show how difficult it is to identify all and only the criminal homicides that are appropriately punished by death (assuming that any are). Individual judges and juries differ in the conclusions they reach. The history of capital punishment for homicides reveals continual efforts, uniformly unsuccessful, to identify before the fact those homicides for which the slayer should die. Sixty years ago, Benjamin Cardozo, then a justice of the United States Supreme Court, said of the distinction between degrees of murder that it was

> . . . so obscure that no jury hearing it for the first time can fairly be expected to assimilate and understand it. I am not at all sure that I understand it myself after trying to apply it for many years and after diligent study of what has been written in the books. Upon the basis of this fine distinction with its obscure and mystifying psychology, scores of men have gone to their death.[2]

Similar skepticism has been expressed on the reliability and rationality of death-penalty statutes that give the trial court the discretion to sentence to prison or to death. As Justice John Marshall Harlan of the Supreme Court observed more than a decade ago,

> Those who have come to grips with the hard task of actually attempting to draft means of channeling capital sentencing discretion have confirmed the lesson taught by history. . . . To identify before the fact those characteristics of criminal homicide and their perpetrators which call for the death penalty, and to express these characteristics in language which can be fairly understood and applied by the sentencing authority, appear to be tasks which are beyond present human ability.[3]

The abstract principle that the punishment of death best fits the crime of murder turns out to be extremely difficult to interpret and apply.

If we look at the matter from the standpoint of the actual practice of criminal justice, we can only conclude that "a life for a life"; plays little or no role whatever. Plea bargaining (in which a person charged with a crime pleads guilty in exchange for a less severe sentence than he might have received if his case went to trial and he was found guilty), even where murder is concerned, is widespread. Studies of criminal justice reveal that what the courts (trial or appellate) in a given jurisdiction decide on a given day is first-degree murder suitably punished by death could just as well be decided in a neighboring jurisdiction on another day either as second-degree murder or as first degree murder but without the death penalty. The factors that influence prosecutors in determining the charge under which they will prosecute go far beyond the simple principle of "a life for a life." Cynics, of course, will say that these facts show that our society does not care about justice. To put it succinctly, either justice in punishment does not consist of retribution, because there are other principles of justice; or there are other moral considerations besides justice that must be honored; or retributive justice is not adequately expressed in the idea of "a life for a life"; or justice in the criminal justice system is beyond our reach.

Is Death Sufficiently Retributive?

Those who advocate capital punishment for murder on retributive grounds must face the objection that, on their own principles, the death penalty in some cases is morally inadequate. How could death in the electric chair or the gas chamber or before a firing squad or on a gallows suffice as just retribution, given the savage, brutal, wanton character of so many murders? How can retributive justice be served by anything less than equally savage methods of execution? From a retributive point of view, the oft-heard exclamation, "Death is too good for him!" has a certain truth. Are defenders of the death penalty willing to embrace this consequence of their own doctrine?

If they were, they would be stooping to the methods and thus to the squalor of the murderer. Where the quality of the crime sets the limits of just methods of punishment, as it will if we attempt to give exact and literal implementation to *lex talionis*, society will find itself descending to the cruelties and savagery that criminals employ. What is worse, society would be deliberately authorizing such acts, in the cool light of reason, and not (as is often true of vicious criminals) impulsively or in hatred and anger or with an insane or unbalanced mind. Moral restraints, in short, prohibit us from trying to make executions perfectly retributive. Once we grant that such restraints are proper, it is unreasonable to insist that the principle of "a life for a life" nevertheless by itself justifies the execution of murderers.

Other considerations take us in a different direction. Few murders, outside television and movie scripts, involve anything like an execution. An execution, after all, begins with a solemn pronouncement of the death sentence from a judge; this is followed by long detention in maximum security awaiting the date of execution, during which various complex and protracted appeals will be pursued; after this there is a clemency hearing before the governor, and then "the last mile" to the execution chamber itself. As the French writer Albert Camus once remarked,

> For there to be an equivalence, the death penalty would have to punish a criminal who had warned his victim of the date at which he would inflict a horrible death on him and who, from that moment onward, had confined him at his mercy for months. Such a monster is not encountered in private life.[4]

Differential Severity Does Not Require Executions

What, then, emerges from our examination of retributive justice and the death penalty? If retributive justice is thought to consist in *lex talionis*, all one can say is that this principle has never exercised more than a crude and indirect effect on the actual punishments meted out by society. Other principles interfere with a literal and single-minded application of this one. Some homicides seem improperly punished by death at all; others would require methods of execution too horrible to inflict; in still other cases any possible execution is too deliberate and monstrous given the nature of the mo-

tivation culminating in the murder. In any case, proponents of the death penalty rarely confine themselves to reliance on nothing but this principle of just retribution, since they rarely confine themselves to supporting the death penalty only for all murders.

But retributive justice need not be thought of as consisting in *lex talionis*. One may reject that principle as too crude and still embrace the retributive principle that the severity of punishments should be graded according to the gravity of the offense. Even though one need not claim that life imprisonment (or any kind of punishment other than death) "fits" the crime of murder, one can claim that this punishment is the proper one for murder. To do this, the schedule of punishments accepted by society must be arranged so that this mode of imprisonment is the most severe penalty used. Opponents of the death penalty need not reject this principle of retributive justice, even though they must reject a literal *lex talionis*.

Equal Justice and Capital Punishment

During the past generation, the strongest practical objection to the death penalty has been the inequities with which it has been applied. As the late Supreme Court Justice William O. Douglas once observed, "One searches our chronicles in vain for the execution of any member of the affluent strata of this society."[5] One does not search our chronicles in vain for the crime of murder committed by the affluent. All the sociological evidence points to the conclusion that the death penalty is the poor man's justice; hence the slogan, "Those without the capital get the punishment." The death penalty is also racially sensitive. Every study of the death penalty for rape (unconstitutional only since 1977) has confirmed that black male rapists (especially where the victim is a white female) are far more likely to be sentenced to death and executed than white male rapists. Convicted black murderers are more likely to end up on "death row" than are others, and the killers of whites (whether white or nonwhite) are more likely to be sentenced to death than are the killers of nonwhites.

Let us suppose that the factual basis for such a criticism is sound. What follows for the morality of capital punishment? Many defenders of the death penalty have been quick to point out that since there is nothing intrinsic about the crime of murder or rape dictating that the poor or only racial-minority males will commit it, and since there is nothing overly racist about the statutes that authorize the death penalty for murder or rape, capital punishment itself is hardly at fault if in practice it falls with unfair impact on the poor and the black. There is, in short, nothing in the death penalty that requires it to be applied unfairly and with arbitrary or discriminatory results. It is at worst a fault in the system of administering criminal justice. (Some, who dispute the facts cited above, would deny even this.) There is an adequate remedy—execute more whites, women, and affluent murderers.

Presumably, both proponents and opponents of capital punishment would concede that it is a fundamental dictate of justice that a punishment should not be unfairly—inequitably or unevenly—enforced and applied. They should also be able to agree that when the punishment in question is the extremely severe one of death, then the requirement to be fair in using such a punishment becomes even more stringent. There should be no dispute in the death penalty controversy over these principles of justice. The dispute begins as soon as one attempts to connect the principles with the actual use of this punishment.

In this country, many critics of the death penalty have argued, we would long ago have got rid of it entirely if it had been a condition of its use that it be applied equally and fairly. In the words of the attorneys who argued against the death penalty in the Supreme Court during 1972, "It is a freakish aberration, a random extreme act of violence, visibly arbitrary and discriminatory—a penalty reserved for unusual application because, if it were usually used, it would affront universally shared standards of public decency."[6] It is difficult to dispute this judgment, when one considers that there have been in the United States during the past fifty years about half a million criminal homicides but only about 3,900 executions (all but 33 of which were of men).

We can look at these statistics in another way to illustrate the same point. If we could be assured that the nearly 4,000 persons executed were the worst of the bad, repeated offenders incapable of safe incarceration, much less of rehabilitation, the most dangerous murderers in captivity—the ones who had killed more than once and were likely to kill again, and the least likely to be confined in prison without chronic danger to other inmates and the staff—then one might accept half a million murders and a few thousand executions with a sense that rough justice had been done. But the truth is otherwise. Persons are sentenced to death and executed not because they have been found to be uncontrollably violent or hopelessly poor confinement and release risks. Instead, they are executed because they have a poor defense (inexperienced or overworked counsel) at trial; they have no funds to bring sympathetic witnesses to court; they are transients or strangers in the community where they are tried; the prosecuting attorney wants the publicity that goes with "sending a killer to the chair"; there are no funds for an appeal or for a transcript of the trial record; they are members of a despised racial or political minority. In short, the actual study of why particular persons have been sentenced to death and executed does not show any careful winnowing of the worst from the bad. It shows that the executed were usually the unlucky victims of prejudice and discrimination, the losers in an arbitrary lottery that could just as well have spared them, the victims of the disadvantages that almost always go with poverty. A system like this does not enhance human life; it cheapens and degrades it. However heinous murder and other crimes are, the system of capital punishment does not compensate for or erase those crimes. It only tends to add new injuries of its own to the catalogue of human brutality. . . .

Searching for an epigram suitable for our times, in which governments have waged war and suppressed internal dissent by using methods that can only be described as savage and criminal, Camus was prompted to admonish: "Let us be neither victims nor executioners." Perhaps better than any other, this exhortation points the way between forbidden extremes if we are to respect the humanity in each of us.

NOTES

1. Immanuel Kant, *The Metaphysical Elements of Justice*, tr. John Ladd, p. 106.

2. Benjamin Cardozo, "What Medicine Can Do for Law" (1928), reprinted in Margaret E. Hall, ed., *Selected Writings of Benjamin Nathan Cardozo* (1947), p. 204.

3. *McGautha v. California*, 402 U.S. 183 (1971), at p. 204.

4. Albert Camus, *Resistance, Rebellion, and Death* (1961), p. 199.

5. *Furman v. Georgia*, 408 U.S. 238 (1972), at pp. 251–252.

6. NAACP Legal Defense and Education Fund, Brief for Petitioner in *Aikens v. California*, O.T. 1971, No. 68-5027, reprinted in Philip English Mackey, ed., *Voices Against Death: American Opposition to Capital Punishment, 1787-1975* (1975), p. 288.

NO

Ernest van den Haag

THE ULTIMATE PUNISHMENT: A DEFENSE

In an average year about 20,000 homicides occur in the United States. Fewer than 300 convicted murderers are sentenced to death. But because no more than thirty murderers have been executed in any recent year, most convicts sentenced to death are likely to die of old age.[1] Nonetheless, the death penalty looms large in discussions: it raises important moral questions independent of the number of executions.[2]

The death penalty is our harshest punishment.[3] It is irrevocable: it ends the existence of those punished, instead of temporarily imprisoning them. Further, although not intended to cause physical pain, execution is the only corporal punishment still applied to adults.[4] These singular characteristics contribute to the perennial, impassioned controversy about capital punishment.

I. DISTRIBUTION

Consideration of the justice, morality, or usefulness, of capital punishment is often conflated with objections to its alleged discriminatory or capricious distribution among the guilty. Wrongly so. If capital punishment is immoral *in se*, no distribution among the guilty could make it moral. If capital punishment is moral, no distribution would make it immoral. Improper distribution cannot affect the quality of what is distributed, be it punishments or rewards. Discriminatory or capricious distribution thus could not justify abolition of the death penalty. Further, maldistribution inheres no more in capital punishment than in any other punishment.

Maldistribution between the guilty and the innocent is, by definition, unjust. But the injustice does not lie in the nature of the punishment. Because of the finality of the death penalty, the most grievous maldistribution occurs when it is imposed upon the innocent. However, the frequent allegations of discrimination and capriciousness refer to maldistribution among the guilty and not to the punishment of the innocent.

Maldistribution of any punishment among those who deserve it is irrelevant to its justice or morality. Even if poor or black convicts guilty of capital

From Ernest van den Haag, "The Ultimate Punishment: A Defense," *Harvard Law Review*, vol. 99 (May 1986). Copyright © 1986 by the Harvard Law Review Association. Reprinted by permission.

offenses suffer capital punishment, and other convicts equally guilty of the same crimes do not, a more equal distribution, however desirable, would merely be more equal. It would not be more just to the convicts under sentence of death.

Punishments are imposed on persons, not on racial or economic groups. Guilt is personal. The only relevant question is: does the person to be executed deserve the punishment? Whether or not others who deserved the same punishment, whatever their economic or racial group, have avoided execution is irrelevant. If they have, the guilt of the executed convicts would not be diminished, nor would their punishment be less deserved. To put the issue starkly, if the death penalty were imposed on guilty blacks, but not on guilty whites, or, if it were imposed by a lottery among the guilty, this irrationally discriminatory or capricious distribution would neither make the penalty unjust, nor cause anyone to be unjustly punished, despite the undue impunity bestowed on others.[5]

Equality, in short, seems morally less important than justice. And justice is independent of distributional inequalities. The ideal of equal justice demands that justice be equally distributed, not that it be replaced by equality. Justice requires that as many of the guilty as possible be punished, regardless of whether others have avoided punishment. To let these others escape the deserved punishment does not do justice to them, or to society. But it is not unjust to those who could not escape.

These moral considerations are not meant to deny that irrational discrimination, or capriciousness, would be inconsistent with constitutional requirements. But I am satisfied that the Supreme Court has in fact provided for adherence to the constitutional requirement of equality as much as is possible. Some inequality is indeed unavoidable as a practical matter in any system.[6] But, *ultra posse nemo obligatur*. (Nobody is bound beyond ability.)

Recent data reveal little direct racial discrimination in the sentencing of those arrested and convicted of murder. The abrogation of the death penalty for rape has eliminated a major source of racial discrimination. Concededly, some discrimination based on the race of murder victims may exist; yet, this discrimination affects criminal victimizers in an unexpected way. Murderers of whites are thought more likely to be executed than murderers of blacks. Black victims, then, are less fully vindicated than white ones. However, because most black murderers kill blacks, black murderers are spared the death penalty more often than are white murderers. They fare better than most white murderers.[7] The motivation behind unequal distribution of the death penalty may well have been to discriminate against blacks, but the result has favored them. Maldistribution is thus a straw man for empirical as well as analytical reasons.

II. MISCARRIAGES OF JUSTICE

In a recent survey Professors Hugo Adam Bedau and Michael Radelet found that 7000 persons were executed in the United States between 1900 and 1985 and that 25 were innocent of capital crimes.[8] Among the innocents they list Sacco and Vanzetti as well as Ethel and Julius Rosenberg. Although their data may be questionable, I do not doubt that, over a long enough period, miscarriages of justice will occur even in capital cases.

Despite precautions, nearly all human activities, such as trucking, lighting, or construction, cost the lives of some innocent bystanders. We do not give up these activities, because the advantages, moral or material, outweigh the unintended losses.[9] Analogously, for those who think the death penalty just, miscarriages of justice are offset by the moral benefits and the usefulness of doing justice. For those who think the death penalty unjust even when it does not miscarry, miscarriages can hardly be decisive.

III. DETERRENCE

Despite much recent work, there has been no conclusive statistical demonstration that the death penalty is a better deterrent than are alternative punishments.[10] However, deterrence is less than decisive for either side. Most abolitionists acknowledge that they would continue to favor abolition even if the death penalty were shown to deter more murders than alternatives could deter.[11] Abolitionists appear to value the life of a convicted murderer or, at least, his nonexecution, more highly than they value the lives of the innocent victims who might be spared by deterring prospective murderers.

Deterrence is not altogether decisive for me either. I would favor retention of the death penalty as retribution even if it were shown that the threat of execution could not deter prospective murderers not already deterred by the threat of imprisonment.[12] Still, I believe the death penalty, because of its finality, is more feared than imprisonment, and deters some prospective murderers not deterred by the threat of imprisonment. Sparing the lives of even a few prospective victims by deterring their murderers is more important than preserving the lives of convicted murderers because of

the possibility, or even the probability, that executing them would not deter others. Whereas the lives of the victims who might be saved are valuable, that of the murderer has only negative value, because of his crime. Surely the criminal law is meant to protect the lives of potential victims in preference to those actual murderers.

Murder rates are determined by many factors; neither the severity nor the probability of the threatened sanction is always decisive. However, for the long run, I share the view of Sir James Fitzjames Stephen: "Some men, probably, abstain from murder because they fear that if they committed murder they would be hanged. Hundreds of thousands abstain from it because they regard it with horror. One great reason why they regard it with horror is that murderers are hanged."[13] Penal sanctions are useful in the long run for the formation of the internal restraints so necessary to control crime. The severity and finality of the death penalty is appropriate to the seriousness and the finality of murder.

IV. INCIDENTAL ISSUES: COST, RELATIVE SUFFERING, BRUTALIZATION

Many nondecisive issues are associated with capital punishment. Some believe that the monetary cost of appealing a capital sentence is excessive.[14] Yet most comparisons of the cost of life imprisonment with the cost of execution, apart from their dubious relevance, are flawed at least by the implied assumption that life prisoners will generate no judicial costs during their imprisonment. At any rate, the actual monetary costs are trumped by the importance of doing justice.

Others insist that a person sentenced to death suffers more than his victim suffered, and that this (excess) suffering is undue according to the *lex talionis* (rule of retaliation).[15] We cannot know whether the murderer on death row suffers more than his victim suffered; however, unlike the murderer, the victim deserved none of the suffering inflicted. Further, the limitations of the *lex talionis* were meant to restrain private vengeance, not the social retribution that has taken its place. Punishment—regardless of the motivation—is not intended to revenge, offset, or compensate for the victim's suffering, or to be measured by it. Punishment is to vindicate the law and the social order undermined by the crime. This is why a kidnapper's penal confinement is not limited to the period for which he imprisoned his victim; nor is a burglar's confinement meant merely to offset the suffering or the harm he caused his victim; nor is it meant only to offset the advantage he gained.[16]

Another argument . . . is that, by killing a murderer, we encourage, endorse or legitimize unlawful killing. Yet, although all punishments are meant to be unpleasant, it is seldom argued that they legitimize the unlawful imposition of identical unpleasantness. Imprisonment is not thought to legitimize kidnapping; neither are fines thought to legitimize robbery. The difference between murder and execution, or between kidnapping and imprisonment, is that the first is unlawful and undeserved, the second a lawful and deserved punishment for an unlawful act. The physical similarities of the punishment to the crime are irrelevant. The relevant difference is not physical, but social.[17]

V. JUSTICE, EXCESS, DEGRADATION

We threaten punishments in order to deter crime. We impose them not only to make the threats credible but also as retribution (justice) for the crimes that were not deterred. Threats and punishments are necessary to deter and deterrence is a sufficient practical justification for them. Retribution is an independent moral justification.[18] Although penalties can be unwise, repulsive, or inappropriate, and those punished can be pitiable, in a sense the infliction of legal punishment on a guilty person cannot be unjust. By committing the crime, the criminal volunteered to assume the risk of receiving a legal punishment that he could have avoided by not committing the crime. The punishment he suffers is the punishment he voluntarily risked suffering and, therefore, it is no more unjust to him than any other event for which one knowingly volunteers to assume the risk. Thus, the death penalty cannot be unjust to the guilty criminal.[19]

There remain, however, two moral objections. The penalty may be regarded as always excessive as retribution and always morally degrading. To regard the death penalty as always excessive one must believe that no crime—no matter how heinous—could possibly justify capital punishment. Such a belief can be neither corroborated nor refuted; it is an article of faith.

Alternatively, or concurrently, one may believe that everybody, the murderer no less than the victim, has an imprescriptible (natural?) right to life. The law therefore should not deprive anyone of life. I share Jeremy Bentham's view that any such "natural and imprescriptible rights" are "nonsense upon stilts."[20]

Justice Brennan has insisted that the death penalty is "uncivilized," "inhuman," inconsistent with "human dignity" and with "the sanctity of life,"[21] that it "treats members of the human race as nonhumans, as objects to be toyed with and discarded,"[22] that it is "uniquely degrading to human dignity"[23] and "by its very nature, [involves] a denial of the executed person's humanity."[24] Justice Brennan does not say why he thinks execution "uncivilized." Hitherto most civilizations have had the death penalty, although it has been discarded in Western Europe, where it is currently unfashionable probably because of its abuse by totalitarian regimes.

By "degrading," Justice Brennan seems to mean that execution degrades the executed convicts. Yet philosophers, such as Immanuel Kant and G. F. W. Hegel, have insisted that, when deserved, execution, far from degrading the executed convict, affirms his humanity by affirming his rationality and his responsibility for his actions. They thought that execution, when deserved, is required for the sake of the convict's dignity. (Does not life imprisonment violate human dignity more than execution, by keeping alive a prisoner deprived of all autonomy?)[25]

Common sense indicates that it cannot be death—our common fate—that is inhuman. Therefore, Justice Brennan must mean that death degrades when it comes not as a natural or accidental event, but as a deliberate social imposition. The murderer learns through his punishment that his fellow men have found him unworthy of living; that because he has murdered, he is being expelled from the community of the living. This degradation is self-inflicted. By murdering, the murderer has so dehumanized himself that he cannot remain among the living.

The social recognition of his self-degradation is the punitive essence of execution. To believe, as Justice Brennan appears to, that the degradation is inflicted by the execution reverses the direction of causality.

Execution of those who have committed heinous murders may deter only one murder per year. If it does, it seems quite warranted. It is also the only fitting retribution for murder I can think of.

NOTES

1. Death row as a semipermanent residence is cruel, because convicts are denied the normal amenities of prison life. Thus, unless death row residents are integrated into the prison population, the continuing accumulation of convicts on death row should lead us to accelerate either the rate of executions or the rate of commutations. I find little objection to integration.
2. The debate about the insanity defense is important for analogous reasons.
3. Some writers . . . have thought that life imprisonment is more severe . . . Jacques Barzun . . . has expressed this view. See Barzun, In Favor of Capital Punishment, in THE DEATH PENALTY IN AMERICA 154 (H. Bedau ed. 1964). However, the overwhelming majority of both abolitionists and of convicts under death sentence prefer life imprisonment to execution.
4. For a discussion of the sources of opposition to corporal punishment, see E. VAN DEN HAAG, PUNISHING CRIMINALS 196–206 (1975).
5. Justice Douglas, concurring in Furman v. Georgia, 408 U.S. 238 (1972), wrote that "a law which . . . reaches that [discriminatory] result in practice has no more sanctity than a law which in terms provides the same." Id. at 256 (Douglas, J., concurring). Indeed, a law legislating this result "in terms" would be inconsistent with the "equal protection of the laws" provided by the fourteenth amendment, as would the discriminatory result reached in practice. But that result could be changed by changing the distributional practice. Thus, Justice Douglas notwithstanding, a discriminatory result does not make the death penalty unconstitutional, unless the penalty ineluctably must produce that result to an unconstitutional degree.
6. The ideal of equality, unlike the ideal of retributive justice (which can be approximated separately in each instance), is clearly unattainable unless all guilty persons are apprehended, and thereafter tried, convicted and sentenced by

the same court, at the same time. Unequal justice is the best we can do; it is still better than the injustice, equal or unequal, which occurs if, for the sake of equality, we deliberately allow some who could be punished to escape.

7. It barely need be said that any discrimination *against* (for example, black murderers of whites) must also be discrimination *for* (for example, black murderers of blacks).

8. Bedau & Radelet, *Miscarriages of Justice in Potentially Capital Cases* (1st draft, Oct. 1985) (on file at Harvard Law School Library).

9. An excessive number of trucking accidents or of miscarriages of justice could offset the benefits gained by trucking or the practice of doing justice. We are, however, far from this situation.

10. For a sample of conflicting views on the subject, see Baldus & Cole, *A Comparison of the Work of Thorsten Sellin and Isaac Ehrlich on the Deterrent Effect of Capital Punishment*, 85 YALE L.J. 170 (1975); Bowers & Pierce, *Deterrence or Brutalization: What Is the Effect of Executions?*, 26 CRIME & DELINQ. 453 (1980); Bowers & Pierce, *The Illusion of Deterrence in Isaac Ehrlich's Research on Capital Punishment*, 85 YALE L.J. 187 (1975); Ehrlich, *Fear of Deterrence: A Critical Evaluation of the "Report of the Panel on Research on Deterrent and Incapacitative Effects"*, 6 J. LEGAL STUD. 293 (1977); Ehrlich, *The Deterrent Effect of Capital Punishment: A Question of Life and Death*, 65 AM. ECON. REV. 397, 415–16 (1975); Ehrlich & Gibbons, *On the Measurement of the Deterrent Effect of Capital Punishment and the Theory of Deterrence*, 6 J. LEGAL STUD. 35 (1977).

11. For most abolitionists, the discrimination argument . . . is similarly nondecisive: they would favor abolition even if there could be no racial discrimination.

12. If executions were shown to increase the murder rate in the long run, I would favor abolition. Sparing the innocent victims who would be spared, *ex hypothesi*, by the nonexecution of murderers would be more important to me than the execution, however just, of murderers. But although there is a lively discussion of the subject, no serious evidence exists to support the hypothesis that executions produce a higher murder rate. Cf. Phillips, *The Deterrent Effect of Capital Punishment: New Evidence an Old Controversy*, 86 AM. J. SOC. 139 (1980) (arguing that murder rates drop immediately after executions of criminals).

13. H. GROSS, A THEORY OF CRIMINAL JUSTICE 489 (1979) (attributing this passage to Sir James Fitzjames Stephen).

14. Cf. Kaplan, *Administering Capital Punishment*, 36 U. FLA. L. REV. 177, 178, 190–91 (1984) (noting the high cost of appealing a capital sentence).

15. For an example of this view, see A. CAMUS, REFLECTIONS ON THE GUILLOTINE 24–30 (1959). On the limitations allegedly imposed by the *lex talionis*, see Reiman, *Justice, Civilization, and the Death Penalty: Answering van den Haag*, 14 PHIL. & PUB. AFF. 115, 119–34 (1985).

16. Thus restitution (a civil liability) cannot satisfy the punitive purpose of penal sanctions, whether the purpose be retributive or deterrent.

17. Some abolitionists challenge: if the death penalty is just and serves as a deterrent, why not televise executions? The answer is simple. The death even of a murderer, however well-deserved, should not serve as public entertainment. It so served in earlier centuries. But in this respect our sensibility has changed for the better, I believe. Further, television unavoidably would trivialize executions, wedged in, as they would be, between game shows, situation comedies and the like. Finally, because televised executions would focus on the physical aspects of the punishment, rather than the nature of the crime and the suffering of the victim, a televised execution would present the murderer as the victim of the state. Far from communicating the moral significance of the execution, television would shift the focus to the pitiable fear of the murderer. We no longer place in cages those sentenced to imprisonment to expose them to public view. Why should we expose those sentenced to execution?

18. *See* van den Haag, *Punishment as a Device for Controlling the Crime Rate*, 33 RUTGERS L. REV. 706, 719 (1981) (explaining why the desire for retribution, although independent, would have to be satisfied even if deterrence were the only purpose of punishment.)

19. An explicit threat of punitive action is necessary to the justification of any legal punishment: *nulla poena sine lege* (no punishment without [preexisting] law). To be sufficiently justified, the threat must in turn have a rational and legitimate purpose. "Your money or your life" does not qualify; nor does the threat of an unjust law; nor, finally, does a threat that is altogether disproportionate to the importance of its purpose. In short, preannouncement legitimizes the threatened punishment only if the threat is warranted. But this leaves a very wide range of justified threats. Furthermore, the punished person is aware of the penalty for his actions and thus volunteers to take the risk even of an unjust punishment. His victim, however, did not volunteer to risk anything. The question whether any self-inflicted injury—such as a legal punishment—ever can be unjust to a person who knowingly risked it is a matter that requires more analysis than is possible here.

20. 2 THE WORKS OF JEREMY BENTHAM 105 (J. Bowring ed. 1972). However, I would be more

polite about prescriptible natural rights, which Bentham described as "simple nonsense." *Id.* (It does not matter whether natural rights are called "moral" or "human" rights as they currently are by most writers.)

21. THE DEATH PENALTY IN AMERICA 256–63 (H. Bedau ed., 3d ed. 1982) (quoting Furman v. Georgia, 408 U.S. 238, 286, 305 (1972) (Brennan, J., concurring).

22. *Id.* at 272–73; *see also* Gregg v. Georgia, 428 U.S. 153, 230 (1976) (Brennan, J., dissenting).

23. Furman v. Georgia, 408 U.S. 238, 291 (1972) (Brennan, J., concurring).

24. *Id.* at 290.

25. *See* Barzun, *supra* note 3, *passim.*

POSTSCRIPT

Should Capital Punishment Be Abolished?

The argument is sometimes made that even if capital punishment is not a deterrent (or, more radically, even if capital punishment actually encourages crime), justice demands that certain criminals be executed. For example, former Nazis who killed many people are today tracked down and brought to trial. Usually these are elderly men who have lived many years without killing anyone. If the death penalty is demanded for these people, would this demand receive support from the deterrence line of reasoning? Probably not. First, these people have already stopped killing and so do not need to be deterred. Second, should we suppose that executing them will deter potential future Nazis, neo-Aryans, and other racists from murder? More likely, in these cases, the argument is that these former Nazis must die for what they have done as a matter of justice.

Studies of capital punishment and deterrence can be found in I. Ehrlich, "Deterrence: Evidence and Inference," *Yale Law Review* (1975); P. Passell, "The Deterrence Effect of the Death Penalty: A Statistical Test," *Stanford Law Review* (1975); Jack Gibbs, *Crime, Punishment and Deterrence* (Elsevier, 1975); and H. Zeisel, "The Deterrent Effects of the Death Penalty: Facts v. Faith," in P. E. Kurland, ed., *The Supreme Court Review* (University of Chicago Press, 1976).

A special issue for Americans is whether the death penalty is constitutional. The Eighth Amendment to the Constitution reads: "Excessive bail shall not be required, nor excessive fines imposed, nor cruel and unusual punishments inflicted." Raoul Berger argues, in *Death Penalties: The Supreme Court's Obstacle Course* (Harvard University Press, 1982), that the death penalty is not cruel and unusual and is not unconstitutional. Earlier, in a series of important legal cases (including *Furman v. Georgia*, 1972, and *Gregg v. Georgia*, 1976), the U.S. Supreme Court ruled that the death penalty was not *in principle* unconstitutional. However, the Court also found that how the death penalty was *applied* in many actual cases was indeed cruel and unusual.

The most thorough coverage of all aspects of capital punishment is Hugo Adam Bedau, ed., *The Death Penalty in America*, 3rd ed. (Oxford University Press, 1982). See also Arthur Koestler, *Reflections on Hanging* (Macmillan, 1957); Ernest van den Haag and John P. Conrad, *The Death Penalty: A Debate* (Plenum Press, 1983); Hugo Adam Bedau, *Death Is Different: Studies in the Morality, Law, and the Politics of Capital Punishment* (Northeastern University Press, 1987); and Stephen Nathanson, *An Eye for an Eye? The Morality of Punishing by Death* (Rowman & Littlefield, 1987).

ISSUE 16

Is Euthanasia Immoral?

YES: J. Gay-Williams, from "The Wrongfulness of Euthanasia," in Ronald Munson, ed., *Intervention and Reflection: Basic Issues in Medical Ethics* (Wadsworth, 1979)

NO: Richard Brandt, from "A Moral Principle About Killing," in Marvin Kohl, ed., *Beneficent Euthanasia* (Prometheus Books, 1975)

ISSUE SUMMARY

YES: J. Gay-Williams believes that euthanasia is immoral because it violates one's natural personal will to survive. In addition, he points out, a public policy that allows euthanasia would have severe negative practical effects. **NO:** Moral philosopher Richard Brandt argues that killing human beings ordinarily injures them and violates their preferences. In cases of euthanasia, when both of these conditions are lacking, the killing could be allowable.

The word *euthanasia* comes from two Greek elements: the prefix *eu* (meaning good, easy, or fortunate) and the word *thanatos* (meaning death). The root idea is that in euthanasia one undergoes a good death, or an easy or fortunate one.

Euthanasia means more than this, however. We do not use the term unless we are referring to a case in which someone kills another person in order to give that person an easy death. Suppose your grandmother lives to a great age and, having put all her personal affairs in order, dies a painless death while asleep. However good or easy a death this might have been—and however much we might hope that when we or other loved ones die this will be the way—such a case is *not* one of euthanasia. The key element of a person killing a person is absent. It is precisely this element that makes euthanasia morally controversial.

Now the fact that any one person kills another does not automatically make euthanasia wrong. There are killings in a "just" war, in self-defense, and in state executions. Although some might well claim that any one of these three is wrong, it would be difficult indeed to maintain that all three of these are always wrong.

One difference between euthanasia and the three cases mentioned above is that in those three cases the person who is killed is regarded by the killer as an enemy, an attacker, or a criminally guilty person. But the person who dies in euthanasia is not regarded as such. Often the person killed is a relative, a friend, or a medical patient of the killer. A common phrase used for euthanasia that recognizes this feature is "mercy killing."

Proponents of euthanasia generally do perceive euthanasia as a merciful practice, one that offers a way out—perhaps the only way out—of a painful existence. For example, consider the following true story. A physicist who had worked with X rays for many years developed skin cancer. As a result of this disease, he lost part of his jaw, his upper lip, his nose, his left hand, two fingers from his right hand, and his sight. Blind and in great pain, he was given about a year to live by his doctors, who could neither cure the cancer nor eliminate the pain. He begged for death. He wanted one of his three brothers to kill him. Two refused, but the third, to whom he had always felt the closest, reluctantly shot him to death.

Opponents of euthanasia, on the other hand, point out that euthanasia—far from resembling justified killing—fits the standard definition for murder: the killing of an innocent person.

Moreover, if this killing is tolerated, where will it stop? The possibilities are many. Suppose the physicist in the previous case had become mentally incapacitated before expressing a wish to die. Would his brothers or his doctors then make a judgment about euthanasia? Suppose the patient has no relatives and no money and lives on public funds. Would taxpayers then decide? Perhaps various groups—the old, the infirm, those with incurable diseases, the insane, or even those with undesirable character traits—would be killed in this way. Opponents of euthanasia ask: Where will the line be drawn once the killing of the innocent is condoned? They rule out *all* euthanasia, thus eliminating the need to draw such a line.

In the following selections, J. Gay-Williams argues that euthanasia is intrinsically wrong and also likely to lead to disagreeable consequences. Support for euthanasia, he suspects, is the result of an unthinking sentimentalism. Richard Brandt presents what he believes is a rational analysis of what is wrong with killing human beings. He argues that euthanasia that is free of these elements is not wrong.

YES

J. Gay-Williams

THE WRONGFULNESS OF EUTHANASIA

My impression is that euthanasia—the idea, if not the practice—is slowly gaining acceptance within our society. Cynics might attribute this to an increasing tendency to devalue human life, but I do not believe this is the major factor. Well-publicized, tragic stories like that of Karen Quinlan elicit from us deep feelings of compassion. We think to ourselves, "She and her family would be better off if she were dead." It is an easy step from this very human response to the view that if someone (and others) would be better off dead, then it must be all right to kill that person.[1] Although I respect the compassion that leads to this conclusion, I believe the conclusion is wrong. I want to show that euthanasia is wrong. It is inherently wrong, but it is also wrong judged from the standpoints of self-interest and of practical effects.

Before presenting my arguments to support this claim, it would be well to define "euthanasia." An essential aspect of euthanasia is that it involves taking a human life, either one's own or that of another. Also, the person whose life is taken must be someone who is believed to be suffering from some disease or injury from which recovery cannot reasonably be expected. Finally, the action must be deliberate and intentional. Thus, euthanasia is intentionally taking the life of a presumably hopeless person. Whether the life is one's own or that of another, the taking of it is still euthanasia.

It is important to be clear about the deliberate and intentional aspect of the killing. If a hopeless person is given an injection of the wrong drug by mistake and this causes his death, this is wrongful killing but not euthanasia. The killing cannot be the result of accident. Furthermore, if the person is given an injection of a drug that is believed to be necessary to treat his disease or better his condition and the person dies as a result, then this is neither wrongful killing nor euthanasia. The intention was to make the patient well, not kill him. Similarly, when a patient's condition is such that it is not reasonable to hope that any medical procedures or treatments will save his life, a failure to implement the procedures or treatments is not eutha-

From J. Gay-Williams, "The Wrongfulness of Euthanasia," in Ronald Munson, ed., *Intervention and Reflection: Basic Issues in Medical Ethics* (Wadsworth, 1979). Copyright © 1979 by Ronald Munson. Reprinted by permission.

nasia. If the person dies, this will be as a result of his injuries or disease and not because of his failure to receive treatment.

The failure to continue treatment after it has been realized that the patient has little chance of benefitting from it has been characterized by some as "passive euthanasia." This phrase is misleading and mistaken.[2] In such cases, the person involved is not killed (the first essential aspect of euthanasia), nor is the death of the person intended by the withholding of additional treatment (the third essential aspect of euthanasia). The aim may be to spare the person additional and unjustifiable pain, to save him from the indignities of hopeless manipulations, and to avoid increasing the financial and emotional burden of the family. When I buy a pencil it is so that I can use it to write, not to contribute to an increase in the gross national product. This may be the unintended consequence of my action, but it is not the aim of my action. So it is with failing to continue the treatment of a dying person. I intend his death no more than I intend to reduce the GNP by not using medical supplies. His is an unintended dying, and so-called "passive euthanasia" is not euthanasia at all.

1. THE ARGUMENT FROM NATURE

Every human being has a natural inclination to continue living. Our reflexes and responses fit us to fight attackers, flee wild animals, and dodge out of the way of trucks. In our daily lives we exercise the caution and care necessary to protect ourselves. Our bodies are similarly structured for survival right down to the molecular level. When we are cut, our capillaries seal shut, our blood clots, and fibrogen is produced to start the process of healing the wound. When we are invaded by bacteria, antibodies are produced to fight against the alien organisms, and their remains are swept out of the body by special cells designed for clean-up work.

Euthanasia does violence to this natural goal of survival. It is literally acting against nature because all the processes of nature are bent towards the end of bodily survival. Euthanasia defeats these subtle mechanisms in a way that, in a particular case, disease and injury might not.

It is possible, but not necessary, to make an appeal to revealed religion in this connection.[3] Man as trustee of his body acts against God, its rightful possessor, when he takes his own life. He also violates the commandment to hold life sacred and never to take it without just and compelling cause. But since this appeal will persuade only those who are prepared to accept that religion has access to revealed truths, I shall not employ this line of argument.

It is enough, I believe, to recognize that the organization of the human body and our patterns of behavioral responses make the continuation of life a natural goal. By reason alone, then, we can recognize that euthanasia sets us against our own nature.[4] Furthermore, in doing so, euthanasia does violence to our dignity. Our dignity comes from seeking our ends. When one of our goals is survival, and actions are taken that eliminate the goal, then our natural dignity suffers. Unlike animals, we are conscious through reason of our nature and our ends. Euthanasia involves acting as if this dual nature—inclination towards survival and awareness of this as an end—did not exist. Thus, euthanasia denies our basic human character and requires that we regard ourselves or others as something less than fully human.

2. THE ARGUMENT FROM SELF-INTEREST

The above arguments are, I believe, sufficient to show that euthanasia is inherently wrong. But there are reasons for considering it wrong when judged by standards other than reason. Because death is final and irreversible, euthanasia contains within it the possibility that we will work against our own interest if we practice it or allow it to be practiced on us.

Contemporary medicine has high standards of excellence and a proven record of accomplishment, but it does not possess perfect and complete knowledge. A mistaken diagnosis is possible, and so is a mistaken prognosis. Consequently, we may believe that we are dying of a disease when, as a matter of fact, we may not be. We may think that we have no hope of recovery when, as a matter of fact, our chances are quite good. In such circumstances, if euthanasia were permitted, we would die needlessly. Death is final and the chance of error too great to approve the practice of euthanasia.

Also, there is always the possibility that an experimental procedure or a hitherto untried technique will pull us through. We should at least keep this option open, but euthanasia closes it off. Furthermore, spontaneous remission does occur in many cases. For no apparent reason, a patient simply recovers when those all around him, including his physicians, expected him to die. Euthanasia would just guarantee their expectations and leave no room for the "miraculous" recoveries that frequently occur.

Finally, knowing that we can take our life at any time (or ask another to take it) might well incline us to give up too easily. The will to live is strong in all of us, but it can be weakened by pain and suffering and feelings of hopelessness. If during a bad time we allow ourselves to be killed, we never have a chance to reconsider. Recovery from a serious illness requires that we fight for it, and anything that weakens our determination by suggesting that there is an easy way out is ultimately against our own interest. Also, we may be inclined towards euthanasia because of our concern for others. If we see our sickness and suffering as an emotional and financial burden on our family, we may feel that to leave our life is to make their lives easier.[5] The very presence of the possibility of euthanasia may keep us from surviving when we might.

3. THE ARGUMENT FROM PRACTICAL EFFECTS

Doctors and nurses are, for the most part, totally committed to saving lives. A life lost is, for them, almost a personal failure, an insult to their skills and knowledge. Euthanasia as a practice might well alter this. It could have a corrupting influence so that in any case that is severe doctors and nurses might not try hard enough to save the patient. They might decide that the patient would simply be "better off dead" and take the steps necessary to make that come about. This attitude could then carry over to their dealings with patients less seriously ill. The result would be an overall decline in the quality of medical care.

Finally, euthanasia as a policy is a slippery slope. A person apparently hopelessly ill may be allowed to take his own life. Then he may be permitted to deputize others to do it for him should he no longer be able to act. The judgment of others then becomes the ruling factor. Already at this point euthanasia is not personal and voluntary, for others are acting "on behalf of" the patient as they see fit. This may well incline them to act on behalf of other patients who have not authorized them to exercise their judgment. It is only a short step, then, from voluntary euthanasia (self-inflicted or authorized), to directed euthanasia administered to a patient who has given no authorization, to involuntary euthanasia conducted as part of a social policy.[6] Recently many psychiatrists and sociologists have argued that we define as "mental illness" those forms of behavior that we disapprove of.[7] This gives us license then to lock up those who display the behavior. The category of the "hopelessly ill" provides the possibility of even worse abuse. Embedded in a social policy, it would give society or its representatives the authority to eliminate all those who might be considered too "ill" to function normally any longer. The dangers of euthanasia are too great to all to run the risk of approving it in any form. The first slippery step may well lead to a serious and harmful fall.

I hope that I have succeeded in showing why the benevolence that inclines us to give approval of euthanasia is misplaced. Euthanasia is inherently wrong because it violates the nature and dignity of human beings. But even those who are not convinced by this must be persuaded that the potential personal and social dangers inherent in euthanasia are sufficient to forbid our approving it either as a personal practice or as a public policy.

Suffering is surely a terrible thing, and we have a clear duty to comfort those in need and to ease their suffering when we can. But suffering is also a natural part of life with values for the individual and for others that we should not overlook. We may legitimately seek for others and for ourselves an easeful death, as Arthur Dyck has pointed out.[8] Euthanasia, however, is not just an easeful death. It is a wrongful death. Euthanasia is not just dying. It is killing.

NOTES

1. For a sophisticated defense of this position see Philippa Foot, "Euthanasia," *Philosophy and Public Affairs*, vol. 6 (1977), pp. 85-112. Foot does not endorse the radical conclusion that euthanasia, voluntary and involuntary, is always right.

2. James Rachels rejects the distinction between active and passive euthanasia as morally irrelevant in his "Active and Passive Euthanasia," *New England Journal of Medicine*, vol. 292, pp. 78-80. But see the criticism by Foot, pp. 100-103.

3. For a defense of this view see J.V. Sullivan, "The Immorality of Euthanasia," in Marvin Kohl, ed., *Beneficent Euthanasia* (Buffalo, New York: Prometheus Books, 1975), pp. 34-44.

4. This point is made by Ray V. McIntyre in "Voluntary Euthanasia: The Ultimate Perversion," *Medical Counterpoint*, vol. 2, pp. 26-29.

5. See McIntyre, p. 28.

6. See Sullivan, "The Immorality of Euthanasia," pp. 34-44, for a fuller argument in support of this view.

7. See, for example, Thomas S. Szasz, *The Myth of Mental Illness*, rev. ed. (New York: Harper & Row, 1974).

8. Arthur Dyck, "Beneficent Euthanasia and Benemortasia," Kohl; *op. cit.*, pp. 117-129.

NO
Richard Brandt

A MORAL PRINCIPLE ABOUT KILLING

One of the Ten Commandments states: "Thou shalt not kill." The command-ment does not supply an object for the verb, but the traditional Catholic view has been that the proper object of the verb is "innocent human beings" (except in cases of extreme necessity), where "innocent" is taken to exclude persons convicted of a capital crime or engaged in an unjust assault aimed at killing, such as members of the armed forces of a country prosecuting an unjust war. Thus construed, the prohibition is taken to extend to suicide and abortion. (There is a qualification: that we are not to count cases in which the death is not wanted for itself or intended as a *means* to a goal that is wanted for itself, provided that in either case the aim of the act is the avoidance of some evil greater than the death of the person.) Can this view that all killing of innocent human beings is morally wrong be defended, and if not, what alternative principle can be?

This question is one of the ground rules for answering which are far from a matter of agreement. I should myself be content if a principle were identified that could be shown to be one that would be included in any moral system that rational and benevolent persons would support for a society in which they expected to live. Apparently others would not be so content; so in what follows I shall simply aim to make some observations that I hope will identify a principle with which the consciences of intelligent people will be comfort-able. I believe the rough principle I will suggest is also one that would belong to the moral system rational and benevolent people would want for their society.

Let us begin by reflecting on what it is to kill. The first thing to notice is that *kill* is a biological term. For example, a weed may be killed by being sprayed with a chemical. The verb *kill* involves essentially the broad notion of death—the change from the state of being biologically alive to the state of being dead. It is beyond my powers to give any general characterization of this transition, and it may be impossible to give one. If there is one, it is one that human beings, flies, and ferns all share; and to kill is in some sense to bring that transition about. The next thing to notice is that at least human

From Richard Brandt, "A Moral Principle About Killing," in Marvin Kohl, ed., *Beneficent Euthanasia* (Prometheus Books, 1975). Copyright © 1975 by Prometheus Books, Inc. Reprinted by permission.

beings do not live forever, and hence killing a human being at a given time must be construed as *advancing the date* of its death, or as *shortening its life*. Thus it may be brought about that the termination of the life of a person occurs at the time t instead of at the time $t + k$. Killing is thus shortening the span of organic life of something.

There is a third thing to notice about *kill*. It is a term of causal agency and has roots in the legal tradition. As such, it involves complications. For instance, suppose I push a boulder down a mountainside, aiming it at a person X and it indeed strikes X, and he is dead after impact and not before (and not from a coincidental heart attack); in that case we would say that I killed X. On the other hand, suppose I tell Y that X is in bed with Y's wife, and Y hurries to the scene, discovers them, and shoots X to death; in that case, although the unfolding of events from my action may be as much a matter of causal law as the path of the boulder, we should *not* say that I killed X. Fortunately, for the purpose of principles of the morally right, we can sidestep such complications. For suppose I am choosing whether to do A or B (where one or the other of these "acts" may be construed as essentially *inaction*—for example, *not* doing what I know is the one thing that will *prevent* someone's death); then it is enough if I know, or have reason to think it highly probable, that were I to do A, a state of the world including the death of some person or persons would ensue, whereas were I to do B, a state of the world of some specified different sort would ensue. If a moral principle will tell me in this case whether I am to do A or B, that is all I need. It could be that a moral principle would tell me that I am absolutely never

to perform any action A, such that were I to do it the death of some innocent human being would ensue, provided there is some alternative action I might perform, such that were I to do it no such death would ensue.

It is helpful, I think, to reformulate the traditional Catholic view in a way that preserves the spirit and intent of that view (although some philosophers would disagree with this assessment) and at the same time avoids some conceptions that are both vague and more appropriate to a principle about when a person is morally blameworthy for doing something than to a principle about what a person ought morally to do. The terminology I use goes back, in philosophical literature, to a phrase introduced by W. D. Ross, but the conception is quite familiar. The alternative proposal is that there is a *strong prima facie obligation* not to kill any human being except in justifiable self-defense; in the sense (of prima facie) that it is morally *wrong* to kill any human being except in justifiable self-defense *unless* there is an even stronger prima facie moral obligation to do something that cannot be done without killing. (The term *innocent* can now be omitted, since if a person is not innocent, there may be a stronger moral obligation that can only be discharged by killing him; and this change is to the good since it is not obvious that we have no prima facie obligation to avoid killing people even if they are not innocent.) This formulation has the result that sometimes, to decide what is morally right, we have to compare the stringencies of conflicting moral obligations—and that is an elusive business; but the other formulation either conceals the same problem by putting it in another place, or else leads to objectionable implications. (Consider one implication of the traditional formulation, for a party of spelunkers in a cave by the oceanside. It is found that a rising tide is bringing water into the cave and all will be drowned unless they escape at once. Unfortunately, the first man to try to squeeze through the exit is fat and gets wedged inextricably in the opening, with his head inside the cave. Somebody in the party has a stick of dynamite. Either they blast the fat man out, killing him, or all of them, including him, will drown. The traditional formulation leads to the conclusion that all must drown.)

Let us then consider the principle: "There is a strong prima facie moral obligation not to kill any human being except in justifiable self-defense." I do not believe we want to accept this principle without further qualification; indeed, its status seems not to be that of a basic principle at all, but derivative from some more-basic principles. W. D. Ross listed what he thought were the main basic prima facie moral obligations; it is noteworthy that he listed a prima facie duty not to *cause injury*, but he did not include an obligation not to kill. Presumably this was no oversight. He might have thought that killing a human being is always an injury, so that the additional listing of an obligation not to kill would be redundant; but he might also have thought that killing is sometimes *not* an injury and that it is prima facie obligatory not to kill only when, and because, so doing would injure a sentient being.

What might be a noninjurious killing? If I come upon a cat that has been mangled but not quite killed by several dogs and is writhing in pain, and I pull myself together and put it out of its misery, I have killed the cat but surely not *injured* it. I do not injure something by relieving its pain. If someone is being tortured and

roasted to death and I know he wishes nothing more than a merciful termination of life, I have not injured him if I shoot him; I have done him a favor. In general, it seems I have not injured a person if I treat him in a way in which he would want me to treat him if he were fully rational, or in a way to which he would be indifferent if he were fully rational. (I do not think that terminating the life of a human fetus in the third month is an injury; I admit this view requires discussion.[1])

Consider another type of killing that is not an injury. Consider the case of a human being who has become unconscious and will not, it is known, regain consciousness. He is in a hospital and is being kept alive only through expensive supportive measures. Is there a strong prima facie moral obligation not to withdraw these measures and not to take positive steps to terminate his life? It seems obvious that if he is on the only kidney machine and its use could *save* the life of another person, who would lead a normal life after temporary use, it would be wrong not to take him off. Is there an obligation to continue, or not to terminate, if there is no countering obligation? I would think not, with an exception to be mentioned; and this coincides with the fact that he is *beyond* injury. There is also not an obligation *not* to preserve his life, say, in order to have his organs available for use when they are needed.

There seems, however, to be another morally relevant consideration in such a case—knowledge of the patient's own wishes when he was conscious and in possession of his faculties. Suppose he had feared such an eventuality and prepared a sworn statement requesting his doctor to terminate his life at once in such circumstances. Now, if it is morally obligatory to some degree to carry out a person's wishes for disposal of his body and possessions after his death, it would seem to be equally morally obligatory to respect his wishes in case he becomes a "vegetable." In the event of the existence of such a document, I would think that if he can no longer be injured we are free to withdraw life-sustaining measures and also to take positive steps to terminate life—and are even morally bound, prima facie, to do so. (If, however, the patient had prepared a document directing that his body be preserved alive as long as possible in such circumstances, then there would be a prima facie obligation *not* to cease life-sustaining measures and not to terminate. It would seem obvious, however, that such an obligation would fall far short of giving the patient the right to continued use of a kidney machine when its use by another could save that person's life.) Some persons would not hesitate to discontinue life-sustaining procedures in such a situation, but would balk at more positive measures. But the hesitation to use more positive procedures, which veterinarians employ frequently with animals, is surely nothing but squeamishness; if a person is in the state described, there can be no injury to him in positive termination more than or less than that in allowing him to wither by withdrawing life-supportive procedures.

If I am right in my analysis of this case, we must phrase our basic principle about killing in such a way as to take into account (1) whether the killing would be an injury and (2) the person's own wishes and directives. And perhaps, more important, any moral principle about killing must be viewed simply as an implicate of more basic principles about these matters.

Let us look for corroboration of this proposal to how we feel about another type of case, one in which termination would be of positive benefit to the agent. Let us suppose that a patient has a terminal illness and is in severe pain, subject only to brief remissions, with no prospect of any event that could make his life good, either in the short or long term. It might seem that here, with the patient in severe pain, at least life-supportive measures should be discontinued, or positive termination adopted. But I do not think we would accept this inference, for in this situation the patient, let us suppose, has his preferences and is able to express them. The patient may have strong religious convictions and prefer to go on living despite the pain; if so, surely there is a prima facie moral obligation not positively to terminate his life. Even if, as seemingly in this case, the situation is one in which it would be *rational* for the agent, from the point of view of his own welfare, to direct termination of his life,[2] it seems that if he (irrationally) does the opposite, there is a prima facie moral obligation not to terminate and some prima facie obligation to sustain it. Evidently a person's own expressed wishes have moral force. (I believe, however, that we think a person's expressed wishes have *less* moral force when we think the wishes are irrational.)

What is the effect, in this case, if the patient himself expresses a preference for termination and would, if he were given the means, terminate his own existence? Is there a prima facie obligation to sustain his life—and pain—against his will? Surely not. Or is there an obligation *not* to take positive measures to terminate his life immediately, thereby saving the patient much discomfort? Again, surely not. What possible reason could be offered to justify the claim that the answer is affirmative, beyond theological ones about God's will and our being bound to stay alive at His pleasure? The only argument I can think of is that there is some consideration of public policy, to the effect that a recognition of such moral permission might lead to abuses or to some other detriment to society in the long run. Such an argument does seem weak.

It might be questioned whether a patient's request should be honored, if made at a time when he is in pain, on the grounds that it is not rational. (The physician may be in a position to see, however, that the patient is quite right about his prospects and that his personal welfare would be maximized by termination.) It might also be questioned whether a patient's formal declaration, written earlier, requesting termination if he were ever in his present circumstances, should be honored, on the grounds that at the earlier time he did not know what it would be like to be in his present situation. It would seem odd, however, if *no* circumstances are identifiable in which a patient's request for termination is deemed to have moral force, when his request *not* to terminate is thought morally weighty in the same circumstances, even when this request is clearly irrational. I think we may ignore such arguments and hold that, in a situation in which it is rational for a person to choose termination of his life, his expressed wish is morally definitive and removes both the obligation to sustain life and the obligation not to terminate.

Indeed, there is a question whether or not in these circumstances a physician has not a moral obligation at least to withdraw life-supporting measures, and perhaps positively to terminate life. At least there seems to be a general moral obligation to render assistance when a person is in need, when it can be given at small cost to oneself, and when it is requested. The obligation is the stronger when one happens to be the only person in a position to receive such a request or to know about the situation. Furthermore, the physician has acquired a special obligation if there has been a long-standing personal relationship with the patient—just as a friend or relative has special obligations. But since we are discussing not the possible obligation to terminate but the obligation *not* to terminate, I shall not pursue this issue.

The patient's own expression of preference or consent, then, seems to be weighty. But suppose he is unable to express his preference; suppose that his terminal disease not only causes him great pain but has attacked his brain in such a way that he is incapable of thought and of rational speech. May the physician, then, after consultation, take matters into his own hands? We often think we know what is best for another, but we think one person should not make decisions for another. Just as we must respect the decision of a person who has decided after careful reflection that he wants to commit suicide, so we must not take the liberty of deciding to bring another's life to a close contrary to his wishes. So what may be done? Must a person suffer simply because he cannot express consent? There is evidence that can be gathered about what conclusions a person would draw if he were in a state to draw and express them. The patient's friends will have some recollection of things he has said in the past, of his values and general ethical views. Just as we can have good reason to think, for example, that he would vote Democratic if voting for president in a certain year, so we can have good reason to think he would take a certain stand about the termination of his own life in various circumstances. We can know of some persons who because of their religious views would want to keep on living until natural processes bring their lives to a close. About others we can know that they decidedly would not take this view. We can also know what would be the *rational* choice for them to make, and our knowledge of this can be *evidence* about what they would request if they were able. There are, of course, practical complications in the mechanics of a review board of some kind making a determination of this sort, but they are hardly insurmountable.

I wish to consider one other type of case, that of a person who, say, has had a stroke and is leading, and for some time can continue to lead, a life that is comfortable but one on a very low level, *and* who has antecedently requested that his life be terminated if he comes, incurably, into such a situation. May he then be terminated? In this case unlike the others, there are probably ongoing pleasant experiences, perhaps on the level of some animals, that seem to be a good thing. One can hardly say that *injury* is being done such a person by keeping him alive; and one might say that some slight injury is being done him by terminating his existence. There is a real problem here. Can the (slight) goodness of these experiences stand against the weight of an earlier firm declaration requesting that life be terminated in a situation of hopeless senility? There is no *injury* in keeping the person alive despite his request, but there seems something *indecent* about keeping a mind alive after a severe stroke, when we know quite well

that, could he have anticipated it, his own action would have been to terminate his life. I think that the person's own request should be honored; it should be if a person's expressed preferences have as much moral weight as I think they should have.

What general conclusions are warranted by the preceding discussion? I shall emphasize two. First, there is a prima facie obligation *not* to terminate a person's existence when this would injure him (except in cases of self-defense or of senility of a person whose known wish is to be terminated in such a condition) *or* if he wishes not to be terminated. Second, there is *not* a prima facie obligation not to terminate when there would be *no* injury, or when there would be a positive benefit (release from pain) in so doing, provided the patient has not declared himself otherwise or there is evidence that his wishes are to that effect. Obviously there are two things that are decisive for the morality of terminating a person's life: whether so doing would be *injury* and whether it conforms to what is known of his *preferences*.

I remarked at the outset that I would be content with some moral principles if it could be made out that rational persons would want those principles incorporated in the consciences of a group among whom they were to live. It is obvious why rational persons would want these principles. They would want injury avoided both because they would not wish others to injure them and because, if they are benevolent, they would not wish others injured. Moreover, they would want weight given to a person's own known preferences. Rational people do want the decision about the termination of their lives, where that is possible; for they would be uncomfortable if they thought it possible that others would be free to terminate their lives without consent. The threat of serious illness is bad enough without that prospect. On the other hand, this discomfort would be removed if they know that termination would not be undertaken on their behalf without their explicit consent, except after a careful inquiry had been made, both into whether termination would constitute an injury and whether they would request termination under the circumstances if they were in a position to do so.

If I am right in all this, then it appears that killing a person is not something that is just prima facie wrong *in itself*; it is wrong roughly only if and because it is an *injury* of someone, or if and because it is contrary to the *known preferences* of

someone. It would seem that a principle about the prima facie wrongness of killing is *derivative* from principles about when we are prima facie obligated not to injure and when we are prima facie obligated to respect a person's wishes, at least about what happens to his own body. I do not, however, have any suggestions for a general statement of principles of this latter sort.

NOTES

1. See my "The Morality of Abortion" in *The Monist*, 56 (1972), pp. 503–26; and, in revised form, in a forthcoming volume edited by R. L. Perkins.

2. See my "The Morality and Rationality of Suicide," in James Rachels, ed., *Moral Problems* (in press); and, in revised form, in E. S. Shneidman, ed., *Suicidology: Current Developments* (forthcoming).

POSTSCRIPT

Is Euthanasia Immoral?

One of the puzzles in the euthanasia debate is whether there is a morally significant difference between "active" euthanasia and "passive" euthanasia. Supposedly, the difference between these two is that in the first case you take active measures in order to bring about death, while in the latter case you passively allow death to happen (although it is possible that you could prevent the death). An example of the first case would be the shooting of the physicist by his brother, which was mentioned in the introduction to this issue. An example of the latter case would be the failure to operate on a patient when the operation could be lifesaving. Take the example of a baby born with several physical and mental problems who is allowed to die because a relatively routine operation that would make food digestion possible is not performed. Parents may withhold permission for surgery in such cases because, although alive after the surgery, the baby would remain disabled.

Much of the popular discussion about euthanasia refers to "pulling the plug" on life-support systems. Is this passive euthanasia, because the patient is then allowed to die of natural causes, or is it active euthanasia, because if the action of pulling the plug were not taken, the patient would still be alive? James Rachels has challenged the supposition that active euthanasia is morally worse than passive euthanasia in an important article, "Active and Passive Euthanasia," originally published in *The New England Journal of Medicine* (January 9, 1975). A response to Rachels can be found in Thomas D. Sullivan, "Active and Passive Euthanasia: An Impertinent Distinction?" *Human Life Review* (Summer 1977).

Another issue that arises in discussions of euthanasia is whether permitting euthanasia in any form is likely to lead to something else. Once euthanasia has taken its first life, is there a danger that *programs* of euthanasia will become widespread? There are those who believe that allowing euthanasia in some cases puts us on a course of action toward killing anyone judged unfit for life. Peter Singer discusses this objection in his *Practical Ethics* (Cambridge University Press, 1979).

Both moral and legal questions concerning euthanasia are discussed in "Euthanasia," by James Rachels, in Tom Regan, ed., *Matters of Life and Death*, 2d ed. (Random House, 1986). See also James Rachels, *The End of Life* (Oxford University Press, 1986).

ISSUE 17

Is Affirmative Action Morally Justifiable?

YES: Richard Wasserstrom, from "A Defense of Programs of Preferential Treatment," *National Forum: The Phi Kappa Phi Journal* (Winter 1978)

NO: Barry R. Gross, from "Is Turn About Fair Play?" in Barry R. Gross, ed., *Reverse Discrimination* (Prometheus Books, 1977)

ISSUE SUMMARY

YES: Professor of philosophy Richard Wasserstrom, in defense of affirmative action programs, refutes criticisms designed to persuade that, however well-intentioned affirmative action programs might be, they are fundamentally flawed.
NO: Philosopher Barry R. Gross argues that programs of affirmative action fail to fit any reasonable model of reparation or compensation, and they introduce undesirable consequences of their own. They are all cases of reverse discrimination and are all fundamentally unjust.

Throughout history, women and minority groups have been discriminated against in the United States. However, it might be difficult for many of us today to appreciate the extent of past discrimination and the ways in which social, legal, and political institutions were discriminatory.

Slavery is probably the most blatant form of past racism. We know that people were bought and sold, but the words are so familiar that the realities they stand for may never rise to consciousness. Many particular events and experiences lie behind a simple word like slavery. For example, the importation of slaves to this country was illegal before slaveholding itself became so. When ships at sea bringing African slaves to America found themselves in danger of being confronted by the law, it was easy to do what smugglers on the high seas always do with their contraband: the blacks, chained together and weighted down, were dropped overboard. Even after the Civil War, blacks were denied the right to vote, to testify in court, to own land, or to make contracts. In many states, laws restricted blacks in every conceivable aspect of their lives, including education, employment, and housing.

With respect to discrimination against women, consider the following, written by U.S. Supreme Court Justice Joseph Bradley in concurring with the Court's decision (in *Bradwell v. Illinois*, 1873) that the state of Illinois was justified in denying Myra Bradwell a license to practice law on the grounds that she was a woman:

[T]he civil law, as well as nature herself, has always recognized a wide difference in the respective spheres and destinies of man and woman. Man is, or should be, woman's protector and defender. The natural and proper timidity and delicacy which belongs to the female sex evidently unfits it for many of the occupations of civil life. The constitution of the family organization, which is founded in the divine ordinance, as well as in the nature of things, indicates the domestic sphere as that which properly belongs to the domain and functions of womanhood. The harmony . . . of interests and views which belong . . . to the family institution is repugnant to the idea of a woman adopting a distinct and independent career from that of her husband. . . . The paramount destiny and mission of woman are to fulfill the noble and benign offices of wife and mother.

Such thoughts are rarely openly expressed these days, and racial segregation and discrimination do not have legal support. One wonders, though, how much attitudes have actually changed. The law can change, but old attitudes persist, and they can even be preserved and passed down from generation to generation. Moreover, the results of past social injustices are with us today. The question we now face and cannot turn away from is what to do about the consequences of past discrimination.

In the following selections, Richard Wasserstrom argues that the social realities of today do not allow us to say that programs of affirmative action and preferential treatment constitute discrimination against whites, men, and so on. He speaks specifically of the *Bakke* case, decided by the U.S. Supreme Court in 1978. Allan Bakke was a white male applicant for medical school at the University of California at Davis. He was denied admittance, although some minority group members who had lower overall scores (based on such criteria as interviews and Medical College Admissions Test scores) were accepted. These minority group members had applied through a special program that set aside sixteen of the one hundred places in the entering class for disadvantaged students. The Court's decision was a complicated one. The Court ruled, by a 5–4 vote, that the Davis plan was not legal; but it also ruled, by a different 5–4 vote, that a plan that takes racial considerations into account is not automatically unconstitutional.

Barry R. Gross argues that programs of affirmative action actually go too far. They start out addressing problems of discrimination but end up promoting a kind of discrimination of their own. Gross warns against making the assumption that if a specific group (Jews, the Irish, and WASPs, for example) are not represented in a given profession or job category in percentages equal to the group's percentage of the general population, there must be discrimination. He goes on to consider possible justifications for affirmative action programs but concludes that none of them would work.

YES

Richard Wasserstrom

A DEFENSE OF PROGRAMS OF PREFERENTIAL TREATMENT

Many justifications of programs of preferential treatment depend upon the claim that in one respect or another such programs have good consequences or that they are effective means by which to bring about some desirable end, e.g., an integrated, equalitarian society. I mean by "programs of preferential treatment" to refer to programs such as those at issue in the *Bakke* case—programs which set aside a certain number of places (for example, in a law school) as to which members of minority groups (for example, persons who are non-white or female) who possess certain minimum qualifications (in terms of grades and test scores) may be preferred for admission to those places over some members of the majority group who possess higher qualifications (in terms of grades and test scores).

Many criticisms of programs of preferential treatment claim that such programs, even if effective, are unjustifiable because they are in some important sense unfair or unjust. In this paper I present a limited defense of such programs by showing that two of the chief arguments offered for the unfairness or injustice of these programs do not work in the way or to the degree supposed by critics of these programs.

The first argument is this. Opponents of preferential treatment programs sometimes assert that proponents of these programs are guilty of intellectual inconsistency, if not racism or sexism. For, as is now readily acknowledged, at times past employers, universities, and many other social institutions did have racial or sexual quotas (when they did not practice overt racial or sexual exclusion), and many of those who were most concerned to bring about the eradication of those racial quotas are now untroubled by the new programs which reinstitute them. And this, it is claimed, is inconsistent. If it was wrong to take race or sex into account when blacks and women were the objects of racial and sexual policies and practices of exclusion, then it is wrong to take race or sex into account when the objects of the policies have their race or sex reversed. Simple considerations of intellectual consistency—of what it means to give racism or sexism as a reason for condemning these

From Richard Wasserstrom, "A Defense of Programs of Preferential Treatment," *National Forum: The Phi Kappa Phi Journal*, vol. 58, no. 1 (Winter 1978), pp. 15–18. Copyright © 1978 by *National Forum: The Phi Kappa Phi Journal*. Reprinted by permission.

social policies and practices—require that what was a good reason then is still a good reason now.

The problem with this argument is that despite appearances, there is no inconsistency involved in holding both views. Even if contemporary preferential treatment programs which contain quotas are wrong, they are not wrong for the reasons that made quotas against blacks and women pernicious. The reason why is that the social realities do make an enormous difference. The fundamental evil of programs that discriminated against blacks or women was that these programs were a part of a larger social universe which systematically maintained a network of institutions that unjustifiably concentrated power, authority, and goods in the hands of white male individuals, and which systematically consigned blacks and women to subordinate positions in the society.

Whatever may be wrong with today's affirmative action programs and quota systems, it should be clear that the evil, if any, is just not the same. Racial and sexual minorities do not constitute the dominant social group. Nor is the conception of who is a fully developed member of the moral and social community one of an individual who is either female or black. Quotas that prefer women or blacks do not add to an already relatively overabundant supply of resources and opportunities at the disposal of members of these groups in the way in which the quotas of the past did maintain and augment the overabundant supply of resources and opportunities already available to white males.

The same point can be made in a somewhat different way. Sometimes people say that what was wrong, for example, with the system of racial discrimination in the South was that it took an irrelevant characteristic, namely race, and used it systematically to allocate social benefits and burdens of various sorts. The defect was the irrelevance of the characteristic used—race—for that meant that individuals ended up being treated in a manner that was arbitrary and capricious.

I do not think that was the central flaw at all. Take, for instance, the most hideous of the practices, human slavery. The primary thing that was wrong with the institution was not that the particular individuals who were assigned the place of slaves were assigned there arbitrarily because the assignment was made in virtue of an irrelevant characteristic, their race. Rather, it seems to me that the primary thing that was and is wrong with slavery is the practice itself—the fact of some individuals being able to own other individuals and all that goes with that practice. It would not matter by what criterion individuals were assigned; human slavery would still be wrong. And the same can be said for most if not all of the other discrete practices and institutions which comprised the system of racial discrimination even after human slavery was abolished. The practices were unjustifiable—they were oppressive—and they would have been so no matter how the assignment of victims had been made. What made it worse, still, was that the institutions and the supporting ideology all interlocked to create a system of human oppression whose effects on those living under it were as devastating as they were unjustifiable.

Again, if there is anything wrong with the programs of preferential treatment, it should be evident that the social realities in respect to the distribution of resources and opportunities make the difference. Apart from everything else, there is simply no way in which all of these programs taken together could plausibly be viewed as capable of relegating white males to the kind of genuinely oppressive status characteristically bestowed upon women and blacks by the dominant social institutions and ideology.

The second objection is that preferential treatment programs are wrong because they take race or sex into account rather than the only thing that does matter—that is, an individual's qualifications. What all such programs have in common and what makes them all objectionable, so this argument goes, is that they ignore the persons who are more qualified by bestowing a preference on those who are less qualified in virtue of their being either black or female.

There are, I think, a number of things wrong with this objection based on qualifications, and not the least of them is that we do not live in a society in which there is even the serious pretense of a qualification requirement for many jobs of substantial power and authority. Would anyone claim, for example, that the persons who comprise the judiciary are there because they are the most qualified lawyers or the most qualified persons to be judges? Would anyone claim that Henry Ford II is the head of the Ford Motor Company because he is the most qualified person for the job? Part of what is wrong with even talking about qualifications and merit is that the argument derives some of its force from the erroneous notion that we would have a meritocracy were it not for programs of preferential treatment. In fact, the higher one goes in terms of prestige, power and the like, the less qualifications seem ever to be decisive. It is only for certain jobs and certain places that qualifications are used to do more than establish the possession of certain minimum competencies.

But difficulties such as these to one side, there are theoretical difficulties as well which cut much more deeply into the argument about qualifications. To begin with, it is important to see that there is a serious inconsistency present if the person who favors "pure qualifications" does so on the ground that the most qualified ought to be selected because this promotes maximum efficiency. Let us suppose that the argument is that if we have the most qualified performing the relevant tasks we will get those tasks done in the most economical and efficient manner. There is nothing wrong in principle with arguments based upon good consequences that will flow from maintaining a social practice in a certain way. But it is inconsistent for the opponent of preferential treatment to attach much weight to qualifications on this ground, because it was an analogous appeal to the good consequences that the opponent of preferential treatment thought was wrong in the first place. That is to say, if the chief thing to be said in favor of strict qualifications and preferring the most qualified is that it is the most efficient way of getting things done, then we are right back to an assessment of the different consequences that will flow from different programs, and we are far removed from the considerations of justice or fairness that were thought to weigh so heavily against these programs.

It is important to note, too, that qualifications—at least in the educational context—are often not connected at all closely with any plausible conception of social effectiveness. To admit the most qualified students to law school, for example—given the way qualifications are now determined—is primarily to admit those who have the greatest chance of scoring the highest grades at law school. This says little about efficiency except perhaps that these students are the easiest for the faculty to teach. However, since we know so little about what constitutes being a good, or even successful lawyer, and even less about the correlation between being a very good law student and being a very good lawyer, we can hardly claim very confidently that the legal system will operate most effectively if we admit only the most qualified students to law school.

To be at all decisive, the argument for qualifications must be that those who are the most qualified deserve to receive the benefits (the job, the place in law school, etc.) because they are the most qualified. The introduction of the concept of desert now makes it an objection as to justice or fairness of the sort promised by the original criticism of the programs. But now the problem is that there is no reason to think that there is any strong sense of "desert" in which it is correct that the most qualified deserve anything.

Let us consider more closely one case, that of preferential treatment in respect to admission to college or graduate school. There is a logical gap in the inference from the claim that a person is most qualified to perform a task, e.g., to be a good student, to the conclusion that he or she deserves to be admitted as a student. Of course, those who deserve to be admitted should be admitted. But why do the most qualified deserve anything? There is simply no necessary connection between academic merit (in the sense of being most qualified) and deserving to be a member of a student body. Suppose, for instance, that there is only one tennis court in the community. Is it clear that the two best tennis players ought to be the ones permitted to use it? Why not those who were there first? Or those who will enjoy playing the most? Or those who are the worst and, therefore, need the greatest opportunity to practice? Or those who have the chance to play least frequently?

We might, of course, have a rule that says that the best tennis players get to use the court before the others. Under such a rule the best players would deserve the court more than the poorer ones. But that is just to push the inquiry back on stage. Is there any reason to think that we ought to have a rule giving good tennis players such a preference? Indeed, the arguments that might be given for or against such a rule are many and varied. And few if any of the arguments that might support the rule would depend upon a connection between ability and desert.

Someone might reply, however, that the most able students deserve to be admitted to the university because all of their earlier schooling was a kind of competition, with university admission being the prize awarded to the winners. They deserve to be admitted because that is what the rule of the competition provides. In addition, it might be argued, it would be unfair now to exclude them in favor of others, given the reasonable expectations they developed about the way in which their industry and performance would be rewarded. Minority-admission programs, which inevitably prefer some who are less qualified over some who are more qualified, all possess this flaw.

There are several problems with this argument. The most substantial of them is that it is an empirically implausible picture of our social world. Most of what are regarded as the decisive characteristics for higher education have a great deal to do with things over which the individual has neither control nor responsibility: such things as home environment, socioeconomic class of parents, and, of course, the quality of the primary and secondary schools attended. Since individuals do not deserve having had any of these things vis-á-vis other individuals, they do not, for the most part, deserve their qualifications. And since they do not deserve their abilities they do not in any strong sense deserve to be admitted because of their abilities.

To be sure, if there has been a rule which connects say, performance at high school with admission to college, then there is a weak sense in which those who do well at high school deserve, for that reason alone, to be admitted to college. In addition, if persons have built up or relied upon their reasonable expectations concerning performance and admission, they have a claim to be admitted on this ground as well. But it is certainly not obvious that these claims of desert are any stronger or more compelling than the competing claims based upon the needs of or advantages to women or blacks from programs of preferential treatment. And as I have indicated, all rule-based claims of desert are very weak unless and until the rule which creates the claim is itself shown to be a justified one. Unless one has a strong preference for the status quo, and unless one can defend that preference, the practice within a system of allocating places in a certain way does not go very far at all in showing that that is the right or the just way to allocate those places in the future.

A proponent of programs of preferential treatment is not at all committed to the view that qualifications ought to be wholly irrelevant. He or she can agree that, given the existing structure of any institution, there is probably some minimal set of qualifications without which one cannot participate meaningfully within the institution. In addition, it can be granted that the qualifications of those involved will affect the way the institution works and the way it affects others in the society. And the consequences will vary depending upon the particular institution. But all of this only establishes that qualifications, in this sense, are relevant, not that they are decisive. This is wholly consistent with the claim that race or sex should today also be relevant when it comes to matters such as admission to college or law school. And that is all that any preferential treatment program—even one with the kind of quota used in the *Bakke* case—has ever tried to do.

I have not attempted to establish that programs of preferential treatment are right and desirable. There are empirical issues concerning the consequences of these programs that I have not discussed, and certainly not settled. Nor, for that matter, have I considered the argument that justice may permit, if not require, these programs as a way to provide compensation or reparation for injuries suffered in the recent as well as distant past, or as a way to remove benefits that are undeservedly enjoyed by those of the dominant group. What I have tried to do is show that it is wrong to think that programs of preferential treatment are objectionable in the centrally important sense in which many past and present discriminatory features of our society have been and are racist and sexist. The social realities as to power and opportunity do make a fundamental difference. It is also wrong to think that programs of preferential treatment are in any strong sense either unjust or unprincipled. The case for programs of preferential treatment could, therefore, plausibly rest both on the view that such programs are not unfair to white males (except in the weak, rule-dependent sense described above) and on the view that it is unfair to continue the present set of unjust—often racist and sexist—institutions that comprise the social reality. And the case for these programs could rest as well on the proposition that, given the distribution of power and influence in the United States today, such programs may reasonably be viewed as potentially valuable, effective means by which to achieve admirable and significant social ideals of equality and integration.

NO

IS TURN ABOUT FAIR PLAY?

Men born to freedom are naturally alert to repel invasion of liberty by evil-minded rulers. The greatest danger to liberty lurks in insidious encroachment by the men of zeal, well-meaning but without understanding.

—Louis D. Brandeis

No rule on the subject recommends itself so strongly to the primitive and spontaneous sentiment of justice as the *lex talionis*, an eye for an eye and a tooth for a tooth. Though this principle of the Jewish and Mohammedan law has been generally abandoned in Europe as a practical maxim, there is, I suspect, in most minds, a secret hankering after it; and when retribution accidentally falls on an offender in that precise shape, the general feeling of satisfaction evidenced bears witness how natural is the sentiment to which its repayment in kind is acceptable.

—John Stuart Mill

The balance of argument weighs against reverse discrimination for four interrelated sets of reasons. First, the procedures designed to isolate the discriminated are flawed. Second, the practice has undesirable and dangerous consequences. Third, it fails to fit any of the models of compensation or reparations. Fourth, it falls unjustly upon both those it favors and those it disfavors. I conclude that if to eliminate discrimination against the members of one group we find ourselves discriminating against another, we have gone too far.

Sociologically, groups are simply not represented in various jobs and at various levels in percentages closely approximately their percentage of the population. When universities in general and medical schools in particular discriminated heavily against them, Jews were represented in the medical profession in far greater percentages than their percentage of the population. At the same time, they were represented in far lower percentages in banking, finance, construction, and engineering than their percentage in the population, especially the population of New York City. A similar analysis by crudely drawn group traits—Jew, Roman Catholic, WASP, Irish, and so forth—of almost any trade, business or profession would yield similar results.

From Barry R. Gross, "Is Turn About Fair Play?" in Barry R. Gross, ed., *Reverse Discrimination* (Prometheus Books, 1977). Copyright © 1975 by the *Journal of Critical Analysis*. Reprinted by permission. This article first appeared in *Journal of Critical Analysis*, vol. 5, no. 4 (January/April 1975).

But the argument from population percentages may be meant not as an analysis of what is the case, but as an analysis of what ought to be the case. A proponent might put it this way: It is true that groups are not usually represented in the work force by their percentage in the population at large, but minority C has been systematically excluded from the good places. Therefore, in order to make sure that they get some of them, we should now systematically include them in the good places, and a clear way of doing it is by their percentage in the populations. Or we might conclude instead: therefore, in order to make up for past exclusion, they should be included in the good places as reparation, and an easy way to do it is by their percentage in the population.

If the definition of a minority discriminated against is ipso facto their representation in certain jobs in percentages less than their percentage in the general population, then one has to remark that the reasoning is circular. For we are trying to prove: (1) that minority C is discriminated against.

We use as a premise (3) that minority C is underrepresented in good jobs. Since (1) does not follow from (3) (mere underrepresentation not being even prima facie evidence of discrimination), it is necessary to insert (2) that their underrepresentation is due to discrimination. But this completes the circle.

A critic might reply that we know perfectly well what is meant. The groups discriminated against are blacks, Puerto Ricans, Mexican-Americans, American Indians, and women. He is correct, though his answer does not tell us how to find out who is discriminated against. This critic, for example, left out Jews and Orientals. If he should reply that Jews and Orien-

tals do well enough, we point out that the question was not "Who fails to do well?" but rather, "Who is discriminated against?" This argument shows that the mechanisms for identifying the victims of discrimination and for remedying it are seriously deficient.

Even if we allow that the percentage of the group in the work force versus its percentage in the population is the criterion of discrimination, who is discriminated against will vary depending upon how we divide the groups. We may discover that Republicans are discriminated against by our literary or intellectual journals—*New York Review, Dissent, Commentary.* We may also discover that wealthy Boston residents are discriminated against by the Los Angeles Dodgers, that women are discriminated against by the Army, and that idiots (we hope) are discriminated against by universities.

What employment or profession a person chooses depends upon a number of variables—background, wealth, parents' employment, schooling, intelligence, drive, ambition, skill, and not least, luck. Moreover, the analysis will differ depending upon what group identification or stratification you choose. None seems to have priority over the others. Every person can be typed according to many of these classifications. It seems, therefore, that the relevant analysis cannot even be made, much less justified.

In addition, some proponents of the population-percentage argument seem to hold: (4) From the contingent fact that members of the group C were discriminated against, it follows necessarily that they are underrepresented in the good positions. They then go on to assert (5) if members of group C were not discriminated against they would not be underrepresented, or (6) if they are underrepresented, then they are discriminated against.

But clearly (4) is itself a contingent, not a necessary truth. Clearly also neither (5) nor (6) follows from it, (5) being the fallacy of denying the antecedent and (6) the fallacy of affirming the consequent. Lastly, neither (5) nor (6) is necessarily true. The members of a group might simply lack interest in certain jobs (for example, Italians in the public-school system are in short supply). Could one argue that, even though neither (4), (5), nor (6) is *necessarily* true, the mere fact of underrepresentation in certain occupations does provide evidence of discrimination? The answer is no—no more than the fact of "overrepresentation" in certain occupations is evidence of favoritism.

At most, underrepresenation can be used to support the contention of discrimination when there is *other* evidence as well.

FAIR PLAY: OUGHT WE TO DISCRIMINATE IN REVERSE?

There are at least three difficulties with reverse discrimination: first, it is inconsistent; second, it licenses discrimination; third, it is unfair.

If we believe the principle that equal opportunity is a right of everyone, then if members of group C are excluded from enjoying certain opportunities merely because they are members of group C, their right is being abrogated. They are entitled to this right, but so is everybody else, even those persons who presently deny it to them. If both are made to enjoy equal opportunity, then both are enjoying their right. To give either oppressors or oppressed more than equal opportunity is equally to deny the rights of one

or the other in violation of the principle of equal opportunity.

Proponents of reverse discrimination seem to be caught on the horns of a dilemma: either discrimination is illegitimate or it is not. If it is illegitimate, then it ought not to be practiced against anyone. If it is not, then there exists no reason for *now* favoring blacks, Puerto Ricans, Chicanos, Indians, women, and so forth over whites.

Two strategies present themselves. Either we can analyze one disjunct with a view to showing that distinctions can be made which require compensation or reparations in the form of reverse discrimination to be made to wronged individuals or groups; or we can try to soften one of the disjuncts so as to make a case for exceptions in favor of the wronged. The first appeals both to our reason and our sense of justice. The second appeals to our emotions. I shall argue that neither strategy works.[1]

Now reverse discrimination can take several forms, but I think that what many of its proponents have in mind is a strong form of compensation—a form which requires us to discriminate against non-C members and favor C members even if less qualified. One may well wonder whether there is not a little retribution hidden in this form of compensation.

THE "SOFTENED" GENERAL PRINCIPLE

The argument for construing reverse discrimination as compensation or reparation has a great appeal which can be brought out by contrasting it with another approach. One might agree that as a general rule reverse discrimination is illegitimate but that it need not be seen as universally illegitimate. In particular, in the case where people have been so heavily discriminated against as to make it impossible for them now to gain a good life, there is no possibility of their having a fair chance, no possibility of their starting out on anything like equal terms, then and only then is it legitimate to discriminate in their favor and hence against anyone else.

Against this "softened" general principle I shall urge two sorts of objections which I call respectively "practical" and "pragmatic." Against the reparations type of argument, I shall urge first that there is some reason to think the conditions for exacting and accepting them are lacking, and second that, owing to the peculiar nature of the reparations to be exacted (reverse discrimination), the very exaction of them is unreasonable and unfair to both parties—exactors and exactees.

I mention briefly two sorts of practical objections to the "softened" general principle. First, it is simply the case that when discrimination is made in favor of someone regardless of his qualifications, there is the greatest possible danger that the person getting the position will not be competent to fill it. Second, when a person is placed in a position because of discrimination in his favor, he may come to feel himself inferior.[2] This may easily lead to the permanent conferral of inferior status on the group, an inferiority which is all the stronger because self-induced. Its psychological effects should not be underestimated.

The pragmatic objection to the "softened" general principle is much stronger. Discrimination in any form is invidious. Once licensed, its licenses rebound upon its perpetrators as well as others. Principles tend to be generalized without consideration of restrictions or the circumstances to which they were intended to apply. Students of the Nazi movement will have noticed that in licensing the discrimination, isolation, persecution, and "final solution" of the Jews, the Nazis (foreign and German) licensed their own. (Hitler's plans for extermination included political groups, for example, the Rohm faction of the SA, as well as other racial groups, for example, Slavs and Balts who fought on the German side.) It is necessary to be quite careful what principles one adopts. In view of the long and bloody history of discrimination, one ought to be very chary of sanctioning it.

COMPENSATION, REPARATIONS, AND RESTITUTION

Because it escapes most of these objections, the reparations argument becomes very attractive. What is more obvious than the principle that people ought to be compensated for monetary loss, pain and suffering inflicted by others acting either as agents of government or as individuals? From the negligence suit to reparations for war damage, the principle is comfortable, familiar, and best of all, legal. For victims of broken sidewalks, open wells, ignored stop signs, the conditions under which damages are awarded are quite clear. (1) There is specific injury, specific victim, specific time and place. (2) A specific individual or set of individuals must be found responsible either (a) by actually having done the injury, or (b) by failing to act in such a way (for example, repairing the sidewalk, sealing the well) so as to remove a particular potential source of injury on their property. (3) A reasonable assessment of the monetary value of the claim can be made. In such cases no moral blame is attached to the person forced to pay compensation.

But reparations are somewhat less clear. How much does Germany owe France for causing (losing?) World War I? Can we say that *Germany* caused the war? Can we say that Germany *caused* the war? Germany did pay, at least in part, based upon rough calculations of the cost of the Allied armies, including pensions, the loss of allied GNP, indemnities for death and for the destruction of property.

Besides the ability to calculate the indemnities, reparations between countries require at least three other conditions to be met: (1) Responsibility for the events must be able to be assigned and accepted. (2) There must be governments or government-like agencies between which the transfer of goods and services and money takes place. (3) There must be a *modus agendi* worked out. The transfer of vast amounts of goods, money, and services is immensely complicated. In the end Germany could refuse to pay and the Allies to accept large parts of the reparations. Part of the Allied refusal is instructive. Britain, for example, simply could not absorb the payments without extreme economic dislocation.

The meaning of *reparations* was extended to cover payments to Israel and payments to individuals both in and out of Germany who suffered losses through the actions of the Third Reich. The payments to Israel, which did not exist during the war, were to reimburse that state, as the representative of the Jewish people, for the expenses incurred by Jewish organizations during the war in resettling persons uprooted by persecutions and made victims of "unspeakable Nazi crimes."[3]

German payments to individuals were called *Wiedergutmachung* (restitution). *Wiedergutmachung* was awarded not merely for damages or injuries but in order to restore a person to his former position in life. It was calculated on a precise basis. You could be indemnified for: (1) loss of property; (2) loss of income; (3) loss of family; (4) length and type of imprisonment; (5) what you would have earned based upon a reasonable calculation, if you were young and had not yet begun a career. To qualify for indemnities, one had to produce, respectively, proof of ownership and value of property, a calculation of the difference between what one earned as a refugee and would have earned, proof of loss of family, proof of imprisonment.

INAPPLICABILITY OF THESE PARADIGMS

Can reverse discrimination be construed to fit any of these paradigms? Can favoring blacks, Chicanos, Indians, women, and so forth over whites or males be seen as compensation, reparations, or restitution? The answer is no for two general reasons and for several which are specific to the various paradigms. The general reasons are, first, that responsibility for discrimination past and present and for its deleterious consequences is neither clearly assigned nor accepted. Some seem to think that the mere fact of its existence makes all whites (or males in the case of antifeminism) responsible.[4] But I do not know an analysis of responsibility which bears out this claim. Second, there is a great difficulty, if not an impossibility, in assigning a monetary value to the damage done and the compensation allegedly owed—that is to say, reverse discrimination.

If we turn to the negligence paradigm, all the conditions seem to fail. *Specific* injury is lacking, *specific* individual responsibility is lacking, and there is no way to assess the monetary value of the "loss." Indeed, in the case of reverse discrimination it is not monetary value which is claimed but preferential treatment. Under the large-scale reparations paradigm two conditions beyond responsibility are lacking. There are no governments or government-like agencies between which the transfer could take place, and there is no *modus agendi* for the transfer to take place.

Where the transfer is to be of preferential treatment, it is unclear how it is even to be begun. So we come to the third paradigm: individual restitution. This is much closer, for it deals with compensating individual victims of persecution. Again, however, it fails to provide a model, first, because reverse discrimination cannot be looked at in monetary terms, and second, even if it could, the restitution is designed to bring a person back to where he was before the deprivation. In the case of the minorities in question, there can be no question of restoring them to former positions or property. Precisely, the point of the reparation is to pay them for what they, because of immoral social practices, never had in the first place.

But doesn't Condition 5 under *Wiedergutmachung* seem ready-made for the purpose here? Does it not require calculation of what the person would have earned had his life not been blighted? If A was a doctor, lawyer, office manager, beginning a career, or even a mere student, you could get a rough estimate of what he might earn based upon his family position, the average earnings for that occupation, and so forth. But suppose A is young, uneducated, unskilled, unemployed, from a broken home; what might he have been had circumstances been different? Anything. And that is the tragedy. But how can you calculate his earnings on that basis, and how can you translate them into reverse discrimination?

JUSTICE

Finally, if we ignore all that has been said and simply go ahead and discriminate in reverse, calling it reparation, it remains to ask whether it would be either reasonable or just? I think the answer is no. It is possible to hold that in some set of cases, other things being equal, compensation is required and yet to argue either that since other things are not equal compensation is not required, or that even if some compensation is required it ought not to take the form of reverse discrimination. Certainly, from the fact that some form of compensation or reparation must be made it does not follow that any *specific* form of compensation is in order. If X is discriminated against in awarding professorships because he is a member of C group, it scarcely follows that if compensation is in order it *must* take the form of his being discriminated in favor of for another professorship, at least not without adopting the principle of "an eye for an eye" (and only an *eye* for an eye?). Consider X being turned down for an apartment because he is a C member. Must compensation consist just in his being offered another ahead of anybody else? Even if he has one already? To go from the relatively innocuous principle that where *possible* we ought to compensate for damages, to sanction reverse discrimination as the proper or preferred form of redress, requires us to go beyond mere compensation to some principle very much like "let the punishment mirror the crime." But here the person "punished," the person from whom the compensation is exacted, is often not the "criminal." Nor will it help to say that the person deprived of a job or advancement by reverse discrimination is not really being punished or deprived, since the job did not belong to him in the first place. Of course it didn't; nor did it belong to the successful candidate. What belonged to both is equal consideration, and that is what one of them is being deprived of.[5]

There is an element of injustice or unfairness in all reparations. The money derived from taxes paid by all citizens is used for reparations regardless of whether they were responsible for, did nothing about, opposed, or actually fought the policies or government in question. Yet we say that this is the only way it can be done, that the element of unfairness is not great, and that on the whole it is better that this relatively painless way of appropriating money from Jones, who is innocent, be used than that the victims of persecution or crime go uncompensated. But the consequences of reverse discrimination are quite different, especially when it is based upon group membership rather than individual desert. It is possible and is sometimes the case that though most C members are discriminated against, Y is a C member who has met with no discrimination at all. Under the principle that all C members should be discriminated in favor of, we would offer "compensation" to Y. But what are we compensating him *for*? By hypothesis he was no victim of discrimination. Do we compensate him for what happened to others? Do we pay Jones for what we buy from Smith? We seem to be compensating him for being a C member, but why? Do we secretly hold C members inferior? Some claim that society as a whole must bear the burden of repara-

tion. But then reverse discrimination will hardly do the trick. It does not exact redress from the government, or even from all white (responsible?) citizens equally, but falls solely against those who apply for admissions, or jobs *for which blacks or other minorities are applying at the same time.* By the same token, it does not compensate or "reparate" all minority persons equally but merely those applying for admission, jobs, promotions, and so forth. Those whose positions are secure would not be made to pay, and those who do not apply for anything would not be paid. A white person who fought for civil rights for blacks may be passed over for promotion or displaced, a victim of reverse discrimination, while a Ku Klux Klan man at the top of the job ladder pays nothing. This would be a laughably flawed system if it were not seriously advocated by responsible people, and partly implemented by the government. Surely, it violates the principles of both compensatory and distributive justice.

NOTES

1. For examples of these strategies, see the articles by J. W. Nickel, L. J. Cowan, and Paul Taylor [in Barry Gross, ed., *Reverse Discrimination* (Prometheus 1977)].
2. *Contra* this objection see Irving Thalberg, "Justifications of Institutional Racism," *The Philosophical Forum*, Winter 1972.
3. See the text of the reparations agreement in Rolf Vogel, *The German Path to Israel* (Dufour Editions, 1969), pp. 56ff.
4. See Thalberg. For an interesting catalogue of "irresponsible uses of 'responsibility' " see Robert Stover, "Responsibility for the Cold War—A Case Study in Historical Responsibility," *History and Theory*, 1972. For a clear-cut analysis that more than mere presence on the scene is required to show responsibility, see S. Levinson, "Responsibility for Crimes of War," *Philosophy and Public Affairs*, Spring 1973.
5. See Gertrude Ezorsky, "It's Mine," *Philosophy and Public Affairs*, Spring 1974.

POSTSCRIPT

Is Affirmative Action Morally Justifiable?

That racial discrimination and sex discrimination have existed in this country is a matter of historical record and beyond dispute. But the question remains, what follows for us here and now?

Opponents of affirmative action say that nothing at all follows, except perhaps that we might be more careful and vigilant about allowing any form of discrimination, including modern forms of reverse discrimination.

Proponents of strong affirmative action say that although these views might *look* fair and aim to *be* fair, they are not fair. This approach would simply freeze an unfairly established *status quo*. As American society is now, blacks are just not represented in the professions, in graduate schools, in business boardrooms, or in positions of social and political leadership in a way that is consistent with their numbers in the population. This is not for lack of interest or ability; it is a legacy of social injustice. To insist that we now freeze this *status quo* and proceed "fairly," on a case-by-case basis, will guarantee that the white-biased social momentum will continue for at least the foreseeable future. Advocates of affirmative action want to eradicate the effects of past discrimination and to put an end to the bias in momentum as soon as possible. They call for active measures to ensure that representative numbers of blacks are in positions of authority. Programs of affirmative action have their work cut out for them, supporters say, but once the work is done, the programs will have no value and should be dismantled.

Other sources that are relevant to this issue include Lisa H. Newton, "Reverse Discrimination as Unjustified," *Ethics* (July 1973); Nathan Glazer, *Affirmative Discrimination: Ethnic Inequality and Public Policy* (Basic Books, 1975); Barry R. Gross, *Discrimination in Reverse* (New York University Press, 1978); Bernard Boxhill, *Blacks and Social Justice* (Rowman & Littlefield, 1984); Kathanne W. Greene, *Affirmative Action and the Principles of Justice* (Greenwood Press, 1989); Gertrude Ezorsky, *Racism and Justice: The Case for Affirmative Action* (Cornell University Press, 1991); Stephen L. Carter, *Reflections of an Affirmative Action Baby* (Basic Books, 1991); and Michel Rosenfeld, *Affirmative Action and Justice: A Philosophical and Constitutional Inquiry* (Yale University Press, 1991).

UN PHOTO 164669/JOHN ISAAC

PART 5

Morality and the International Scene

Do moral concerns transcend political and geographical boundaries? Or are some moral concerns inescapably limited by political boundaries and physical distances? For example, how should Americans respond to poor or famine-stricken people in distant lands? Where should Americans stand with regard to war and terrorism? The issues in this section go beyond societal problems and raise questions about interaction among different societies.

Do Rich Nations Have an Obligation to Help Poor Nations?

Is Terrorism Ever Justified?

Can Modern War Be Just?

ISSUE 18

Do Rich Nations Have an Obligation to Help Poor Nations?

YES: Peter Singer, from *Practical Ethics* (Cambridge University Press, 1979)

NO: Garrett Hardin, from "Lifeboat Ethics: The Case Against Helping the Poor," *Psychology Today* (September 1974)

ISSUE SUMMARY

YES: Professor of philosophy Peter Singer argues that citizens of rich nations can help those in poor nations without great harm to themselves and that, therefore, they *should* help.

NO: Biologist Garrett Hardin argues that since birthrates in poorer nations are high and the Earth can provide only finite resources, future generations of all nations will be hurt if wealthy nations help poor nations.

If the wealth of a community were concentrated in the hands of a few people, while many other people were so poor that they would likely die of exposure or starve to death, it would be reasonable to say that the wealthy had an obligation to help their neighbors. If the wealth of a nation were concentrated in the hands of a relatively small number of people, while the majority were in dire need, again it would be reasonable to say that the wealthy had an obligation to help their countrymen.

Other questions are worth exploring in order to understand the relationship between rich and poor. For instance, did the wealthy acquire their wealth at the expense of the needy? If so, it is clear that the wealthy have an obligation to help the needy, since they are to some extent responsible for the others' condition. How great is the discrepancy between the two classes of the rich and the poor? The greater the discrepancy, the stronger the case for obligation. How poor are the poor? There may be no limit to the riches that one can acquire, but there is an absolute bottom limit to the level of poverty to which one can descend; at some point one dies. The greater the absolute need of the needy, the better the case for obligation on the part of the wealthy.

How great a burden will fall on the "haves" if they come to the assistance of the "have nots"? If the discrepancy between the two groups is very large, and if the needy are very poor indeed, then the wealthy can help the poor and needy without falling too many rungs on the ladder of wealth.

These questions all concern the distribution of wealth among the members of a community and among members of a nation. Should we also ask these questions with respect to the entire human race? Our world is divided into countries, some of which are quite wealthy, including the United States, Western European industrial nations, and oil-rich Arab countries. These countries, although in the minority, control most of the world's wealth. It is also true that the discrepancy between the rich nations and the poor nations is great, and that the level of existence in many poor nations is abysmally low. The outlook for inhabitants of poor countries is even worse during times of war, drought, political oppression, flood, famine, and epidemic disease.

Is the community of nations different from a community of individuals? Does the same reasoning apply to both cases? We wouldn't let someone die of exposure or starvation on our own doorstep, but should this concern extend over vast distances?

In the following selections, Peter Singer argues that needy nations are quite needy, that wealthy nations are quite wealthy, and that the wealthy nations can help the distant needy at a relatively low cost. Therefore, he says, rich nations *should* help poor ones. Singer dismisses the idea that moral obligations to others vary according to geographical location. Garrett Hardin argues that although the people in question may be very bad off, wealthy nations are not in a position to help them. If aid were rendered to poor nations, future generations of all countries would be hurt because such aid would support high birthrates in poor countries, thereby depleting the Earth's finite resources.

YES

Peter Singer

RICH AND POOR

SOME FACTS

Consider these facts: by the most cautious estimates, 400 million people lack the calories, protein, vitamins and minerals needed for a normally healthy life. Millions are constantly hungry; others suffer from deficiency diseases and from infections they would be able to resist on a better diet. Children are worst affected. According to one estimate, 15 million children under five die every year from the combined effects of malnutrition and infection. In some areas, half the children born can be expected to die before their fifth birthday.

Nor is lack of food the only hardship of the poor. To give a broader picture, Robert McNamara, President of the World Bank, has suggested the term 'absolute poverty'. The poverty we are familiar with in industrialized nations is relative poverty—meaning that some citizens are poor, relative to the wealth enjoyed by their neighbours. People living in relative poverty in Australia might be quite comfortably off by comparison with old-age pensioners in Britain, and British old-age pensioners are not poor in comparison with the poverty that exists in Mali or Ethiopia. Absolute poverty, on the other hand, is poverty by any standard. In McNamara's words:

Poverty at the absolute level . . . is life at the very margin of existence.

The absolute poor are severely deprived human beings struggling to survive in a set of squalid and degraded circumstances almost beyond the power of our sophisticated imaginations and privileged circumstances to conceive.

Compared to those fortunate enough to live in developed countries, individuals in the poorest nations have:

An infant mortality rate eight times higher

A life expectancy one-third lower

An adult literacy rate 60% less

A nutritional level, for one out of every two in the population, below acceptable standards; and for millions of infants, less protein than is sufficient to permit optimum development of the brain.

And McNamara has summed up absolute poverty as:

> a condition of life so characterized by malnutrition, illiteracy, disease, squalid surroundings, high infant mortality and low life expectancy as to be beneath any reasonable definition of human decency.

Absolute poverty is, as McNamara has said, responsible for the loss of countless lives, especially among infants and young children. When absolute poverty does not cause death it still causes misery of a kind not often seen in the affluent nations. Malnutrition in young children stunts both physical and mental development. It has been estimated that the health, growth and learning capacity of nearly half the young children in developing countries are affected by malnutrition. Millions of people on poor diets suffer from deficiency diseases, like goitre, or blindness caused by a lack of vitamin A. The food value of what the poor eat is further reduced by parasites such as hookworm and ringworm, which are endemic in conditions of poor sanitation and health education.

Death and disease apart, absolute poverty remains a miserable condition of life, with inadequate food, shelter, clothing, sanitation, health services and education. According to World Bank estimates which define absolute poverty in terms of income levels insufficient to provide adequate nutrition, something like 800 million people—almost 40 percent of the people of developing countries—live in absolute poverty. Absolute poverty is probably the principal cause of human misery today.

This is the background situation, the situation that prevails on our planet all the time. It does not make headlines. People died from malnutrition and related diseases yesterday, and more will die tomorrow. The occasional droughts, cyclones, earthquakes and floods that take the lives of tens of thousands in one place and at one time are more newsworthy. They add greatly to the total amount of human suffering; but it is wrong to assume that when there are no major calamities reported, all is well.

The problem is not that the world cannot produce enough to feed and shelter its people. People in the poor countries consume, on average, 400 lbs of grain a year, while North Americans average more than 2000 lbs. The difference is caused by the fact that in the rich countries we feed most of our grain to animals, converting it into meat, milk and eggs. Because this is an inefficient process, wasting up to 95 percent of the food value of the animal feed, people in rich countries are responsible for the consumption of far more food than those in poor countries who eat few animal products. If we stopped feeding animals on grains, soybeans and fishmeal the amount of food saved would—if distributed to those who need it—be more than enough to end hunger throughout the world.

These facts about animal food do not mean that we can easily solve the world food problem by cutting down on animal products, but they show that the problem is essentially one of distribution rather than production. The world does produce enough food. Moreover the poorer nations themselves could produce far more if they made more use of improved agricultural techniques.

So why are people hungry? Poor people cannot afford to buy grain grown by American farmers. Poor farmers cannot afford to buy improved seeds, or fertilizers, or the machinery needed for drilling wells and pumping water. Only by transferring some of the wealth of the developed nations to the poor of the undeveloped nations can the situation be changed.

That this wealth exists is clear. Against the picture of absolute poverty that McNamara has painted, one might pose a picture of 'absolute affluence'. Those who are absolutely affluent are not necessarily affluent by comparison with their neighbours, but they are affluent by any reasonable definition of human needs. This means that they have more income than they need to provide themselves adequately with all the basic necessities of life. After buying food, shelter, clothing, necessary health services and education, the absolutely affluent are still able to spend money on luxuries. The absolutely affluent choose their food for the pleasures of the palate, not to stop hunger; they buy new clothes to look fashionable, not to keep warm; they move house to be in a better neighbourhood or have a play room for the children, not to keep out the rain; and after all this there is still money to spend on books and records, colour television, and overseas holidays.

At this stage I am making no ethical judgments about absolute affluence, merely pointing out that it exists. Its defining characteristic is a significant amount of income above the level necessary to provide for the basic human needs of oneself and one's dependents. By this standard Western Europe, North America, Japan, Australia, New Zealand and the oil-rich Middle Eastern states are all absolutely affluent, and so are many, if not all, of their citizens. The USSR and Eastern Europe might also be included on this list. To quote McNamara once more:

> The average citizen of a developed country enjoys wealth beyond the wildest dreams of the one billion people in countries with per capita incomes under $200. . . .

These, therefore, are the countries—and individuals—who have wealth which they could, without threatening their own basic welfare, transfer to the absolutely poor.

At present, very little is being transferred. Members of the Organization of Petroleum Exporting Countries lead the way, giving an average of 2.1 percent of their Gross National Product. Apart from them, only Sweden, The Netherlands and Norway have reached the modest UN target of 0.7 percent of GNP. Britain gives 0.38 percent of its GNP in official development assistance and a small additional amount in unofficial aid from voluntary organizations. The total comes to less than £1 per month per person, and compares with 5.5 percent of GNP spent on alcohol, and 3 percent on tobacco. Other, even wealthier nations, give still less: Germany gives 0.27 percent, the United States 0.22 percent and Japan 0.21 percent. . . .

THE OBLIGATION TO ASSIST

The Argument for an Obligation to Assist

The path from the library at my university to the Humanities lecture theatre passes a shallow ornamental pond. Suppose that on my way to give a lecture I notice that a small child has fallen in and is in danger of drowning. Would anyone deny that I ought to wade in and pull the child out? This will mean getting my clothes muddy, and either cancelling my lecture or delaying it until I can find something dry to change into; but compared with the avoidable death of a child this is insignificant.

A plausible principle that would support the judgment that I ought to pull the child out is this: if it is in our power to prevent something very bad happening, without thereby sacrificing anything of comparable moral significance, we ought to do it. This principle seems uncontroversial. . . .

Nevertheless the uncontroversial appearance of the principle that we ought to prevent what is bad when we can do so without sacrificing anything of comparable moral significance is deceptive. If it were taken seriously and acted upon, our lives and our world would be fundamentally changed. For the principle applies, not just to rare situations in which one can save a child from a pond, but to the everyday situation in which we can assist those living in absolute poverty. In saying this I assume that absolute poverty, with its hunger and malnutrition, lack of shelter, illiteracy, disease, high infant mortality and low life expectancy, is a bad thing. And I assume that it is within the power of the affluent to reduce absolute poverty, without sacrificing anything of comparable moral significance. If these two assumptions and the principle we have been discussing are correct, we have an obligation to help those in absolute poverty which is not less strong than our obligation to rescue a drowning child from a pond. Not to help would be wrong, whether or not it is intrinsically equivalent to killing. Helping is not, as conventionally thought, a charitable act which it is praiseworthy to do, but not wrong to omit; it is something that everyone ought to do.

This is the argument for an obligation to assist. Set out more formally, it would look like this.

FIRST PREMISE: If we can prevent something bad without sacrificing anything of comparable significance, we ought to do it.

SECOND PREMISE: Absolute poverty is bad.

THIRD PREMISE: There is some absolute poverty we can prevent without sacrificing anything of comparable moral significance.

CONCLUSION: We ought to prevent some absolute poverty.

The first premise is the substantive moral premise on which the argument rests, and I have tried to show that it can be accepted by people who hold a variety of ethical positions.

The second premise is unlikely to be challenged. Absolute poverty is, as McNamara put it, 'beneath any reasonable definition of human decency' and it would be hard to find a plausible ethical view which did not regard it as a bad thing.

The third premise is more controversial, even though it is cautiously framed. It claims only that some absolute poverty can be prevented without the sacrifice of anything of comparable moral significance. It thus avoids the objection that any aid I can give is just 'drops in the ocean' for the point is not whether my personal contribution will make any noticeable impression on world poverty as a whole (of course it won't) but whether it will prevent some poverty. This is all the argument needs to sustain its conclusion, since the second premise says that any absolute poverty is bad, and not merely the total amount of absolute poverty. If without sacrificing anything of comparable moral significance we can provide just one family with the means to raise itself out of absolute poverty, the third premise is vindicated.

I have left the notion of moral significance unexamined in order to show that the argument does not depend on any specific values or ethical principles. I think the third premise is true for most people living in industrialized nations, on any defensible view of what is morally significant. Our affluence means that we have income we can dispose of without giving up the basic necessities of life, and we can use this income to reduce absolute poverty. Just how much we will think ourselves obliged to give up will depend on what we consider to be of comparable moral significance to the poverty we could prevent: colour television, stylish clothes, expensive dinners, a sophisticated stereo system, overseas holidays, a (second?) car, a larger house, private schools for our children. . . .

Objections to the Argument

Taking Care of Our Own

Anyone who has worked to increase overseas aid will have come across the argument that we should look after those near us, our families and then the poor in our own country, before we think about poverty in distant places.

No doubt we do instinctively prefer to help those who are close to us. Few could stand by and watch a child drown; many can ignore a famine in Africa. But the question is not what we usually do, but what we ought to do, and it is difficult to see any sound moral justification for the view that distance, or community membership, makes a crucial difference to our obligations.

Consider, for instance, racial affinities. Should whites help poor whites before helping poor blacks? Most of us would reject such a suggestion out of hand . . . people's need for food has nothing to do with their race, and if blacks need food more than whites, it would be a violation of the principle of equal consideration to give preference to whites.

The same point applies to citizenship or nationhood. Every affluent nation has some relatively poor citizens, but absolute poverty is limited largely to the poor nations. Those living on the streets of Calcutta, or in a drought-stricken region of the Sahel, are experiencing poverty unknown in the West. Under these circumstances it would be wrong to decide that only those fortunate enough to be citizens of our own community will share our abundance.

We feel obligations of kinship more strongly than those of citizenship. Which parents could give away their last bowl of rice if their own children were starving? To do so would seem unnatural, contrary to our nature as biologically evolved beings—although whether it would be wrong is another question altogether. In any case, we are not faced with that situation, but with one in which our own children are well-fed, well-clothed, well-educated, and would now like new bikes, a stereo set, or their own car. In these circumstances any special obligations we might have to our children have been fulfilled, and the needs of strangers make a stronger claim upon us. . . .

Property Rights

Do people have a right to private property, a right which contradicts the view that they are under an obligation to give some of their wealth away to those in absolute poverty? According to some theories of rights (for instance, Robert Nozick's) provided one has acquired one's property without the use of unjust means like force and fraud, one may be entitled to enormous wealth while others starve. This individualistic conception of rights is in contrast to other views, like the early Christian doctrine to be found in the works of Thomas Aquinas, which holds that since property exists for the satisfaction of human needs, 'whatever a man has in superabundance is owed, of natural right, to the poor for their sustenance'. A socialist would also, of course, see wealth as belonging to the community rather than the individual, while utilitarians, whether socialist or not, would be prepared to override property rights to prevent great evils.

Does the argument for an obligation to assist others therefore presuppose one of these other theories of property rights, and not an individualistic theory like Nozick's? Not necessarily. A theory of property rights can insist on our *right* to retain wealth without pronouncing on whether the rich *ought* to give to the poor. Nozick, for example, rejects the use of compulsory means like taxation to redistribute income, but suggests that we can achieve the ends we deem morally desirable by voluntary means. So Nozick would reject the claim that rich people have an 'obligation' to give to the poor, in so far as this implies that the poor have a right to our aid, but might accept that giving is something we ought to do and failing to give, though within one's rights, is wrong—for rights is not all there is to ethics.

The argument for an obligation to assist can survive, with only minor modifications, even if we accept an individualistic theory of property rights. In any case, however, I do not think we should accept such a theory. It leaves too much to chance to be an acceptable ethical view. For instance, those whose forefathers happened to inhabit some sandy wastes around the Persian Gulf are now fabulously wealthy, because oil lay under those sands; while those whose forefathers settled on better land south of the Sahara live in absolute poverty, because of drought and bad harvests. Can this distribution be acceptable from an impartial point of view? If we imagine ourselves about to begin life as a citizen of either Kuwait or Chad—but we do not know which—would we accept the principle that citizens of Kuwait are under no obligation to assist people living in Chad?

Population and the Ethics of Triage
Perhaps the most serious objection to the argument that we have an obligation to assist is that since the major cause of absolute poverty is overpopulation, helping those now in poverty will only ensure that yet more people are born to live in poverty in the future.

In its most extreme form, this objection is taken to show that we should adopt a policy of 'triage'. The term comes from medical policies adopted in wartime. With too few doctors to cope with all the casualties, the wounded were divided into three categories: those who would probably survive without medical assistance, those who might survive if they received assistance, but otherwise probably would not, and those who even with medical assistance probably would not survive. Only those in the middle category were given medical assistance. The idea, of course, was to use limited medical resources as effectively as possible. For those in the first category, medical treatment was not strictly necessary; for those in the third category, it was likely to be useless. It has been suggested that we should apply the same policies to countries, according to their prospects of becoming self-sustaining. We would not aid countries which even without our help will soon be able to feed their populations. We would not aid countries which, even with our help, will not be able to limit their population to a level they can feed. We would aid those countries where our help might make the difference between success and failure in bringing food and population into balance. . . .

In support of this view Garrett Hardin has offered a metaphor: we in the rich nations are like the occupants of a crowded lifeboat adrift in a sea full of drowning people. If we try to save the drowning by bringing them aboard our boat will be overloaded and we shall all drown. Since it is better that some survive than none, we should leave the others to drown. In the world today, according to Hardin, 'lifeboat ethics' apply. The rich should leave the poor to starve, for otherwise the poor will drag the rich down with them. . . .

Putting aside the controversial issue of the extent to which food production might one day be increased, it is true, as we have already seen, that the world now produces enough to feed its inhabitants—the amount lost by being fed to animals itself being enough to meet existing grain shortages. Nevertheless population growth cannot be ignored. Bangladesh could, with land reform and using better techniques, feed its present population of 80 million; but by the year 2000, according to World Bank estimates, its population will be 146 million. The enormous effort that will have to go into feeding an extra 66 million people, all added to the population within a quarter of a century, means that Bangladesh must develop at full speed to stay where she is. Other low income countries are in similar situations. By the end of the century, Ethiopia's population is expected to rise from 29 to 54 million; Somalia's from 3 to 7 million, India's from 620 to 958 million, Zaire's from 25 to 47 million.

What will happen then? Population cannot grow indefinitely. It will be checked by a decline in birth rates or a rise in death rates. Those who advocate triage are proposing that we allow the population growth of some countries to be checked by a rise in death rates—that is, by increased malnutrition, and related diseases; by widespread famines; by increased infant mortality; and by epidemics of infectious diseases.

The consequences of triage on this scale are so horrible that we are inclined to reject it without further argument. How could we sit by our television sets, watching millions starve while we do nothing? Would not that . . . be the end of all notions of human equality and respect for human life? Don't people have a right to our assistance, irrespective of the consequences?

Anyone whose initial reaction to triage was not one of repugnance would be an unpleasant sort of person. Yet initial reactions based on strong feelings are not always reliable guides. . . .

. . . The question is: how probable is this forecast that continued assistance now will lead to greater disasters in the future?

Forecasts of population growth are notoriously fallible, and theories about the factors which affect it remain speculative. One theory, at least as plausible as any other, is that countries pass through a 'demographic transition' as their standard of living rises. When people are very poor and have no access to modern medicine their fertility is high, but population is kept in check by high death rates. The introduction of sanitation, modern medical techniques and other improvements reduces the death rate, but initially has little effect on the birth rate. Then population grows rapidly.

Most poor countries are now in this phase. If standards of living continue to rise, however, couples begin to realize that to have the same number of children surviving to maturity as in the past, they do not need to give birth to as many children as their parents did. The need for children to provide economic support in old age diminishes. Improved education and the emancipation and employment of women also reduce the birthrate, and so population growth begins to level off. Most rich nations have reached this stage, and their populations are growing only very slowly.

If this theory is right, there is an alternative to the disasters accepted as inevitable by supporters of triage. We can assist poor countries to raise the living standards of the poorest members of their population. We can encourage the governments of these countries to enact land reform measures, improve education, and liberate women from a purely child-bearing role. We can also help other countries to make contraception and sterilization widely available. There is a fair chance that these measures will hasten the onset of the demographic transition and bring population growth down to a manageable level. Success cannot be guaranteed; but the evidence that improved economic security and education reduce population growth is strong enough to make triage ethically unacceptable. We cannot allow millions to die from starvation and disease when there is a reasonable probability that population can be brought under control without such horrors.

Population growth is therefore not a reason against giving overseas aid, although it should make us think about the kind of aid to give. Instead of food handouts, it may be better to give aid that hastens the demographic transition. This may mean agricultural assistance for the rural poor, or assistance with education, or the provision of contraceptive services. Whatever kind of aid proves most effective in specific circumstances, the obligation to assist is not reduced.

NO

Garrett Hardin

LIFEBOAT ETHICS:
THE CASE AGAINST HELPING THE POOR

Environmentalists use the metaphor of the earth as a "spaceship" in trying to persuade countries, industries and people to stop wasting and polluting our natural resources. Since we all share life on this planet, they argue, no single person or institution has the right to destroy, waste, or use more than a fair share of its resources.

But does everyone on earth have an equal right to an equal share of its resources? The spaceship metaphor can be dangerous when used by misguided idealists to justify suicidal policies for sharing our resources through uncontrolled immigration and foreign aid. In their enthusiastic but unrealistic generosity, they confuse the ethics of a spaceship with those of a lifeboat.

A true spaceship would have to be under the control of a captain, since no ship could possibly survive if its course were determined by committee. Spaceship Earth certainly has no captain; the United Nations is merely a toothless tiger, with little power to enforce any policy upon its bickering members.

If we divide the world crudely into rich nations and poor nations, two thirds of them are desperately poor, and only one third comparatively rich, with the United States the wealthiest of all. Metaphorically each rich nation can be seen as a lifeboat full of comparatively rich people. In the ocean outside each lifeboat swim the poor of the world, who would like to get in, or at least to share some of the wealth. What should the lifeboat passengers do?

First, we must recognize the limited capacity of any lifeboat. For example, a nation's land has a limited capacity to support a population and as the current energy crisis has shown us, in some ways we have already exceeded the carrying capacity of our land.

ADRIFT IN A MORAL SEA

So here we sit, say fifty people in our lifeboat. To be generous, let us assume it has room for ten more, making a total capacity of sixty. Suppose the fifty of us in the lifeboat see 100 others swimming in the water outside, begging for admission to our boat or for handouts. We have several options: we may be tempted to try to live by the Christian ideal of being "our brother's keeper," or by the Marxist ideal of "to each according to his needs." Since the needs of all in the water are the same, and since they can all be seen as "our brothers," we could take them all into our boat, making a total of 150 in a boat designed for sixty. The boat swamps, everyone drowns. Complete justice, complete catastrophe.

Since the boat has an unused excess capacity of ten more passengers, we could admit just ten more to it. But which ten do we let in? How do we choose? Do we pick the best ten, the neediest ten, "first come, first served"? And what do we say to the ninety we exclude? If we do let an extra ten into our lifeboat, we will have lost our "safety factor," an engineering principle of critical importance. For example, if we don't leave room for excess capacity as a safety factor in our country's agriculture, a new plant disease or a bad change in the weather could have disastrous consequences.

Suppose we decide to preserve our small safety factor and admit no more to the lifeboat. Our survival is then possible, although we shall have to be constantly on guard against boarding parties.

While this last solution clearly offers the only means of our survival, it is morally abhorrent to many people. Some say they feel guilty about their good luck. My reply is simple: "Get out and yield your place to others." This may solve the problem of the guilt-ridden person's conscience, but it does not change the ethics of the lifeboat. The needy person to whom the guilt-ridden person yields his place will not himself feel guilty about

his good luck. If he did, he would not climb aboard. The net result of conscience-stricken people giving up their unjustly held seats is the elimination of that sort of conscience from the lifeboat.

This is the basic metaphor within which we must work out our solutions. Let us now enrich the image, step by step, with substantive additions from the real world, a world that must solve real and pressing problems of overpopulation and hunger.

The harsh ethics of the lifeboat become even harsher when we consider the reproductive differences between the rich nations and the poor nations. The people inside the lifeboats are doubling in numbers every eighty-seven years; those swimming around outside are doubling, on the average, every thirty-five years, more than twice as fast as the rich. And since the world's resources are dwindling, the difference in prosperity between the rich and the poor can only increase.

As of 1973, the U.S. had a population of 210 million people, who were increasing by 0.8 percent per year. Outside our lifeboat, let us imagine another 210 million people, (say the combined populations of Columbia, Ecuador, Venezuela, Morocco, Pakistan, Thailand, and the Philippines) who are increasing at a rate of 3.3 percent per year. Put differently, the doubling time for this aggregate population is twenty-one years, compared to eighty-seven years for the U.S.

MULTIPLYING THE RICH AND THE POOR

Now suppose the U.S. agreed to pool its resources with those seven countries, with everyone receiving an equal share. Initially the ratio of Americans to non-

Americans in this model would be one-to-one. But consider what the ratio would be after eighty-seven years, by which time the Americans would have doubled to a population of 420 million. By then, doubling every twenty-one years, the other group would have swollen to 3.54 billion. Each American would have to share the available resources with more than eight people.

But, one could argue, this discussion assumes that current population trends will continue, and they may not. Quite so. Most likely the rate of population increase will decline much faster in the U.S. than it will in the other countries, and there does not seem to be much we can do about it. In sharing with "each according to his needs," we must recognize that needs are determined by population size, which is determined by the rate of reproduction, which at present is regarded as a sovereign right of every nation, poor or not. This being so, the philanthropic load created by the sharing ethic of the spaceship can only increase.

THE TRAGEDY OF THE COMMONS

The fundamental error of spaceship ethics, and the sharing it requires, is that it leads to what I call "tragedy of the commons." Under a system of private property, the men who own property recognize their responsibility to care for it, for if they don't they will eventually suffer. A farmer, for instance, will allow no more cattle in a pasture than its carrying capacity justifies. If he overloads it, erosion sets in, weeds take over, and he loses the use of the pasture.

If a pasture becomes a commons open to all, the right of each to use it may not be matched by a corresponding responsibility to protect it. Asking everyone to use it with discretion will hardly do, for the considerate herdsman who refrains from overloading the commons suffers more than a selfish one who says his needs are greater. If everyone would restrain himself, all would be well; but it takes only one less than everyone to ruin a system of voluntary restraint. In a crowded world of less than perfect human beings, mutual ruin is inevitable if there are no controls. This is the tragedy of the commons.

One of the major tasks of education today should be the creation of such an acute awareness of the dangers of the commons that people will recognize its many varieties. For example, the air and water have become polluted because they are treated as commons. Further growth in the population or per capita conversion of natural resources into pollutants will only make the problem worse. The same holds true for the fish of the oceans. Fishing fleets have nearly disappeared in many parts of the world, technological improvements in the art of fishing are hastening the day of complete ruin. Only the replacement of the system of the commons with a responsible system of control will save the land, air, water and oceanic fisheries.

THE WORLD FOOD BANK

In recent years there has been a push to create a new commons called a World Food Bank, an international depository of food reserves to which nations would contribute according to their abilities and from which they would draw according to their needs. This humanitarian proposal has received support from many liberal international groups, and from such prominent citizens as Margaret Mead, U.N. Secretary General Kurt Waldheim, and Senators Edward Kennedy and George McGovern.

A world food bank appeals powerfully to our humanitarian impulses. But before we rush ahead with such a plan, let us recognize where the greatest political push comes from, lest we be disillusioned later. Our experience with the "Food for Peace program," or Public Law 480, gives us the answer. This program moved billions of dollars worth of U.S. surplus grain to food-short, population-long countries during the past two decades. But when P.L. 480 first became law, a headline in the business magazine *Forbes* revealed the real power behind it: "Feeding the World's Hungry Millions: How It Will Mean Billions for U.S. Business."

And indeed it did. In the years 1960 to 1970, U.S. taxpayers spent a total of $7.9 billion on the Food for Peace Program. Between 1948 and 1970, they also paid an additional $50 billion for other economic-aid programs, some of which went for food and food-producing machinery and technology. Though all U.S. taxpayers were forced to contribute to the cost of P.L. 480, certain special interest groups gained handsomely under the program. Farmers did not have to contribute the grain; the Government, or rather the taxpayers, bought it from them at full market prices. The increased demand raised prices of farm products generally. The manufacturers of farm machinery, fertilizers and pesticides benefited by the farmers' extra efforts to grow more food. Grain elevators profited from storing the surplus until it could be shipped. Railroads made money hauling it to ports, and shipping lines profited from carrying it overseas. The implementation of P.L. 480 required the creation of a vast Government bureaucracy, which then acquired its own vested interest in continuing the program regardless of its merits.

EXTRACTING DOLLARS

Those who proposed and defended the Food for Peace program in public rarely mentioned its importance to any of these special interests. The public emphasis was always on its humanitarian effects. The combination of silent selfish interests and highly vocal humanitarian apologists made a powerful and successful lobby for extracting money from taxpayers. We can expect the same lobby to push now for the creation of a World Food Bank.

However great the potential benefit to selfish interests, it should not be a decisive argument against a truly humanitarian program. We must ask if such a program would actually do more good than harm, not only momentarily but also in the long run. Those who propose the food bank usually refer to a current "emergency" or "crisis" in terms of world food supply. But what is an emergency? Although they may be infrequent and sudden, everyone knows that emergencies will occur from time to time. A well-run family, company, organization or country prepares for the likelihood of accidents and emergencies. It expects them, budgets for them, it saves for them.

LEARNING THE HARD WAY

What happens if some organizations or countries budget for accidents and others do not? If each country is solely responsible for its own well-being, poorly managed ones will suffer. But they can learn from experience. They may mend their ways, and learn to budget for infrequent but certain emergencies. For example, the weather varies from year to year, and periodic crop failures are certain. A wise and competent government saves out of the production of the good years in anticipation of bad years to come. Joseph taught this policy to Pharaoh in Egypt more than 2,000 years ago. Yet the great majority of the governments in the world today do not follow such a policy. They lack either the wisdom or the competence, or both. Should those nations that do manage to put something aside be forced to come to the rescue each time an emergency occurs among the poor nations?

"But it isn't their fault!" some kind-hearted liberals argue. "How can we blame the poor people who are caught in an emergency? Why must they suffer for the sins of their governments?" The concept of blame is simply not relevant here. The real question is, what are the operational consequences of establishing a world food bank? If it is open to every country every time a need develops, slovenly rulers will not be motivated to take Joseph's advice. Someone will always come to their aid. Some countries will deposit food in the world food bank, and others will withdraw it. There will be almost no overlap. As a result of such solutions to food shortage emergencies, the poor countries will not learn to mend their ways, and will suffer progressively greater emergencies as their populations grow.

POPULATION CONTROL
THE CRUDE WAY

On the average, poor countries undergo a 2.5 percent increase in population each year; rich countries, about 0.8 percent.

Only rich countries have anything in the way of food reserves set aside, and even they do not have as much as they should. Poor countries have none. If poor countries received no food from the outside, the rate of their population growth would be periodically checked by crop failures and famines. But if they can always draw on a world food bank in time of need, their population can continue to grow unchecked, and so will their "need" for aid. In the short run, a world food bank may diminish that need, but in the long run it actually increases the need without limit.

Without some system of worldwide food sharing, the proportion of people in the rich and poor nations might eventually stabilize. The overpopulated poor countries would decrease in numbers, while the rich countries that had room for more people would increase. But with a well-meaning system of sharing, such as a world food bank, the growth differential between the rich and the poor countries will not only persist, it will increase. Because of the higher rate of population growth in the poor countries of the world, 88 percent of today's children are born poor, and only 12 percent rich. Year by year the ratio becomes worse, as the fast-reproducing poor outnumber the slow-reproducing rich.

A world food bank is thus a commons in disguise. People will have more motivation to draw from it than to add to any common store. The less provident and less able will multiply at the expense of the abler and more provident, bringing eventual ruin upon all who share in the commons. Besides, any system of "sharing" that amounts to foreign aid from the rich nations to the poor nations will carry the taint of charity, which will contribute little to the world peace so devoutly desired by those who support the idea of a world food bank. . . .

CHINESE FISH AND MIRACLE RICE

The modern approach to foreign aid stresses the export of technology and advice, rather than money and food. As an ancient Chinese proverb goes: "Give a man a fish and he will eat for a day, teach him how to fish and he will eat for the rest of his days." Acting on this advice, the Rockefeller and Ford Foundations have financed a number of programs for improving agriculture in the hungry nations. Known as the "Green Revolution," these programs have led to the development of "miracle rice" and "miracle wheat," new strains that offer bigger harvests and greater resistance to crop damage. Norman Borlaug, the Nobel Prize winning agronomist who, supported by the Rockefeller Foundation, developed "miracle wheat," is one of the most prominent advocates of a world food bank. . . .

OVERLOADING THE ENVIRONMENT

Every human born constitutes a draft on all aspects of the environment: food, air, water, forests, beaches, wildlife, scenery and solitude. Food can, perhaps, be significantly increased to meet a growing demand. But what about clean beaches, unspoiled forests, and solitude? If we satisfy a growing population's need for food, we necessarily decrease its per capita supply of the other resources needed by men.

India, for example, now has a population of 600 million, which increases by 15 million each year. This population already puts a huge load on a relatively impoverished environment. The country's forests are now only a small fraction of what they were three centuries ago, and floods and erosion continually destroy the insufficient farmland that remains. Every one of the 15 million new lives added to India's population puts an additional burden on the environment, and increases the economic and social costs of crowding. However humanitarian our intent, every Indian life saved through medical or nutritional assistance from abroad diminishes the quality of life for those who remain, and for subsequent generations. If rich countries make it possible, through foreign aid, for 600 million Indians to swell to 1.2 billion in a mere twenty-eight years, as their current growth rate threatens, will future generations of Indians thank us for hastening the destruction of their environment? Will our good intentions be sufficient excuse for the consequences of our actions?

My final example of a commons in action is one for which the public has the least desire for rational discussion—immigration. Anyone who publicly questions the wisdom of current U.S. immigration policy is promptly charged with bigotry, prejudice, ethnocentrism, chauvinism, isolationism or selfishness. . . .

IMMIGRATION VS. FOOD SUPPLY

World food banks *move food to the people,* hastening the exhaustion of the environment of the poor countries. Unrestricted immigration, on the other hand, *move people to the food,* thus speeding up the destruction of the environment of the rich countries. We can easily understand why poor people should want to make this latter transfer, but why should rich hosts encourage it?

As in the case of foreign-aid programs, immigration receives support from selfish interests and humanitarian impulses. The primary selfish interest in unimpeded immigration is the desire of employers for cheap labor, particularly in industries and trades that offer degrading work. In the past, one wave of foreigners after another was brought into the U.S. to work at wretched jobs for wretched wages. In recent years the Cubans, Puerto Ricans and Mexicans have had this dubious honor. The interests of the employers of cheap labor mesh well with the guilty silence of the country's liberal intelligentsia. White Anglo-Saxon Protestants are particularly reluctant to call for a closing of the doors to immigration for fear of being called bigots.

But not all countries have such reluctant leadership. Most educated Hawaiians, for example, are keenly aware of the limits of their environment, particularly in terms of population growth. There is only so much room on the islands, and the islanders know it. To Hawaiians, immigrants from the other forty-nine states present as great a threat to those from other nations. At a recent meeting of Hawaiian government officials in Honolulu, I had the ironic delight of hearing a speaker, who like most of his audience was of Japanese ancestry, ask how the country might practically and constitutionally close its doors to further immigration. One member of the audience countered: "How can we shut the door now! We have many friends and relatives in Japan that we'd like to bring here some day so that they can enjoy Hawaii too." The Japanese-American speaker smiled sympathetically and answered: "Yes, but we have children now, and someday we'll have grandchildren too. We can bring more people here from Japan only by giving away some of the land that we hope to pass on to our grandchildren some day. What right do we have to do that?"

At this point, I can hear U. S. liberals asking: "How can you justify slamming the door once you're inside? You say that immigrants should be kept out. But aren't we all immigrants, or the descendants of immigrants? If we insist on staying, must we not admit all others?" Our craving for intellectual order leads us to seek and prefer symmetrical rules and morals: a single rule for me and everybody else; the same rule yesterday, today, and tomorrow. Justice, we feel, should not change with time and place.

We Americans of non-Indian ancestry can look upon ourselves as the descendants of thieves who are guilty morally, if not legally, of stealing this land from its Indian owners. Should we then give back the land to the now living American descendants of those Indians? However morally or logically sound this proposal may be, I, for one, am unwilling to live by it and I know no one else who is. Besides, the logical consequence would be absurd. Suppose that, intoxicated with a sense of pure justice, we should decide to turn our land over to the Indians. Since all our wealth has also been derived from the land, wouldn't we be morally obliged to give that back to the Indians too?

PURE JUSTICE VS. REALITY

Clearly, the concept of pure justice produces an infinite regression to absurdity. Centuries ago, wise men invented statutes of limitations to justify the rejection of such pure justice, in the interest of preventing continual disorder. The law zealously defends property rights, but only relatively recent property rights. Drawing a line after an arbitrary time has elapsed may be unjust, but the alternatives are worse.

We are all the descendants of thieves, and the world's resources are inequitably distributed. But we must begin the journey to tomorrow from the point where we are today. We cannot remake the past. We cannot safely divide the wealth equitably among all peoples so long as people reproduce at different rates. To do so would guarantee that our grandchildren, and everyone else's grandchildren, would have only a ruined world to inherit.

To be generous with one's own possessions is quite different from being generous with those of posterity. We should call this point to the attention of those who, from a commendable love of justice and equality, would institute a system of the commons, either in the form of a world food bank, or of unrestricted immigration. We must convince them if we wish to save at least some parts of the world from environmental ruin.

Without a true world government to control reproduction and the use of available resources, the sharing ethic of the spaceship is impossible. For the foreseeable future, our survival demands that we govern our actions by the ethics of a lifeboat, harsh though they may be. Posterity will be satisfied with nothing else.

POSTSCRIPT

Do Rich Nations Have an Obligation to Help Poor Nations?

The wealth of the Earth is unevenly distributed. Some nations find oil in their deserts, and others only sand. Some are hit by severe droughts or floods, and others are not. Some countries benefit from the foresight of their politicians, while others suffer from revolution or political corruption. All of these factors have an impact on the life prospects of an individual. But to what extent, if any, do these matters affect a rich nation's responsibility to a poor one?

Singer argues that the need in poor countries is indeed great and that wealthy nations have the ability to help. By cutting back on luxuries, he says, the well-to-do can prevent people from starving to death. Moreover, because great good can be accomplished at a relatively low cost, wealthy nations have a positive obligation to do so.

Hardin questions whether the cost is really so low. Good can be done, suffering can be relieved, and lives can be saved, but the populations of poor countries will rise at faster rates than will the populations of rich countries. Consequently, in the end, the suffering has only been postponed, and more lives will be devastated.

Singer can accommodate some of this criticism. If Hardin is right that the countries in question have population problems and extremely high rates of population growth, then *these* are problems that rich nations should address. Singer's overseas aid would include contraceptive devices, information, and programs, in addition to food and medicine.

Of course, there is always the possibility that a given nation will be opposed to contraception or population control and that its population will grow unchecked. In such a case, Hardin would be on stronger ground. The sovereignty of nations comes into play here. One nation is simply not empowered to diagnose a problem in another country and to prescribe and apply a remedy for it. What is often sad in these cases is that the inhabitants of the poor country themselves may lack political power; they are then at the mercy of those who do have control.

Further discussions of these problems, from different political and moral points of view, can be found in the following sources: The Report of the Presidential Commission on World Hunger, *Overcoming World Hunger: The Challenge Ahead* (Government Printing Office, 1980); William Aiken and Hugh La Follette, eds., *World Hunger and Moral Obligation* (Prentice Hall, 1977); Peter G. Brown and Henry Shue, eds., *Food Policy: The Responsibility of the United States in the Life and Death Choices* (The Free Press, 1977); Susan George, *How the Other Half Dies: The Real Reasons for World Hunger* (Allanheld, 1977); and Onora O'Neill, *Faces of Hunger* (Allen and Unwin, 1985). Arline T. Golkin, *Famine: A Heritage of Hunger* (Regina Books, 1987) provides background information, empirical data, and extensive bibliographical references.

ISSUE 19

Is Terrorism Ever Justified?

YES: Virginia Held, from "Violence, Terrorism, and Moral Inquiry," *The Monist* (October 1984)

NO: Alfred Louch, from "Terrorism: The Immorality of Belief," in David C. Rapoport and Yonah Alexander, eds., *The Morality of Terrorism: Religious and Secular Justifications* (Pergamon Press, 1982)

ISSUE SUMMARY

YES: Professor of philosophy Virginia Held admits that a limited terrorism, directed to those in political power or their protectors, may be justifiable. She agrees that no violent, illegal acts *should* be morally justifiable, but if a terrorist act is the only way to counter state-inspired terrorism, and if it is likely to succeed, then it may be justified.
NO: Professor of philosophy Alfred Louch argues that terrorism of any sort cannot be justified. He believes that terrorists' concerns, which seem only to extend to the destruction of present institutions and not to the possible good that may or may not result from terrorist actions, are not sufficient motives to warrant the type of violence that they employ.

There are great problems in defining terrorism. The main problem is the one embodied in the saying, "One man's terrorist is another man's freedom fighter." Part of the idea here seems to be that whether one views a person as a terrorist or a freedom fighter depends on one's own political views. This suggests that only the enemy can practice terrorism, but who the enemy is depends on which side one is on. However, it seems that people on both sides of a political struggle can practice terrorism.

The word *terrorist* should be regarded as more synonymous with the word *killer* than with the word *murderer*. A murderer is a person who commits a wrongful killing. The concept of murder already includes the idea of killing and the idea of wrongfulness; but the idea of a killer includes only the idea of killing and says nothing about wrongfulness. A killing can be justified, and not wrong at all, such as in the case of killing in self-defense. For this issue it is best to use a definition of *terrorist* that does not inherently suggest that the terrorist is in the wrong.

One point that any definition of terrorism should include is that the intention of terrorist activity is ultimately political. This should distinguish terrorists from ordinary criminals, who generally have no political agenda. Also, even though terrorism is often pictured as the work of individuals, any good definition of terrorism should allow that nations themselves can practice terrorism. Furthermore, one of the distinguishing features of terrorism is that terrorism can strike at any time. Elements of surprise and publicity seem essential to terrorist activity, since its most immediate aim is to cause fear. Terrorism generally cannot cause fear unless it strikes suddenly and without warning, and news of the terrorist act must spread.

That publicity is essential can be established by considering what would happen if the public never heard any news of the terrorist activity that takes place. The terrorists would see their actions as pointless and ineffective and be defeated. Note that although authorities can take measures to prevent the spread of news concerning terrorist activities, they have very little control over rumor and word-of-mouth communication. These latter methods of spreading news are quite effective in spreading both news and fear.

Targeting innocent people for its victims is sometimes thought of as essential to terrorism. But attacking innocent victims could be only an effective means toward gaining publicity and causing fear. It is also possible for terrorists to pick their victims carefully and to try to avoid injury to innocent bystanders. Of course, even if terrorists try to avoid such injury, there is no guarantee of success. They also try to avoid getting captured or blown up by their own bombs, but sometimes such things happen. Apparently, in all such cases, the political cause that they are fighting for is of greater concern to them. Presumably, for example, Irish terrorists fighting for the removal of British power from Northern Ireland would rather attack and kill high British officials than ordinary British soldiers, and they would rather attack and kill ordinary British soldiers than a random group of civilian shoppers in London. But as a matter of fact, they have done all three. Each act brings them publicity and contributes to the climate of fear.

In any case, many terrorists would not consider their targets to be innocent, anyway. Palestinian terrorists, for example, would be unlikely to entertain the idea that there may be *innocent* Jews living in the occupied West Bank.

One of the troublesome features of the moral examination of terrorists is that we want to distinguish them from common criminals and troublemakers (and this desire in turn tends to make us want to treat them as a special case), but we also want to be able to condemn them if they go too far or step out of bounds. The permissiveness entailed by the former desire gets in the way of the strictness entailed by the latter. Terrorists generally do not consider themselves to be criminals. But, if they believe enough in their causes and the terrorist activities that support their political goals, they tend to feel that any lengths they go to in order to reach their goals can never be considered "going too far."

In the following selections, Virginia Held argues that violence and terrorism are justified in certain cases. Alfred Louch condemns terrorism to a category of actions that are so abominable that they can never be justified.

YES

Virginia Held

VIOLENCE, TERRORISM, AND MORAL INQUIRY

What shall we say about those acts of moral agents in which violence or terror are used to achieve moral objectives? Can they ever be justified? And what, if anything, can our deliberations in this domain indicate about the methods by which we ought to conduct moral inquiry?

In developing the arguments of this paper, I shall concentrate on the question of the justifiability of violence. I shall then briefly consider whether the arguments apply also to terrorism, and if not, why not. . . .

VIOLENCE

It is sometimes suggested that violence is by definition wrong, but to maintain this is not a satisfactory position. It is easy enough to think of examples of acts of violence of which it is meaningful to ask whether they were wrong or not. One of the clearest examples would be the 1944 bomb plot against Hitler. To answer questions about the justifiability of acts of violence requires that the issues not be construed as ones which can be settled merely by appealing to a definition.

Violence can be defined as action, usually sudden, predictably and coercively inflicting injury upon or damage harming a person.[1] The threat of such action is a violent threat. Property damage is sometimes called "violence" by those who deplore it, but should only be included insofar as it risks injury or harm to persons.[2] . . .

Harm can be inflicted through psychological as well as physical pressure, and the injury caused by violence may be physical or psychological.

A dissident who blows up a car, intentionally killing its occupants, is violent. The police who capture him with guns threaten violence to do so. If he is wounded or killed in the capture, violence has been used against him. A competent doctor operating on a patient is not inflicting harm. An honest tennis player injuring another does not do so predictably. Automobile driving predictably risks injury, but to the extent that it is voluntarily engaged in, it does not do so coercively. . . .

POLITICAL VIOLENCE

To consider whether violence can be politically justified we need to distinguish political violence from other forms of violence. We may say that political violence is violent action against individuals or groups for political or social reasons. Usually, we can consider any attacks upon public officials to be instances of political violence, unless they are for obviously personal non-political reasons. And when agents of government employ violence beyond what is needed for the enforcement of justifiable law, this is political violence. . . .

Assuming that acts of political violence sometimes cause political changes that are significant improvements, politically and morally, can they then be justifiable within the political system? The difficulty of saying yes or no is effectively portrayed by Sorel:

> Certain acts of violence have rendered such great services to democracy that the latter has often consecrated as great men those who, at the peril of their lives, have tried to rid it of its enemies. . . . Each time an outrage occurs, the doctors of the ethico-social sciences, who swarm in journalism, indulge in reflections on the question, Can the criminal act be excused, or sometimes even justified, from the point of view of the highest justice? Then there is an irruption into the democratic press of that casuistry for which the Jesuits have so many times been reproached.[3]

There may always be the danger, empirically well-established, that violence is hard to control, no matter how rational the original intentions of those deciding to employ it. As Hannah Arendt suggested, " . . . the danger of the practice of violence, even if it moves within a non-extremist framework of short-term goals, will always be that the means overwhelm the end. . . . The practice of violence, like all action, changes the world, but the most probable change is a more violent world."[4] . . .

The danger that violent action will produce consequences which are worse than the situation under attack is often severe. The successful use of violence almost certainly requires a tight discipline and capacity for secrecy in direct conflict with the open, participatory decision processes its advocates sometimes espouse. Still, an outbreak of violence may provide a signal that the political system, in its own interest, should heed. It may increase the likelihood that more moderate leaders will be paid attention to by those who would rather ignore the issues raised by the discontented. This may well have been the situation in which progress in civil rights was achieved in the U.S. in the 1960's.[5] Since those with political power are often insensitive to the distress of others, and since those who are sensitive so often lack political power, it may be that violence can provide a shock which will lead to improvement in an area of distress in a political system.

THE JUSTIFICATION OF VIOLENCE

Let us suppose, then, that an intentional act of political violence, Vp, does not lead to additional, more extensive, unintended violence, and does produce what can be taken to be, in a sense to be considered, good results. What can be meant by holding the judgment "Vp was justifiable" valid within political system P?

We may well argue that one of the primary functions of a political system is the validation of political positions as justifiable or non-justifiable, just as one of the primary functions of a legal system is the validation of legal claims as justifiable or non-justifiable. The grounds upon which a judgment may be valid may be different in the two systems, but both provide a method of deciding between conflicting claims.

If an act not permitted by existing laws but concerning which there are strongly felt conflicting positions turns out to have results which are generally considered to contribute to the well-being of the political system, the act will be considered justifiable within this system. And if we can make a decision at a moral level that the continued well-being of that political system is at least better than its destruction, then the act, even if it is an act of violence, may not only be *considered* justifiable within a political system, but may be politically justifiable. . . .

[W]e cannot say that *only* the future can justify violence, though political violence should normally be judged by its results.

Political justification, I wish to argue, presupposes the existence of a political system with methods of deciding between conflicting claims, just as legal justification presupposes the existence of a legal system.

Within various established political systems now in existence, some acts of violence seem to be capable of being found justifiable if they have the following characteristics:

1. They do not lead to additional, more extensive violence;
2. They directly and promptly bring about political consequences which are more decisively approved within the political system than the actions were disapproved.

3. No effective alternative means of bringing about these consequences were possible. Perhaps acts of violence can be justifiable on other grounds as well; I am trying to suggest characteristics such that, if an act has them, it is justifiable. I intentionally evade the language of necessary and sufficient conditions.

A few words about (1) above: it is not meant to require that other acts of violence not occur, since the same kinds of reasons or causes that lead to one act of violence may lead to another, but it suggests that each act needs to be justified independently, and that a given act of political violence has this characteristic only if *it* does not produce further, more extensive violence.

Since violence is the inflicting of injury and damage rather than the creation of any political good, we may say that the only consequences it is in fact capable of producing, in (2) above, are negative ones: the harm to or the destruction or removal of some person or power or obstacle. But sometimes this is a result that will be widely approved, and that will make possible further good consequences. And we can further note that although political systems ought to develop in ways such that characteristic (3) is, in fact, *never* present, until they do, violence can sometimes be politically justifiable.

Whenever the conditions are present that would give what Joan Bondurant calls "the process of creative conflict"[6] a chance of successes, it should be favored. The Gandhian method of winning over one's opponents through non-violent pressure may well be more effective than violence in undermining the attachment people have to mistaken views. But one should not ask peoples willingly to accept genocide, even if one believes—and it would be a position for which little evidence could be marshalled—that the world would be so shocked it would be the last case of genocide. And one should not assume that non-violent protest is always worth the risk. Walter Laqueur believes that "civil disobedience would not have had the slightest effect in Nazi Germany; Gandhi was quite mistaken when he recommended it."[7] He may be mistaken. Joan Bondurant points out that "had the Jews offered satyagraha against the Nazi regime their losses could scarcely have been greater. . . . Had the Jews of Germany been schooled in the art of satyagraha, an organized effort of satyagraha might have got underway. The chances for success are certainly as great as are the chances for violent revolution under the modern police-state system.[8] But if the empirical judgment is made that those preventing the alternative means in characteristic (3) from being available are totally unlikely to change, then refraining from violence might be harder to justify than resorting to it. . . .

CAN VIOLENCE BE MORALLY JUSTIFIABLE?

Just as there is some civil disobedience that will be found legally justifiable by future judicial decisions about constitutionality, and some which will never be found legally justifiable within a given legal system but is still morally justifiable, so there can be violence aimed at changing a political system that will be found acceptable within that system, and also violence aimed at changing a system that, though it will never be found politically justifiable by that system, may

nevertheless be morally justifiable. An example might be a violent political protest against the jailing of political opponents in a state which will never reform itself in such a way as to find the protest justifiable.

If an individual has no sincere expectation that her act of political violence may be found justifiable within the political system in which she takes it, dependent as that system must be for its very existence on certain configurations of prevailing power, she may consider whether the action can be morally justifiable. An act of political violence may be morally justifiable, I think, if it has the following characteristics:

1. It does not lead to additional, more extensive violence;

Either,

2. It directly and promptly brings about consequences which are, in terms of a justifiable moral system, of sufficient greater moral good than evil to outweigh the violence itself, and no effective alternative means of bringing about these consequences are possible;

Or,

3. It is prescribed by a moral rule or principle which is valid and applicable to a situation before the individual, and no alternative way of fulfilling this rule is possible. . . .

Moral justification presupposes the existence of a moral system in some sense, but not in the sense of being able to impose and enforce its decisions. A moral system should be authoritative because it is able to win the voluntary assent of free moral agents in a way comparable to that by which a scientific system gains authority by winning the acceptance of free and impartial inquirers. Conflicts between moral systems, obviously rife at present, should be settled by argument and persuasion on the basis of sincere and impartial deliberation and extensive moral experience. But some states refuse to allow this process to occur. Though it can proceed to some extent even under conditions of repression, it ought to be enabled to develop freely.

If the effectiveness of a moral system should depend upon its power to win voluntary agreement, one may wonder whether any moral rule can ever prescribe a violent act, or any good consequences justify such an act.

Kant argued that "everyone may use violent means to compel another to enter into a juridical state of society."[9] But we might agree that a state, with legal provisions allowing violence in self-defense but forbidding it generally, would be better and stronger if founded on agreement rather than on forcible imposition. Those who agree might use violence to defend themselves *against* those who do not, but this would be collective self-defense, not imposing a legal system on those who do not accept it.

The most plausible view, then, might be that we are not justified in using violence to force others to cooperate with us, but that we may defend ourselves against those who prevent us from entering into cooperative, morally justifiable relations. And we may use violence to defend our moral rights to express our views on why others ought to join in arrangements for the resolution of conflict through argument and political decision rather than through violence.

When there is no viable alternative way to defend our moral rights to free expression or to be given a hearing, violence may be morally justifiable. This view reflects the primacy that is often felt for the moral rights of freedom of thought, of expression, of conscience.

VIOLENCE AND THE SELF

. . . If . . . an existing political system refuses to allow the expression of moral arguments designed to transform it, and if an act of political violence can constitute such an expression, it may be morally justifiable. There will be grave danger that any violent political act will cause unforeseeable consequences, and even graver danger that a violent action intended to change a political system will instead be seen as, and unleash the responses that would attend, an action intended to destroy that system. . . . [E]vidence of sincerity is . . . difficult to offer in the case of violent action that is not justifiable within the political system, but it is not impossible. The provision of fair warning to minimize unnecessary injury, the offering of unmistakable evidence of restraint that the violence can be ended in as disciplined a way as it is being taken, may all contribute.

When those to whom a political system fails to give a voice constitute a large number of that system's members, the argument may be persuasive that an act of violence which warns that system of possible danger to itself, may have to be justifiable within that political system or it will not be justifiable at all. But when those to whom a political system denies a voice are too small a minority or too powerless to represent a significant threat to the existence or even the health of that system, the requirement that for an act of violence to be morally justifiable it must also be politically justifiable, may be mistaken. Political systems have been known to be long-lived, though highly immoral.

Quite clearly, the world should be such that violent but illegal actions are *never* morally justifiable. Persuasion and argument should always be the forms through which moral judgment succeeds in being authoritative for political actions. Political systems should be such as to provide the forums within which moral argument can take place, and to transform the clash of forces behind the arguments into an interaction of minds, wills, and political power rather than of violent actions.

Polemarchus' observation to Socrates on the road from Piraeus is, however, still with us: you cannot persuade those who will not listen.[10]

Although it is almost never the case, if an act of violence is the only way to open the possibilities for persuasion and argument through non-violent forms, to channel intractable conflicts into intellectual, political and legal processes of resolution, or to express non-acceptance of the despicable acts of evil regimes, it may be morally justifiable. War to end war has been a miserable failure; violence to end violence is no less likely to fail. But the requirements for an act of violence to be morally justifiable may not be impossible to meet, logically or empirically.

DESTRUCTION OF THE STATE

. . . Can violence to destroy a state and to defend a new one being brought into existence then be morally justifiable? Account will need to be taken of the possibilities of uncontrolled violence and vicious repression, as the system seeks to defend its existence and as its attackers increase their stake in success. Assessments should continually be made of the chances for new non-violent measures to bring about the changes sought, after every breakdown of such measures. The inability of destruction to provide, of itself, any better alternative system, should never be forgotten. Nevertheless, in some circumstances, violent action may result in less violence than otherwise, and may, I think, be justified.

If one believes that it may be morally justifiable to punish criminals, the same sorts of arguments would provide moral justification of the "punishment" on moral grounds of tyrants and torturers where existing law and political power allow them otherwise to go unpunished. Even though there may be, in a given situation, no realistic expectation of vindication within a given political system, the victims or intended victims or defenders of such victims of torture or of political violence carried out by tyrants may be morally justified in trying to assure that those who commit evil deeds cannot do so without cost to themselves. Violence to punish torturers and tyrants may be more justifiable than violence to uphold unjust regimes. And where no other way exists to punish the violent and immoral use of power, violence to do so may be justified if punishment ever is, though one may well doubt that punishment can ever be justified.

Of course there is the danger that those judging whether a given case of torture or tyranny deserves punishment are making a mistaken judgment, but we must allow for the possibility that such judgments are correct. We should not make the faulty assumption that those with political power are always more nearly right than those without it. . . .

CAN TERRORISM BE JUSTIFIED?

Do the arguments I have considered concerning violence apply also to terrorism? Terrorism is sometimes defined as "the systematic use of murder, injury, and destruction" to create terror and despair through "indiscriminate" attacks in which "no distinction" is made that might exempt the innocent from being targets of such attacks.[11] Terrorists are sometimes said to "sacrifice all moral and humanitarian considerations for the sake of some political end."[12] If terrorism is defined this way, we may be unable even to raise the question of whether it could be justifiable. As with violence, the question should be open, not shut by definition. Any adequate definition of terrorism must be able to include terrorism carried out by a government as well as by its opponents. If, as some report, terrorist acts "are often viewed in many Third World countries as noble acts of 'freedom fighters,' "[13] we should be able to examine the reasons without having precluded them by definitional fiat.

Robert Young, in an article on terrorism, agrees with most definitions that terrorism is "intimidatory in intent,"[14] but does not agree that terrorist attacks need be "indiscriminate." The targets of terrorism may be the armed forces, the police, and those with political power responsible for repression. Although surprise is "central to the potency of terrorism,"[15] this is not inconsistent with warnings to minimize harm to the innocent. In Young's view, terrorism should only be tactic of last resort where other means of political action are not available. However, as part of an ideological "program of revolutionary struggle," it may be justified, he thinks, as certain wars can be. Its casualties and violence are very limited compared to war. A program including terrorist acts may in his view be the only realistic means to counter state-inspired terrorism, and, if its cause is just and success likely, terrorism may thus be justified.

In one of the most comprehensive discussions, Grant Wardlaw defines political terrorism as "the systematic threat of violence to secure political goals."[16] The purposes may be very varied: "Whilst the primary effect is to create fear and alarm the objectives may be to gain concessions, obtain maximum publicity for a cause, provoke repression, break down social order, build morale in the movement or enforce obedience to it. Several of the objectives may be accomplished simultaneously by a single incident."[17]

Amar Ouzegane, a leader of the Algerian FLN movement trying to gain Algerian independence against the French, wrote of the functions of terrorism that "urban terrorism, our liberating terrorism, functioned as a safety valve. It permitted patriots ulcerated by the unequal struggle, revolted by French injustice . . ., to liberate themselves from an unconscious psychological complex, to keep cool heads, to respect revolutionary discipline."[18]

Interestingly, those who defend terrorism often employ arguments familiar from "just war" discussions. John Dugard writes that "the Third World argument is based largely on a Western philosophical tradition: that of the 'just war.' "[19] He points out that many states "including the major Western powers, have on occasion engaged in acts of terror against civilian populations which completely overshadow the acts of terror committed by national liberation movements . . ."[20] While prohibitions against state terrorism remain unenforced, "it is asking too much," he thinks, "of Third World countries to collaborate in the suppression of the most effective means to counter terror available to national liberation movements."[21]

We might conclude that *if* war can be justified, terrorist acts can be also, if they have certain characteristics. But if terrorism includes, not by definition but in fact, the unnecessary killing of the innocent, it is at least not more justified than war in doing so, though the scale may be smaller. And if comparable good results can be accomplished with far less killing, an alternative to war that would achieve these results through acts intrinsically no worse than those that occur in war would be more justifiable.

But it is almost always possible to show that as limited terrorism is better than war, less violent alternatives to terrorism are better than terrorism, and non-violent pressures are better than violent ones. We might agree that the causing of war, whether through aggression, violent repression, the extermination or expulsion of unwanted populations, or by depriving people of the means to maintain life, is the ultimate crime of violence. If war to prevent the success of those who cause war can be justified, lesser uses of terror and violence can also, sometimes, be justified. But the more tyrants and torturers depend on the support of those around them, the better may be the chances of eroding that support through non-violent pressure. The opponents of evil should not have to sacrifice their lives. But those who use violence must also be prepared to risk their lives.[22] To risk one's life in non-violent protest, if the risk is no greater, and the chance of success and the rightness of the cause are only no less, is surely more justifiable.

NOTES

1. The discussions of more complex and refined definitions in *Violence*, edited by Jerome A. Shaffler (New York: McKay, 1971) are helpful. See also Francis C. Wade, "On Violence," *Journal of Philosophy*, LXVIII, 12 (June 17, 1971), and Joseph Betz, "Violence, Garver's Definition and a Deweyan Correction," *Ethics* 87:4 (July 1977). I shall concentrate in this paper on questions of justification rather than explore those of definition.

2. For arguments concerning what our moral rights to property should and should not include, see Virginia Held, ed., *Property, Profits, and Economic Justice* (Belmont, CA: Wadsworth, 1980). What, from a moral point of view, our "property" is taken to include may affect whether we are "harmed" by its destruction. I shall not in this paper explore the meaning of "harm."

3. Georges Sorel, *Reflections on Violence*, Trans. T. E. Hulme and J. Roth. (London: Collier-Macmillan, 1961) pp. 58–59.

4. Hannah Arendt, "Civil Disobedience," *The New Yorker*, September 12, 1970, pp. 7–105.

5. See e.g. Addison Gayle, Jr., *The Black Situation* (New York: Dell, 1970). See also Stokely Carmichael and Charles V. Hamilton, *Black Power. The Politics of Liberation in America* (New York: Random House, 1967).

6. Joan Bondurant, *Conquest of Violence* (Berkeley, CA: University of California Press, 1965), p. viii.

7. Walter Laqueur, "The Anatomy of Terrorism," in *Ten Years of Terrorism. Collected Views*, eds. Jennifer Shaw, E. F. Gueritz, and A. E. Younger. Royal United Services for Defense Studies. (London: Crane, Russak & Co., 1979) p. 20.

8. Joan Bondurant, see n6 above, p. 227.

9. Immanuel Kant, *The Metaphysical Elements of Justice*, trans. John Ladd (New York: Liberal Arts, 1965) pp. 76–77.

10. Plato, *The Republic*, 328.

11. Paul Wilkinson, "The Laws of War and Terrorism," in *The Morality of Terrorism. Religious and Secular Justifications*, eds. David C. Rapoport and Yonah Alexander (New York: Pergamon Press, 1982) pp. 310–11. See also Michael Walzer, *Just and Unjust Wars* (New York: Basic Books, 1977) especially ch. 12.

12. Paul Wilkinson, *Political Terrorism* (London: Macmillan, 1974) p. 17.

13. John Dugard, "International Terrorism and the Just War," *Stanford Journal of International Studies* XII, 21–37. p. 77.

14. Robert Young, "Revolutionary Terrorism, Crime and Morality," *Social Theory and Practice* vol. 4, no. 3 (Fall 1977) 287–302. p. 288.

15. Ibid., p. 289.

16. Grant Wardlaw, *Political Terrorism* (Cambridge: Cambridge University Press, 1982) p. 13.

17. Ibid., pp. 41–42.

18. Amar Ouzegane, *Le Meilleur Combat* (Paris: Julliard, 1962) p. 257, quoted in Wardlaw, see n16 above, p. 41.

19. John Dugard, see n13 above, p. 77.

20. Ibid., p. 91.

21. Ibid.

22. See Joan Bondurant, n6 above, ch. VI.

NO

Alfred Louch

TERRORISM: THE IMMORALITY
OF BELIEF

Are there actions so abominable that no reasons could justify or contexts excuse them? Answers, I suppose, may differ. My list would include torture, killing for the fun of it, and blowing up the innocent in order to demoralize those one supposes guilty. Others will say, the first two surely . . . but the third, in spite of the apparent atrocity of it, is after all the response to atrocity. The innocent suffer and that is unfortunate, but their death and dismemberment are stages in a radical social surgery. At the end of that process is the millennium, when repression and exploitation will cease.

If we believe that only terror can bring about the millennium, we will be well on the way toward admitting its necessity. Even so, we may find it hard to shake off a rather different impression of the terrorist—the person who carries out the ghastly assignment. This may be so for two related reasons. First, terrorists, like kidnappers, put us in the unenviable position of acceding to their illegitimate demands or becoming accessories to their atrocities. If we comply we only make further demands more likely; if we refuse we feel a joint responsibility for the fate of their victims. Rage is the natural response to this dilemma, and rage does not exactly diminish feelings of moral, as well as personal, distaste.

Second, it is cowardly to attack the defenseless. It speaks of an indifference to violence that is not suitable psychological material for the millennium. Most of all, terrorists are arrogant, acting on beliefs about social causality that the available evidence does not license. Their moral perceptions are equally dulled, since they seem quite unable to distinguish between the repressiveness of totalitarian regimes—Hitler's, Amin's or Stalin's—and those, like the Western democracies, that, even if they limit human freedom, do so within recognizable constraints on political or economic power, and in an atmosphere that allows for some freedom of opinion. They are, in short, fanatics, and fanatics are not part of the good society. They are the effluvia of social unrest, ambition, frustration, and hatred. Even if we allowed that only through fanaticism are great social objectives ever attained, we would still be repelled by the fanatic.

Are we hypocrites if we tacitly approve the consequences while condemning the doer and the deed? It has been suggested to me by my friend and former student, Professor Keith Quincy, that morality has to do with what is done, not with the agent who does it. So we might consistently approve a deed and condemn the doer—approve terror and condemn the terrorist. On the face of it, this distinction amounts to a utilitarian account of action. Of the act we ask: does it result in a balance of good over evil? Of the person: is he or she someone we could like, trust, or regard as a friend? But if we reject a utilitarian calculus—as unworkable or as false to our moral intuitions—we might believe that the judgments about persons are a better index of the morality of actions than the consequences that issue from them. If, along these lines, we saw that only a repulsive character could perform certain acts, we should find this a reason to condemn them.

And this applies to jailers, secret agents, soldiers, informers, and all sorts of people whose business and talent it is to do violent, sordid, and unpleasant things, as well as to terrorists. But most of us acknowledge the necessity of nasty functions, and try not to think about the agency of them, even while condemning noninstitutionalized terror. . . . So the first question is: do we have a leg to stand on in condemning terror?

Another question arises also from our equivocal attitude toward violence. We don't condemn all instances of random or sudden violence. We applaud the act, and from a distance admire the actor, where terror is directed against regimes so hideous and oppressive as Nazi Germany. Many, though obviously not all, will feel similarly equivocal about the methods of internal warfare employed to bring down Chiang Kai-shek, Batista, or Somoza, or to establish the state of Israel. We say that the evil against which we fight is both serious and powerful; only by fighting fire with fire can we hope for a remedy. If at the same time we condemn the PLO, the Red Brigade, the IRA, or the SLA, it must be because we think the targets of these groups are neither evil enough nor powerful enough to warrant such extreme measures. Or we may feel rather more fastidious than they about targets—it is one thing, we say, to blow up dictators, banks, or bridges, quite another to plant bombs in supermarkets where the victims are innocent. We must then ask, is our condemnation of terror selective? And if so, does our distinction between allowed and disallowed forms of terror rest on an assumption that Western societies are really not so bad? We shall doubtless feel at least somewhat tepid about this assumption—embarrassed, perhaps, at finding it in our ideological baggage. This is a second challenge to the moral condemnation of terrorism.

Finally, we shall need to face up to the moral strains under which terror places us. What are we to think of terrorists, and how are we to respond to them? Terrorists commit us to a response which is itself violent, for they are outside the reach of law because they do not acknowledge its authority. They are thus outlaws. But we have few, if any, instructive precedents for dealing with outlaws. This is perhaps the most important dimension of terrorism, but I have, alas, the least to say about it.

I.

Are we hypocrites in condemning terror? Or without sin in casting stones? Suppose we draw the following distinction: there is all the (moral) difference in the world between public institutional sanctions and random individual reprisals. The difference is that the first commands community consent and gives advance warning of the consequences of acting in certain ways. The second raises an idiosyncratic conception of the good, or the just, above the consensus, and applies sanctions without warning. In a community dominated by terror, there is no way that citizens could know their guilt or how to avoid it. In contrast, settled communities have at least institutionalized their barbarities (allowing for the sake of argument that all forms of force applied by the state on individuals are barbaric). An individual has grounds for predicting the state's use of force, and knows how to act in order to avoid it.

Now terrorists say the distinction is meaningless. Law and authority are illusions that tempt the imperceptive to cooperate in their own exploitation. It is odd that this argument has so often paralyzed moral judgment, for it is the most transparent instance of a *tu quoque*. We don't appeal to examples of admitted wickedness as models and justifications of our own conduct. Corporations, banks and the democratic process, in their various ways, may be instruments of exploitation and coercion; for that very reason they hardly serve as an excuse for greater violence. That would be like using the existence of capital punishment in one jurisdiction as a motive for another to resort to torture.

But to construe the argument this way is to miss its effect. Political societies are described in the language of exploitation not to license violence but to paralyze the will of those who give at least tepid allegiance to such societies. We bourgeois feel, hearing the charges, the twinge of guilt at our own practices or those in which we have acquiesced. We are people in glass houses, and that is a frame of mind in which we lose our grip on the important distinction between practices admittedly needing improvement or rectification, and those that are incorrigibly evil.

Nonetheless, here is a sketch of an attempt to maintain that distinction. Unless we are fanatics, we don't believe that a perfect society is possible. Bourgeois regimes, which are so often villified by revolutionaries as the paradigms of exploitation and repression, are marked by severe disparities of advantage and opportunity and by obstacles to legitimate pursuits and the airing of righteous grievances. Nonetheless, some mitigation of these evils is better than none. A state in which, for example, it is possible to appeal through the courts to win relief from police misconduct has to be preferred to one in which the police are wholly immune from citizen complaints, and brutality and torture are the rule. We shall not, having made that judgment, justify the brutality of our own police, or fail to take note of gross injustice, to which venality or race or class consciousness of public officials exposes us. But we will argue that a system like ours, with its partially working constraints on police power, is immensely to be preferred to one in which torture or imprisonment without trial are accepted practices. We don't want to be complacent about our faults, but neither do we want to obliterate the distinction between capricious and lawlike exercises of the police function, simply because both rest on coercion. The policeman's even reluctant reading of the *Miranda* warning to the quaking suspect is not to be compared to the interrogations of a secret police or the staged executions of the terrorist justice. If we cannot find it in our hearts to condemn the terrorist because the police carry guns and sometimes use them too rashly, we evidently believe that violence is evil. Otherwise the example of police brutality would not embarrass us. If we do believe thus, we should be able to distinguish greater and lesser degrees of violence, or greater and lesser control over it. I therefore see no reason to suffer paralysis of judgment on account of *tu quoque* arguments. Let us agree: the act of terror is evil.

II.

If anything more is to be said, it must be by way of extenuation. The terrorist's reasons, or the context of his action, must make a difference. And here, I think, the friends of terror say one of two things. First, they say, you must sometimes fight fire with fire, a slogan designed to show that violence is the only means to a worthy or a necessary end. Second, they complain that systematic (and cunningly disguised) repression prevents legitimate points of view from being heard; violence is the only remaining way to express a certain range of beliefs about politics and society. Let us look at these apologies in turn.

1. If the fighting-fire-with-fire principle applies, terrorists must have good reason to believe either that worse things will happen unless he throws his bombs, or that a more than offsetting good will be brought about, and can only be brought about, in this way. Terrorists seldom

trouble themselves about the eventual good; their future extends only to the destruction of present institutions. So we and they don't know what positive qualities of life the destruction of society aims at. To kill in the name of unspecified and unspecifiable benefits is to kill for no reason at all. This is gratuitous violence, for which no extenuation is produced or sought. It is an immorality of thought as well as act.

Terror as preventive action may seem more promising. Most of us allow that violence might be necessary in self-defense, or to subdue a madman, or to assassinate a tyrant. These cases sometimes—even in the critical light of hindsight—warrant violence. Hitler and Amin are not open to persuasion or vulnerable to other lawful pressures. We know, moreover, that they will certainly commit further atrocities if we fail to kill them. If we are lucky, a single bullet may put an end to the imminent evil. But usually the method is more like war. There will be regretted casualties, as war always brings in its wake; but still more will die, and still more rot in prisons, if the chance isn't taken.

The argument is not unpersuasive. But before it can be assessed to help the terrorist, distinctions must be made. The assassin and guerrilla soldier kill so that atrocities may cease. They may be mistaken, but it is at least plausible to believe that on occasion they are not. It is possible that the evidence supports their actions and excuses the suffering they cause.

But are guerrillas soldiers or terrorists? I have no zeal for definitional disputes, but a matter of importance hangs on the answer to this question. Terrorism, guerrilla warfare and assassination share a form of extenuation. Bloody work is done to prevent bloodier consequences. But in attempting wicked things for virtuous ends, stronger than usual evidence is required to show that the work will indeed bring about the desired future, that it will not have unforeseen effects that cancel out the accomplished good, and that other options for action are unavailable. The Vietnam War protester who sits on the White House lawn may or may not have adequate grounds for his views about the evil of the war or the consequences of withdrawing from it, but because his action is not itself morally momentous—causing at most minor inconvenience to public officials and passersby—we do not oblige him to prove his case beyond the shadow of a doubt. He is, we say, entitled to his opinion. But the assassin who supposes a president must die to end the conflict, or the terrorist who sees the war as a symptom of social malaise and attempts to destroy society by random violence, cannot claim immunity because these are privately held opinions. Can an assassin ever be sure that with the death of his or her target evil will cease, or that it will not bring other unforeseen evils in its wake? Rarely, we say. And those cases for which we may find the grounds sufficient are tyrannies in which present evils are so frightful that our inability to rule out untoward consequences of tyrannicide simply cannot matter. Can the terrorist's theories of social repression ever offer grounds for capricious violence? Here, I think, the answer is that the anti-bourgeois terrorist cannot profit by sharing a common label with the guerrilla or the assassin of lunatic despots. Those who rail against bourgeois society and attempt to bring it to its knees by leaving bombs in supermarkets cannot claim to be frustrating demonstrable and about to

be committed evils. They do not know what specific evils they are preventing; the rhetorical flourishes of repression and exploitation do not serve to identify the alleged evils. They have no evidence to show that the social structure will crack under the pressure of their sporadic violence. And nothing, surely, is more horrifying than the use of tendentious slogans of social theories as bills of indictment against individuals. Yet this is the proposed extenuation offered on behalf of terrorists in the Western world, in Ireland, or in Palestine. No greater atrocity will be prevented by their exploding bombs. Such reasons do not mitigate violence, but simply make light of it.

2. Sometimes terrorists are described as seeking an audience for their views in the only way open to them. We cannot therefore accuse them of doing terrible deeds on the merest pretext of evidence as to their efficacy, because efficacy is not part of the terrorists' immediate intention. Rather, their bombs dramatize their condemnation of the social order. I find this idea bewildering. The message of dismembered housewives is at the very least unclear. By what twisted reasoning can it be supposed that the exploitation of persons will succeed in stating a message about exploitation? Should I be awakened to my status as a wage slave or a manipulated consumer by contemplating this ultimate use of people as means? Why should I not learn instead the lesson that my current exploited state is much to be preferred to the exploitation I may expect at terrorist hands? Those who can say that terrorists are only expressing opinions they have a right to hold and express have failed to appreciate what the exploitation of persons means. They can demonstrate it in their social theories, and fail to notice it in

dreadful fact. These are threadbare defenses indeed.

One last effort at extenuation. Sometimes it is argued that no man is innocent, therefore the terrorist is not guilty—or at least not of slaughtering the innocent. This argument shifts the grounds of mitigation from the reasons for acting to the context in which it takes place. But what can that mean? Not, surely, some Kafka-like eschatology, which when applied to practical affairs converts killers into agents of divine retribution, even though an element of just such madness can be detected in the minds of many terrorists. In a more mundane spirit, one might suppose that the loss of the status of being innocent means only that a state of total war exists. Many who could not be connected positively to the war effort died at Dresden and Hiroshima, but their presence there made them accidental victims of a strategy with a rightful cause, the defeat of the Axis powers. So terrorists are at war with society, fighting for its demise through tactics imposed on them by the logic of the situation. To argue in this way, whether about bombing Hiroshima or the Bank of America, sidesteps the issue as to whether the probabilities of good results can justify such atrocities. We might answer—as many friends of terrorism would—that we lacked such warrant in Dresden or Hiroshima. What, then, would lead us to suppose that the terrorist declaration of total war is any different? Indeed, it is ludicrous to suppose that a half-dozen self-appointed rescuers of humanity are in any position to declare war, total or otherwise, or to appoint themselves just executioners of the wicked against a nation of 50 or 250 million people. Such a defense is just another instance of banal reasons thought adequate for the commission of violent crimes.

It is, of course, part of the terrorist's eschatology to believe that citizens of modern states are hopelessly corrupted by their affiliation, and by their exploitation. To say no one is innocent may mean just this—some are exploiters and die for that, others are exploited and are thus past saving. So in pulling down prisons as centers of repression, guards should die as agents of repression, and the prisoners as victims of it. Such a bloody salvation can only be self-immolating; terrorists must be victims of the social order also. At least they do not, as far as I know, come down from the sky, though some of them, or their defenders on university campuses, may appear to have come up out of the earth.

III.

So much for extenuation. But what of us? Terror is a fact of life to which we must respond somehow or other. Terror tempts us to violent reprisal because it strikes us as irrationally violent. By the same token, we want to say that terrorists are mad. And so our minds are diverted to thoughts of therapy and commiseration. This response is self-deceiving, unless we remember [Joseph] Conrad's remark in Lord Jim: "how much certain forms of evil are akin to madness, derived from intense egotism, inflamed by resistance." On the other hand, a violent response to violence caters to the propaganda of terror. Our violence supports the terrorist's otherwise shabby case, or seems to do so for many. And so we seek accommodation, which appears as a sign of the success of terrorist methods. In the end, we must reluctantly admit that the terrorist's uncompromising position makes it impossible to treat him or her as other than the enemy—as an outlaw. Except in war we lack the conventions of violent reprisal. And even in war we maintain the minimum conventions of civility; we recognize that our enemies hold other, but still plausible, allegiances. Men and women who blow up supermarkets and glory in their deed have moved beyond the reach of that courtesy. But what it means to treat someone as an outlaw is a matter on which I fear I have no more to say, except to say that it is what we ought to think about.

POSTSCRIPT

Is Terrorism Ever Justified?

Held carries out a very careful analysis of violence and terrorism. One particularly relevant point she makes is this: you cannot persuade those who will not listen. In an open and democratic society, there are generally many voices and many opportunities for persuasion. But in some cases, such as in the case of repressive regimes, the opportunities for persuasion do not exist. To say that there may be no terrorist activities in these cases seems to rule in support of the repressive regimes. On the other hand, Held issues the warning that any such terrorist actions may completely backfire: an increase in violent and criminal activity of all kinds, or even more governmental repression, may result. In any case, there are usually less drastic (and less unpredictable) alternative actions than terrorist ones, and she recommends these.

Louch often seems to presuppose that terrorists are acting within an open and democratic society, and so concludes that they have no place. But sometimes, especially when he mentions specific repressive leaders—Hitler, Amin, and Stalin, for example—he hints at another view. He sometimes credits terrorists with beliefs that they may not have, such as the belief that their terrorist activities might lead to a utopia or to what he sometimes calls "the millennium." Louch's criticism may apply to some groups. However, many of the most famous terrorist groups do not seek a utopia. Rather, they desire a radically improved political situation, usually of quite local extent. For example, Palestinian terrorists seek a Palestinian homeland on the West Bank of the Jordan River. They want Jerusalem, and they have various ideas about the legitimacy of the state of Israel and the presence of the Jews in the Middle East. Also, Irish terrorism against the British is generally focused on eliminating the British from Northern Ireland and reunifying all of Ireland.

These terrorist concerns are typical in their scope. They aim only for a limited and rather specific political change.

The current political situations, which are always subject to change, and the history of actual terrorist programs may be gathered from recent national histories and news concerning places of terrorist activity, such as Northern Ireland and Israel. Such sources are useful for investigating particular terrorist organizations.

A very thorough examination of terrorism is given in Grant Wardlaw, *Political Terrorism: Theory, Tactics, and Counter-Measures*, 2d ed. (Cambridge University Press, 1989). See also chapter 12 of Michael Walszer's *Just and Unjust Wars* (Basic Books, 1977).

ISSUE 20

Can Modern War Be Just?

YES: Robert L. Phillips, from *War and Justice* (University of Oklahoma Press, 1984)

NO: Robert L. Holmes, from *On War and Morality* (Princeton University Press, 1989)

ISSUE SUMMARY

YES: Professor of philosophy Robert L. Phillips argues that modern war, like any other war, can indeed be just if it is initiated and conducted within the requirements for a just war, which he specifies.

NO: Professor of philosophy Robert L. Holmes argues that war in the modern world is not justified. He dissociates himself from an absolute pacifism and argues that modern war involves means that always violate justice.

People sometimes think that "anything goes" in war and that morality does not apply. They think that during war, people are not morally accountable for their actions. One response to this idea is to consider the fact that in most (if not all) wars, soldiers have raped civilians. Are these rapes acceptable because they occurred during a war? Or is the idea that "anything goes" wrong in this case? The defender of the "anything goes" position could still say that while soldiers must observe ordinary moral demands with respect to civilians, they are nevertheless freed from observing any moral demands when dealing with enemy soldiers. But what about people who work in munitions factories but are not soldiers, soldiers who are medics, and nonmilitary politicians who vote for and support the war? Does the "anything goes" position allow that enemy soldiers could be tortured, held without food or water, or made the subjects of medical experiments, but the politicians who voted for the war and supply the funds for the purchase of military hardware must be safeguarded? One who maintains that "anything goes" in war seems to sidestep the responsibility of having to make moral distinctions. Does it seem true that war can somehow excuse all action, and that war can always make all right what would otherwise have been serious wrongs?

Furthermore, even if the "anything goes" position can be framed in a defensible way, it still has to face an important question. *If* what would have been morally wrong in peacetime is excused by wartime conditions, then it becomes very important to discriminate between the time of peace and the time of war and to monitor carefully the transition from peacetime to wartime. Should we say that soldiers of one army who wish to destroy the soldiers of another army should make sure that war is declared first so that whatever they do is all acceptable? If morality applies in peacetime but not in wartime, and since most wars are declared in peacetime, then the declaration of war will have to conform to moral demands. So even if we grant some version of the view that "anything goes" in war, morality still applies at the time when a declaration of war is being considered.

One reason to be concerned so much with the "anything goes" view is that the view seems to be popular, although most people who think seriously about war do not subscribe to the view at all. As much as they differ, both authors of the following selections agree that morality applies to war as much as it applies to anything else.

Perhaps one reason why some people subscribe to the view that morality does not apply to war is because they fear that war will be unable to pass moral muster, but they still want to reserve the right to go to war.

Robert L. Phillips believes that wars will continue to be waged. He also believes that it is important that they be declared and carried out in a just way. He supports what has traditionally been called the just war, or *bellum justum*, theory. There are two parts to the just war theory, which correspond to the two objections that were raised above with respect to the "anything goes" view. There are the demands for *jus ad bellum*, which are moral demands for justice in going to war, and there are the demands for *jus in bello*, which are moral demands for the proper conduct of the war itself. Justice in war also requires adherence to what has become known as the principle of double effect, which Phillips also defends. This principle is designed to show that it is morally justified to bomb enemy military targets even if one knows that at the same time innocent civilians will be killed.

Robert L. Holmes, who opposes Phillips on the overall issue, agrees that in order to fulfill the demands of the just war theory, we would have to satisfy the demands of both *just ad bellum* and *jus in bello*, but he stresses the point that these two sorts of demands are not independent of each other. If going to war is to be justified, he argues, then the necessary means to waging war must be justified. But in the modern world, the means that we would have to use are *not* justified, so going to war is not justified in the first place.

YES

Robert L. Phillips

WAR AND JUSTICE

This . . . is a defense of the traditional position on the justified use of force by political states, a doctrine commonly labeled *bellum justum* and subdivided into questions having to do with grounds for initiating combats (*jus ad bellum*) and questions having to do with the correct behavior of combatants in wartime (*jus in bello*). . . .

[S]ince war is probably inevitable it is advisable to attend seriously to the question of how to fight it morally. . . .

I outline below, in point form, the doctrine of the just war, and in the following [text] I shall expand upon the points listed. . . .

BELLUM JUSTUM

Jus ad Bellum

I. Last resort.
II. Declared by legitimate authority.
III. Morally justifiable:
   A. Defense against aggression.
   B. Correction of an injustice that has gone uncorrected by legitimate authority "in another place."
   C. Reestablishment of a social order which will distribute justice.
   D. Undertaken with the intention of bringing about peace.

Jus in Bello

I. Proportionality: The quantity of force employed or threatened must always be morally proportionate to the end being sought in war.
II. Discrimination: Force must never be applied in such a way as to make noncombatants and innocent persons the intentional objects of attack. The only appropriate targets in war are combatants.
   A. The Principle of Double Effect: In a situation where the use of force can be foreseen to have actual or probable multiple effects, some of which are evil, culpability does not attach to the agent if the following conditions are met:

1. The action must carry the intention to produce morally good consequences.
2. The evil effects are not *intended* as ends in themselves or as means to other ends, good or evil.
3. The permission of collateral evil must be justified by considerations of proportionate moral weight.

JUS AD BELLUM

The first thing to note is that the standard translation of *bellum justum* as "just war" may be misleading if it is supposed that war can somehow be itself endowed with moral substance. On the traditional view, war is always an evil insofar as it involves a physical attack upon another person. There may, however, be situations where fighting is the lesser of evils, but in such cases the use of force must be *justified*. Prima facie, attacking another person is evil and, indeed, can never be anything else qua attack. But we may upon occasion find that it is the only means of avoiding an even greater evil. Thus, it may be less misleading to speak of "justified war" instead of "just war."

I. Last Resort

The foregoing is relevant to the first consideration in the outline. Although war may be sometimes justified, it will always be morally correct to effect it only after it is clear that other means are not adequate to resolve the issue. It is a mistake to suppose that "last" necessarily designates the final move in a chronological series of actions. It *may* do so, as when a policeman pursuing a suspect goes through the steps of challenging the fleeing suspect verbally, then firing a warning shot if that fails, and finally firing at him as a last resort. There may also be cases, however, where time does not permit actually attempting less coercive means. If terrorists are holding some hostages and announce that they will kill them all in two minutes, we would certainly be justified in using force as our first act (Entebbe-style), though it would still be as a last resort. . . .

II. Declared by Legitimate Authority.

The claim that war must be declared by legitimate authority only is in some ways ambiguous. . . .

The difficulty here is . . . over the question: Who, or what, *is* legitimate authority? The claim that war may only be undertaken by legitimate authority, while perfectly correct, may involve question-begging where the issue which provoked fighting is precisely a dispute about who is the bearer of that authority. . . .

The paradox is . . . that war itself is most frequently the means whereby questions of legitimacy are decided in the eyes of the community of nations (though rival claimants may not accept this verdict). Thus in the context of a civil war the principle runs into problems. Here again we are faced with a situation where *bellum justum* ramifies into larger issues in political philosophy, particularly with those concerning de facto and de jure authority. . . . The claim that war may be undertaken only by legitimate authority reflects a political reality, namely, that factions at war *will* seek to establish their legitimacy. No matter how divided they may be on other issues, they both seek to be recognized as legitimate by their own people and by the community of nations. Thus they will both agree that the authority to use force is decided by legitimacy. . . . Our attention is thereby turned from questions of simple power to gain control and toward the issue of the right to govern. . . . [O]ne rarely (if ever) finds states basing their claims to use force on force *alone*.

III. Morally Justifiable

(A) The right to self-defense against an aggressor has always been regarded as fundamental by most just-war advocates. . . . [T]he bulk of just-war thinking suggests that, while the death of any person is an evil, an aggressor who refuses to stop what he is doing is responsible for his own death. What a person does not have a right to do is intend the death of the aggressor, in the sense that the purpose of his action should be to stop the aggressor from doing what he is doing. The aggressor's death may thus be accepted or justified as a collateral event if the only means of stopping him is killing. . . .

A state, like an individual, also has the right of defense against aggression. . . .

(B) The traditional version of *bellum justum* holds that a Christian prince has an obligation to intervene in the affairs of another state if there is an unjustice there that continues to be uncorrected by legitimate authority. . . .

(C) If the purpose of political society is the distribution of justice, and if war is a permissible political act, then the purpose of war must ultimately be directed toward reestablishing a just order. This position is formal in the sense that it does not itself specify any particular ideology or social model but is dependent upon such things for its content.

(D) While war may sometimes be justified, it is always morally undesirable as a "state of affairs." Thus the decision to go to war must be accompanied with the intention to effect peace. This rules out various theories which recommend war as therapeutic or as desirable for the glory it brings the sovereign. Another provision which is sometimes attached to (D) holds that war should not be undertaken unless there is a reasonable prospect of winning. This reflects the fact that war is essentially an *agreement* between two states to settle a dispute by arbitrament of arms. A state is not morally justified in resorting to war and subjecting its citizens to death unless there is at least a chance of favorable outcome. . . .

To summarize *jus ad bellum*: Wars of aggression are permitted under the traditional doctrine only if the cause is just; but all wars of aggression are prohibited under the modern interpretation, for no matter how serious the injury to a state, modern warfare is an immoral means for settling grievances and altering existing conditions. This amendment has been made for two reasons. First, the destructiveness of modern war makes it a wholly disproportionate means for the resolution of international disputes and for the redress of grievances, even where they are just. Second, to admit the right of states to initiate combats, even to correct injustice, would impede efforts of the world community to establish a judicial method of outlawing war altogether.

A war of defense against the injustice of aggression is morally permissible in both the traditional and the modern view. This is perceived as in no way a contradiction of the concern for peace, for peace may require defense. . . .

JUS IN BELLO

The "other half" of *bellum justum* is *jus in bello*, or the doctrine of just behavior in combat. We return to the introductory outline:

I. Proportionality

The principle of proportionality holds that in cases where the use of force is justified it cannot be employed in absolutely any measure. Obviously, if the aim of war is the correction of injustice, then the level of force must not be such as to create new and greater injustices. . . .

II. Discrimination

What is true for proportionality is a fortiori true for the principle of discrimination. The notion that force ought to be morally justified only if it can be employed in a discriminate manner lies at the heart of *jus in bello*. The principle of double effect is, in turn, at the heart of discrimination.

(A) Put as simply as possible, by emphasizing intention as the defining feature of moral actions, the supporters of *bellum justum* attempt to mark a difference between killing in war and murder in two different cases. First, the killing of enemy combatants in a justified war may be morally acceptable under some circumstances. Second, the killing of noncombatants incidental to the prosecution of a necessary military operation in a justified war may also be morally acceptable under some circumstances. . . .

Double effect is derived from a quite general criterion of moral judgment enunciated succinctly but clearly by Aquinas: "now moral acts take their species according to what is intended and not according to what is beside the intention, since this is accidental" (*Summa* 2.2, q. 64, art. 7).

Aquinas, I take it, is arguing not that the consequences of actions are morally irrelevant but, rather, that when one raises questions about the morality of a particular action (as opposed to its utility, its beauty, and so on) one is inevitably making reference to the agent's intentions. "Accidental" is used here not exclusively to mean the unforeseen but to include the foreseen but undesired consequences of the action. "Accidental" may be understood as "collateral."

Following this line, we may summarize the principle in the following way: In a situation where the use of force can be seen to have actual or probable multiple effects, some of which are evil, culpability does not attach to the agent if the following conditions are met: (1) the action is intended to produce morally good consequences; (2) the evil effects are not intended as ends in themselves or as means to other ends, good or evil; and (3) the permission of collateral evil must be justified by considerations of proportionate moral weight.

How do these considerations apply to the combat situation? . . .

If force is ever to be morally justified, its employment must be against a target other than a person as such. One must not be directly seeking the death of another human being either as such or as a means to some further end. Therefore, the intention or purpose of the act of force must be toward *restraint* of the aggressor. This is the beginning of an answer to the pacifist. For he and the defender of *bellum justum* are surely in agreement, and correctly so, that the death of another human being ought never to be directly willed if the target is the man himself in his humanity or the man who represents the values of the enemy in a particular historical situation (this prohibition must imply the intrinsic value of other persons). Yet, if force may be justified, then what is the target? The answer must be that the proper target of the discriminate use of force is not the man himself but the combatant *in* the man.

It may be objected that it is a logical impossibility to separate out the totality of actions plus the underlying rationale for such behavior which together constitute the combatant in the man. . . . A soldier going into combat with the intention of restraining or incapacitating combatants must know before he ever lifts a weapon that combat will result in the death of a great many persons.

A utilitarian might put the objection in the following way: Jones and Smith both go into combat armed with machine guns. Jones, a supporter of the traditional view, carries with him the intention to incapacitate or restrain the aggressor, whereas Smith intends merely to kill as many of the enemy as he can in order to avoid being killed himself. On meeting the enemy they both open fire, and they both kill one enemy each. What difference does "intention" make from the moral point of view? In both cases an act of extreme violence, the unleashing of a stream of bullets, has resulted in the death of a person. A corpse lies before both Smith and Jones—this is the brute, ultimate fact which no amount of "intentional" redescription can alter. Thus, there is only *one* action here, the killing (possibly murder) of a human being.

In trying to answer this there are two things that have to be said about intention. The first has to do with the way in which awareness of an agent's intentions is crucial in understanding the meaning of an action and consequently in knowing how correctly to describe it. If one were to universalize the utilitarian's position on the irrelevance of intention, the results would be quite disastrous for any attempt to understand human action. Setting the moral question entirely aside, we would be unable to make intelligible whole classes of human behavior if we supposed that such behavior could even be described as human action without making intention central. That is, there are cases where two quite different actions are identical with respect to result, observable behavior, and foreknowledge of the result; and the *only* way to distinguish the two is by reference to intention. As an example, take the case of self-killing. If we follow the critic's suggestion and consider as relevant only foreknowledge of result, behavior patterns, and end result (a corpse), then suicide would be effectively defined as *any* action which the agent knew would bring about his own death. This is clearly absurd, for it would not permit us to distinguish between an officer who shoots himself in order to avoid a court-martial and an officer of the same regiment who courageously fights a rear-guard action in such a way that he knows he will not survive. In both cases there is foreknowledge of one's own death, there are objective behavior patterns leading to that result, and there is the result itself. They differ importantly only with respect to intention. Intention is what makes them different actions. To put the point in a general way, failure to take account of intention means that we are unable to make the difference between doing x in order that y shall result and doing x knowing that y will result.[1]

Smith and Jones both have foreknowledge of the impending death of the enemy, they both take identical action, and the result is the same—the enemy soldier is dead. And yet there are two different actions here: Jones does x knowing that y will result; Smith does x in order that y shall result. . . .

The crucial difference between Smith and Jones is that the latter is logically committed to behaving differently toward those enemy soldiers who have removed themselves from the role of combatant than is his companion Smith. The belief that force must be directed against the combatant and not against the man is the only presupposition which could provide a moral basis for taking prisoners. . . . To those who argue that there is no relevant difference between killing in war and murder in the case of one combatant killing another, we may reply that it is possible, given a well-thought-out doctrine for the justification of the use of force, to direct forceful actions in such a way that while the death of the enemy may be foreknown it is not willed. The purpose of combats as expressed in the actions of individual soldiers is the incapacitation or restraint of an enemy combatant from doing what he is doing as a soldier in a particular historical situation; it is not the killing of a man. This is the essence of the distinction between killing in war and murder in the case of combatants, and the moral relevance of the premise is exhibited in the obligation to acknowledge prisoner immunity, an obligation not incumbent upon someone who fails to observe the central distinction between the man and the combatant in the man.[2] . . .

So far we have been discussing double effect exclusively in connection with the killing of enemy combatants in an attempt to deal with the criticism that all killing in war is murder. We must now tackle the "other half" of that criticism, namely, that the killing of noncombatants in war is murder. . . .

The problem of noncombatant immunity is frequently thought to center upon the difficulty of distinguishing a separate class of noncombatants, particularly in modern warfare. This is, I think, a large mistake, and it arises in part from an excessively literal reading of war solidarity propaganda. In fact, it is relatively easy to distinguish, in any historical war, whole classes of people who cannot, save in the inflamed world of the propagandist, be said to be combatants in any sense which would make them the object of attack. . . . Generally speaking, classes of people engaged in occupations which they would perform whether or not a war were taking place, or services rendered to combatants both in war and out, are considered immune. This would exempt, for example, farmers and teachers (since education and food are necessities in and out of war) but not merchant sailors transporting war materiel or railway drivers in charge of munitions trains. In other words, the soldiers who are now eating and studying would have to do these things even if they were not soldiers, so that classes of people supplying those sorts of goods and services may be said to be immune from attack, whereas those who are engaged in the production and supply of goods used only in war are not immune. And, of course, certain classes of people may be said to be permanently noncombatant— young children, the mentally defective, and those who are in various ways physically incapacitated. Again, some "hard" or limiting cases will arise, particularly in guerrilla war, but they are less numerous than is sometimes supposed.

The *real* difficulty is not in delineating classes of individuals who merit immunity but in deciding what constitutes a direct attack upon them, for it is plausible to suppose that the deaths of noncombatants can be excused only if their deaths can be construed as collateral or beside the intention of the perpetrators. . . .

Traditional just-war theory distinguishes persons qua persons and persons qua combatants, and it makes this distinction central to its justification of the use of force. Specifically, the death of no *person* should be willed. This maxim constitutes a moral precondition for soldiers fighting in a justified war. . . . [The soldier's] target is the combatant in the person and not the person qua person. . . . War is a morally justified arbitrament of arms aimed at resolving by means of discriminate and proportional force an injustice which is incapable of resolution by other means. . . .

[I]n targeting the combatant and not the person, . . . our concern is to incapacitate the combatant, not to kill or punish the person. Recalling the distinction between doing x that y may result and doing x knowing that y will result, the killing of the enemy soldier may be accepted if that is the only means to remove him from the role of combatant. This is the distinction between killing in war and murder . . .

[I]f mankind is to survive, we must undertake the difficult intellectual work of thinking about how to *restrain* war . . . . [W]ar is not going to go away, . . . [and] the way of salvation in this matter is to achieve a nexus of morality and prudence. *Bellum justum* does precisely that.

NOTES

1. This is a modification of an example in A. MacIntyre, "The Idea of a Social Science," in *Against the Self-Images of the Age* (London: Duckworth, 1971), pp. 211–29.

2. There are many excellent discussions of the problem of prisoner immunity. The best is in M. Ramsey, *The Just War.*

NO

ON WAR AND MORALITY

My contention is that war in the modern world is not morally justified. I say "in the modern world" because my aim is not to try to assess wars that have been fought throughout past history, much less those that might be conceived in the imaginations of philosophers or writers of science fiction. The consideration of some of those is useful for purposes of illustration or the clarification of the finer points of theoretical analysis. But they are not the wars of vital concern to people. The wars that engage our moral sensibilities are those which nations are prepared to wage today, for whose preparation they gear their economies, and into whose waging they pour their wealth, their hopes, and their youth.

The argument is not that wars under all conceivable conditions are morally impermissible, an absolutist position that properly understood, is neither particularly interesting nor defensible. My position differs little in principle from that of the ordinary person. He does not believe that all wars under all conceivable circumstances are justified, but only that war under certain conditions is justified. The difference between his position and mine concerns what the conditions are. He believes that war is justified in circumstances calling for national defense, or to assist in the defense of other nations, and the like, whereas I maintain that the conditions that might theoretically justify war simply are not met in the actual world, hence that war is impermissible in the world as we know it. . . .

When people talk about the morality of war, it is usually to proclaim that we all "know" that war is wrong. However, they usually continue with a "But . . ." and proceed to say that although we all hate war, nonetheless some wars are necessary to avoid greater evils. And in any event, there have always been wars and always will be, and you cannot change that unless you change human nature.

This combination of views—that war is immoral but nonetheless necessary—effectively removes the need to question the morality of war. Its wrongness has already been conceded in a way that allows for the continuation of war and even for a belief in its inevitability.

From Robert L. Holmes, *On War and Morality* (Princeton University Press, 1989). Copyright © 1989 by Princeton University Press. Reprinted by permission.

Those who take this line do not mean that war is wrong in the sense I mean it, however. What they mean is that war is bad, or unfortunate, or tragic, not that it is morally impermissible. And these are different modes of assessment. Plagues, pestilence, floods, and droughts are bad, but they are not immoral. The reason they are not is because they are not the acts of rational beings. Certain of them can be caused by the actions of such beings. But even then it is the act of bringing them about that is immoral, not the phenomenon itself. Everyone but the most fervent glorifier of war agrees that war is bad. That is not the issue. What is at issue is whether it is wrong. What I mean by saying that war is wrong is not only that it is bad but that it ought not to be waged, that governments ought not to declare and fight wars, societies ought not to provide them with the means by which to do so, and individuals ought not to sanction, support, and participate in wars. . . .

MY CONCERN . . . IS WITH THE JUST WAR doctrine in the Western tradition, where it has been heavily influenced by Christianity, and in particular with some of its more recent formulations. I shall not present a history of the evolution of the tradition; that has been done by others and would be beside the point of our present concerns. My aim, rather, is to examine those aspects of the tradition that bear most directly upon my central argument concerning the morality of war and to assess the just war theory as an approach to the morality of war.

Two principal objections have been brought against the just war approach to war, neither of which, in my judgment, is successful, but one of which helps to focus a third objection that I think is decisive.

The first concerns alleged consequences of the prevalence of just war theorizing in certain historical periods. It is sometimes said that the most terrible wars in history occurred during the ascendancy of the just war theory and that the longest periods of relative tranquillity occurred when the theory was in eclipse. . . .

But as tempting as it may be to dismiss the just war approach on these grounds, claims of the preceding sort are difficult to substantiate. . . .

The second objection bears upon the changing character of war in the nuclear age. It holds that the nuclear age, with the threat of annihilation in the case of an all-out war between the superpowers, has rendered the just war theory obsolete. Michael Walzer, for example, speaks of the "monstrous immorality that our policy contemplates, an immorality we can never hope to square with our understanding of justice in war," adding that "nuclear weapons explode the theory of just war."[1] Various just war theorists, including James Turner Johnson, William V. O'Brien, and Robert L. Phillips,[2] defend the theory and argue that it is relevant to the contemporary age and, indeed, represents the only defensible way of thinking about the problem of morality and war. . . .

MOST MODERN THEORISTS . . . DEVOTE LITtle attention to the question of *whether* war is justified; they assume that it is and ask only under what conditions it is justified and how it is to be conducted justly. Their actual prescriptions, in fact, differ little from those of political realists, and apart from the underlying rationales they provide for them it would be difficult to tell them apart. If anything, the just war theorists may be more hardline than political realists, which suggests that adopting a moral perspective does not per se make it less likely that one will be militaristic. They tend to be strongly anticommunist, particularly anti-Soviet, to be pro-nuclear deterrence, and to feel that one is sometimes justified in initiating a war. All of them agree, however, that *jus in bello* requires that the conduct of war be limited. . . .

If now we return to the second of the objections . . . concerning the relevance of the just war approach to the nuclear age, we may observe that [just war theorists] may . . . be correct in saying in response to that objection that a limited use of nuclear weapons would not necessarily escalate into an all-out war. No one can know for certain. If *that* is what is meant by saying that the just war theory is relevant to the nuclear age, the point can be granted and the second objection considered met.

But there is another reply to the objection that is more telling. It is that even if [just war theorists] should be wrong about the possibility of keeping a limited nuclear war limited, all that would follow is that by just war criteria themselves an all-out war would be unjust. The fact that a certain type of war turns out to be unjust does not show that the just war theory is inapplicable to it; it shows only that it yields a certain outcome when applied to that type of war.[3] So if the question is whether the nuclear age has rendered the just war theory obsolete in the sense of showing that its criteria are no longer appropriate for the assessment of war, the answer is that it has not. Whether some, or all, or no nuclear wars turn out to be just by just war criteria is immaterial. That those assessments can be made shows the relevance of the the-

ory to nuclear war in the sense its advocates intend.

The preceding discussion suggests a third and more serious objection to the just war doctrine. . . . [T]here are serious problems in reconciling the claims of *jus ad bellum* with those of *jus in bello* with regard to whether a just cause sometimes warrants, or at least excuses, violations of moral constraints in the conduct of war. A more fundamental question is whether even a war that is just according to both *jus ad bellum* and *jus in bello* criteria will still unavoidably involve the violation of moral constraints; whether, that is, there is something in the very nature of war that renders it wrong and that is not dealt with directly by the just war theory. The just war theory says that if certain conditions are met, it is permissible to go to war; and it says further that if certain other conditions are met, one's manner of conducting the war is moral. What it does not do is to ask whether there are things that one unavoidably does even when *all* of these conditions are met which cannot be justified morally. If there are, then the just war theory is defective in a far more serious way than suggested by either of the first two objections.

I believe that there are. . . . But the issue is complex and requires an examination of the relationship between *jus ad bellum* and *jus in bello*.

A WAR . . . IS JUSTIFIED IF IT IS CHARACTERIZED by *jus ad bellum*: if, that is, the conditions constituting justice in the resort to war are met. These include but are not limited to a just cause. Traditionally . . . one had to have legitimate authority and a right intention as well, with various other requirements often added, such as that the war be a last resort, have a likelihood of success, that the use of force be restrained, and that there be proportionality in the resultant good and evil.

A justified war, however, is not necessarily a just war. To be fully just a war must be characterized by both *jus ad bellum* and *jus in bello*. A war obviously cannot be just if one is unjustified in entering upon it in the first place, but neither can it be just, however just the cause and right the intention, if it utilizes indefensible means.[4] . . .

Notice that I am concerned here with what is morally justified in the conduct of war, not with what is legally justified. There exist certain rules, known as the laws of war, generally accepted as governing the conduct of warfare on all sides. . . . This, however, is not my concern at the moment. My concern is with what is morally justified in warfare, whether or not it coincides with what is legally permissible. . . .

Let us call the principle that one may do whatever is necessary to prosecute a just war a principle of just necessity. . . .

According to this view, . . . whatever justifies resorting to war in the first place justifies the means necessary to winning it (or achieving one's objectives, if they fall short of victory). There are no independent moral constraints upon the conduct of war. This represents what may be called an internalist view of the relationship between *jus ad bellum* and *jus in bello*, in the sense that the standards for judging *jus in bello* are already, as it were, contained in the standards for judging *jus ad bellum*.

Distinguished from this, however, is an externalist view, which holds that there are independent standards for judging *jus in bello*—independent, that is, of *jus ad bellum*. Whatever the justice of one's resort to war, there are in this view limits to what one may do in conducting it. The most prominent of these concerns the treatment of innocent persons, with writers like Ramsey, Phillips, and Anscombe maintaining that there is an absolute prohibition against the intentional killing of such persons.[5] . . .

To justify the pursuit of victory in war requires showing that the necessary means to that end are justified. The permissibility of going to war provides no assurance they will be. One may not even know fully what those means are until the war has progressed, perhaps nearly to its conclusion. Yet, according to the usual thinking in just war theory, one may know in advance of going to war whether or not he is justified in so doing. If that is true, then the standards for *jus ad bellum* cannot by themselves, determine the standards for *jus in bello*.

This means that the internalist position, and with it the principle of just necessity, must be rejected. It is not the end that justifies the means but the means (among other things) that justify the end.[6]

This has even more far-reaching implications. Both the internalist and the externalist assume that war may be just; they differ only over the criteria for *jus in bello*. But if the impermissibility of the means necessary to win a war means that one may not justly pursue victory in that war, then the impermissibility of the acts necessary to the very *waging* of war mean that one may not justly wage war, whatever one's objectives. Waging war requires justifying the means of so doing as much as winning a war requires justifying the means to that end.[7]

To justify going to war, then, that is, to establish *jus ad bellum* in the first place, requires showing that what one would be doing by waging it is justified. If a way is justified, then the necessary means to waging it will indeed *be* justified—but not because they are legitimated by the justice of the war assessed independently of those means. They will be justified because to be justified in going to war requires establishing antecedently that those means are permissible. Again, it is not the end that justifies the means but the permissibility of the means (including the killing and destroying that are part of the nature of warfare) that, along with satisfaction of the other requirements of *jus ad bellum*, justifies the end.

The point is that killing and destruction are inherent in warfare, and unless they can be justified, war cannot be justified. It will by its very nature be wrong. . . .

The relevant question . . . is whether all of what one does in the course of fighting a war can be morally justified (by which I mean, all of what one does that is associated with the nature of war; obviously one can do many gratuitously barbarous things that are unessential to the aims of war and that are morally prohibited). . . . [I]n addition to justifying the *means* of conducting war as part of justifying the resort to war, one must also justify those acts which are *constitutive* of the waging of war by whatever means. War by its nature is organized violence, the deliberate, systematic causing of death and destruction. This is true whether the means employed are nuclear bombs or bows and arrows. Often it is the doing of psychological violence as well. And . . . it is presumptively wrong to do violence to persons in these ways. So given that one can know to a virtual certainty that he commits himself to doing these things in going to war, fully to

justify going to war requires justifying these acts as well. A necessary condition of the justifiable pursuit of *any objectives* in war, by *any means* whatever (hence a necessary condition of the satisfaction of the criteria of both *jus ad bellum* and *jus in bello*), is that one be justified in engaging in such killing and violence in the first place. . . .

[T]his means that most attempts to justify war from the early just war theorists to the present day are inadequate. For they do not meet this necessary condition. . . .

Most just war theorists proceed . . . as though they assume that one can justify the resort to war independently of, and antecedently to, justifying both the necessary means of conducting it and the acts constitutive of waging it. . . .

[A]ttention in *jus ad bellum* must be shifted away from the almost exclusive concern with the offenses and ancillary conditions commonly thought to justify war to a consideration of the precise nature of what one is doing in the waging of it; not, as in traditional accounts of *jus in bello*, starting from the assumption that war is justified and needs only to be waged humanely, but rather starting with an open mind about whether it is ever justified in the first place. *Unless one can justify the actions necessary to waging war, he cannot justify the conduct of war and the pursuit of its objectives; and if he cannot do this, he cannot justify going to war.* . . .

IF THE MEANS NECESSARY TO WAGING WAR cannot be justified, then war cannot be justified and no war can be just. Not only must there be moral constraints upon the *conduct* of war even if the war is in all other particulars justified; the possibility must be recognized that there are moral constraints upon the treatment of persons that prohibit the *waging* of war in the first place, that is, even engaging in the limited killing and destruction that otherwise just wars entail. . . .

My concern [here] shall be with the killing of innocent persons. Nothing is more central to the moral assessment of war, and this issue is at the heart of the question whether the waging of war can be justified, whatever other limitations are imposed upon its conduct. . . . [T]here is no stronger moral presumption than that against the doing of violence to innocent persons. And knowingly killing them against their will is to do violence to them. This does not . . . of itself mean that such killing is never justified; whether that is so is beyond my present concerns. But it does mean that the burden is upon those who would kill innocent persons to justify so doing, not upon those who believe it wrong to show that it is wrong. . . .

WHETHER WAR, OR AT LEAST MODERN WAR, which shall be our concern henceforth, inevitably entails the killing of innocent persons cannot be answered independently of a consideration of what constitutes innocence. Here one encounters disagreement. Some argue that virtually everyone in wars between states is non-innocent, others that nearly everyone in such wars is innocent. The most common strategy is to substitute the categories of noncombatancy and combatancy for innocence and noninnocence and to ignore the problems associated with the killing of innocents.[8] But I shall maintain that this will not do. . . .

Modern warfare . . . will inevitably kill innocent persons, most likely even on the side that acts unjustly in the initiation of the war. Not only the character of modern weaponry but also the principles on which most nations conduct war make this clear. . . .

Given the presumption that killing innocent persons is wrong, the fact that war inevitably kills such persons means, in light of our argument that war can be neither just nor justified if the means necessary to waging it are not justified, that modern war is presumptively wrong. . . .

CAN THE PRESUMPTION OF THE WRONGNESS of war be undercut by defeating the presumption that killing innocent persons in wartime is wrong? Most attempts to justify such killing maintain either that there are clear cases in which it is permissible or that there are circumstances, however ambiguous, in which overriding considerations allow it. . . .

[Some just war theorists argue as follows.] Acts may sometimes have both good effects and bad, and what it important from a moral standpoint is to intend only the good. This by itself is usually not thought sufficient to make an act right, and other conditions are commonly incorporated into the notion of double effect, such as that the act itself be good or at least indifferent, the bad effect not be a means to the production of the good, and the good of the good effect be proportionate to the bad, in the sense of being greater than it or at least not less. . . .

Writing in this tradition, Elizabeth Anscombe brings out the importance of this distinction for Christian ethics:

> The distinction between the intended, and the merely foreseen, effects of a voluntary action is indeed absolutely essential to Christian ethics. For Christianity forbids a number of things as being bad in themselves. But if I am answerable for the foreseen consequences

of an action or refusal, as much as for the action itself, then these prohibitions will break down. If someone innocent will die unless I do a wicked thing, then on this view I am his murderer in refusing: so all that is left to me is to weigh up evils. Here the theologian steps in with the principle of double effect and says: "No, you are no murderer, if the man's death was neither your aim nor your chosen means, and if you had to act in the way that led to it or else do something absolutely forbidden." Without understanding of this principle, anything can be—and is wont to be—justified, and the Christian teaching that in no circumstances may one commit murder, adultery, apostasy . . . goes by the board. These absolute prohibitions of Christianity by no means exhaust its ethic; . . . But the prohibitions are bedrock, and without them the Christian ethic goes to pieces. Hence the necessity of the notion of double effect.[9]

The point usually extracted from such reasoning, though Anscombe does not do so in this passage, is that one can prohibit the killing of innocent persons, even prohibit it *absolutely,* and yet proceed to kill such persons provided in so doing their deaths are merely foreseen and not intended. . . .

Technically this is an externalist position. It does impose a restriction upon what one may do in the conduct of war. But in effect it is internalist, since it enables one to wage war in ways indistinguishable from those sanctioned by just necessity, which legitimizes all means necessary to the prosecution of a justified war. . . . [D]ouble effect legitimizes every action legitimized by just necessity, provided only that one not intend the harm that he does. In fact no action whatsoever is prohibited by the principle

of double effect so long as one acts from a good intention. . . .

[T]he principle of double effect . . . lends itself to the justification of virtually any action its user wants. On the assumption that we can "direct" or "aim" intentions as we please, any action whatever can be performed with a good intention or, at any rate, can be described as being performed with a good intention. . . . This is as true of pillage, rape, and torture as of killing. One suspects that defenders of the principle find that it invariably justifies just those actions they are antecedently disposed to believe are right. . . .

If this is correct, then the particular externalist position we have been examining fails. If one prohibits the killing of innocents, he cannot then invoke good intentions to justify proceeding to kill them. . . .

THE KILLING OF INNOCENTS BY AN AGGRESsor is no worse *as such* than the killing of innocents by those who would oppose him by waging war. Human beings have as much right to be spared destruction by good people as by bad. If an aggressor poses a threat to innocent persons it is presumably because killing them will be a means to achieving certain ends, or because killing them is at least a by-product of adopting those means. If I choose to kill innocent persons in order to prevent the deaths of others at the hands of an aggressor, I, no less than and perhaps even more than he (if his killing of innocents is only incidental to his attaining his ends) am using innocent persons as a means to an end. If this is correct, the presumption against killing innocents is not defeated by this reasoning.

LET ME DRAW TOGETHER OUR MAIN CON-
clusions at this point. I have argued that
doing violence to persons is presumptively wrong, and that war by its nature
does such violence. Because realist attempts to insulate war either wholly or
partially from moral consideration do not
succeed, this fact must be at the center of
the assessment of war. It means, if I am
correct, that attention needs to be fo-
cussed away from the standard conditions dealt with in the just war tradition
and upon the nature of what one is
doing in the very *waging* of war, however
just one's cause and however carefully
one otherwise abides by the standard
rules for its conduct. This reveals, I maintain, that modern war inevitably kills
innocent persons. And this, I contend,
makes modern war presumptively wrong.
What I consider the strongest arguments
to defeat that presumption, by way of
trying to defeat the presumption against
the killing of innocent persons, also do
not succeed. If that is the case, then war
has not be shown to be justified, and if it
has not been shown to be justified, then
it is unjustified. This does not of itself
mean that modern war *could* not be justified; to show that something has not
been justified and that the main attempts
to justify it are inadequate can never
logically foreclose the possibility that a
justification might someday be forthcoming. But that justification must be produced. And unless or until it is
produced, war should cease to be in our
repertoire of responses to world problems.

NOTES

1. *Just and Unjust Wars* (New York: Basic Books,
1977), p. 282.
2. See James Turner Johnson, *Can Modern War
Be Just?* (New Haven, Conn.: Yale University
Press, 1984); William V. O'Brien, *The Conduct of a
Just and Limited War* (New York: Praeger, 1981);

William V. O'Brien and John Langan, eds., *The
Nuclear Dilemma and the Just War Tradition* (Lexington, Mass.: Lexington Books, 1986); and Robert L. Phillips, *War and Justice* (Norman:
University of Oklahoma Press, 1984).
3. This point is well made by Phillips in *War
and Justice*, p. xi.
4. On the issue of the relationship between *jus
ad bellum* and *jus in bello*, see Melzer, *Concepts of
Just War*, esp. chap. 2.
5. See Anscombe, "War and Murder," in Wasserstrom ed., *War and Morality*, pp. 42–53; Phillips, *War and Justice*, chap. 2; and Ramsey, *The Just
War*, especially chap. 7.
6. One is justified in performing an act only if
he is justified both in employing the means
necessary to its performance and in performing
any subsidiary acts constitutive of it. I cannot be
justified in watering my garden unless I am
justified in attaching the hose and turning on the
water; or in mowing my lawn unless I am justified in cutting the grass. The justification of the
act is not one thing and the justification of the
means another. What one justifies in the first
place *are* those means; to justify the act *is* to
justify the means (and/or the constitutive acts).
This is the truth in the saying that the end does
not justify the means. . . .
7. I am, for the sake of simplicity, speaking
here as though what one must do in order to
wage war constitutes the means to waging war.
In actuality, those acts are constitutive of waging
war. There are two related but distinguishable
relationships here. One is that of means to end.
It figures in the argument to show that the internalist position is incorrect. It involves showing
that the means to victory in war must be justified
in their own right; their permissibility does not
follow automatically from the fact that the resort
to war may be justified. The other is that of
constituent to whole; it is central to the present
argument regarding the justification of the resort
to war, which involves pointing out that to be
justified in resorting to war one must be justified
in doing all those things that make up the waging of war.
8. Robert L. Phillips argues in his discussion
of the just war that "I have refrained from making any reference to 'the innocent,' despite the
fact that most of the current debate on the morality of war has been about treatment of innocent
parties. This seems to me to represent a major
confusion which has quite unnecessarily complicated the issue." See *War and Justice* (Norman:
University of Oklahoma Press, 1984), p. 56: His
reasons consist principally of the claim that "[it]
is *combatants* who are the objects of attack in war,
and, therefore, moral distinctions will center
upon that notion rather than innocence. This is
necessarily the case, since war is a contest of

strength, an arbitrament of arms carried out under the direction of moral and political aims" (p. 58). It is unclear, however, why this particular characterization of war, even if it should be accepted as something approximating a definition, entails or even implies that noncombatancy is of sole moral importance. In wartime, innocent people are knowingly and often deliberately killed. That fact establishes the relevance of innocence to the assessment of war. If . . . to kill innocent persons is to do violence to them, and to do violence is presumptively wrong, then that suffices to establish that killing innocent persons in wartime is presumptively wrong. And as it is with what is right and wrong in war that morality is concerned, such killing cannot fail to be of the first importance. Phillips contends that to focus upon innocence is to fail to distinguish between the whole person, to whom the notions of guilt and innocence are appropriate (p. 61), and the *role or function* of the person as combatant, to which they are not. But I hope to show that we can both recognize that distinction and see that the notion of innocence applies in each case.

9. "War and Murder," in Wasserstrom, ed., *War and Morality*, pp. 50-51.

POSTSCRIPT

Can Modern War Be Just?

Questions about war and justice go right to the heart of morality. Such questions are impossible to treat seriously without a close analysis of concepts such as intention, consequence, and innocence. Both Phillips and Holmes address these concerns. As different as their final positions turn out to be, they agree to a surprisingly great degree in their methods of inquiry.

One of the most fundamental points of division between Phillips and Holmes is that Phillips thinks that there is such a thing as a just war in the modern world and that the traditional just war theory can explain this idea. In order to show that a modern war can be justified, we have to test it against the two main parts of the just war theory, *jus ad bellum* and *jus in bello*. Phillips thinks that the two tests can be performed independently of each other, while Holmes thinks that without justifying the conduct that is necessary to carry out a war in the modern world (which would be an answer to the question about *jus in bellow*), we cannot answer the question about *jus ad bellum*. According to Holmes, the two parts of the just war theory are tied together.

Another way to consider the differences between Phillips and Holmes is that Phillips thinks that if it is morally permissible to go to war in the first place, as long as we follow the demands of *jus in bello*, we will have a just war. Holmes cautions us not to admit that going to war is just until we see what conduct is entailed by going to war. He believes that once we see wartime conduct, we will not admit that a modern war can be just.

In understanding the principle of double effect, it would be useful to find cases that have nothing to do with war in which this principle seems to give the right result. Are there also cases in which this principle seems to give the wrong results? Or is this such a slippery principle that it can always be adjusted to give the desired results? If this is so, the principle cannot be relied upon to support the just war theory.

For further moral examination of war and morality, see Marshall Cohen, Thomas Nagel, and Thomas Scanlon, eds., *War and Moral Responsibility* (Princeton University Press, 1974); Michael Walzer, *Just and Unjust Wars* (Basic Books, 1977); James Turner Johnson, *Just War Tradition and the Restraint of War* (Princeton University Press, 1981); William V. O'Brien, *The Conduct of Just and Limited War* (Praeger Publishers, 1981); *The Challenge of Peace: God's Promise and Our Response*, U.S. Catholic Conference, *Origins* (April 14, 1983); James Turner Johnson, *Can Modern War Be Just?* (Yale University Press, 1984); L. C. Green, *Essays on the Modern Law of War* (Transactional Publishers, 1985); Jenny Teichman, *Pacifism and the Just War* (Basil Blackwell, 1986); and W. B. Gallie, *Understanding War* (Routledge, 1990).

CONTRIBUTORS
TO THIS VOLUME

EDITOR

STEPHEN SATRIS was born in New York City. He received a bachelor's degree in philosophy from the University of California, Los Angeles, a master's degree in philosophy from the University of Hawaii, Manoa, and a Ph.D. in philosophy from Cambridge University, England. He has written on moral and philosophical issues and is the author of *Ethical Emotivism* (Martinus Nijhoff, 1987). He has taught at several American universities and currently teaches philosophy at Clemson University. Professor Satris is the president of the South Carolina Society for Philosophy (1991–1992).

STAFF

Marguerite L. Egan   Program Manager
Brenda S. Filley   Production Manager
Whit Vye   Designer
Libra Ann Cusack   Typesetting Supervisor
Juliana Arbo   Typesetter
David Brackley   Copy Editor
David Dean   Administrative Assistant
Diane Barker   Editorial Assistant
David Filley   Graphics

AUTHORS

JOHN ARTHUR is a philosopher at the State University of New York at Binghamton. He has published on social, political, and legal philosophy.

RENFORD BAMBROUGH teaches philosophy at Cambridge University in England. An editor of *Philosophy: The Journal of the Royal Institute of Philosophy,* he has written numerous articles and books on reason, truth, knowledge, morality, and metaphysics.

WILLIAM F. BAXTER is a professor of law at Stanford Law School. He has published on government-economic relationships in many areas, including communications, banking, transportation, and pollution.

HUGO ADAM BEDAU is a professor of philosophy at Tufts University. He has written widely on social, political, and legal topics, especially on the death penalty, and is the author of *Death Is Different: Studies in the Morality, Law, and Politics of Capital Punishment* (Northeastern University Press, 1987).

JACK BEMPORAD teaches in the Department of Philosophy and Religion at Southern Methodist University. He has written on faith, reason, and religion.

BRAND BLANSHARD (1892–1987) taught philosophy for many years at Yale University and is the author of numerous books on philosophy and education.

RICHARD BRANDT taught philosophy for many years at Swarthmore College and the University of Michigan. He has written books on moral issues and on the philosophy of Friedrich Schleiermacher, including *A Theory of the Right and the Good* (Oxford University Press, 1979).

PAUL CAMERON is the chairman of the Family Research Institute, Inc., a secular, nonprofit corporation that "deplore[s] the Kinsey, Planned Parenthood, gay rights, and legalization-of-drugs philosophies." He holds a Ph.D. in psychology and has appeared on several television and radio talk shows.

PHILIP E. DEVINE is a professor of philosophy and western civilization at Providence College in Providence, Rhode Island. He has published on ethics, metaphysics, and epistemology, and is the author of *The Ethics of Homicide* (Cornell University Press, 1978) and *Relativism, Nihilism & God* (University of Notre Dame Press, 1989).

JANE ENGLISH (1947–1978) was a philosopher whose published work focuses primarily on feminism and social philosophy.

MARILYN FRENCH is a novelist and literary critic whose publications include *The Women's Room* (Summit Books, 1977) and *James Joyce's Ulysses* (Harvard University Press, 1976). She received a Ph.D. from Harvard University and has taught at Harvard University, Hofstra University, and College of the Holy Cross.

ANN GARRY is a professor of philosophy at California State University, both at the Los Angeles and Northridge campuses. She has published several articles on feminism and the philosophy of mind, and she is a coeditor, with Marilyn Pearsall, of *Women, Knowledge, and Reality: Explorations in Feminist Philosophy* (Unwin Hyman, 1989).

TRUDY GOVIER taught philosophy for 11 years at Trent University. She currently lectures at the University of Calgary and writes on a variety of philosophical topics.

BARRY R. GROSS is a philosopher at York College, City University of New York. He has published books and articles on social philosophy and the philosophy of mind.

GARRETT HARDIN, an ecologist and microbiologist, is best known for his 1968 essay *The Tragedy of the Commons*, which is widely accepted as a fundamental contribution to ecology, population theory, economics, and political science. As a professor of human ecology at the University of California, Santa Barbara, for more than 30 years, he publicly debated the issues of abor-

tion, population control, foreign aid, immigration, and nuclear power. Since his retirement in 1978, he has devoted himself to writing and speaking.

VIRGINIA HELD is a professor of philosophy at Hunter College and the graduate school of the City University of New York. She has written on economic justice, feminism, and political philosophy and is the author of *Rights and Goods: Justifying Social Action* (Free Press, 1984).

MELVILLE J. HERSKOVITS (1895–1963) was a prominent American anthropologist. He conducted field research in West Africa, sub-Saharan Africa, the Caribbean, and South America, and was the founding president of the African Studies Association.

ROBERT L. HOLMES is a professor of philosophy at the University of Rochester. He has published books and articles on ethics, war, and nonviolence.

LAWRENCE E. JOHNSON is a philosopher at Flinders University of South Australia. His research interests are in Oriental philosophy, environmental philosophy, and the theory of truth.

HERBERT T. KRIMMEL is a professor of jurisprudence and bioethics at Southwestern University School of Law in Los Angeles, California, where he has been teaching since 1977. He was recently appointed to the advisory panel of the California Joint Legislative Committee on Surrogate Parenting.

IRVING KRISTOL is the publisher of *The National Interest* and a fellow of the American Enterprise Institute, a privately funded public policy research organization, which is located in Washington, D.C.

MICHAEL LEVIN is a professor of philosophy at City College, City University of New York. He has published books and articles on many social issues, including feminism and the relation between the mind and the body.

C. S. LEWIS (1898–1963), a professor of medieval and Renaissance literature at Cambridge University in England, wrote many books on Christian thought and contemporary society. He is the author of *The Screwtape Letters* (Macmillan, 1942) and *The Chronicles of Narnia* (Macmillan, 1950).

ALFRED LOUCH is a professor of philosophy at the Claremont Graduate School. He has published on moral philosophy, legal philosophy, and the philosophy of Ludwig Wittgenstein.

JOHN L. MACKIE (1917–1981) taught philosophy in New Zealand, Australia, and England. He has written numerous books, including works on causation, probability, belief in God, ethics, the moral philosophy of David Hume, and the philosophy of John Locke.

RUTH MACKLIN is a philosopher and an ethicist in residence at Albert Einstein College of Medicine in the Bronx, New York, and its affiliate hospitals in New York City. She has published works on medical ethics, behavior control, and informed consent, including *Mortal Choices: Bioethics in Today's World* (Pantheon Books, 1987).

DON MARQUIS is a professor of philosophy at the University of Kansas in Lawrence, Kansas. He has written on issues in medical ethics.

KARL MENNINGER (1893–1990) was a psychiatrist who cofounded the Menninger Clinic and the Menninger Foundation, which are institutes devoted to research, training, and public education in psychiatry. He also helped found the Winter Veterans' Administration Hospital, which has the largest psychiatric training program in the world.

RICHARD D. MOHR teaches philosophy at the University of Illinois in Urbana, Illinois. He has written on ancient philosophy, particularly Plato, and on homosexuals in contemporary social life. He is the author of *Gays—Justice: A Study of Ethics, Society, and Law* (Columbia University Press, 1988).

ROBERT L. PHILLIPS is a professor of philosophy and the director of the War and Ethics Program at the University of Connecticut in Hartford, Connecticut. He concentrates primarily on social and political philosophy.

JAMES RACHELS, a philosopher, is dean of the School of Humanities at the University of Alabama in Birmingham. He has written on issues in morality and method ethics and is the author of many books, including *The End of Life* (Oxford University Press, 1986) and *The Elements of Moral Philosophy* (Random House, 1986).

TOM REGAN is a professor of philosophy at North Carolina State University. He has published many books and articles on animal rights, environmental ethics, and the philosophy of G. E. Moore. His publications include *Matters of Life and Death* (Random House, 1985) and *The Struggle for Animal Rights* (ISAR, 1987).

BERTRAND RUSSELL (1872–1970) was a philosopher and logician whose most notable contributions have been to the philosophy of logic and mathematical logic. The author of over 50 books, including *Principia Mathematica* (Cambridge University Press, 1910), with Alfred North Whitehead, and *A History of Western Philosophy* (Allen & Unwin, 1945), he is also famous for espousing unpopular social views and was imprisoned for several months during World War I on account of his pacificism.

G. L. SIMONS is a British writer who has published numerous books on sexuality and on artificial intelligence and computer science.

PETER SINGER is a professor of philosophy at Monash University in Clayton, Victoria, Australia, where he has taught since 1977. He is the director of the Center for Human Bioethics and a coeditor of *Bioethics* journal. His publications include *The Reproduction Revolution* (Charles Scribner, 1984) and *Making Babies: The New Science and Ethics of Conception* (Charles Scribner, 1985) with Deane Wells.

J. J. C. SMART, a professor of philosophy at Australian National University, has published many papers and books on the philosophy of science and moral philosophy.

PAUL W. TAYLOR is a professor of philosophy at Brooklyn College, City University of New York. He has published several books on moral issues, including *Respect for Nature* (Princeton University Press, 1985).

ERNEST van den **HAAG,** formerly the John M. Olin Professor of Jurisprudence and Public Policy at Fordham University, is a distinguished scholar at the Heritage Foundation and a regular lecturer at Columbia University, Yale University, and Harvard University. He is a contributing editor for *National Review* magazine and a coauthor, with John P. Conrad, of *The Death Penalty: A Debate* (Plenum, 1983).

RICHARD WASSERSTROM is a professor of philosophy at the University of California, Santa Cruz.

Chairman of the California Council for the Humanities, he has published in areas of moral philosophy, social philosophy, law, and race relations, including *Today's Moral Problems,* 2d ed. (Macmillan, 1979) and *Philosophy and Social Issues: Five Studies* (University of Notre Dame Press, 1980).

INDEX